Learning to Be Japanese

日本人であるために

LEARNING
TO BE
JAPANESE

Selected Readings
on Japanese Society and Education

Edited by
EDWARD R. BEAUCHAMP

LINNET BOOKS
HAMDEN, CONNECTICUT
1978

© Edward R. Beauchamp 1978

First published 1978 as a Linnet Book,
an imprint of THE SHOE STRING PRESS, INC.
Hamden, Connecticut, 06514

Library of Congress Cataloging in Publication Data

Main entry under title:

Learning to be Japanese.

   Bibliography: p.
     1. Education—Japan—Addresses, essays, lectures.
2. Japan—History—1868- —Addresses, essays, lectures.
I. Beauchamp, Edward R., 1933–
LA1311.L4   370′.952   77–25119
ISBN 0–208–01717–8

Typeset in Apollo by Asco Trade Typesetting Ltd., Hong Kong
Lithoprinted and bound in the United States of America

Dedicated to
Kevin Kenji Beauchamp
and his classmates at Osawa-Dai Primary School
in Mitaka, Japan

CONTENTS

Preface   9

Introduction   11

PART I. THE ROOTS OF CONTEMPORARY JAPANESE EDUCATION

The Legacy   17
    by Ronald Dore
Griffis in Japan: The Fukui Interlude, 1871   42
    by Edward R. Beauchamp
Inoue Kowashi, 1843–1895: and the Formation of Modern Japan   80
    by Joseph Pittau, S. J.
Government Ethics Textbooks in Late Meiji Japan   120
    by Wilbur M. Fridell
The Army, Youth, and Women   137
    by Richard J. Smethurst
The Processes of Army Socialization   167
    by Tsurumi Kazuko
Japan: Under American Occupation   181
    by Victor N. Kobayashi

PART II. SELECTED DIMENSIONS OF CONTEMPORARY
JAPANESE EDUCATION

The Gateway to Salary: Infernal Entrance Examinations   213
    Ezra F. Vogel
The Textbook Controversy   240
    by Benjamin C. Duke
Education: An Agent of Social Change in Ainu Community
    Life   265
    by Fred C. C. Peng
The Sociology of a Student Movement—a Japanese Case
    Study   289
    by Shimbori Michiya
The Conservatives Reform Higher Education   316
    by William K. Cummings
Changing Styles of University Life in Japan   329
    by Thomas R. H. Havens
Report from Japan 1976   338
    by Edward R. Beauchamp

PART III. SOME POSSIBLE FUTURE DIRECTIONS OF
JAPANESE EDUCATION

What Japan's Education Should Be   349
    Japan Teachers Union: Council on Educational
    Reform
Basic Guidelines for the Reform of Elementary and Secondary   372
    Education
    Central Council for Education

Selected Bibliography   399

7

PREFACE

This collection of readings grew out of my own frustrations in trying to find appropriate readings for students in my classes and seminars dealing with education in Japan. I have assigned most of the articles included in this volume to my students, and they have found them to be useful.

As in any collection of readings, there are some materials that I would have liked to include, but was unable to do so because of problems of length, securing the necessary permissions, etc. Despite these problems, however, I feel that this book contains a representative sample of useful materials on the most important dimensions of Japanese education—past and present.

I would like to thank the authors and publishers who have granted permission to reproduce their work. I am sure that they share with me the hope that this volume will, in a modest way, help to encourage the study of Japanese education in the United States and in other western countries.

E. R. B.

Honolulu, Hawaii

INTRODUCTION

In the decades since the end of World War II, Japan has played an increasingly important role in the consciousness of the Western world. Her economic miracle—really not a miracle at all, but based on hard work, self-sacrifice and generous American economic assistance—has won the grudging respect of most of the world. From Mazda to Minolta and Toyota to Toshiba, her products are found in virtually every corner of the world. Less than thirty years after the war, a former Japanese prime minister was the recipient of the Nobel Peace Prize, and a Japanese novelist the winner of the Nobel Prize for Literature. On a more prosaic level, Japanese restaurants are commonly found throughout most of the Western world, and one can view Japanese films and art exhibits in all but the most provincial parts of the world.

Most Americans concede that regardless of how one defines it, Japan is the first (and only) non-Western nation to achieve modernity. At least one American, futurist Herman Kahn of the Hudson Institute, predicted that the twenty-first century will be "Japan's Century." What many Americans do not realize, however, is that Japan's modernity was not achieved full bloom during the period following the Pacific War (as the Japanese refer to World War II), but that its roots extend to at least the days of the Meiji Restoration (1868–1912), and in the case of educational modernity, to the earlier Tokugawa Period (1603–1868).

Although disagreeing on the details, most social scientists and historians generally recognize the important role played by education in the process of modernization, and it is widely acknowleged that education played a particularly important role in the Japanese experience. In fact, one can cogently argue that an understanding of the Japanese educational experience is necessary for an informed view of Japan's past and, perhaps to a greater extent, her present and future.

It must be emphasized that education is not used here merely as as a synonym for schooling. As Bernard Bailyn has argued in his seminal study of the historiography of American education, one should conceive of education "not only as formal pedagogy, but the entire process by which a culture transmits itself across generations."[1] The articles in this collection of readings reflect this definition and, therefore, do not deal exclusively with schools but touch upon others ways in which people learn, and have learned, to be Japanese.

The time span covered is approximately the last century, although one contribution, by Professor Ronald Dore, reaches back into the Tokugawa Period to point out the beginnings of literacy long before intrusion of the West upon Japan's consciousness. The approach is dual, historical, and sociological. Part I deals with historical data although much of that data is informed by sociological insight. Part II provides an overview of some of the more important dimensions of contemporary Japanese education and Part III summarizes some possible future directions. Each of the sections is preceded by a brief introduction. There is a selected bibliography designed to help the interested reader find more detailed information on topics of particular interest. In brief, this collection of readings has been compiled as an educational tool to assist students of Japanese history, society, politics, and education better understand her fascinating past and her important contemporary directions.

1. Bernard Bailyn. *Education in the Forming of American Society.* Chapel Hill: University of North Carolina Press, 1961, page 14.

Part I

The Roots
of Contemporary Japanese Education

This section focuses on education during Japan's pre-Western Tokugawa Period (1603–1868) and the Meiji Period (1868–1912) in which Japan began her rapid development into a world power. For many years the weight of Western scholarship viewed the Tokugawa era as a kind of Eastern "Dark Ages" characterized by little or no educational activity of major significance. A major turning point in the Western view of Tokugawa education was the 1965 publication of Professor Ronald Dore's monograph, *Education in Tokugawa Japan*. Professor Dore paints a detailed and vivid picture of the extent and variety of Japanese education during the two-and-one-half centuries preceding the Meiji Restoration. He concludes that "without the traditions, the teachers, the buildings and the established attitudes of the Tokugawa period the development of the new [Meiji educational] system could never have been accomplished as fast as it was and almost without central government subsidy." It comes as a great surprise to many that the literacy rate during the late Tokugawa period was at least as high as that of contemporary England. This, then, helps to explain how Japan was able to move into the ranks of the world's most powerful nations so quickly.

The arrival of Commodore Matthew C. Perry's "black fleet" off Japan's shores in 1853 set in motion a train of events that led her leaders to conclude that Japan would have to use Western knowledge and technology in what some scholars have described as a strategy of "defensive modernization." Japanese leaders and, to a significant extent, the Japanese masses reacted in a positive way to the Western influx in the 1870s.

The early Meiji fascination with Western technology, which some may describe as a fetish, took two forms: the sending of selected students abroad for study, and the importing of skilled foreign employees (*yatoi*) to Japan to teach the Japanese the secrets of Western power and success. Several thousand of these *yatoi* worked in all kinds of jobs, from agriculture to geology and from education to shipbuilding. Professor Edward Beauchamp offers a colorful case study of one of the earliest of these *yatoi* to arrive in Japan, William Elliot Griffis of Philadelphia. Griffis, an ambitious and talented young man, was later the author of numerous books and articles on Japan, the most noteworthy of which was *The Mikado's Empire* (New York: Harper and Brothers, 1876) which went through twelve editions by 1912. Professor Beauchamp outlines Griffis' experiences—educational and personal—during his ten-month sojourn in the interior castle town of Fukui, as well as his impact on the Japanese with whom he came into contact.

It is clear that the Western educational impact on Japan during the early Meiji period was substantial, in part because a solid intellectual groundwork had been laid during the earlier Tokugawa era, and in part because the Meiji oligarchs recognized that Japan needed to acquire Western science and technology in order to protect herself from possible colonization. In an excellent case study, "Inoue Kawashi, 1843–1895, and the Formation of Modern Japan," Father Joseph Pittau describes how during "the late seventies and early eighties . . . the tempo of change slowed down, and the Meiji leaders set themselves the task of consolidating the new system . . . [and] strove to establish not just a *modern* state along western lines but a modern *Japanese* state."

Education is a tool used, to a greater or lesser degree, by all modern governments to further their ideological and political goals. It appears that as a general rule, the more extreme a government's ideological position, the greater the degree of control that it exerts over the educational system and the greater the ideological content of that system. Certainly the Japan of the period leading to World War II fits this model.

Professor Wilbur Fridell's article deals with some of the roots of this phenomenon in his study of ethics textbooks used in the late Meiji period. He analyzes the contents of these textbooks, designed to inculcate correct ethical values into the youth of the Imperial Japanese Empire, through various editions and concludes that the 1910 edition marks a watershed. This edition, he argues, not only clearly reflected the principles of the Meiji Constitution (1889) and the Imperial Rescript on Education (1890), but also "set a tone, and developed certain basic themes, which greatly influenced later revisions." Thus, when Japanese militarists and ultranationalists took over the reigns of government in the 1930s, their "leaders had only to expand on the foundation laid."

As we are being increasingly reminded today, not all education takes place in the schoolroom. Professor Richard Smethurst offers persuasive evidence of this in his contribution on "The Army, Youth, and Women," in which he describes the "military education networks" established in prewar Japan to complement and supplement the public schools in fostering attitudes and values deemed appropriate to Japanese society. His story is a fascinating account of little known organizations such as those of reservists, youth, and women, all of which played an important role in socialization for nationalism prior to Japan's 1937 invasion of China. Professor Smethurst demonstrates how this network systematically shaped an obedient rural population to support the policy of the militarists. It is an excellent example of what educators today call nonformal education.

The army was also active in socializing its troops to wil-

15

lingly accept the imperatives of the task at hand. In her contribution, Professor Tsurumi Kazuko provides a detailed account of what she vividly describes as "Socialization for Death." Enlivened by excerpts from diaries of soldiers and marines who experienced the process, Professor Tsurumi enables us to better understand the determined resistance, often verging on fanaticism, of Japanese troops in the Pacific War.

One of the most striking lacunae in the study of Japanese education is the period of the American Occupation. For many years the only materials available were either official government documents or personal accounts of various phases of the Occupation written by participants. A hopeful sign that this gap will soon be narrowed can be seen in the beginnings of a trickle of articles and bibliographical materials on generalized aspects of the Occupation. When scholars begin to seriously examine the political and economic consequences of the period, the study of its educational consequences cannot be far behind.

The American Occupation (1945–1952) was one of history's most serious attempts at large-scale social engineering. Its supporters saw it as an idealistic attempt by the United States to transform Japan from an aggressive militaristic power into a peace-loving member of the international community. Critics, on the other hand, charged that it was nothing more than an opportunistic attempt to reshape a defeated and devasted Japan into an anti-Communist satellite of American imperialism.

Probably the single best short study of the educational dimensions of the Occupation is the thoughtful essay of Professor Victor Kobayashi, "Japan Under American Occupation." Professor Kobayashi, a specialist on Japanese education, traces the major educational changes which occurred during this period, and describes how these reforms attempted to make operational the twin concepts of democratization and demilitarization. Regardless of American motives in Japan, the result has clearly been an American dominance of Japanese educational practices since 1945, or, as Kobayashi remarks, "There are amazing similarities between the present curricula of Japan and the U.S."

RONALD DORE

THE LEGACY

If the Tokugawa period was a time of stagnation in many social and technical fields and of cyclical fluctuation in its repeated phases of administrative reform and decline, in the field of education at least there were steady and consistent trends—a trend of growth in the sheer amount of schooling provided and, though much more hesitantly and painfully, an evolution in its content and purposes. Did these developments in any sense condition the changes which took place in Japan in the last quarter of the nineteenth century? Are they germane to an explanation of why Japan, alone among Asian countries, was able to keep her independence and carry through the process of politically directed change which has made her a highly industrialized nation?

Ronald Dore is Professor of Sociology at the Institute for Development Studies at Sussex University in England.

Reprinted from Ronald Dore, *Education in Tokugawa Japan*, copyright © 1965 (Berkeley: University of California Press; London: Routledge & Kegan Paul Ltd, 1965) 291–316, with permission of the publishers.

17

RONALD DORE

Literacy and Its Advantages

However approximate our calculations of the diffusion of popular education must necessarily be, there can be no doubt that the literacy rate in Japan in 1870 was considerably higher than in most of the underdeveloped countries today. It probably compared favourably even then with some contemporary European countries. As late as 1837 a British Select Committee found that in the major industrial towns only one child in four or five was ever getting to school,[1] and it may have been more than a desire to jolt his fellow-countrymen which prompted a Frenchman to write in 1877 that "primary education in Japan has reached a level which should make us blush".[2]

But what does widespread literacy do for a developing country? At the very least it constitutes a training in being trained. The man who has in childhood submitted to some process of disciplined and conscious learning is more likely to respond to further training, be it in a conscript army, in a factory, or at lectures arranged by his village agricultural association. And such training can be more precise and efficient, and more nationally standardized, if the written word can be used to supplement the spoken.

Secondly, the wide diffusion of basic education—and education which was not forced on an unwilling populace but supported by parents' voluntary choice and sacrifice—argues that Japan had already got over the first hurdle in a process of purposeful development, the diffusion of a simple notion of the possibility of "improvement". It was no longer the kind of "traditional society", where things are as they are and the individual does not see himself as offered the choice between doing or not doing anything to alter his society or his position in it. By taking thought one could add an inch to one's child's stature, not only enhance his prestige and his self-respect, but also improve his life-chances in a material sense. It is this latter feature which marks the difference in significance between the high literacy rate in Japan in 1870 and the high literacy rate in Burma in, say, 1930, for popular education in Japan was secular and it was practical. To be sure, it contained a good many elements of traditional formalism, but it nevertheless provided—and this was the main reason why parents were willing to buy it for their children—the kind of knowledge which made men better able to fulfil their economic functions in society. For a few, "self-improvement" meant moving out of one's hereditary position,

18

perhaps "getting a reading and writing job"; for most it meant being a more efficient carpenter, a more respected or a more affluent merchant, than one otherwise would have been. The important thing is that the desire for self-improvement was already awakened, so that when the Meiji period offered new knowledge to be acquired and new levels of self-improvement to be reached, there was no want of candidates for such endeavours. And where the notion of individual self-improvement was widely diffused, the notion of *national* improvement could be more readily understood and accepted.

Note, too, that for some among the commoners, self-improvement did mean "bettering oneself", in the sense of moving out of one's parental occupation to a higher point in the social scale. The growth of schools helped to stimulate such aspirations since they offered a chance of realizing them (the principle that the presence of a bottle on the shelf helps to stimulate a thirst). Education was one of the major means of social ascent in Tokugawa society. Some rich men were able to buy their way into the samurai class, by direct purchase or by making themselves indispensable to a daimyo's financial solvency. But equally a good many poor men were able to get themselves a surname and two swords in a daimyo's service simply by virtue of their mastery of some kind of gakumon—of Chinese, or of Western, learning. This had two consequences. The fact that mobility aspirations were already at a high level meant that when political and technological change created new opportunities in a more fluid Meiji society they were eagerly taken up. It was easier to create a go-getting competitive society because enough people were already psychologically prepared to offer themselves as competitors. Secondly, education continued to be an important mechanism of social ascent. It was by acquiring new knowledge and new skills—not just by entrepreneurial boldness or a keen eye to the main chance—that one moved ahead in Meiji Japan. Education seems to have become the major mechanism of social selection at an earlier stage of industrialization in Japan than in Western countries. Learning was the royal road not only to the professions and to government, but also to business success as well—as the very high proportion of university graduates among Japanese business-men suggests.[3] Undoubtedly one explanation of this fact is that Japan was a late developer, catching up by learning, and hence having more practical use for already systematized knowledge.[4] But the Tokugawa tradition of climbing by one's brush, by the glib solemnity of one's interpretation of the Four Books, or by one's enthusiastic claim to understand a Dutch treatise on saltpetre, was surely also a factor.

The wide diffusion of a basic literacy also meant that Japan had a better chance, when the process of industrialization and political change began, of putting the nation's best intellectual resources to good use. Fewer potential Noguchis or Hoshi Tōrus remained mute and inglorious than would have been the case if a large proportion of the population had not had the chance early in life to get over the first hurdle towards mental training and demonstrate to themselves—and to teachers who might provide access to helpful patronage—such talents as they might have.

Finally, there are the political implications of literacy. Already, in the Tokugawa period, the public notice board was an accepted means of communication between the rulers and the people. Administration by written directive could, in the Japan of 1870, reach down to the lowest level. It may well be, too, that the teachers of the existing popular schools helped to provide channels of communication; they were already there in the village and country towns to act as the carriers of new ideas and of a new national consciousness to the people. The implementation of new decrees, the new land registration system and the new civil registration system, were only possible because basic literacy was sufficiently widespread. The chances of rumour growing wildly out of fearful suspicion and leading to obstruction and revolt were much reduced when a majority even of the peasants could actually read the documents they were required to set their seals to. The early Meiji uprisings could have been much more serious than they were.

In sum, it was important that the Japanese populace was not just a sack of potatoes. The creation of modern Japan was not simply a matter of top-level changes. It was also a cumulation of a mass of small initiatives by large numbers of people who could appreciate new possibilities, make new choices, or at the very least allow themselves to be persuaded to do for the first time something they had never done before. The new educational system which the Restoration Government exerted itself to establish in the 1870s was, of course, much more effective in all these ways than the mixture of mechanical repetition and gentle moralizing purveyed by the terakoya teachers, but this is not to underestimate the legacy of the terakoya system. It ensured that the generation which had passed childhood in 1870 did not have to be written off as hopeless. And without the traditions, the teachers, the buildings and the established attitudes of the Tokugawa period the development of the new system could never have been accomplished as fast as it was—and almost without central government subsidy.[5]

The Nation

One should be careful not to overstate the case. Not every Japanese in 1870 was simmering with intellectual curiosity and social ambition. There were regions where the mass of the people lived lives of boorish drudgery enlivened only by occasional festival fun. In 1880 an official of the Ministry of Education could still urge that it was too soon to allow straight election of education committees because "there are districts where the people still do not appreciate the advantages of education; where they will be only too willing to spend a thousand pieces of gold on a dramatic troupe or a festival, but begrudge ten for a school; where they will lay out the red carpet for actors and wrestlers but show little respect for a teacher".[6] It was, indeed, in the field of popular education—in estimates of school attendance, especially by girls—that the clearest evidence of regional disparities has been given in this book. In education, as in general economic development, south-eastern, central and western-central Japan led the way, while the north-east and large parts of Kyūshū lagged behind. Though the pattern was by no means identical, and statistical indicators are not available, it is nevertheless clear that there were also wide differences in samurai education between the progressive and the stagnant fiefs.

This raises another interesting problem. The Meiji Restoration transformed Japan from a collection of separatist fiefs at varying levels of development, each with its own traditions and each jealous of its feudal autonomy, into a centralized nation-state. How far had educational developments prepared the way for this change?

They were obviously not the only factor, for people travelled on pilgrimages and on business, but they must have contributed a great deal. Even in the popular schools there was enough in the content of education to give children a sense that they were not just townsmen of the Shogun's capital or peasants of the lord of Okayama, but also members of the Japanese nation. They learned the names of places and products in distant parts of the country; even the *Teikin ōrai* may have had a "nationalizing" effect, suggesting the contingent arbitrariness of contemporary regional and social divisions by giving children a glimpse

21

of a period when frontiers between fiefs ran very differently, when their ancestors were not so rigidly differentiated into commoners and samurai, and when the Emperor counted for somewhat more than he did in their day. Literacy that is used is almost bound to improve the capacity for "empathy", a precondition of that fellow-feeling which makes compatriots of people who are never likely to meet. Citizens of Edo could read novels written in Osaka; they might even occasionally receive letters from distant cousins in far-off rural areas.

The Confucian education of the samurai was even more effective in making a nation out of a collection of fiefs. Firstly, it formed a very large part of the intellectual culture which was shared by the members of all fiefs, a bond of common interests, common assumptions and common proverbial aphorisms which was much stronger, because of much more substantial content, than a shared interest in the tea ceremony and fencing, or a shared acceptance of the vague and diverse tenets of contemporary Buddhism could alone have provided. Secondly, in most fiefs the samurai's education had come by the end of the period to include, as a matter of course, some study of Japan's own history. However this was taught it would be bound in some measure to enhance the student's sense of his own Japaneseness, and in some fiefs, of course, it was taught in an intensely nationalistic spirit; Mito, for instance, producing precisely that combination of the Confucian ethic and Shinto-supported racism which was to form the explicit ideology of official Japanese nationalism until 1945. Thirdly, the growth of Confucian scholarship and the teaching profession provided new national channels of communication which ignored fief boundaries. The professional scholars and the intellectually active amateurs read one another's books, exchanged letters, edited one another's poems. They knew one another as individual persons. Hirose Tansō, who never travelled more than fifty miles from his home in Kyūshū, could still write gossip about contemporary scholars he had never met and write it as of colleagues.[7] There is little doubt that he had a sense of membership in a national community of scholars which was stronger than any regional loyalty. In point of fact the stay-at-home Hirose was an exception. Confucian scholars could change their fief of employment with relative ease, and even if they did not, they frequently travelled the length and breadth of the country relying in part on the right a common bond of scholarship gave them to expect the hospitality of their colleagues.[8]

22

The development of a national consciousness had to overcome not only regional divisiveness but also the barriers of class. Perhaps the single most important factor which transformed Japan in the space of half a century from a society of hereditary "estates" with clearly institutionalized boundaries to a society in which few people knew or cared to what estate his neighbours' ancestors had belonged, was the decision embodied in the decree of 1872 to establish a universal compulsory system of elementary education for all. How was it that the new and still almost exclusively samurai government could so easily abandon the earliest Meiji plans, which assumed as a matter of course the continuation of a dual system of high schools for the samurai and literacy schools for commoners, and decree instead the creation of a unified and universal school system for samurai and commoner alike?

Nowadays it is axiomatic that a literate populace, with some knowledge of geography and history as well as the three R's, is an essential ingredient of a modern civilized state, but in the 1870s this was not so. In Russia, an intellectual concerned with the conditions of economic progress could still say, in the 1890s, that "a good farm and a good factory constitute the best and the only possible school for the people".[9] Indeed, the utilitarian arguments for a universal education system embodied in the 1872 decree had only in 1870 achieved victory in England after a long struggle against the fears of "nearly the whole body of those who are rich [who] dread the consequences of teaching the people more than they dread the effects of their ignorance"[10]—and then only after the growing organization of the working class had won its partial right to the suffrage.

How was it that ideas which had only painfully fought their way to respectability in England in the teeth of class interest and class antagonism aroused no such opposition in Japan? Surely the social cleavage between the samurai and the rest was no less than the gulf which divided the English working class from its betters. To be sure, the distinctions were crumbling; there were mobile men; commoners were being recruited into military formations and tentatively admitted to fief schools even before the period ended, and egalitarianism was strong enough after the Restoration for the principle of equality before the law to be established in most respects. But not in all; and socially the distinctions remained strong. The very growth of education which led to the egalitarian stress on achievement at the same time widened the cultural gap between the samurai who usually had the opportunity

23

to receive that education and the commoners who had not. The cartoons of the Meiji period which show the humble commoner forehead-to-ground before arrogant samurai officials argue that there was a social distance between the classes far greater than even England could match.

Part of the answer lies in the difference of class structure. Social distance between the classes is one thing; class antagonism is another. Japan may have been as much "two nations" as was England, but in England the two nations were at war. Peterloo, the trade unions, the Chartist movement, represented a growing threat to the traditional ruling class and to the new middle class. The samurai, in a pre-industrial Japan, faced no such threat; peasant revolts were the sporadic tantrums of irresponsible children, not symptoms of a growing, systematic disaffection. The lower orders in Japan still knew and accepted their place. There was nothing in the situation which prompted the Restoration leaders to think of a universal education system primarily in terms of its effect on the distribution of political power within the country.

The educational history of the Tokugawa period was in part responsible for this state of affairs. Schools tended always and everywhere to encourage submissive acceptance of the existing order (whereas in England it was often the working-men's study groups and improvement societies which were the centres of disaffection). The only partially educational movement which ever showed the smallest germ of class sentiment—the Shingaku movement with its early appeal to the merchant's battered sense of self-respect—was soon transformed by feudal patronage into yet one more means of social control—encouraging the common man to derive his self-respect from the respect his superiors would show him were he only a loyal and obedient subordinate. It was a circular process. Because, in the Confucian definition, the purposes of education were primarily moral, and because the morality taught concerned chiefly the correct observance of social relations in a hierarchically ordered society, there were small grounds for discouraging the populace from acquiring it. And because popular education proceeded with official approval, and occasionally even encouragement, it was less likely to deviate into subversive ways. The ideological unity of the samurai class was important, too. Education began to seep down into the lower classes of England at a time when the literate middle and upper classes were already ideologically divided, when there were middle-class radicals, free-thinkers and jacobins whose notion of a proper training for the poor did not begin and end with the Catechism and selected portions of the Bible. In Japan popular education began at a time when the ruling class was still intellectually united by a monolithic orthodoxy which held no dangers to the social system and whose diffusion to the people was no threat, but even an advantage.

Given this background there was no reason to suppose in 1872 that universal education would create subversive disaffection. It might rather have been expected to promote loyal obedience. And so, in effect, it did, thanks largely to the ethics courses, in conception and content the element of most direct continuity between the Tokugawa and the modern educational systems. Universal education certainly created the labour movement and the tenants' movement in the 1920s. But the efficacy of the ethics course and related features of primary education was such that these beginnings of class antagonism were easily swamped in a flood-tide of national loyalty in the 'thirties.

It was not, however, until the late 1880s and in particular after the Imperial Rescript on Education of 1890 that this use of popular education to create a loyal and obedient citizenry became a predominant motive in educational policy. The men who drafted the 1872 ordinance and its revisions in 1879 and 1880 seem to have had other ends chiefly in view—as indeed had their forerunners, those few men who were already arguing for universal compulsory education in the preceding two or three decades.

In the first place they were concerned to mobilize all available talent in the pursuit of national goals. This was a reflection of their over-riding nationalism of which we have already spoken.

Secondly, they did have a paternal sense of responsibility towards the mass of the people. In part, doubtless, this too was a consequence as much as a precondition of their nationalism. (The impact of the national danger coming from the Western powers and of the sense of national separateness arising from sudden contacts with Westerners after centuries of seclusion undoubtedly enhanced the samurai's awareness of the common Japaneseness which he shared with the meanest farmer.) But there is more to it than that. For all that the common and popular forms of the Confucian ethic current in Tokugawa Japan did lay almost exclusive stress on the duties of subordinates to superiors, for those who read more widely in the classics, for those, even, who pondered on the *Analects*, there was plenty to remind them of the superior's duty of benevolence to his subordinates. The samurai had come a long way since the bloody suppression of the Shimabara rebellion in 1638. In "pacifying" the samurai class Confucian education also modified its arrogance and contemptuous lack of concern for the welfare of the lower classes, and did do something to breed a sense of paternal responsibility. Smith has well described the "deep sense of the public interest" which to the conscientious samurai was an essential part of "merit" in public officials:

> This was the cultivated sense which alone disciplined the natural self and "interest" (ri), usually thought of as self-interest. It was, for example, what prompted an official to speak out to his superiors fearlessly, yet moderately and tactfully, without an edge of self-regard; to recognize, without envy, ability in others; to listen to unpleasant advice from subordinates without flush of pique or prejudice. In short, it was the ability to think always of the welfare of the people and the state.[11]

Certainly these qualities were not bred in every samurai. What one reads about extortionate tax levies, about peasant revolts and about examples of cruel arbitrariness in the administration of criminal justice is undoubtedly true. One hears less of the local samurai officials who organized famine relief and flood relief measures, of Oshio, the retired Osaka official whose indignation at popular suffering led him into armed revolt against his superiors, of the Bakufu mission to vaccinate the Ainu or of the Kōchi public health service. It was the commoner author of a child's text-book who defined the function of the samurai as being to balance his loyalty to his lord (who requires him to squeeze out the last ounce in taxation) against the claims of the common people on his benevolence[12]—and he was not repeating standard phrases, it seems, but speaking from his observations of the lesser officials with whom he came into contact. Benevolence may still have been a fairly scarce commodity among the samurai, but there would have been much less of it, less chance of a national education system in 1872 and less chance of creating a viable national community, without the development of Confucian education among the samurai in the Tokugawa period.

The Samurai's Intellectual Equipment

How far had the samurai been intellectually prepared by the Tokugawa schools for a useful role as a member of an innovating *elite* in a

035442G

Japan bent on "catching up"? He, too, of course, had been thoroughly imbued with the idea that knowledge and education was a "good thing", and hence was well disposed in principle to the idea of acquiring new kinds of it. He, too, had had in ample measure a training in being trained. The extraordinary thing is that curiosity and the eagerness to learn also survived the education the samurai were given, for it would be difficult to think of a form of education better calculated to kill curiosity than the early stages of Chinese study. Perhaps the truth is that it was only in a fairly small percentage of the most active minds that it did survive. They were able to get through the dulling initial stages quickly enough to be still alert and eager when the later, more potentially stimulating, stages of Chinese study were reached, and they survived to become the indefatigable note-takers on foreign missions, the students who pumped the Clarks and the Janes and the other hired foreign teachers dry of every piece of information they had to give, the government officials and technicians who embarked late in life on the study of foreign languages or sought the instruction of foreign advisers.

And for the other three-quarters, or perhaps nine-tenths, of the samurai class, the traditional education may have prepared them for a useful role in another way. The authoritarian teacher-pupil relations of the fief schools required humility on the part of the pupil. Knowledge was imparted by the teacher to be accepted, not to be improved upon. And this attitude, given the initial decision to learn from the West, produced a humble attentiveness and an assiduous thoroughness. Every detail went down into the notebook; every utterance of the foreign teacher was accorded solemn respect. Had the Tokugawa schools been mainly concerned to "teach people to think", had they encouraged the free play of ideas between teacher and pupil on a footing of near equality, there might have been many more steamships ruined by men who thought they could run them by the light of pure reason before they learned how to keep their boilers full of water.

There is another aspect of the efficacy of a Confucian education which is also more or less independent of the values or knowledge consciously imparted. It "trained the mind". In the words of Tōhata Seiichi, discussing how it was that the samurai were successful industrial pioneers, their education had given them a high "general intellectual level . . . not simply the ability to understand a single concrete body of knowledge, but an ability which could be applied to the understanding of other bodies of knowledge without falling to a lower level".[13] It is a difficult concept to express in these latter days of cultural relativism, when societies may be decently rated in terms of *per capita* income or rates of economic growth but never, in the manner of our Victorian ancestors, by their "level of civilization". Nevertheless, there are real differences of intellectual sophistication for which one might suggest a variety of criteria. One might be the degree of secularization of the intellectual culture; the extent to which the world is seen to be at the mercy of arbitrary supernatural forces, or alternatively governed by regular ascertainable laws. Quite obviously Confucian education had carried the best samurai minds a long way from the superstitions of popular Buddhism and popular Shinto. They might speak of a moral law of just retribution, externally administered by a supernatural agency, but it was often more in a symbolic than in a literal sense that they did so. Even for the terakoya teacher whose precepts are translated in the appendix, the Punishment of Heaven really amounted to the operation of social sanctions.

Another criterion of "intellectual sophistication" might be the richness of the vocabulary available for the discriminating expression of abstract ideas. The new chemists of Meiji had to develop a whole set of new words to express new ways of classifying matter, but the students of politics, law or philosophy found that most of the conceptual distinctions found in their European models were already familiar and could be easily expressed in their own vocabulary. The need of the translators to coin a new word for a "right" is well known. Perhaps the important thing is that so few such neologisms were needed and that the indigenous vocabulary which could be mobilized for the new translations was not the esoteric language of a small intellectual coterie, but the common property of a relatively large section of the nation.[14] The particular character of the Chinese script is also relevant. New words could be easily created in forms which left their etymological components clearly apparent and often made further explanation unnecessary. The reader of Mill in translation might conceivably read and take the sense of the word *"kenri"* without realizing that this was a "new" word to translate the foreign concept of "right".[15]

The sophistication of the political vocabulary which the samurai acquired in Tokugawa schools was perhaps the most important of all. The development of Japan's commercial vocabulary in 1870 reflected simply the contemporary development of Japan's commercial institutions. But the political vocabulary which the samurai had at his disposal enabled him not merely to understand and describe the workings of his own society, but also to conceive of alternative forms of organization. Thanks to their readings in Japanese and Chinese history and legal codes, the samurai had had some training in comparing and contrasting different principles of political organization. This may not have been a particularly refined or subtle knowledge, but, for instance, the mere fact that the contrast between a "feudal system" and a "system of centralized government" was part of the stock-in-trade of the better-educated samurai mind in 1870[16] may explain a lot about the rapidity of political change in early Meiji.

The Samurai's Political Attitudes

We have seen how, from the end of the eighteenth century onwards, there is increasing emphasis on the function of the schools to train efficient and honest administrators. Government needed knowledge. Likewise, the purpose of knowledge was government. The Confucian schools generally rejected any attempt to teach useful facts or skills for administrators—this was a field left to be preempted by Western learning. Rather, "useful" education for men of talent in the departments of Chinese learning was primarily concerned with ends rather than with means, with the study of history as a road to knowledge of guiding precedents in government, concerned, in other words, with politics.

This overriding preoccupation with politics was perhaps fortified by the samurai's training in swordsmanship which brought him face to face with the elemental power situation in which the strong and skilful holds, but must exercise with discretion, the power of life and death over the weak and inept. It was certainly strengthened by the decentralized feudal system of administration. In the bureaucracies of the fiefs very large numbers of men held, or could reasonably seek to hold, positions which offered scope for political initiative—a scope which was progressively widened in the fluid Bakumatsu period as traditional restraints gave way and routine administrative responses became inadequate to cope with new situations.

In this sense, it has been suggested, the feudal system provided an admirable training ground for political and administrative talent which stood the Meiji regime in good stead.[17] The fief bureaucracies were, to pervert de Tocqueville's phrase, "the grade schools of oligarchy". One might add that they were the grade schools of opposition and revolt as

29

well. The rebellions of the first decade, the Popular Rights Movement, the early development of party politics, the popular nationalism of the early twentieth century, the plots and assassinations of the terrorist *shishi* tradition right up to the present day, spring from much the same roots. Japan did not have to wait for the development of a middle-class chafing under governmental restriction of its economic activity before a large section of the nation began to hold political opinions and seek to express them in action. The samurai, thanks in large part to the high political content of nineteenth-century Confucian education, began the period of industrialization with their political consciousness well developed. Yamaji Aizan was not untypical when he declared:

> Politics is my mistress. I love politics, I adore politics, I live and breathe politics. My fate is bound up with the fate of the Japanese nation. "The governance of the state, the bringing of peace to the world" has been my study since youth.[18]

The phrase he quoted is taken from the *Greater Learning*.

A slightly closer look at the nature of these political preoccupations is necessary to explain why, among the opposition movements of post-Restoration Japan, one should see the Popular Rights movement and the young officers' *coup d'état* as especially rooted in this Tokugawa tradition, but not, say, the activities of the Seiyukai or the suffrage movement. Excluding for the moment motives of personal pecuniary gain, a passionate concern with national politics might partake (the division is a rough and ready one) in varying proportions of three elements: (a) a desire to further the interests of sectional groups within the nation, (b) a predilection for political activity as a vocation, the activity in itself, and the exercise of power if that activity is successful, providing intrinsic satisfaction, and (c) a desire to promote policies which are conceived to be necessary for the welfare of the nation as a whole.

As for the first of these, there can be no doubt that a good many samurai worked to promote the interests of their own fief, to preserve the privileges of the samurai as a class, to further the sectional interests of business-men or of officials when they became such. But this, in the Confucian scheme of things, was so little a respectable motive for action that they rarely did so openly and avowedly. And those who were most obviously activated by sectional interests rarely achieved positions of much power or prestige.

Nor, to be sure, did the second motive find explicit sanction in Confucian teachings. The exercise of political leadership was not, for the samurai, supposed to be an acknowledged source of personal gratification, but a fulfilment of duty. So much for the explicit moral teachings; but the effect of studying history on youthful members of a military class could only too easily produce a different orientation. In large measure the history they read was the history of military adventure in which government and warfare, the responsibilities of power and the glories of military victory, were inextricably intertwined. Government might be a duty in the Tokugawa Confucian ethic, but military adventure, in the less codified samurai tradition nurtured by family legends of the exploits of sixteenth-century ancestors and by Rai Sanyō's descriptions of the heroes of Japanese history, was exciting and pleasurable. Jansen has described the zestful enjoyment with which Sakamoto Ryōma pursued his youthful career as a political activist in the last years of the Tokugawa period,[19] and it was still in a spirit of military adventure that the heirs of the post-Perry *shishi* approached politics in the 1880s—and in 1936. Tokutomi Sohō complained in 1886 that too many of his friends in the Popular Rights movement looked "on politics as a kind of sport, a form of amusement like letting off fireworks", and their bombastic rhetoric was always shooting off into flights of fantasy in which they pictured themselves riding bravely along the banks of the Yalu, banners streaming in the wind. Better for Japanese youth, he said sadly, if they had chosen as their heroes Adam Smith and John Watt instead of Napoleon and Bismarck, the idols of his day.[20] One might well argue that it is because a passionate concern with politics was in its origins allied in this way with the spirit of military adventure that the pattern of private enterprise violence has persisted in Japanese politics to a more advanced level of industrial and constitutional development than in most other countries.

It was above all the third kind of passionate concern with politics, the desire to promote policies considered to be necessary for the nation as a whole, which was most specifically nurtured by the education samurai received. In the Confucian tradition politics was not the art of the possible, the choice of lesser evils, the achievement of the best compromise between conflicting interests. A good policy was one which would benefit *everyone*. It was the political philosophy of an uncomplex society in which the chief potential conflict of interest lay between the producing ruled and the consuming rulers. Enlightened government consisted in the kind of benevolence which would enable the ruled to produce more in contentment to the benefit of all. When sectional conflict did rear its head among the ruled, as between peasant and merchant, it was resolved by a simple scale of priorities; the peasantry was of the greater importance to the welfare of the whole; hence its interests should be paramount. It is hardly surprising that men who received training in this kind of political philosophy—and received it at a time when the Japanese nation as a whole did have, in defence against foreign attack, one overriding common concern overshadowing all other political issues—should have developed a concern with politics of this nationally oriented, rather than sectionally oriented, kind. They were *yūkoku no shi*—men anxious for the fate of the *nation*.

There is another aspect of Confucian political training which is directly relevant to the opposition movements of post-Restoration Japan. It was, at least implicitly, a training in *principles*. As such it opened the possibility for every man to become his own arbiter of the correct application of principle to particular situations. True, one of the major principles inculcated was *loyalty*—to the head of one's household or to the head of one's fief—and it is true that in a dominant version of this ethic loyalty meant blind obedience. But Maruyama has shown the persistence in the Tokugawa period of a different tradition which required the loyal servant to be his own judge of what was really in his lord's interest, even his own judge of what constituted benevolent rule in his lord (which he should support) and what constituted wickedness (against which he should remonstrate).[21] Such judgments required criteria over and above the simple principle of loyalty, and these criteria history could offer, for history was chiefly concerned to record and judge the deeds of rulers at the pinnacle of loyalties, for whom loyalty in this sense of blind obedience could provide no guide. We have seen how Rai Sanyō showed the late Tokugawa samurai an example of how Confucian criteria (devotion to the "public" as opposed to "private" interests, for instance) could be applied by a Japanese to Japanese history. And if they could be applied to past, they could equally be applied to present, rulers. With a knowledge of the correct principles, the loyal servant could be his *own* judge of what constituted loyalty in a retainer and what constituted good government—true devotion to the public interest of the people as a whole—in a ruler.

The last years of the Tokugawa period provided ample scope for this tradition to grow, the more so because, as Smith has argued, the majority of daimyos had long since forfeited the respect of their subordinates as persons.[22] Craig has described[23] how the loyalists of Chōshū could defy their lord on strictly moral grounds within the Confucian tradition, claiming to be urging on him policies which were in the best interests of the House of Mōri as *they* interpreted them according to *their* principles. The Restoration immeasurably widened the scope for this tradition to develop. The new state had to adopt innovating policies, and innovation, involving a choice between alternatives, requires principles of selection in a way in which the mere routine administration of a system of power may not. There was no lack in the Meiji period of vociferous ex-samurai voices offering to tell the government what those principles should be, and what were the just and proper policies which should follow from them. The point to be made here—a point made by Maruyama in the article just cited—is that one can already find in Tokugawa traditions the source of: (*a*) the hubris which permitted subordinates to offer advice to their superiors, (*b*) the notion that such advice could be offered by any independent thinker who knew the right principles of judgment, and (*c*) some of the content of the principles assumed by government critics in the Meiji period—a notion of the public interest (variously interpreted to mean national glory or popular welfare) and of according with the "trend of the times" (the meaning of *jisei* becoming modified under the influence of Western doctrines of progress).[24] The tradition which produced these attitudes and ideas was one of long standing but it was nurtured by study, particularly historical study, in the schools of the Tokugawa period. Fukuzawa's "spirit of independence", Uchimura's conscience, were not simply grown from foreign roots.

It is an interesting question just how, in those who became the leaders of Meiji society, the three kinds of motive listed earlier combined in their political lives. The fact that the only respectable motive was patriotic devotion to the national good obviously generated a good deal of hypocrisy. The landlords demanding lower land taxes, the importers demanding sugar subsidies, the manufacturers demanding protective tariffs, had to claim that these measures were in *Japan's* interest, not rely on arguments about justice and an equitable satisfaction of their own sectional interests. In fact, as the emphasis of governmental activity shifted from foreign to domestic affairs, the pursuit of sectional interests and the reconciliation of their conflicts actually became an increasingly predominant element of the subject matter of politics. But because it was not respectable it tended to become furtive. "Pressure group" may be a dirty word in other societies besides Japan, but it is not often that, as in Japan even today, the pressure group which is open and above board in its activities and blatantly unsecretive about its pursuit of private interests does not thereby mitigate its offence but compounds it.[25]

Equally there can be no doubt that the idealistic patriotism of the politician devoted to the national interest was rarely unalloyed with the personal pursuit and enjoyment of prestige and power. But as long as the overt ideology stressed collective goals, prestige, and in the long run power, too, depended on some real performance in the service of the nation, so that these two motives could work in harness rather than in conflict. It was otherwise when the pursuit of "private" interests took a material form. The business-man, perhaps, could still combine patriotism and the profit motive as long as what was good for Mitsubishi could be thought to be good for the nation. But the politician could only enrich himself at the expense of the public purse. "The road to private aggrandisement was often the road of public service", Bellah has remarked of the Tokugawa period,[26] and Fukuzawa was once explicit and sweeping in his condemnation of samurai hypocrisy. They were, he said,

> to all outward appearances model retainers, given to large talk of loyalty and service to the fief—"Poverty is the rule of the samurai". "He who is nourished as a retainer should die in his master's service."—One would think they were about to seek their death in battle at any moment.

And yet these men who posed as *chun-tzu*, as Confucius's "superior men",

> were nothing but gilded pseudo-*chun-tzu* ... Commissioners of Works would take kickbacks from carpenters, Exchequer officials would take bribes from merchants, and such behaviour was almost standard practice in the households of the three hundred daimyos[27]

Meiji Japan was by no means free of such officials. Not even the leaders of the government were notably abstemious in their enjoyment of the good things of life. Official salary scales were generous, so were expense accounts, and statesmen were not above corruption, not only from patriotic motives (buying the votes of despised politicians in the national interest) but also for personal ends. Tani Kanjō, in an excoriating memorandum written after he resigned from government service in 1887, denounces the corruption of his colleagues and predicts that Japan, too, might well follow in the path of Egypt whose drive for national regeneration under Mahomet Ali foundered in its leaders' self-indulgence.[28]

He was, however, proved wrong. The official ethic may have been unable entirely to eliminate personal cupidity, but it did serve to keep it within bounds. Corruption remained, for the most part, a matter of misusing official position to give favours to friends and allies; it rarely, if ever, reached the more overt level of the contractual sale of favours to the highest bidder. And personal enrichment was held within limits by the ideal. Even if there was a large element of hypocrisy in the statesmen's professedly selfless patriotism, the virtue to which vice thus paid tribute had its restraining effects. Policy was always the result of a dialectic between the ideal and private interest, never solely guided by the latter.

Merit and Competition

Chapter VI attempted to show how the development of samurai education accelerated the trend infief administrations to give more explicit recognition to "merit" in the appointment of administrators. Smith has justly argued that the merit ideal spread much faster than its application in practice. Among the liveliest and most public-spirited lower samurai, therefore, there was a growing sense of frustration at the gap between their ideal of justice and the real world they had to live in, a sense of frustration which eventually destroyed their loyalty to their fief superiors and made them enthusiasts for a regime which would destroy the feudal system.[29]

One might further generalize from the growing emphasis on the need for the merit system in administration and argue that this development prepared the way for the creation of a society which should in all spheres award prestige and power and income predominantly on the basis of performance. When Fukuzawa Yukichi urged that it was not hereditary status but contribution to society which made a man worthy of respect and began his preface to the *Encouragement of Learning* with his most famous phrase: "Heaven did not create men above men, nor set men below men"[30] he was not simply introducing a startling new Western idea; he was succinctly summarizing a current of thought long since developing in Tokugawa society.

Tokugawa Confucianism, despite the particularism of the obligations its ethic enjoined, was in principle universalistic in two senses. It was the Way of Man, and as such Confucian scholarship was not to be forbidden even to the commoner classes. Secondly, its standards of excellence were objective. Although it had its schools and coteries they never became as exclusive as they did in the military arts, the dramatic arts or traditional religion; there were no licences of proficiency granted by teachers whose award might be motivated by favouritism rather than the honest assessment of merit. A scholar's knowledge of the classics, the quality of his Chinese poems, were in principle exposed to the judgment of strangers as well as of teachers and friends, and there were objective standards by which to judge them. Even for the ordinary samurai, the introduction of school education meant that a large part of a boy's life was now occupied by a new activity which required him to meet objectively measured standards of performance. These standards were probably more rigorous than those of the only pre-existing comparable activity—his military training. Even if they were not, the mere addition of a new field doubled the proportion of his youthful time spent in such tasks and must thereby have increased his general "achievement-orientation".

It also provided a new field in which differences of ability—of natural endowment, of application and of achievement—could become apparent. We have seen how wary teachers were of making use of this fact to stimulate a spirit of competition for fear of the impurity of the motives which would be awakened. Yet competitiveness did develop. It is a remarkable fact that for all the emphasis on collective goals in the ideology there was little in the actual experience of the young samurai to develop a "team spirit" and everything to encourage individualistic self-assertion. Military training was a matter of individual skill at individual combat. Similarly in the schools, with the possible exception of the licensed gangs for younger pupils at Aizu, there was no organization of "houses" or of any other kind of groups whose collective performance could be pitted one against the other. The playing fields of Eton, or at least of Dr Arnold's Rugby, would have been much more suitably congruent with the collectivism of the

Tokugawa ideology than either the classrooms or the military sheds of the fief schools.

This odd mixture was probably an important ingredient of Japan's recipe for development. The combination of an individualistic will to succeed in the individual personality together with an emphasis on collective goals in the ideology was one which helped to accelerate the rate of economic and social change and at the same time to keep individual efforts within a framework of national objectives. It drove statesmen and business-men to work with zealous energy in order to distinguish themselves, to achieve success. But that success could only be sanctified and could only bring them real honour if it was, or could be represented as, service to the nation.

The Balance Sheet

Every man likes to think well of his subject, but a cautious writer ought perhaps to have stopped before this and asked himself whether he has not exaggerated the beneficent influences of Tokugawa education on Japan's subsequent history. Let us therefore qualify. While it is true that the economic growth of Japan since 1870 is widely regarded as a success story, there are equally, in the social and political sphere, a good many phases of Japan's modern development which most people would agree are much less worthy of admiration. And the Tokugawa schools probably contributed about equally to each side of the balance sheet.

The terrorism of modern ultra-nationalist activists and the furtiveness and hypocrisy attaching to interest group politics were already mentioned in passing in this chapter. One might add that the tradition of benevolent paternalism, too, though really productive of a good deal of enlightened social reform, was also productive of a good deal of self-righteous hypocrisy and oppression—one has only to think of the conciliation societies and the improvement societies which were hastily started in the 'twenties to mollify and emasculate the protest movements of the workers, the tenants and the *eta* outcasts. Again, the use of schools to propagate among the mass of the people a morality of docile submissiveness was an aspect of Tokugawa education which remained unchanged in the modern period (or more particularly between 1900 and 1945) except that it was carried out with immensely improved efficiency. That very combination of a debased form of the Confucian ethic with beliefs in Japanese racial uniqueness and Imperial divinity—the Japanism which hung like a pall of sanctimonious smog, not only over the schools but over the whole of Japanese intellectual and political life until 1945—was first effectively formulated at Mito, in one of the fief schools of the Tokugawa period. Equally the emphasis on collective goals in the ideology inherited from the Tokugawa period led to militarism and disaster as well as to economic advance. The scorn of the public-spirited man for the sordid trivialities of internal politics and his exclusive concentration on foreign affairs (in which it was clearly the interests and glory of *Japan* that were at stake) worked together with the traditions kept alive in the military half of the Tokugawa schools to produce irresistible pressure for the pursuit of military glory and territorial expansion. In 1905 this did not so much matter, perhaps. Japan got away with it against Russia and she did so with honour, for her actions accorded with the morality of the times. But so strong were these pressures and so great the sense of self-righteousness which Japanese nationalism drew from its distant Confucian sources that Japan remained unchanged—or rather moved backwards—when the rest of the world, or most of it, had moved on. As a result she was led into the same kind of venture thirty years later at a time when she could neither gain honour nor, as it turned out, any longer get away with it.

Altogether it is a significant and undeniable fact that it was in the 1930s that pilgrimages to the Mito school became popular, that educational historians began writing fulsome books of praise about their Tokugawa forerunners, that the Shingaku movement was revived, that Tokugawa-style swordsmanship was brought back into the schools and that the selected writings of certain Tokugawa Confucianists became most popular in high school curricula. The decade when Japanese society was being reduced at the hands of fanatics to its most stifling condition of oppressive irrationalism was the decade in which the ideals of the Japanese educational world were closer to those of its Tokugawa past than at any time since 1870.

In some respects the "good" and the "bad" sides of the balance sheet are inextricably intermixed; the same features of the legacy bequeathed to modern Japan by Tokugawa educators probably helped to promote both economic growth and militaristic expansionism, and it is doubtful if Japan could have had the one without the other. The very slogan which summed up early government policy as "enriching the country and strengthening the army" underlines the connection. But in other respects there *are* two sides; some among the descendants of the Tokugawa samurai *were* concerned with popular welfare, whereas others were concerned only with popular loyalties; some used the self-righteous rhetoric of idealism to cover the protection of their own private interests, whereas others helped the weak and downtrodden to organize to protect themselves; some were interested in objective truth, others only in spiritual and ideological unity; some genuinely tried to create a society which would provide equal opportunities for all its citizens, others were more concerned to see that each man knew and kept his proper place. And always the men who were most hypocritical, most jealous of privilege, most concerned with spiritual unity, harmony and proper hierarchy, were the ones who were at the same time most anxious to preserve, or revive, the forms of Tokugawa education in the modern period. Perhaps the best that can be said of the legacy which Tokugawa educators bequeathed to the modern period is that in some of their ideals—in the rationalism, the stress on selflessness and benevolence and the need to put knowledge to the service of others which they taught in theory but failed very often to exhibit in practice—there was still a sufficient glimmer of inspiration to make rebels of the best of their pupils, and to ensure that when the time and opportunity came the latter would seek to destroy the educational traditions which had formed them.

1. B. Simon, *Studies in the History of Education*, p. 170.
2. G. Bousquet, *Le Japon de nos jours*, I, p. 337.
3. J. Abegglen and H. Mannari, "Leaders of Modern Japan".
4. See Smith, "Landlords' sons in the business elite".
5. After the first fine flourish of the 1872 programme with its bold intentions of creating over 54,000 new primary schools *de novo*, the central government was finally forced to accommodate itself to the cloth from which its coat had to be cut. The revised ordinances of 1879 and 1880 permitted private schools (i.e. the existing terakoya) to function as substitutes for public schools if certified as efficient, and in the Ministry's explanation to the Senate of the 1880 order it is admitted that even in the public schools nine-tenths of the teachers had received no training from the new training colleges, and that most of them

RONALD DORE

were 'priests, monks (*shūgen*) or teachers of calligraphy'—i.e. former terakoya teachers (Mombushō, *Kaisei kyōikurei seitei riyū*, pp. 399. 307).

6. *Ibid.*, p. 401.

7. *Jurin-hyō (Zenshū*, 2).

8. Hirose Tansō forbade his students to travel on the expectation of hospitality in other students' homes. It had reached the point that many parents were reluctant to allow their children to take up scholarship seriously for fear of the stream of unwelcome visitors it might lead to (*Kangien kiyaku kokuyu*, p. 9).

9. Alexander Gerschenkron, "Economic development in Russian intellectual history", p. 30. (Quoting D. I. Pisarev.)

10. Francis Place, writing in 1830. Quoted in B. Simon, *Studies in the History of Education*, p. 169.

11. "'Merit' in Tokugawa bureaucracy."

12. See p. 286, Dore, *Education in Tokugawa Japan*.

13. Arisawa *et al.*, *Keizai shutaisei kōza*, 3, p. 17.

14. If one takes, as an example, a random page from an official memorandum justifying the imposition of compulsory education by arguments clearly derived from Western sources, a few of the new words stand out: "the *rights* of minors", "the government, i.e. the *collective force of society*", in the "*eye of the law*". But these are a small proportion of the indigenous abstract vocabulary: "to state a reason", "fixed interpretation", "impose a responsibility", "evasion", "essential criterion", "minimum period", etc. (Mombushō, *Kaisei kyōikurei seitei riyū*, pp. 402–3).

15. When Fukuzawa translated *Chambers' Political Economy* in 1866 a Bakufu official objected strongly to its praise of *kyōsō*—the word Fukuzawa had invented to translate "competition". He had no difficulty in understanding the meaning of the word, only in accepting the notion that anything involving "conflict" (the basic meaning of one of the characters used) could be considered praiseworthy (Carmen Blacker, *Fukuzawa Yukichi*, p. 28). Another linguistic feature helped in the popular diffusion of new words as well as of erudite old ones. In popular decrees it was common to write beside difficult words written in Chinese characters an approximate synonym from common speech written in the phonetic script. It is as if in, say, "anyone creating a disturbance", the word "disturbance" had the gloss "noise" written beside it.

16. The distinction is found even in Yamamoto's mediocre little compendium of Chinese grammar, written not for samurai but for commoners. In a series of short general-knowledge sections at the end, the main point made under the heading of history is that there were systems of government, *hōken-seido* and *gunken-seido*, and that China started with the first and went on to the second, while Japan reversed the process (Yamamoto Shōitsu, *Dojitsū*).

17. Matsuda Michio, "Nihon no chishikijin", p. 13.

18. Quoted (from *Aru hito ni kotooru sho*) in Uchida and Shioda, "Chishiki seinen no shoruikei", p. 249.

19. M. B. Jansen, *Sakamoto Ryōma and the Meiji Restoration*, esp. pp. 153, 156, 171.

40

20. *Shōrai no Nihon*, pp. 204, 95.

21. "Chūsei to hangyaku" pp. 393–7.

22. " 'Merit' in Tokugawa bureaucracy."

23. A. Craig, *Chōshū in the Meiji Restoration*, pp. 160–1, 224, 352.

24. See Carmen Blacker, *Fukuzawa Yukichi*, pp. 127–36, for a comparison of Fukuzawa's concept of *jisei* as a "general state of public opinion" limiting the actions of great men, with that of Rai Sanyō. See also Tokutomi Sohō's *Shōrai no Nihon* (esp. pp. 193, 210) for a related but more Spencerian concept of *hitsuzen no ikioi*, a kind of dynamic force impelling society along a road of inevitable progression from the military to the productive form of society.

25. For excellent elaborations of this point see the remarks of Kyōgoku Junichi in Oka, *Gendai Nihon no seiji katei*, p. 475, and M. Maruyama, *Thought and behaviour in modern Japanese Politics*, pp. 6–7.

26. *Tokugawa religion*, p. 37.

27. Quoted (from *Gakumon no susume*) in Maruyama, "Chūsei to hangyaku", p. 391.

28. *Ikensho*, in Yoshino, *Meiji bunka zenshū*, 13, p. 469.

29. " 'Merit' in Tokugawa bureaucracy."

30. *Gakumon no susume*, pref. These words are now inscribed at the base of his statue in his home town of Nakatsu, and on the bars of chocolate sold in the booths beside it.

EDWARD R. BEAUCHAMP

GRIFFIS IN JAPAN: THE FUKUI
INTERLUDE, 1871

A characteristic of the decades following the arrival in Japanese waters of Commodore Matthew C. Perry's "black ships" in 1853–4 was the increasing frequency of intercourse between Japan and the United States. After more than two centuries of virtual isolation from the rest of the world, Japan's veil of seclusion was stripped away and her policy of self-imposed exile brought to an end. The Meiji Restoration of 1868 marked the beginning of an official government policy aimed at acquiring Western knowledge so as to strengthen the nation and to enable Japan to confront the Western intruders on a basis of parity. An important element of this policy was the reformation of Japanese education along Western lines.

The promulgation of the Imperial Charter Oath in 1868 by the young Meiji Emperor laid down the aims of the new government, called on the people to eschew old-fashioned ways, and insisted that "Know-

Edward R. Beauchamp is Associate Professor of History of Education at the University of Hawaii.

Reprinted from *Monumenta Nipponica* XXX, 4 (Winter, 1975), with permission of the author and publisher. This material, in a different form, appears in *An American Teacher in Early Meiji Japan* by E. R. Beauchamp (Honolulu: University Press of Hawaii, 1976).

ledge be sought throughout the world."[1] In response to this call, many Japanese students journeyed at government expense to the United States and to Western Europe seeking to learn the mysteries of Western power and prestige so that Japan could join the ranks of the powerful. A slightly different manifestation of the Emperor's charge was the employment of foreign specialists as teachers, technicians and experts by both the new government in Tokyo and several of the *han* governments in order to foster rapid development. It has been estimated that between 3,000 and 4,000 of these people were employed by the Japanese during the first two decades of the Meiji Period.[2]

Of these so-called *yatoi*,[3] or foreign employees, one of the earliest and most interesting was William Elliot Griffis. Born in Philadelphia on 17 September 1843, Griffis was the second son and fourth child of Anna Marie (Hess) Griffis and Captain John Limeburner Griffis. William's paternal grandfather, a Welshman, came to the United States as supercargo aboard a merchant ship in the years preceding the American Revolution, and established himself as a tea merchant in Philadelphia. However, his stubborn opposition to the colonial policies of King George III, combined with the outbreak of war in 1776, resulted in his remaining in Philadelphia instead of returning to his native land. The elder Griffis struck up a friendship with Benjamin Franklin, and is buried near him in Philadelphia's Arch Street Cemetery.[4]

Young "Willie" Griffis, as his family and friends called him, acquired his earliest education from his mother, and between 1848 and 1850 attended a local dame school before entering one of Philadelphia's newly established elementary schools. There is some evidence that the Griffis family fortune might have declined in the mid-1850s, causing economic problems, but Willie continued his schooling at Central High School, graduating in 1859.[5]

At an early age, Griffis witnessed the launching of Commodore Perry's future flagship, the U.S.S. *Susquehanna*, from his father's coal wharf on the Delaware River. His father, an old seafaring man, had a number of friends at the local navy yard and indeed the Commanding Officer at the time allowed the Griffis boys a great deal of freedom in the shipyard. As a result, Willie saw the ship being constructed during his frequent visits.[6]

Almost ten years later, on 9 June 1860, Griffis witnessed the first Japanese Embassy to the U.S. when it arrived in Philadelphia to visit the local sights, and he was able to meet several of its members. Years later, he wrote, "From the first, I took the Japanese seriously. In many respects our equals, in others they seemed to be our superiors."[7] Although he occasionally became disillusioned with the Japanese, for example, in their treatment of Korea, this was a judgment which he maintained to the end of his long life.

William Elliot Griffis was, above all, a deeply religious man. His first religious experiences were as a Presbyterian, but at the age of twenty he gravitated to the Second Dutch Reformed Church of Philadelphia when he disagreed with his pastor's pro-slavery sentiments. It was in his new church, on 24 May 1863, that he heard the sermon that gave his life a direction that had been lacking. The sermon, delivered by Rutgers President William Henry Campbell, inspired Griffis "to enter the ministry, to study at Rutgers, and eventually to go to Japan."[8] Interestingly enough, his mother had attended a commencement twenty years earlier at Rutgers and was so moved that she vowed that should one of her boys be called to the ministry he would study at Rutgers.[9]

While visiting an uncle in Baltimore, Griffis learned of General Lee's invasion of Pennsylvania and hurried home in June 1863 to enlist in the Union Army. During the course of his ninety-day enlistment, he served with H Company of the 44th Pennsylvania Regiment, and missed seeing action at the Battle of Gettysburg only because his unit, fortunately, arrived a few days too late to participate in the carnage. Upon his discharge from the army, Griffis returned home, engaged a tutor to help prepare himself for college, and entered Rutgers in the autumn of 1865.

Although Griffis planned to enter the ministry, he chose to follow the new scientific curriculum rather than the more traditional classical path to a degree. This decision was typical of Griffis; he possessed a lively curiosity and always resisted pressures to confine his interests within narrowly prescribed channels. While at Rutgers he studied, among other subjects, mathematics, astronomy, chemistry, physics, botany, Latin, Greek, philosophy, German, French, Hebrew and history. This intellectual breadth and an active extracurricular schedule did not prevent him from graduating fifth in his class with a 93.6% average.[10]

Another link with Japan was forged by Griffis during his Rutgers years. In 1866, several Japanese students arrived in New Brunswick under the auspices of the Board of Foreign Missions of the Reformed

Church. Griffis soon met these young men, whom he described as the "equals of American students in good-breeding, courtesy, and mental acumen."[11] Griffis tutored several of them, including Kusakabe Tarō,[12] and when Kusakabe died before his graduation, it was Griffis who personally delivered the deceased youth's Phi Beta Kappa key and personal effects to his family in Echizen when Griffis went to Fukui in 1871.

Upon graduation in 1869, Griffis traveled through Europe with his sister Margaret. At the end of that long pleasant summer, he entered the New Brunswick Theological Seminary, taught at Rutgers Preparatory School, and even did some preaching. In September 1870, the daimyo of Echizen *han*, Matsudaira Shungaku,[13] requested Guido Verbeck, the well-known Dutch-American missionary in Japan, to recommend a qualified person to establish "a scientific school on the American principle and teach the natural sciences" in his provincial capital of Fukui facing the Sea of Japan.[14] Verbeck, anxious to secure a fellow-member of the Dutch Reformed for this position, passed the request on to friends at Rutgers,[15] who in turn recommended Griffis for the post.

Verbeck had made it clear that whoever was sent to Japan would be expected to teach chemistry and physics at an annual salary of $2,400, plus a European-style house and a horse. He added that under these terms a man could live adequately on about $800 per year. He warned, however, that the conditions would be trying and the temptations great; the country was filled with those who had fallen into a dissolute way of life.[16]

Sometime during the first week in September 1870, Griffis was offered the position. Although it was an attractive one, he hesitated before accepting it. His urge for adventure and the obvious financial benefits offered by the position were tempered by his attraction to a young lady, Ellen G. Johnson, whom it seems he expected to marry. Her intentions, however, were not so certain as his, and her decision to take an extended trip to Europe disappointed him bitterly. At the urging of the Japanese students at Rutgers and his classmate, Robert Pruyn, whose father had been the American Minister to Japan, Griffis reconsidered his initial decision and accepted the offer. In a letter to his sister Margaret, dated 26 September 1870, he justified his decision in these words, "*I can study and be ordained there, and God willing, return to my native land, only one year later than if I stayed.* Besides the grand opportunities and culture, travel and good climate, and being under the special protection of the Prince, I can not only study my theology but collect materials to write a book. I can support my family at home, at least *pay the rent, and carpet the floors and send handsome sums home, too.*" [17]

The news of this position in Japan did not, however, meet with complete support in the Griffis household. One of his sister's "tears flowed so copiously that she appeared to disolved [sic]," and another sister "fled to her chamber there in secret to give vent to her grief." His pious mother, however, told Willie that "the fact that you believe yourself called of him is sufficient to me." [18]

The two months between his acceptance of the position and his departure were filled with activities related to closing out his affairs, packing, studying, etc. Griffis expressed chagrin that "insuarance [sic] companies would not, except at a heavy premium, insure the life of me going inside Japan." He recalled the "incredulity and surprise expressed by businessmen that 'an intelligent young man should trust a people like the Japanese to keep a financial arrangement'." [19]

Finally, on 13 November 1870, young William Elliot Griffis set out from Philadelphia to cross the continent by train. After a long and arduous journey, he caught sight of "the waters of the Pacific gleaming into view, the Golden Gate in sight." [20] On 1 December Griffis boarded the steamer *Great Republic* and soon left his country behind him. On the morning of 29 December, he rose to see Japan for the first time. "Hills, crested with timber, line the bay, and the beaches are dotted with thatched huts and white store-houses. Fisherman's boats, manned and moving over the bay, are near enough for us to distinguish their occupants. Tall and muscular men, with skins of dirty copper color, in long loose dress, their mid-scalps shaven . . . are the first natives of Japan whom we see at home." [21]

The Japan that Griffis found upon his arrival was a land known at first hand by few Westerners. In terms of numbers, the only substantial Western enclaves were found at Yokohama, and to a lesser extent at Tokyo. In the former, there were approximately 2,000 foreigners, half of them Western military and security forces, while Tokyo sheltered only 100 Westerners, including two or three women. It was in Tokyo, at the home of Guido Verbeck, that Griffis stayed for several weeks before journeying to Fukui to commence his work. He put to good use the time he spent in the capital; the curious newcomer filled his hours exploring the city and its environs, sometimes with Verbeck guiding him, studying Japanese, reading, and substitute teaching in the local Western school. He also began collecting a wide variety of materials on Japan and the Japanese that would inform his numerous books and articles.[22] The excitement and vitality of the capital were not a good preparation for the harsher reality he would find in Fukui, located 200 miles west of the capital in one of the most remote parts of Japan. While Fukui was still a backwater, Tokyo was described by a contemporary as a place where

> Something was always going on, and pleasant society was not wanting, whenever one felt the need for it. Evening parties and entertainments were frequent among the foreign residents, and the elegance and style seen on such occasions reminded one more of the fashionable life at home than residence in a foreign city.[23]

Despite the genteel aspects of a cultivated foreigner's life in the capital during the 1870s, the situation also had its unsavory side. Griffis summed up this aspect when he suggested, "It is doubtful whether vice in Edo was ever more rampant than in the third quarter of the nineteenth century . . . life was held to be cheaper than dirt by the swashbucklers, ronins and other strange characters and outlaws . . . infesting Tokyo."[24] Anti-foreign feeling ran so high among the *rōnin* that they often felt that it was an act of the highest patriotism to cut down a foreign "barbarian" in the street. Griffis had been forewarned of this danger by his Japanese friends at Rutgers, and it seems that upon their advice he purchased a Smith & Wesson revolver before leaving New Brunswick. He later wrote that he was "not certain that the mere gesture of putting my hand into my bosom was more than once a means of impressing upon some scowling patriot that he had better not draw."[25]

Although one wonders how much embellishment this situation received from Griffis' romantic imagination, the reality of the danger was demonstrated shortly after his arrival in Tokyo. Early in the evening of 13 January 1871, two teachers, by name of Dallas and Ring, dismissed their bodyguards assigned to escort them whenever they left the teachers' compound, and sought out female companionship. While walking down the road, "suspicious of nothing", they were attacked from the rear by two sword-wielding *rōnin*. Dallas suffered a severe wound from his right ear to his left shoulder, "about 8 inches long and three inches deep". Ring's assailant cut him "across the neck and shoulder", and when Ring tried to escape, slashed his back "severing one of the ribs and touching the spine."[26] In a letter to his sister, Griffis assured his family that the incident would be exaggerated at home, but if one took reasonable precautions, there was little danger. He added that he had little sympathy for those who "deliberately reject all guards, & go unarmed."[27]

Finally, on 3 February 1871, all was in readiness for Griffis to leave for Echizen. He confided to his sister Margaret that he was actually offered a choice of going to the interior or staying with Verbeck in the capital, but he chose the former because it would not have been "fair to disappoint Prince Echizen", who had been responsible for his coming to Japan. He did not protest, however, when Verbeck interceded with the Prince to obtain for him $3,600 per year rather than the original $2,400 which had been offered to him in New Brunswick.[28]

In late February 1871, Griffis began the last leg of his journey to Fukui. The city which greeted Griffis on 4 March 1871 offered sharp contrast to both the relatively sophisticated Tokyo which he had recently left, and his anticipated image of Fukuo. After an arduous journey of twelve days over several hundred miles, "escorted by twelve knights on horseback",[29] Griffis entered the ancient capital of Echizen fief amid "wind, light showers, and fitful flakes of snow, alternating with rifts of sunlight."[30]

One student of the period described Fukui at about the time of Griffis' arrival in 1871 as "a typical provincial city of its time, containing some 12,000 inhabitants, 2,849 homes, 25 inns and 34 streets along the center of which clear mountain water was conducted through stone channels [in which] the citizens washed their dishes and their clothes."[31] Nearby were both an important paper mill, famous throughout Japan, and a prosperous silk industry, which Griffis described in a letter to his sister.[32]

In his often fertile imagination, Griffis had envisioned Fukui as an opulent Asian city, indeed, "the ideal Fukui was a grand city." As he rode through the streets, however, "expecting at last to emerge into some splendid avenue . . . the scales", he wrote, "fell from my eyes." Suffering from nothing more serious than a case of "culture shock", Griffis wrote, "I was amazed at the utter poverty of the people, the contemptible houses, and the tumble-down look of the city, as compared with the trim dwellings of an American town. . . . I realized what a Japanese—an Asiatic city—was [and] I was disgusted."[33]

48

In an article written a few days later, and subsequently published in *The Christian Intelligencer*, he rhetorically asked, "How *could* a nineteenth century New Yorker live in the twelfth century?" After a full week in Fukui, Griffis, a nineteenth-century Philadelphian, managed to adjust, a fact he attributed to his missionary impulse. "It is", he wrote, "no loss to live in a social desert, if [one] can help the people upward to God."[34] As is not uncommon, the passage of time mellowed Griffis' early opinion of Fukui. Years later, in a more generous mood, he claimed, "I was proud and delighted that my lot was cast in Fukui, a city which in eminence and intellectual and moral progress was set, as it were, upon a hill."[35]

This later judgment was, at least in an objective sense, partially accurate. Fukui was the capital of Echizen *han* whose daimyo, Matsudaira Shungaku, was one of Japan's wisest and most progressive leaders. Adamantly opposed to the Western challenge at the outset, he quickly came to see the futility of that position and reversed himself.[36] Sir George Sansom has written that even prior to Matsudaira's change of heart in 1863, "foreign studies had made good progress" in Echizen, and Marius Jansen has described Matsudaira as "one of the outstanding lords' of his era.[37]

Assuming the position of daimyo of Echizen in 1838, Matsudaira set out to rebuild the *han's* shaky financial structure and to strengthen its military posture.

In 1848 cannon on Western models were cast at Fukui. Echizen sent some of the young men to study medicine of the Dutch at Nagasaki, and, without ordering, advised European practice. To stay the ravages of smallpox he petitioned the Shogun to have general vaccination attempted throughout the country. Failing in this, in 1850 he opened at Fukui an office at which his own people could receive the pure vaccine virus. The next year he introduced the Dutch artillery, drill and infantry tactics. In 1852 he abolished archery, as the Samurai's accomplishment, and ordered rifle shooting at the butts.[38]

Education was not neglected in this burst of reform-oriented energy. Several years after Matsudaira became daimyo, Yokoi Shōnan,[39] a Kumamoto samurai and a well-known scholar, paid his first of several visits to Fukui in 1847. Although Matsudaira was in Edo at the time of this visit, Yokoi met with a number of the daimyo's advisers, whom he impressed with his wide knowledge. Yokoi's views on education were largely shaped by his conviction that, in Sansom's words, "the modern samurai were taken up, besotted almost, with art over letters, to the neglect of political and social studies which the times demanded; and the aim of his teaching was described as the encouragement of real, practical learning."[40] He felt that education and politics were inseparable as young men pursued formal education to better prepare themselves for political activities. This type of "imaginative and politically conscious education" was attractive to Matsudaira and his advisers.[41]

As a result of the enthusiasm generated by Yokoi's ideas, a school was established on 2 May 1855, called the *Meidōkan*.[42] "At first the *Meidōkan* taught the Confucian classics, military arts, national history, Chinese philosophies other than Confucianism, ceremonial affairs, poetics, writing, arithmetic, calendar reading, medicine and Dutch Studies."[43] Hashimoto Sanai,[44] son of a prominent Fukui doctor, had been studying in Edo since 1854 and returned to Fukui in the summer of 1856 "as an instructor in charge of Dutch studies at the new *han* academy . . . , and by February 1857, he had become the school's headmaster." During his tenure he encouraged "a new and more utilitarian curriculum".[45] On 6 May 1857, "a foreign literature training department, with a curriculum of study, with textbooks based on the Dutch model, was established."[46]

Hashimoto was anxious to have the *Meidōkan's* effectiveness increased and he wrote,

> The appointment of able men is important in any age. It is especially important now when the *han* government is being reformed and the organization of the *han* is being reestablished. At present, men of ability have been appointed, but this is as yet insufficient. Thus we need to educate the young people and cultivate their talent. The school should hold fast to educational policy and provide for the future of the *han* government. . . . In order to achieve this educational policy of the unification of study and politics, it is not enough to do our best for school education. The *han* authorities have to appoint men of ability positively and in large numbers, giving great encouragement to general students. Otherwise, without a proper place for themselves, men of talent would lose all hope, complain and be dissatisfied. In the end, this educational policy would create a damaging effect on the school education itself.[47]

In order to lend "encouragement to general students", Hashimoto arranged for the establishment of four schools outside the castle walls to serve as a branch for training in the martial arts.

Between the time of Yokoi's first visit to Fukui in 1847 and the 1870 decision to invite foreign teachers to Fukui, the major goal of education in the *han* had shifted from the training of hereditary warriors loyal to the Prince, to the training of men of ability who would serve in positions of governmental power and responsibility. This shift was reflected in a proclamation issued by the Prince in December 1869, suggesting that since all were now, more than ever, subjects of the Emperor, "the school has to bring up men of talent who would be useful to the Imperial Government by widening the students' knowledge and improving their morality."[48] Thus, Western teachers were welcomed for the knowledge and skills they could transmit to the Emperor's subjects.

Riding through the crowded streets and surrounded by curious people trying to get a look at the blue-eyed foreigner from across the seas, Griffis was greeted by "several officers, all in their best silks, swords, sandals, and top-knots, with bows, and such awkward but hearty handshakings as men unused to it might be supposed to achieve."[49] After these formalities, Griffis was quickly escorted to his temporary quarters, "an old mansion, nearly 150 years old, once belonging to an ancient Japanese family, and still bearing the crest of the Tokugawa family on the lofty painted gable."[50] The house contained Western furnishings, and was heated by Fukui coal.

Griffis admitted that he was "agreeably surprised ... to find how comfortable they had my own house." These first quarters were actually the *yashiki* of a *han* officer, and contained "a large and handsome canopied iron bedstead and matress, bureau, and cheerful little stove, all fitted with pipe, set in a stove basin, and sending out a cheerful glow with the coal recently discovered in Fukui."

He informed his sister Maggie of his complete satisfaction with the treatment he had received and exclaimed that his hosts, so far at least, had "acted so generously *above* their contract, that it sometimes moves me almost to tears." Somewhat suspiciously he attributed this treatment to the fear of the Japanese hosts that he would "be disgusted with the loneliness and uncivilized condition of the country and leave."[51]

The day following his initial meeting with the Prince, Griffis began his educational work in earnest. Settled in his temporary quarters, he contemplated with satisfaction the plans of the Western-style house that the authorities had promised to build for his comfort. Then he visited the school, met with the other teachers, and began to plan for his classes and to set up his own classroom and laboratory. He wrote,

> I was surprised to find it so large and flourishing. There were in all about eight hundred students, comprised in the English, Chinese, Japanese, medical, and military departments. A few had been studying English for two or three years, under native teachers who had been in Nagasaki. In the medical department. I found a good collection of Dutch books, chiefly medical and scientific, and a fine pair of French dissection models, of both varieties of the human body. In the military school was a library of foreign works on military subjects, chiefly in English, several of which had been translated into Japanese. In one part of the yard young men, book, diagram or trowel in hand, were constructing a miniature earth-work. The school library, of English and American books—among which were all of Kusakabe's—was quite respectable. In the Chinese school I found thousands of boxes, with sliding lids, filled with Chinese and Japanese books. Several hundred boys and young men were squatted on the floor, with their teachers, read-ing or committing lessons to memory, or writing the Chinese characters.[52]

Griffis informed Maggie that the school stood in "the very heart of the old castle and lies inside the innermost of the three circuits of walls and moats." He went on to mention, "Some of the rooms are gorgeously decorated in golden and lacquered designs." The laboratory in which he initially worked, however, "was in the daimio's ladies boudoir."[53]

In honor of Griffis' first visit to the school, young men performed *kendō*, wrestling and other physical-martial arts. Griffis admitted being "highly impressed with the display, and could not fail to admire the splendid, manly physique of many of the lads." Nevertheless, as Griffis returned to his quarters, he "wondered how long it would require to civilize such "barbarians"."[54]

7 March 1871 saw him teach his first class, which he felt "succeeded quite well." In appreciation of his efforts and in honor of the occasion, the director of the school made him a personal gift of a plump goose, and another officer, Sasaki Gonroku,[55] gave him "two bottles of champagne and carved monkeys".[56]

Charged with enthusiasm, Griffis confided to his sister his major goal: "to make Fukuwi College the best in Japan, and to make a national text-book on Chemistry, to advocate the education of women, to abolish the drinking of sake, the wearing of swords, the promiscuous bathing of the sexes."[57] "I want the Prince to feel that I am more than a time-serving foreigner." He invited the Prince and other high-ranking officials and with them, "I discuss my ideas for the welfare of Japan, and have every reason to believe they are deeply influenced. Various evidences that all I do for the people is appreciated and is leavening opinion, come to me in various ways."[58]

In the early spring of 1871, Griffis found that "my pupils at present number less than 90, divided into four classes,"[59] and that he was expected to teach four hours per day, six days per week. Sunday was a free day in keeping with his Christian conscience and the terms of his contract. Characteristically, Griffis planned to throw himself completely into his work. He expected to "have my hands full of all sorts of teaching and work . . . , all of which will be entirely voluntary outside of school hours." His typical inclination to do more than expected of him was reinforced by his feeling that his employers had been so generous toward him "that it sometimes moves me almost to tears; not a day so far, but some present, which although small, testifies to a kind heart."[60]

The first few weeks of his teaching took on a routine form; he taught his classes in the morning, received gifts of food from various people in both the school and the town, worked on the plans for his new laboratory, took afternoon rides and evening walks, and taught various subjects to his students and townspeople in the evening. "It is only by keeping incessantly busy in school, at study, or at exercise," he confided to his sister, "that I shall be able to drive off home-sickness and occasional dejection."[61]

Griffis attempted to counter his isolation with a continual round of activities. Only three weeks after arriving in Fukui, he announced that his "heart and soul, body and mind are for the present given to Japan. From early morn till near midnight, I am busy, and I go to bed, weared [sic] out. I dare not have time to be homesick, or country-sick." He explained why he did not mind doing more than his contract called for in order to remain busy, but even with this extra work, "I cannot tell you how much and how often I think of and long for the One I left behind, on whom all my love centered."[62]

During his first weeks in Fukui, Griffis arranged voluntarily to teach German to a class of six medical students for three hours per week. He also planned to "begin evening classes for the study of History, Physiology, U.S. Constitution, the Bible" through his interpreter, whom "I like very much."[63]

Griffis quite clearly derived great personal satisfaction from his work, but was frustrated by the restrictions placed upon him in his role as a *yatoi*. The general attitude of the Japanese authorities, both in Tokyo and in Fukui, toward the *yatoi* whom they hired to teach them the secrets of Western power was the source of much of Griffis' frustration. The Japanese had no intention of allowing foreigners any real control over actual policy-making functions. The "Japanese only look upon foreigners as schoolmasters. As long as they cannot help themselves, they make use of them; and they send them about their business."[64] To his credit, Griffis recognized this fact of life early in his tour in Echizen. Writing in the *Scientific American*, he warned those contemplating coming to Japan that the country was already overstocked.

I should advise no American to come to Japan, unless he has a position secured before he comes. A man can do well here if he comes to Japan having been appointed in America. It gives him *prestige* over those who are trying to get employment here. . . . In regard to men appointed to offices with high sounding names and large salaries, I am afraid many people will be disappointed concerning Japan. The Japanese simply want helpers and advisors. They propose to keep the "bossing", officering and the power all in their own hands. . . . Nearly every appointee comes here "to revolutionize" his department, but the Japanese don't want that. They want the foreigners to get into the traces, and pull just as fast as, and no faster than, their mighty enterprises can bear. . . .

Therefore, if a man means real hard work that takes off his coat, and is willing to run the risk of going hungry occasionally, and if he has patience enough to wait until an experience taught people can trust him, and he isn't a born brigadier-general, and is willing to help without "taking charge" of everything, let him try Japan. If he expects that the Japanese people wish to make him a Secretary of State, or Minister of Education, or Postmaster General, etc., he had better stay at home, because the Japanese people like to be officers themselves, and are neither children nor weak-minded.[65]

Despite this, however, William Elliot Griffis was instrumental in promoting the growth of Western science in Fukui, although it would be going too far to claim any seminal or national influence for his efforts. Nakamura Takeshi describes how, in the decades preceding the Meiji Restoration, the Dutch "taught navigation, the theory and practice of shipbuilding, artillery and other military crafts, as well as astronomy, land surveying and mathematics."[66] Frances Helbig suggests that Fukui was not alone in encouraging instruction in Western science, for "all of the stronger and more enlightened han were moving swiftly in this direction," and, in fact, "three other provincial chemical laboratories [were] functioning about the same time ... presided over by the Germans."[67]

This having been said, it is important to point out that Griffis' role within Fukui was a significant one. His Japanese hosts saw Griffis as having a great deal to teach them. This is shown by their greeting him with such respect and enthusiasm, giving him a one-third increase in salary before his arriving in Fukui, and treating him with deference and consideration during his sojourn in Matsudaira's realm.

Settling down to his work, Griffis was pleased to find "I have a good interpreter and the officers have provided me with a good blacksmith, tinsman and joiner to make my apparatus." Not worried about the limits to their talents, Griffis would simply "send to America for what I cannot get here."[68] A careful search through the shops of Yokohama, however, yielded "a few glass tubes, some utensils and materials" which enabled him to begin his classes.[69] Despite the skill of his Japanese artisans and his own "Yankee ingenuity", Griffis soon found that he had to order certain items from America and England. He had high praise for "the Japanese skill, fineness of work and ability to "catch on" to the foreigner's ideas. . . . The great trouble was that without models for copying and both chemical facts and nomenclature not being then familiar either to the educated or to the plain folk, progress at times was slow."[70]

Griffis was constantly chafing over the long time lag between the placement of orders and the arrival of his materials, and he consistently reminded his sister Margaret, who acted as his agent, to be sure to account for every cent that he sent her for supplies. He was very sensitive that he was an expensive "item to the government" with his high salary, expensive laboratory and housing costs, not to mention his interpreter's salary.[71]

The lack of proper equipment was only part of his problem in teaching modern science to the Japanese. Both his patience and ingenuity were severely taxed when, only three days after his arrival in Fukui, he was asked "to teach the men in the war departments . . . of Echizen how to blow up a man of war with submarine mines!"[72] In another place he revealed, "When I tried to show in the course of years an iron spike would not only rust, but "eat" away the timber in which it was once tightly pounded, the school officials wondered what that had to do with science."[73]

According to his diary, among the subjects that Griffis covered in his chemistry classes were water, air, voltaic batteries, sulphur, hydrogen, carbon dioxide, iodine, mercury, silver, air pumps, magnetism, and arsenic, and his students' response to his teaching appears to have been a positive one. For example, he wrote in his diary on 23 March that he had experimented with oxygen in his class with "70 spectators in my room", which he found "exciting work to teach".[74]

The large and airy hall in which Griffis delivered his lectures was located in Matsudaira's castle. Helbig describes it as "about thirty-five feet by twenty feet with the southwest side of the room almost entirely of glass", and topped by a large skylight. Shortly after Griffis' arrival, the Prince began to build a new laboratory for him in a garden adjoining the lecture hall.[75] Three months later the laboratory was not quite completed, but Griffis was pleased that it was "already roofed and ceiled, and when finished, will be as fine as any laboratory in the U.S. except of course the great Sheffield and Lawrence laboratories of Yale & Harvard."[76] His anticipation was justified, for upon its completion, in early September 1871, he wrote to Margaret, "I wish you could fly over to Japan some day, and see my lecture room and laboratory. All in fine order and arranged in best American college style." The only major problem was that "*no apparatus* has arrived in Fukuwi, though several boxes have been in Yokohama since July 28th."[77]

Despite the lack of materials, Griffis was able to proceed using a few utensils that he had purchased in Yokohama and with what could be made from local materials. Fortunately the hospital in Fukui provided his classes with a minimum of chemicals needed for simple experiments until the overseas orders were filled.[78] At about this time, Griffis informed his sister, "I teach about 4 hours each day except Sunday, and will soon have my hands full of all sorts of teaching and work for them, all of which will be entirely voluntary outside of school hours."[79]

Griffis devoted one of his earliest projects to "organizing a staff of scholarly interpreters who put into the vernacular many of the traditional terms as well as the newly coined and more exact scientific terminology."[80] For another project, Griffis planned a chemistry text-book in the vernacular that would be relevant to Japan. Writing in a slightly different context, Robert Schwantes credited Griffis with being one of the "few American teachers [who] have tried to devise materials specially adapted to Japanese needs."[81] Griffis recognized that "all our books are adapted to our style of life and civilization," so "my aim is to search all good English and American textbooks, and with my own notes, arrangement and illustrations, to produce a book for the Japanese and translate it into Japanese."[82] He made preliminary arrangements with Hatakeyama Yoshinari,[83] a young Japanese who had been a student at Rutgers, was converted to Christianity, and who had briefly attended the Second Reformed Church of Philadelphia with Griffis, to translate the proposed text into Japanese.[84]

Although no evidence has yet been found that this book was ever completed, the fact of his intention to write such a volume is, in itself, revealing. During his entire life, Griffis perceived himself as a conscious bridge between Japan and America, an interpreter of the Japanese to his fellow countrymen. This textbook project had much of the same flavor, except in this case Griffis was to act as an interpreter of the best Western scientific knowledge to the Japanese, to whom the book would be directed. Much of his informal social contact with the Japanese during his three-and-one-half years in Japan also had this character.

Perhaps some of Griffis' most rewarding teaching occurred outside of school, and a substantial amount of it dealt with modern science. He wrote to Margaret, "Three or four evenings in the week I hold evening classes in my own house. On Mondays I lecture on Physiology, on which evening my hearers, about 16 in number, are from the Medical School and hospital."[85] Another typical evening was spent "with several of the scholars, who had come from the school and about a half dozen or more principal men of the village, who had come to hear the foreigner tell of all the wonderful things in his country, to answer questions in science, manufactures, etc."[86]

Griffis' audiences included not only schoolboys and older men from town, but also the highest figures in local government. He described how "the two chief officers of the Prince came to witness chemical experiments, and were highly pleased."[87] On at least one occasion the Prince attended one of Griffis' lectures, and "expressed himself delighted" after he had "listened and questioned very attentively" during a Saturday morning lecture lasting ninety minutes.[88]

Griffis looked back on his first eight months in Fukui with evident satisfaction:

> We have nearly 125 promising pupils in chemistry and physics, and with two good interpreters, apparatus from America, a printing press, and earnest young men to help in translating and applying the knowledge gained in school, we hope to make the "Fukui Scientific School" one of the centers whence shall radiate the new civilization.[89]

Griffis' methods of teaching were not uncommon for the age in which he lived, but it would perhaps be helpful to discuss briefly a few of the fundamental assumptions that he brought with him to the classroom. The single most pervasive characteristic that runs as a leitmotif through all of his teaching, preaching, and writing was a didactic one. The teacher, Griffis, was the instructor of others and at the center of each learning or teaching situation; *he* was the disseminator of knowledge and his students or audience were the receptacles.

He criticized the Japanese teachers of Tokugawa Japan whose major qualification was their personal knowledge of the Chinese classics, and as Griffis saw it, their "chief duty was to stuff and cram the minds of... pupils. To expand or develop the mental powers of a boy, to enlarge his mental visions, to teach him to think for himself, would have been doing precisely what it was the teacher's business to prevent."[90] What Griffis opposed, however, was neither the centrality of the teacher to the learning process nor his propensity "to stuff and cram the minds of his pupils". Instead, he argued that "the native teacher of the future must depend less on traditional authority, and more on the resources of a *richly furnished* mind." He suggested that while the "old teacher was a drill master, the new one must be that and more. The old one stifled questioning; the new one must encourage it."[91] Griffis' concern was primarily to modify the traditional lecture method in ways which would make it more effective. He was a reformer, but not a radical.

He explained how in his own teaching he "introduced largely, the blackboard system of instruction" in which "all the teaching has been by experiments and lectures verbally translated."[92] Thus most of his formal teaching consisted of his either lecturing or demonstrating an experiment, and using the blackboard for listing formulae or illustrating various points. His interpreters translated the abstract ideas he presented into the vernacular as best they could, given the state of the Japanese language at the time. Since Griffis' knowledge of Japanese was only elementary, he required translation assistance for all but the most rudimentary communication with his students.[93] One wonders how much was lost in the process.

As a man or as a teacher, Griffis was very serious in everything that he did. He always stressed the importance of securing a sound knowledge of fundamentals before attempting to master any field of knowledge. He consistently emphasized the importance "of a thorough *elementary* training", the lack of which could "never be fully made up". He wrote approvingly, for example, that the Rutgers Grammar School "aims first to lay the sure foundations of a good English education, by continual drilling and practice."[94] In advising his sister Margaret on the education of one of his relatives, Griffis urged that he "learn the Greek alphabet, the structure of Greek and Latin prefixes, affixes, changes of verb roots, sentences, etc." and stressed the necessity of being "drilled thoroughly in the formation of scientific knowledge and terms of science."[95]

Griffis' solution to teaching large classes of students containing a wide variety of ability levels was a very conventional one. Given what has been said so far about his educational views, it is not surprising that he did what he could to control carefully the selection of students and worked in special classes with the cleverer ones. With satisfaction he reported,

> I do not have large classes as I had at first, but that is because the novelty is over and as chemistry means work, I have weeded out the lazy ones, and have about $\frac{1}{2}$ the former number, but all earnest, patient students. My class of 15 boys in French are doing well, so are the seven older German scholars, and the 15 small boys in German, under Masaki, my best pupil.[96]

Another technique to cope with large classes that he used was the so-called "Lancasterian System" in which one teacher instructed a number of older pupils who in turn taught younger ones carefully prescribed lessons. Griffis wrote, "In school I have organized new

classes, setting the assistants to work at teaching, give private lessons
to the smartest and best students in German & French—in my house
and set them to teaching in the schools."[97] Of his students he wrote,

> All were bare-headed, with the top-knot, cue and shaven mid-
> scalp, most of them with bare feet on their clogs, and with their
> characteristic dress, swagger, fierce looks, bare skin exposed at
> the scalp, neck, arms, calves, and feet, with their murderous
> swords in their belts, they impressed upon my memory a picture
> of feudalism I shall never forget. As I walked, I wondered how
> long it would require to civilize such "barbarians". Here were
> nearly a thousand young samurai. What was one teacher among
> so many? Could it be possible that these could be trained to be
> disciplined students? . . . A few months later, and I had won their
> confidence and love. I found they were quite able to instruct me
> in many things. I need fear to lose neither politeness nor sense
> of honor among these earnest youth. In pride and dignity of
> character, in diligence, courage, gentlemanly conduct, refinement
> and affection, truth and honesty, good morals, in so far as I knew
> or could see, they were my peers.[98]

In another place he described the "average Japanese student" as
"bright, quick, eager, earnest and faithful". A Japanese student,
Griffis recorded, "delights his teacher's heart by his docility, his industry, his obedience, his reverence, his politeness. In the course of
five years, the writer can remember no instance of rudeness, no case
of slander, no uncanny trick, no impudent reply from any of his many
pupils."[99]

Griffis took many of them into his home, and by the end of October
1871, he had seven young students living with him. In that active
house Griffis spent much time informally instructing them in the virtues
of the American constitution and in the wisdom of the Western world.
As was perhaps inevitable, he had his favorites, especially one lad
named Kasawara whom Griffis described as "a pretty boy of lovely
disposition and very bright".[100]

In return for Griffis' attention to them, either as part of their school
assignments or as goodwill gestures to their host, these students
provided their teacher with a great deal of first-hand information on
Japanese life that eventually found its way into print in his articles

and books. The Griffis Collection at Rutgers contains several score of essays written by Griffis' young students. The numerous topics covered the students' native cities and towns, the geography of their provinces, games played by Japanese children, Japanese money, signs and theaters, burial customs, their first impressions of foreigners, etc. One does not have to read very far into Griffis' extensive writings to recognize the source of much of his information.

Griffis' scholarly reputation was strong enough to attract four young men from Higo (present-day Kumamoto) who were "cousins of one of my old pupils in America [Numagawa, whom he had taught at Rutgers] who came 600 miles to study with me although they have a foreigner in Higo." Upon their arrival in Fukui, the four students gave Griffis a basket of eggs and arranged an "entertainment in my honor" which convinced him that "the Japanese are by no means an ungrateful race." [101]

The people of Fukui, from daimyo to commoner, clearly appreciated Griffis' efforts to help them achieve progress, and they plied him with gifts and kind sentiments. He later wrote that during his months in Fukui "unceasing kindnesses were showered upon me. . . . I have nothing to record but respect, consideration, sympathy, and kindness. My eyes were opened. I needed no revolver, nor were guards necessary . . . and among the happiest memories are those of Fukui." [102]

Despite these mutual feelings of warmth, affection, and satisfaction with his work, Griffis was troubled by his role in Japan's modernization efforts. Often during late-night walks beneath the stars, he felt an occasional twinge of doubt.

> I had come hither to be a builder of knowledge, to help bring the new civilization that must destroy the old. Yet it was hard to be an iconoclast. I often asked myself the question—Why not leave these people alone? They seem to be happy enough; and he that increaseth knowledge increaseth sorrow. [103]

Reflecting upon living in an ancient Japanese home, he worried that the "sacredness of human belief and reverence had consecrated even the old shrine, and other hands than mine must remove the stones of the deserted fane. What vulgarity to make a dining-room of the family oratory, where the ancestral tablets once stood, and the sacred lights and incense burned." [104]

61

Despite misgivings of this sort, Griffis was an articulate advocate of Japanese modernization. In many ways he saw the United States as the model that Japan "ought" to emulate. He was convinced, for example, that one of the primary reasons for America's rapid development lay in her people's willingness to roll up their sleeves and dirty their hands. He therefore argued that "Japan can never be a great country while it is a disgrace to labor with [one's] hands."[105] On those occasions when he was invited to dine with the Prince, usually with a fellow teacher named Lucy, he pushed this point very hard.

> Mr. Lucy and I . . . were invited to meet with the Prince in his summer mansion, about 2 miles from the college. We rode out and met him there, with four of his head officers, and found a gorgeous dinner spread out, cooked by our trained cook, served by the pages and in thorough style. And eaten properly, chairs, tables, plates, knives and forks were of the best. The courses numbered 10, the wine and beer of course were there; and finding the officers and Prince Matsudaira in good humor, I told him of our glorious country with its free schools, free institutions, where labor with the hands was not in disgrace, where our chief magistrate came from the people, where we educate our women as highly as ourselves. We told them that Japan could never be a great country until they honored labor, trade, the privileged classes work, educated their women, and elevated and cared for the common people. Think of it! in a despotic country, and in a Daimio's presence, promulgating such revolutionary ideas.[106]

Although Griffis' domestic life in Fukui was materially comfortable and quite varied, he often complained to his sister about his gnawing sense of loneliness and his unhappiness over his diet. As early as 23 March 1871, he wrote, "I don't grieve over beefsteak. . . . I have always found that a temperate diet enabled me to do about twice the work of ordinary students and kept me in fair health. I do not propose to change being mainly satisfied with rice and fish." In the same letter he revealed, "I use the chop sticks splendidly, & the 'nerve-fluids' flow most exuberantly, and my liver is in good state."[107]

A month later, however, he suggested, "I am indeed at the ends of the earth," but "I am beginning to enter into and understand Japanese life quite well." After describing his activities to Margaret, Griffis explained, "I fear lest you think that I have fallen into satisfied exile content to be stranded out here at the ends of the earth caring scarcely for those at home." He reassured her that this was emphatically not the case and concluded, "I cannot put my heart on paper, I cannot write what I feel...." [108]

By the end of May he had, however, settled into a comfortable domestic life which he described as "quite perfect" with a "pull bell for door and servant, regular meals in good civilized style, good furniture, mosquito netting that makes my bed room an object of delight and wonder to the Japs." [109]

With the departure of Lucy (whose contract was not renewed) from Fukui in July 1871, Griffis' one contact with his Western heritage was lost to him. [110] He fell into increasingly lonely moods. At about the same time, his interpreter and companion, Iwabuchi, married "a blushing damsel of 15". But Griffis prudently added, "It must be remembered that the Japanese girls develop at least two years sooner than American or European girls." [111] This marriage took Iwabuchi away from his "close connection with me, & leaves me more lonely than ever." [112]

By the middle of August, Griffis' spirits were lifted by the completion of the European house which the Prince had ordered built for him. But this meant new expenses for Griffis, and he informed Margaret on 17 August that he "must take on a new servant and be under other expenses." She was a "girl of about 17, who will wait on the table, and take care of my room specially." [113]

It is not surprising that this new situation proved to be more than young Griffis was able to handle. As early as 28 March 1871, he recognized the temptations facing a Christian man in Japan, and confided to his sister that he was having doubts as to the wisdom of trying to find a position for his younger brother. Indeed, he wrote, it is "little less than madness to bring even a brother to this land of fearful temptations and no restraints." [114] Three months later, he informed Maggie that "my saddest and sorest need is for something to love, something to caress or at least some congenial soul and presence. The temptations to a lonely man here are fearful. I dare not have an idle moment." [115]

In light of these feelings, it is not surprising that young Griffis experienced a moral crisis when his acute loneliness, an attractive young woman in his house, and his sexual mores intersected during late August and early September 1871. His ambivalence and inner turmoil can be seen in the following passage of a letter written to Margaret on 9 September:

> In my own household, I have made another change. The young girl . . . whom I took for a servant to wait specifically on me proved to be very faithful, diligent and pleasant in every way, anticipated my every want, and made my house almost as comfortable as a home; I like her very much. All of which to a sometimes weary and home-sick young man must necessarily be a strong temptation in his lonely hours. I found after two weeks, that she made too much comfort for me, and was too attractive herself. After having her [for] 11 days, I sent her away, before temptation turned into sin . . . and now, though with less comfort and a more lonely house, I can let all my inner life be known to you without shame.[116]

Faced with this personal crisis, Griffis had written to Guido Verbeck in Tokyo to seek support during his difficult time. In a letter to Griffis, dated 30 September, Verbeck reacted as a minister of the Dutch Reformed Church.

> Do not think of *temptations*! If your religion does not hold you up, think of your parents & sisters, of your *future* wife. *Put* it *out of the question.* . . . Nonsense! Don't frighten a man with such mean trash! *Name, influence, respect, future happiness, present peace,* all would be irretrievably gone! Be a true man & Christian. Friends far & near are watching you—& so is God—no, no, you only meant to stir me up & you have done it.[117]

This experience served two useful purposes for Griffis. He reminded Margaret in a letter, dated 3 December, that "out of weakness, make strong," and he was sure that this was the ultimate effect upon his own person. Finally, this incident appears to have strengthened his determination to keep his younger brother, who wanted to join him in Japan, at home in Philadelphia. He wrote, "I am sure you see now the madness, the folly of sending anyone here, but one clothed in whole armor. . . . So, let this subject pass forever."[118]

It was also about this time that Griffis seems to have decided to leave Fukui. While he had been excited to have "lived in Fukui . . . , within what, in 1871, was still the pulsing body of feudalism,"[119] he was now anxious to rejoin the nineteenth century. The winds of change were beginning to reach Fukui. As Jacob Burckhardt wrote in another context, "The historical process is suddenly accelerated in terrifying fashion. Developments which otherwise take centuries seem to flit by like phantoms in months or weeks, and are fulfilled."[120]

While Griffis was busying himself with his everyday duties, vast changes were in process throughout Japan. Although even his earliest diary entries and letters home indicated that he sensed at least some of the drama of a nation in flux, there is no evidence to suggest that he was particularly well informed as to exactly what was in the wind. His diary entry of 18 July 1871 records the decision of the Imperial government "dispensing with officers and reducing incomes—excitement among thousands of families all over Japan . . . & in the school."[121] Looking back on the day, in *The Mikado's Empire*, he wrote with much more detail and a great deal more dramatic effect:

> The thunder-bolt has fallen! The political earthquake has shaken Japan to its centre. . . . Intense excitement reigns in the homes of the samurai of the city to-day. I hear that some of them are threatening to kill Mitsuoka, who receives income for meritorious services in 1868, and who has long been the exponent of reform and of national progress in Fukui.
>
> At ten o'clock this morning, a messenger from Tokio arrived at the *han-chō*. Suddenly there was a commotion in the school. All the native teachers and officials were summoned to the directors' room. I saw them a few minutes afterward. Pale faces and excited nerves were in the majority. The manner in which some of them strode to the door, thrust their swords into their belts, stepped intotheirclogs,andsetoffwithflowinggarmentsandsilkcoat-tails into their clogs, and set off with flowing garments and silk coat-tails flapping to the leeward, was quite theatrical, and just like the pictures in Japanese books.[122]

Soon after these events, Tokyo abolished the remnants of feudal practices by dissolving the *han*, and ordering the old feudal lords from their domains to the capital. This action was decisive in accelerating the process of drawing the best young minds from the provinces to the capital. In any event, the exodus of students from Fukui overseas or to Tokyo, which had begun to increase in the spring of 1871, turned into a torrent after the *han* were abolished. In May 1871 Griffis was asked to appoint two Fukui students to study in the West after an initial course of study in Tokyo, and gradually more and more students began to leave Fukui on their own account for the capital. In mid-July, for example, he complained to Margaret that Kinoshita, "one of my best scholars, leaves Fukuwi to go to Yokohama . . . to remain several years and perhaps permanently. He will learn some trade or business there."[123] By the middle of September, "No less than six students left school this week," but Griffis could not bring himself to blame them. "I do not wonder," he informed Maggie, "at anyone leaving their dull provincial city for the gay capital or the new and lively Yokohama." What bothered him most about this exodus of students was that "the grown-up young men are liable . . . to break off study and go [into] business." As a result, "I care more for, and place my hopes on the smaller boys, many of them bright and quick."[124]

On 28 October, Griffis complained, "There seems to be a perpetual exodus to Edo," and in the previous month he had noted that even several of the civil servants "have been called to Edo."[125] In November he wrote to Maggie, "At least *700 men* have made exodus from Fukui alone, since March, the retired prince, all the former chief officers and scores of the most talented young men have gone. . . . "[126] This was not a completely negative trend, for he observed:

> Of course I have lost some good scholars, but in the main, have improved and condensed rather than suffered loss, besides, in the developments of the future, it is better . . . to have my chief friends, and those I most influenced . . . go to the Imperial Government as high officers, instead of being petty local dignitaries.[127]

Despite this, Griffis was not happy with the situation. In a letter to Maggie, he described his last meeting with the prince.

> The Prince leaves for Tokio, early tomorrow morning [2 October]. He will never again, most probably return to Fukuwi. . . . It is a new era for Japan, destined to be the grandest of her history. . . . Yet there is always sadness, even though I am here for the very purpose of laying, or helping to lay the foundation of modern civilization on the ruins of the old past.[128]

Prior to leaving Fukui for the last time, the Prince was bid farewell in an impressive ceremony, which Griffis recorded in *The Mikado's Empire*.

> I went over to the main hall at nine o' clock. I shall never forget the impressive scene. . . . Arranged in the order of their rank, each in his starched robes of ceremony, with shaven-crown, and gun-hammer top knot, with hands clasped on the hilt of his sword resting upright before him as he sat on his knees, were the three thousand samurai of the Fukui clan. . . . It was more than a farewell to their feudal lord. It was the solemn burial of the institutions under which their fathers had lived for seven hundred years.[129]

Griffis was the only foreigner to witness this event, and he was later honored by the prince with a thirty-minute visit to his home to bid him farewell. Griffis confessed, "I am feeling more than unusually lonely today."[130]

The loneliness that Griffis felt was both real and understandable. While his first few months in Fukui had opened up to him an exotic world which his fellow Americans at home were anxious to hear about, the vast changes that were sweeping Japan had, in a very profound sense, made Fukui obsolete. The abolition of the *han* accelerated the already significant brain drain to Yokohama and Tokyo. In addition, the loss of Mr Lucy several months earlier had robbed Griffis of Western companionship, and the departure of the prince for Tokyo led him to conclude, "The glory of Fukuwi as well as many another province has departed."[131]

In order to follow this "glory", Griffis set in motion a train of events that would culminate in his appointment to a position in Tokyo. Shortly after Prince Matsudaira's departure from Fukui, Griffis "addressed a communication to the Minister of Public Instruction in Tokio, urging the establishment of a polytechnic school."[132] In a letter written to Griffis on 26 November, Edward Warren Clark,[133] who was teaching in Shizuoka, hinted that Guido Verbeck was seriously considering bringing Griffis to Tokyo. Although Griffis did not mention this proposal for the establishment of a technical school in Tokyo, he did inform his sister Maggie that he had "written to one or two high officers" in the capital "relative to a National system of education and for providing for the first and greatest educational need of Japan—good teachers. I have suggested that six or eight National *Normal* schools be established,'' and added that ''a higher position [in Tokyo] may be in store for me.'' To further confuse the issue, in the same letter to Maggie, Griffis revealed,

> I know I am highly appreciated by the men of Fukuwi, and am more than willing to stay here, patiently and laboriously training the young men of Fukuwi. In a few weeks I shall choose out ten of the brightest of my advanced class, give them special lessons in chem[istry] with practical experimenting by each one, and thus in time send forth ten . . . good teachers.[134]

As he waited for a response from Tokyo answering his queries and suggestions, Griffis continued his busy Fukui schedule in addition to planning a serious study of the Japanese language. Admitting that ''since I came to Japan, I had done almost nothing at the language'' because of a busy schedule and several extremely competent and congenial interpreters, he wrote, ''I have resolved to go manfully at the language & have trained my ears to distingush & my brain to think in Japanese, so . . . that my progress is fairly good.''[135]

Keeping busy was small consolation, however, and Griffis continued to long for a change. Many of his letters reflected this theme and he was particularly frustrated by the loss of students to Tokyo. The major problem that he grappled with, however, seems to have been his feeling that events were passing him by as long as he remained in Fukui.

Finally, on 10 January 1872, several long-awaited letters from the capital arrived, and he happily informed Maggie,

> Letters came from Edo to-day, deciding a matter which had been in abeyance for several weeks of which I had said nothing in my letters to you, waiting until some definite decision had been made. That decision is, by invitation of the Minister of Instruction and at the urgent desire of Mr. Verbeck, I shall go to Edo. A few months ago, I wrote to the Department of Education, urging them to adopt a National System of Education, and the establishment of several Polytechnic or Scientific schools in various parts of the country. Clarkie [Edward Warren Clark] hinted in a letter Nov. 26 that Mr Verbeck wanted me in Edo. On the same day I was called to the Gov't. office and informed that the Department of Education in Edo had sent to Fukuwi, ordering them to transfer me to Edo,

but the Echizen officers had so earnestly remonstrated and wished to keep me, that all that was needed to keep the Fukuwi school in prosperity was my cordial assent to remain in Fukuwi. I told them I should consult with my best friend in Japan, and leave the decision to him. I wrote to Mr. Verbeck, stating the whole matter, and telling him, that if the call were repeated, I should gladly come to Edo.[136]

Soon afterwards Verbeck told Griffis exactly what he had hoped to hear. "Do you ask my advice?—I say, come by all means."[137] With this approval from his "best friend in Japan", Griffis informed the Fukui officials of his decision to leave for Tokyo. They were not, however, prepared to allow their foreign teacher to exit so easily. Murata Ujihisa,[138] the chief school officer in Fukui, whom Griffis described as "determined and strong-willed", refused to acquiesce to the teacher's departure. The reason for this, Griffis was convinced, was based on "the very fact that I had worked hard day and night, and the laboratory and classes here are in such good condition and progress."[139]

Griffis, on the other hand, was just as determined to leave for the capital. Both his isolation from "civilization" and his feeling that he was far removed from the important events of the day led him to complain,

For over six months I have not seen one of my own race. The tax on the nervous system of being isolated, looked at as a stranger and a curiosity, made the target of so many eyes, and the constant friction and chafing of one Caucasian against a multitude of sharp angles of an Asiatic civilization, as represented by servants, petty officials, and ignorant people; and the more delicate work of polite fencing with intellectual rapiers against cultured men educated under other systems of morals and ideas; the ruin of temper and principle which such a lonely life threatens, are more than I wish to attempt to bear, when duty as well as pleasure seems to invite me to the capital.[140]

Griffis was adamant in the face of Murata's determined opposition to his leaving Fukui for Tokyo. He submitted a request to the provincial authorities for twenty-five days' leave so that he could visit Yokohama and Tokyo during February, "though it is not laid down in the contract, and I of course wanted them to pay all expenses & my salary during the holiday." He rationalized this request by pointing out that twelve of the days would fall during the Japanese New Year holiday. "They refused," Griffis wrote, "to let me go at the time I specified . . . but said if I would wait one month (Just too late to receive any appointment. . . .) I could go & take *40* days, all expenses paid." Angered by their refusal, Griffis sent back word *that I must go* on my expected & promised visit, starting from Fukuwi *Jan. 14th* and should go even if *I went alone & on foot* in the snow, whether in disgrace or in honor."[141]

One of the most interesting aspects of this dispute with the Japanese was Griffis' sensitivity to the cultural context in which he had to conduct his case. He writes that he had two interviews, each lasting two hours, with Murata in the Government office, and the official "used all his keen mind to frame unnumbered arguments to deter me from my purpose, & to keep me in Fukuwi till all danger of appointment in Edo was over." This is apparently a reference to Murata's offer of forty days' leave rather than twenty-five days, which would have, in effect, kept Griffis in Fukui until it was too late for him to take up the Tokyo position. Griffis, however, did not fall into that trap and countered by moving his departure date forward by fifteen days. He recognized that both "skill and patience" were required "to overcome these polished Japanese officers". Any other approach, he suggested, was self-defeating. "Although intense feelings may scald the veins and jar the heart, even though life and death may hang in the scales, all is done with perfect and polished etiquette. Any angry or loud tones or hasty speech—and the case is lost."[142]

Either before, or as a result of the two meetings, Griffis wrote a draft of a letter to Murata. There is no decisive evidence that he ever sent the letter, but the draft version reflects his anxiety and frustrations over the situation. In addition, it would not have been out of character for him to have sent the letter.[143] The American began by offering his regrets that his leaving would cause hardship to the Fukui school, and he suggested that his departure was not so sudden as it seemed. "Months ago," he claimed, "I wrote and told friends in America, Yokohama, Yedo and . . . Shidzoka [Shizuoka] that I should be in Yokohama" in early February, "and now I must fulfill that promise and attend to urgent business in Yokohama." He requested permission for his departure, but made it clear that, permission or not, he would leave. Furthermore, somewhat disingenuously, he argued that "I have known for months past and so have my friends that I shall leave at this time, therefore, it is hard for me to understand it, when you say I leave in a hurry." While it is true that Griffis wanted to leave months earlier, he did not know that a Tokyo assignment was in the offing until Clark's letter of 26 November reached him, and it was not until a month later that the official invitation was received. To argue that he knew that he was to leave at this time does not seem completely truthful. Even had Griffis known this, it still does not explain why Murata and the other officials were not notified until the last moment.

As though he sensed that the above arguments were not compelling, Griffis then took a different tack, promising that "if I am dismissed with honor, I shall strenuously endeavor to get the Tokio officers to continue the school here. If you wish, I shall be most happy to write a letter now to the *Mombusho* urging them to continue the school with a good teacher." Griffis was, at best, naive in using this argument for it was clear to most *yatoi* that their influence with the Japanese authorities did not extend beyond the day-to-day details of their own particular sphere of expertise. Finally, in what can only be described as a bald-faced lie, Griffis claimed, "I left a good position in America, with a salary nearly equal to what I receive now." No part-time teacher at the Rutgers' Preparatory School was making anywhere near $3,600 per year in addition to having a house, horse and servants furnished.

These arguments advanced by Griffis illustrate his desperation to leave Fukui for the capital. He ended his letter by pleading with Murata,

> Please do not let me go away alone and in disgrace to Yokohama. If I were a drunkard or whoremaster you would be glad to be rid of me. Please treat me as well as you would a servant. I wish to go to Tokio and ask them to keep up the Fukuwi school, I don't want to see my work scattered . . . but in honor or dishonor, alone or attended I must leave Fukuwi on the 14th day of this month and whether I come back to Fukuwi or not, whether I am lost in the snow, come good, come harm, I have a clear conscience in doing what I have looked forward to for so many months. . . . Please be kind to me, and grant my request. Do not treat me harshly but as a father.[144]

Whether or not Murata ever saw this letter, Griffis finally succeeded. As Griffis conceded, "By the contract . . . they were right; and they had the full power to deny my request." On the other hand, they had little to gain by refusing this adamant young man their permission to leave.

He had, it appears, persuaded them that he was not bluffing, and that he would leave, preferably with their permission, but in any event, he would leave on his own terms. As he later wrote, "They could let me go alone, pay me only up to the day of leaving Fukui and brand me a contract-breaker according to the letter." As he informed his sister Maggie, however,

> ...they missed their man if they thought they could force me into any rough word, hasty speech or loud voice. The battle was with rapiers, not with bludgeons, and I knew it. I was firm as a rock, was fully resolved to set out alone, if necessary, in spite of snow, mountains, speechlessness or robbers. I answered every argument, and by one happy stroke, which Iwaboochi translated splendidly, I got them laughing, upset their dignity, and finally *won*. They gave me an officer as an escort, pay my expenses, continue my salary until a new contract is made, gave a grand final merry-making at the chief eating house & saloon here. . . .

Despite his tone of self-righteousness, Griffis felt some pangs of conscience over his insistence on leaving Fukui. In reaching an accommodation between his actions and their effect on Fukui, Griffis listed several "unanswerable reasons" to justify his leaving.

> 1st, Fukuwi is changed, it is no longer a province dependent on itself, but is merged into all Japan, and the Imperial Gov't. who now pays my salary have a right to take me. 2nd, Mr. Verbeck first sent me here & he now urgently calls me away. . . . 3rd, All my best students are continually leaving Fukuwi for Edo thus spoiling my plans. 4th, at least 15 of my best students are in raptures of my going, because they will follow me. . . . To say nothing of an *exiles* personal reasons, my duty to *Dai Nippon*, would call me away.[145]

A closer analysis of these reasons seems to indicate that the first is the only one which may have had some degree of validity. The fact remains, however, that Fukui originally hired Griffis, not the central government, and it was only later that the central government began to assume his salary and expenses. The second, third and fourth reasons listed seem to be all of a self-serving nature, having nothing to do with the terms of the contract which he agreed to abide by with his signature. It seems obvious that Griffis' fundamental reasons for leaving Fukui are contained in his phrase "an *exiles* personal reasons". If one examines the question of *who* would benefit by Griffis' departure from Fukui before the end of his contract, one can only conclude that it would be Griffis himself.

Both Griffis and his Japanese hosts put a good face on the situation, and the townspeople and officials graciously feted him prior to his departure on 22 January 1872. Writing to Maggie just before leaving that morning, Griffis noted that it had been snowing for five days and the snow was piled up to three feet deep. Despite this harsh weather, he continued, "about 50 of my pupils and citizens will accompany me three miles and then bid me good-bye. The chief officer [Murata] of the school & about 12 others will go 12 miles with me."

> All day yesterday, my house was filled by my pupils, officers, citizens, and everybody generally, who came to bid me farewell. All bring presents in money, lacquer ware, confectionary, curios, etc. My tables are filled with all kinds of things, the smallest a present of 2 *shu* (13 cents) and the greatest, a handsome inlaid Jap table, (small and low) from Murata, the chief officer, and an ancient silver-mounted flute (very peculiar) and 1 pair very handsome gilt and gorgeous screens, a Jap sword, etc.[146]

In light of this send-off, it is interesting to note that Griffis forgot whatever pangs of conscience he may have had over the circumstances of his departure. His letters and diary are silent on this question, but he made it a point to tell Maggie, "I go away in honor and regreted by all. Many students have already made ready to follow me, but all but 5 have been hindered by the gov[ernment] until I am fairly settled in Edo."[147]

After a hard journey across the snowy terrain, broken only by a brief visit to an old Rutgers classmate in Shizuoka, Griffis arrived in Yokohama on 2 February 1872. He rested briefly in the home of an American missionary, and journeyed on to Tokyo "blistered, weary & sore and faint from loss of rest, sleep & the effects of a Japanese 13 day diet."[148]

So ended the Fukui experience of William Elliot Griffis. He remained in Japan, teaching at one of the predecessors of the University of Tokyo, until July 1874, while taking an active part in the social, intellectual and religious life of the foreign community. Upon his return to the United States he published one of the best known and widely read histories of

Japan, *The Mikado's Empire*, which went through twelve editions between 1876 and 1913. In addition, he published several other books and over a hundred articles on Japan and the Japanese, virtually all of them informed by his stay of three and a half years in Japan, and especially his Fukui year.

William Elliot Griffis was not only a precursor of what has become, since the end of World War II, a common phenomenon—the Western educational expert in a developing nation—but also one of the first "old Japan hands" who helped, through his prolific writing, to place some of the first "scratches on our minds" about Japan.

1. The full text of the Imperial Charter Oath may be found in W. W. McLaren, "Japanese Government Documents", in TASJ, XLII, 1914, p. 8. An excellent brief description of the dominance of Western education thought in the early Meiji period is given in Herbert Passin, *Society and Education in Japan*, New York, 1965, pp. 63–80.

2. Probably the most thorough research on this subject has been done by Professor Hazel Jones, whose dissertation, "The Meiji Government and Foreign Employees, 1868–1900" (University of Michigan, 1967) contains much valuable information. See also her articles in *MN*, XXIII, 1968, pp. 9–30, & XXIX, 1974, pp. 305–27.

3. 雇

4. William Elliot Griffis, "British and American Cooperation in Asia", in *Landmark*, VII, London, 1925, pp. 553–6.

5. Central High School, in the judgment of a leading education journal of the day, was in "the discipline and course of study . . . superior to any institution of this grade with which we are acquainted." *Connecticut Common School Journal*, III, 1841, p. 162.

6. William Elliot Griffis, "The Launching of Commodore Perry's Flagship, 1850', unpublished manuscript, GC.

7. Ardath Burks, "Reflections of 100 Years of Cultural Exchange" (unpublished paper delivered before the Japan Society's Meiji Centennial Lecture Series, Rutgers University, 13 November 1967), p. 10.

8. Ibid., p. 9.

9. William Elliot Griffis, "Intimate Glimpses", in *Rutgers Alumni Quarterly*, II, April 1916, p. 134.

10. For details of Rutgers in this period, see Richard Demarest, *A History of Rutgers College, 1776–1924*, Rutgers University Press, 1924.

11. Griffis, *The Mikado's Empire* [ME], Harper & Brothers, New York, 1876, p. 8. Hereafter all references are to the 12th edition, 1913, unless otherwise specified.

12. 日下部太郎

13. 松平春嶽

14. Foster Rhea Dulles, *Yankees and Samurai: America's Role in the Emergence of Modern Japan*, New York, 1965, p. 156.

15. Although it later became a land-grant college, in its early days Rutgers had very close ties with the Dutch Reformed Church. Even today a theological school is found on its main campus.

16. Verbeck to J. W. Ferris, 21 July 1870, GC.

17. William Elliot Griffis [WEG] to Margaret Clark Griffis [MCG], 12 Sept 1870, GC.

18. Anna Marie Griffis to WEG, 10 Oct 1870, GC.

19. Griffis, *Verbeck of Japan: A Citizen of No Country*, New York, 1900, pp. 217–8.

20. WEG to MCG, 27/28 Nov 1870, GC.

21. Griffis, "First Glimpses of Japan", in *Christian Intelligencer*, New York, 2 March 1871, n.p. Also see ME, pp. 327–32.

22. This part of Griffis' career is detailed in Edward R. Beauchamp, "'Scratches on Our Minds': William Elliot Griffis as Interpreter of Japan", in *Asian Profile*, I, 3, December 1973.

23. Edward Warren Clark, *Life and Adventure in Japan*, American Tract Society, New York, 1878, p. 147.

24. Griffis, *Verbeck*, p. 245.

25. ME, p. 377, and Griffis, *Verbeck*, p. 237.

26. WEG to MCG, 15 Jan 1871, GC.

27. Ibid.

28. WEG to MCG, 3 Feb 1871, GC.

29. Postcard, WEG to Miss Bella Swan, 26 Feb 1924, GC.

30. ME, p. 423.

31. Pat Barr, *The Deer Cry Pavilion: The Story of Westerners in Japan, 1868–1905*, New York, 1968, p. 50. In a letter, 2 April 1871, Griffis told his sister Margaret that Fukui's population was between 85,000 and 100,000. Yazaki Takeo, in *Social Change and the City in Japan*, San Francisco, 1968, estimates the population at 27,000 in 1878 and 43,000 in 1897. Griffis' figure is probably inflated and Fukui's actual population in 1871 seems to have been somewhere between Barr's 12,000 and Yazaki's 27,000.

32. WEG to MCG, 2 April 1871, GC.

33. ME, p. 430.

34. Griffis, "In the Heart of Japan", in *Christian Intelligencer*, 27 April 1871, n.p.

35. Griffis, "Japan at the Time of Townsend Harris", in William Elliot Griffis & Hugh Byas, *Japan: A Comparison*, The Japan Society, New York, 1923, p. 14.

36. George M. Wilson, "The Bakumatsu Intellectual in Action: Hashimoto Sanai in the Political Crisis of 1858", in Albert Craig & Donald Shively, *Persona-*

lity in Japanese History, Berkeley, 1970, p. 241.

37. G. B. Sansom, *The Western World and Japan*, New York, 1950, p. 303; Marius B. Jansen, *Sakamoto Ryōma and the Meiji Restoration*, Princeton U. P., 1961, p. 408.

38. Griffis, *The Mikado: Institution and Person; A Study of the Internal Political Force of Japan*, Princeton U. P., 1915, p. 68.

39. 横井小楠

40. Sansom, pp. 266–7.

41. Ronald P. Dore, *Education in Tokugawa Japan*, Berkeley, 1965, p. 265.

42. 明道館, "School of Enlightened Methods".

43. Kanai Madoka, "Fukui, the Domain of a Tokugawa Collateral Daimyō: Its Tradition and Transition", unpublished paper delivered at the "Rutgers-Japan Conference, April 1967: Centennial Celebration of One Hundred Years of Cultural Exchange".

44. 橋本左内

45. Wilson, p. 237.

46. Griffis, *Mikado*, p. 69.

47. Quoted in Motoyama Yukihiko, "The Educational Policy of Fukui Han and William Elliot Griffis", unpublished paper delivered at the Rutgers-Japan Conference, April 1967.

48. Ibid.

49. ME, p. 424.

50. WEG to MCG, 2 April 1971, GC.

51. WEG to MCG, 9 March 1871, GC.

52. ME, p. 431.

53. Griffis, "The New World of Books in Japan", clipping, no identification, no date, p. 130, GC.

54. ME, pp. 433–4.

55. 佐々木元禄

56. WEG diary, 7 March 1871, GC.

57. WEG to MCG, 23 March 1871, GC.

58. WEG to MCG, 22 July 1871, GC.

59. WEG to MCG, 12 March 1871, GC.

60. WEG to MCG, 26 March 1871, GC.

61. WEG to MCG, 15 July 1871, GC.

62. WEG to MCG, 26 March 1871, GC.

63. WEG to MCG, 12 March 1871, GC.

64. John Black, *Young Japan: Yokohama and Yedo* . . . , Kelly & Co., Yokohama, 1883, II, p. 425.

65. WEG to the Editor of *Scientific American*, 18 July 1872, quoted in Frances Y. Helbig, "William Elliot Griffis: Entrepreneur of Ideas" (M.A. thesis, University of Rochester, 1966), pp. 57–8.

66. Nakamura Takeshi, "The Contribution of Foreigners", in *Journal of World History*, IX, 2, (1965), esp. pp. 295–305; quotation given on p. 294.

67. Helbig, p. 56.

68. WEG to MCG, 9 March 1871, GC.

69. Griffis, "Introduction of Chemistry into Japan: An Appreciation of the

Services of Charles William Eliot as a Chemist'', in *Chemical Age*, 3, 17 April 1924, galley proofs, GC.

70. Ibid.

71. WEG to MCG, 2 April 1871, GC.

72. WEG to *New York Tribune*, 4 Sept 1904, GC.

73. Griffis, ''Pioneering in Chemistry in Japan'', in *Industrial and Engineering Chemistry*, XVI, 11 (November 1924), quoted in Helbig, p. 63.

74. WEG Diary, 23 March 1871, GC.

75. Helbig, pp. 58–9.

76. WEG to MCG, 5 June 1871, GC.

77. WEG to MCG, 3 Sept 1871, GC.

78. Griffis, ''Introduction'', n.p.

79. WEG to MCG, 9 March 1871, GC.

80. Griffis, ''Introduction'', n.p.

81. Robert Schwantes, *Japanese and Americans: A Century of Cultural Relations*, New York, 1955, p. 188.

82. WEG to MCG, 12 March 1871, GC.

83. 畠山義就

84. Edward Warren Clark to WEG, 17 Oct 1871, GC; also quoted in Clark, *Life and Adventures in Japan*, American Tract Society, New York, 1878, p. 139.

85. WEG to MCG, 28 April 1871, GC.

86. WEG to MCG, 10 April 1871, GC.

87. WEG to MCG, 18 June 1871, GC.

88. WEG to MCG, 17 Sept 1871, GC.

89. Helbig, p. 64.

90. Griffis, ''Education in Japan'', in *The College Courant*, 16, 16 May 1874, n.p., GC.

91. Ibid.

92. WEG to MCG, 9 Sept & 3 Dec 1871, GC.

93. Helbig, p. 63.

94. Griffis, ''Primary School and Elementary Teaching'', unpublished manuscript in ''Griffis Scrapbook'', p. 64, GC.

95. WEG to MCG, 5 July 1871, GC.

96. Ibid.

97. WEG to MCG, 9 Sept 1871, GC.

98. ME, p. 434.

99. Griffis, ''Education'', n.p.

100. WEG to MCG, 1 Nov 1871, GC.

101. WEG to MCG, 23 March 1871, GC.

102. ME, p. 429.

103. Ibid., pp. 439–40.

104. Ibid., p. 440.

105. WEG Diary, 15 March 1871, GC.

106. WEG to MCG, 2 April 1871, GC.

107. WEG to MCG, 23 March 1871, GC.

108. WEG to MCG, 12 May 1871, GC.

109. Ibid.

110. Alfred Lucy, an English teacher and British subject whom Griffis had met earlier in Tokyo, had been teaching in Japan for five years and in Fukui for six months prior to Griffis' arrival in Japan. Although the two men appear to have got on well together, Griffis critized Lucy's moral laxity. He wrote to Margaret that Lucy "like the 99 of every hundred single men in Japan, had taken a temporary wife, but put her away just before I came." WEG to MCG, 5 July 1871, GC.

111. WEG to MCG, 17 Aug 1871, GC.

112. WEG to MCG, 18 Aug 1871, GC.

113. WEG to MCG, 17 Aug 1871, GC.

114. WEG to MCG, 28 March 1871, GC.

115. WEG to MCG, 25 June 1871, GC.

116. WEG to MCG, 9 Sept 1871, GC.

117. Verbeck to WEG, 30 Sept 1871, GC.

118. WEG to MCG, 3 Dec 1871, GC.

119. Griffis, *Some of Japan's Contributions to Civilization, Direct and Indirect*, Japan Society, New York, 1928, p. 39.

120. Quoted in Kenneth B. Pyle, *The New Generation in Meiji Japan*, Stanford, 1969, p. 1.

121. WEG Diary, 18 July 1871, GC.

122. ME, p. 526.

123. WEG to MCG, 15 July 1871, GC.

124. WEG to MCG, 9 Sept 1871, GC.

125. Ibid.

126. WEG to MCG, 26 Nov 1871, GC.

127. Ibid.

128. WEG to MCG, 1 Oct 1871, GC.

129. ME, p. 534.

130. WEG to MCG, 1 Oct 1871, GC.

131. WEG to MCG, 26 Nov 1871, GC.

132. ME, p. 538.

133. A college classmate of Griffis.

134. WEG to MCG, 1 Oct 1871, GC.

135. WEG to MCG, 28 Oct 1871, GC.

136. WEG to MCG, 10 Jan 1872, GC.

137. Ibid.

138. 村田氏懿

139. WEG to MCG, 20 Jan 1872, GC.

140. ME, p. 539.

141. WEG to MCG, 29 Jan 1872, GC.

142. Ibid.

143. Draft, WEG to Murata, "12 mo. 9 day" [1871], GC; this date corresponds to 18 January. WEG Diary, 16 Jan 1872: a messenger "returned with my letter to Muratta, not having been able to get audience of Muratta, he being very busy with officers from other Hans, etc. Resolved, if hindered to go to Yedo, (alone even) Jan. 23rd." On the following day, 17 January, he describes a meeting that he had had with Murata culminating in his decision "that

whether in honor or disgrace, alone or attended, I should set out for Yedo, overland, Jan. 23rd." He also reveals, "Wrote a letter to Muratta, in answer to his official letter rec'd this evening 7 PM which was read and ex-explained [to me] to-day." The day after Griffis wrote this letter, he received a message from the Fukui officials saying, "All Right".

144. Ibid.
145. WEG to MCG, 29 Jan 1872, GC.
146. WEG to MCG, 22 Jan 1872, GC; see also, ME, p. 540.
147. Ibid.
148. WEG to MCG, 4 Feb 1872, GC.

JOSEPH PITTAU, S.J.

INOUE KOWASHI, 1843–1895:
AND THE FORMATION OF
MODERN JAPAN

The first decade of the Meiji era (1868–1878) was characterized by the exhilarating craze for things western, not only techniques but also customs, ideas and values. The Meiji leaders and Meiji society in general were dominated by an irresistible urge for social, cultural, economic and political change. In the late seventies and early eighties, however, the tempo of change slowed down, and the Meiji leaders set themselves the task of consolidating the new system and formulating a new identity in politics as well as in ideology and morals. The span between 1878 and 1890 saw a systematic attempt at rediscovering the old, building a new, Japanese physiognomy. They strove to establish not just a *modern* state along western lines but a modern *Japanese* state.

In this new formulation three fields were given priority: the political or constitutional aspect, the power or military element, and the moral and educational formation. These elements, put together, gave modern

Joseph Pittau, S. J., is President of Sophia University in Tokyo.

Reprinted from *Monumenta Nipponica* XX, 3–4 (1965), pp. 253–282, with permission of the author and publisher.

DATE	BORROWER'S NAME	

Japan the ideological and political framework which kept the country united until the end of the second world war.

If a single man can be pointed out as the outstanding contributor to the codification of the political and educational system of early Meiji Japan, it would be Inoue Kowashi. His thought is extremely important for understanding the ideals that inspired the Meiji Constitution and the Imperial Rescript on Education. Since Inoue was very seldom in the limelight of Meiji politics, his role is somewhat obscured by the more evident contributions of the famous leaders of Meiji Japan. Because of this, there has been no monographic study thus far in any western language on this dedicated bureaucrat and great thinker. There has been very little published even in Japanese on Inoue's role, and we are still waiting for a long study of his work and his thought.[1]

Inoue Kowashi was born in Takebe, Kumamoto *han*,[2] on December 18, 1843. Though his father, Iida Gongobei,[3] had been adopted into the Iida family, Kowashi, the third son, inherited the early family name of Inoue. The Iida family was poor and Kowashi had to suffer many difficulties in order to receive a good education. Inoue was what might be called an infant prodigy and at the early age of four or five he was able to repeat by heart the One Hundred Poems by One Hundred Poets.[4]

At ten he entered the Yoneda school, and because of his remarkable record he was granted a scholarship. When he was fourteen, he was selected by the *han* leader, Nagaoka Kemmotsu,[5] and sent to the school directed by Kinoshita Seitan[6] (1805–1867), a great Confucian scholar, who had also been the teacher of Yokoi Shōnan and Motoda Eifu.[7]

In 1862 Inoue became a boarding student at the Kumamoto domain school, the *Jishūkan*,[8] where the brightest youngsters of the whole *han* were prepared to become the future leaders. The purpose of the *Jishūkan* as stated in the act of foundation in 1755 was to prepare the *han* for "national emergencies by encouraging the literary and military arts and cultivating men of ability."[9] The training was not reserved to samurai but was opened to all students excellent in learning and earnest in applying themselves to study. Yokoi Shōnan had been head master of the *Jishūkan* a few years before Kowashi went there. A special brand of Confucianism was taught at the Kumamoto school: officially it was *Shushigaku* (Chu Hsi School of Confucianism) but also *Soraigaku* (the school based on Ogyū Sorai's teaching) was accepted and taught, and *Jitsugaku*[10] (practical learning) too, was considered very important. A mixture of ancient principles and modern applications was the characteristic of the curriculum taught at the *Jishūkan*. In 1865 Inoue left the boarding school, though he was allowed to attend the lectures as before.

While he was at the boarding school Inoue had a long discussion with Yokoi Shōnan on the pros and cons of Christianity and Buddhism. When Inoue asked which of the two, Buddhism or Christianity, would do greater harm to Japanese society, Shōnan answered: "If Christ upholds ethics and Buddha discards morals, then the evil of Buddha's doctrine is greater."[11] Buddhists did not go beyond their pure-hearted austerities and neglected the study of the fundamental principles of society. Since Buddhism discarded ethics, it was something that must be rejected, even more than Christianity. But at the same time Shōnan recognized that due to the divisions and religious wars among Christian sects in Europe and due to the fact that Buddhism had a long history and deep-rooted foundations in Japan, if Christianity was propagated in Japan there would emerge religious and social unrest. Listening to this opinion Inoue asked what was the best way to prevent Christianity from taking root in Japan. Shōnan answered that they had only to revise the textbooks and strengthen the minds of the people. Inoue, not satisfied with this answer, pointed out that when the two religions clash either Christianity will lose and be absorbed into Buddhism or Buddhism will lose and be absorbed into Christianity.

Though these talks Inoue deepened his interest in the relationship between religion and politics, which lasted till the end of his life. He started also the study of Christianity by reading the Bible and reached the conclusion that Christian thought compared with Confucianism was shallow and fictitious, and not founded in the natural principles which constitute the basis of a political community. Confucianism was the only system which gave clear norms to govern the country and tranquilize the people.

This attitude against Christianity became even stronger during his period of study in Edo and Yokohama. In 1867 Inoue was sent by the *han* authorities to study French in Edo. Inoue studied also at the *Sankeijuku*[12] of Yasui Sokken[13] in Yokohama from December 1867 to April 1868, when he had to leave Edo because the political turmoil following the restoration was not conducive to peaceful study. The influence of Yasui Sokken must have been extremely deep in Inoue's formation. Yasui is known for a small booklet, *Bemmō* (Vindication), written in 1873, in which he violently refuted the teaching of Christianity, attacking the descriptions of the Old Testament and the narrations of the Gospel from the point of view of Confucianism. It has been said that *Bemmō* represented the strongest attack against Christianity in the Meiji era.[14] Though the booklet was written five years after Inoue had left Yasui's school we might surmise that Yasui propagated his ideas among the students of his academy.

Inoue returned to Kumamoto in April 1868. After a few months of study in Nagasaki he went back to Tokyo to finish his courses in French and western learning. In the training of his early youth we can already observe a few interesting features which are the key to his later work and thought. The Kumamoto curriculum was based on the spirit of Confucianism but at the same time it was open to new things, the practical learning and science of the West. This ambivalence explains many of Inoue's later contributions. The early contact with Confucianism was to remain the ideological basis of his political and moral program through his whole life; similarly his rejection of Christianity in particular and religion in general was already decided during this formative period. In this aspect he was very close to Motoda Eifu, the emperor's reader and adviser and, like Inoue, a bureaucrat from Kumamoto.[15] Inoue's open mindedness toward change and new trends and his contact with foreign ideas and currents of thought through the study of foreign languages made him, however, very different from Motoda. While in Inoue Confucianism could be described as a social device to reach definite political aims, in Motoda Confucianism remained the final goal which had once and for all solved all social and political problems.

Inoue's training received its last polish in his European tour as a member of the Etō Shimpei mission in 1872, sent to investigate the legal systems of Europe.[16] Inoue had started his government service in 1871 by joining the Department of Justice, whose chief was Etō Shimpei. Inoue was most probably selected for the European tour because of his fluency in French. In those days there were two classic routes followed by those who wanted rapid achievements: knowledge of foreign languages and travel and study abroad. Inoue Kowashi had the opportunity to follow both of these routes after a solid formation in the traditional curriculum in his native Kumamoto.

During the European tour Inoue attended for three months lectures on legal problems given by Gustave Boissonade at the Sorbonne, and he was able to observe first-hand the workings of the French and German legal and political systems. His admiration for the Prussian institutions goes back to his visit to Europe in 1872–1873, though at that time his constitutional ideas were still closer to the French and English tradition. He noticed that France was always in turmoil, though it prided itself on having a constitution based on a social contract. Prussia, on the contrary, was peaceful, and the relations between monarch and people were well defined and stable. The Prussian Constitution was not derived from a social contract, but it had been granted by the monarch.[17]

After his return from Europe in November 1873 Inoue was engaged in the translation of western legal and constitutional documents. In 1874 he translated the French Penal Code, and in 1875 he wrote *Ōkoku kenkoku hō* (Monarchical Constitutions). This book, completed in February 1875, was a translation of a French work published in 1869 which contained the constitutions of many European and American countries. Inoue translated only the parts related to monarchical governments in Europe; he also wrote a few pages of introduction. In his brief introduction to *Ōkuko kenkoku hō*[18] Inoue describes the basic concepts of a monarchical constitution. The constitution of a country is the fundamental law through which the monarch's rights are fixed and limited, the bureaucratic powers are subject to rules, and the people's rights are protected. The fundamental law forms the framework of a political system and it is inseparable from the country itself; the constitution lives together with the country and together it dies. Civil rights imply the principle of equality of all citizens, freedom of movement and abode, freedom of speech, religion and association. In a despotic country, the monarch alone makes rules and laws; in a constitutional country, however, the king and parliament share the legislative power. In a constitutional country taxes and the budget are determined only upon the consent of the elected representatives of the people. Inoue concludes his brief introduction with words to the effect that a country without a constitution is like a house without supporting pillars or a wagon without an axle.

The early research he made in foreign constitutions and legal codes gave Inoue a privileged position in the Meiji government and opened for him the way to rapid promotions. The relationship between Etō Shimpei and Inoue Kowashi was short lived. Etō was forced out of the government when the adovocates of a strong policy towards Korea

84

lost the debate against the moderate party which was under the leadership of Ōkubo Toshimichi, Kido Takayoshi and Iwakura Tomomi.[19]
After Etō's departure Inoue came to work under Ōkubo. Inoue's
relationship with Ōkubo started during the Formosan Incident. In
order to appease the disgruntled samurai the government decided to
embark on some small-scale foreign adventure. An overseas expedition
would serve as a safety valve to release the pent-up energies and
grievances of the discontented ex-samurai. The Formosan Incident
seemed to be a preordained opportunity for such a plan.[20]

In the spring of 1874 the Japanese government sent an expedition
to Formosa under the command of Saigō Tsugumichi.[21] When the
Chinese protested, Ōkubo was dispatched at his own request to China
with full powers to negotiate a treaty for the settlement of the Formosan
dispute. Ōkubo chose the Frenchman Gustave Boissonade as his legal
adviser for the mission. Before Ōkubo's departure Inoue prepared a
secret document on the Chinese problem. The document was so well
written and manifested such incisive insight in the questions involved
that Ōkubo, who was already on the point of departure from Kobe,
sent a cable calling Inoue immediately to join him on the mission to
Peking.[22] During the Ōkubo Mission to Peking, Inoue had new chances
to develop both his relationship with Boissonade and his knowledge
of foreign legislation.

In 1875 Inoue was discovered by Itō Hirobumi,[23] who after the death
of Kido, Ōkubo and Iwakura, was to become the leading figure of the
Meiji government and in a certain sense the heir to all their plans and
ideals. Inoue had accompanied Kishira Ken'yō[24] of the Department of
Justice on an inspection tour of Kyushu. On his return to Tokyo, Inoue
had drafted the report on the situation of the Kyushu population and
on the problems facing the government there. Itō Hirobumi read the
report and was greatly impressed by the competent way in which it
was written. Through investigation Itō learned that the author of the
report had been Inoue Kowashi and immediately took him as one of
his close advisers. From that time on Inoue worked faithfully for Itō,
and as Itō himself subsequently acknowledged: "from that time till
he died, Inoue participated in almost all matters related to state legislation."[25]

In the same year of 1875 Inoue also accompanied Mori Arinori[26] on
his mission to China to reach a solution on the Korean problem. He was
also Itō's confidant at the Osaka conference when efforts were made

to discover a new basis for unity among the Meiji leaders.

Inoue had joined the government service in 1871. In four years' time he had achieved remarkable successes and had come in contact with the most prominent leaders of the time. Mastery of foreign languages and knowledge of international law and foreign legal constitutional systems were in early Meiji Japan rare phenomenona, and these were the keys which easily opened the door to rapid promotion. Moreover, his classical Japanese style was very useful for the drafting of official documents. His relationship with Ōkubo as well as with Itō arose because these two statesmen were deeply impressed by his ability in writing official reports. Unaffiliated with *han* cliques, he was able to collaborate with all the outstanding leaders without ever losing his individuality or his freedom in formulating ideas and plans. That he was able to work closely with the in-group of the Court party, with Satsuma and Chōshū leaders, is in itself a proof of his diplomatic and agreeable spirit. While all the other bureaucrats under the sway of the great Meiji leaders either lost their individuality or their jobs, Inoue was able to retain both till his death.

I. THE POLITICAL CRISIS OF 1881

IMPORTANT as Inoue's services were in the early seventies, those functions were only of secondary importance compared to his role in the structuring of the Meiji Constitution, and in the formulating of principles concerning education. With the death of Ōkubo Toshimichi the first period of the Meiji government came to an end. By the spring of 1878, the original triumvirate of the Meiji Restoration, Ōkubo, Kido, and Saigō Takamori[27] had ceased to exist. Kido died on May 26, 1877. Saigō perished by his own hand in September of 1877 during the last battle of the Satsuma rebellion; and Ōkubo was assassinated on May 14, 1878, while on his way to his office. The assassination of Ōkubo marked the end of the era of centralized power. The time had come to rationalize the government and to find more efficient ways to fullfill the promises and expectations of the restoration.

There was fundamental agreement that the new political system had to be in constitutional form.[28] The problem was not whether to have a constitution, but when and what kind of a constitution. The debates raging in the late seventies and early eighties concerned timing and the nature of the constitution. The opposition was in favor of immediately establishing a system of government based upon the English tradition of constitutionalism. The ruling group was in favor of gradualism: they upheld the position that the Japan of the seventies and early eighties was not ready yet for such a constitution.

In June 1878, the senate (Genrōin) presented a draft constitution (*Nihon kokken an*).[29] The primary purpose of this draft was described in an accompanying memorial as a system that distributes the power into executive, legislative and judicial branches so that each branch would have specific functions and responsibilities. The hope was expressed that a government so constituted would bring great benefit not merely to a well disciplined administration but to the nation at large. On the whole this draft made important concessions to the democratic ideal, and clear checks and balances were established to limit the powers of the emperor and of the central government.[30]

Iwakura Tomomi who had replaced Ōkubo as the leading figure in the government did not like the implicit democratic tendencies of the Genrōin draft. Moreover he felt that the government must take action soon because of the growth of the people's rights movement and the increasing number of memorials which demanded the establishment of a national assembly. Thus in 1879, Iwakura Tomomi petitioned the Throne to order the junior councilors to report their views on the constitutional problem so that the elements most suitable to the traditional Japanese pattern of government could be singled out by the emperor as the basis for a constitution.[31] As a result the views of Yamagata Aritomo, Kuroda Kiyotaka, Yamada Akiyoshi, Inoue Kaoru, Itō Hirobumi, Ōki Takatō and Ōkuma Shigenobu were presented to the emperor between December 1879 and March 1881.[32]

After having examined the memorials of the Junior Councilors, Iwakura sent Sanjō and Arisugawa two documents, the first presenting his "Opinion on the Constitution," the second explaining the "General Principles" to be included in the future constitution. These two documents, as the historians Suzuki Yasuzō and Inada Masatsugu have clearly proved, were written by Inoue Kowashi in strict collaboration with Hermann Roesler, a German legal adviser.[33] The central ideas of Inoue's constitutionalism are already present in these documents of 1881, and for this reason they deserve close analysis.

Inoue started from the point of view that although the purpose of constitutional government was generally the same, the methods and procedures differed according to the different levels of civilization, national polity and customs. Japan, too, had to find the right methods and procedures according to the peculiar Japanese situation and the unique *kokutai*. The choice must be made whether Japan wanted to preserve the traditional imperial system or whether the emperor should become a mere ornament, as in the case of the British monarch who reigned but did not govern. The British system thus was a monarchy only in name; the Prussian system on the contrary was based on the monarchic principle in which the king became the repository of sovereign power and the link of union for the various groups and elements of the country.

Moreover, said Inoue, Japan was not ready yet for a system of government based on political parties like those in England. In Japan there were no parties, only factions, and there was no alternative to the leadership of the ruling group. In case of change there would be only chaos with everybody struggling for personal power.

In the "General Principles" Inoue laid down his fundamental points for the future constitution.

1. The constitution shall emanate from the Emperor, and the policy of gradual approach toward constitutional government shall prevail.
2. The Emperor shall have supreme command over the army and navy, declare war, make peace, conclude treaties, etc.; moreover, the Emperor will direct the national administration.
3. The organization of the cabinet shall not be subjected to the interventions of parliament. Except for those administrative affairs that are of fundamental importance for the state, for which all ministers shall be jointly responsible, each minister shall be individually responsible only for administrative affairs under his official jurisdiction. Ministers shall be responsible to the Emperor and not to parliament.
4. Parliament shall consist of two houses: an upper house composed of members appointed by the emperor and members elected from among the ranks of peers and former samurai; and a lower house of popularly elected representatives.
5. The election law for the lower house shall include a property qualification for the suffrage, while the electors for the peerage and ex-samurai shall not be subjected to property qualifications.
6. All legislative bills shall be initiated by the government.

7. When parliament does not pass an annual budget bill, the government may execute the provisions of the budget of the previous year.

8. With regard to the rights of the citizens, constitutional provisions of other nations shall be consulted.[34]

Inasmuch as many of the principles enumerated above were later embodied in the Meiji Constitution of 1889, it is clear that Japan's fundamental law conformed to the essentials expressed in this document. It is interesting to note that with the exception of the suggestion that only the government could initiate legislation, all the tenets expressed in the "General Principles" were incorporated into the Meiji Constitution.

The political crisis of 1881 was of momentous consequence for the development of Japanese constitutionalism and Japanese thought in general.[35] The role played by Inoue Kowashi in this crisis has been studied in detail by Ōkubo Toshiaki and Inada Masatsugu. Not only did Inoue write the "Opinion on the Constitution" and the "General Principles" but he was also responsible for the whole set of decisions made by the Iwakura-Itō group against Ōkuma and his group.

Inoue showed great political insight and shrewdness in discerning what was the crucial point of the crisis. He saw what was at stake in the battle between the two groups. In a letter to Itō in June 1881, Inoue expressed the fundamental ideas that were to structure the constitution. He wrote:

I have decided to send this opinion to you as I am much worried about the present situation, which, in my opinion, needs a prompt solution. I have no right to discuss the pros and cons of a constitutional form of government since it has been already decided by the Imperial Will that such a government be established. I want only to express my opinion on some fundamental points relating to it. One problem is whether the prime minister should be subject to the vote of confidence of the diet, and the other is whether the taxes should be determined by the diet. If we look at the example of foreign countries, in England the prime minister is subject to the vote of confidence or no confidence of parliament, while in Prussia this is not the case. I suggest that Japan should follow the Prussian example. The reason is as follows: In England there exists the custom that the cabinet be formed by the majority party in parliament. Though the opposition party does not join the cabinet, it is very cooperative. But here in Japan we do not have a system of true political parties, though the term is being used. The so-called parties are just groups of ordinary people, feudalistic and weak, easily split into small factions. Some influential party leader might try to enlarge his power and grasp the reigns of government purely for his own sake. This means that the arena of administrative power would become a battlefield. This is obvious because England also suffered the same troubles in the history of cabinet changes. Our civilization is still young, and our people still consider the sword more important than learning. So it is natural that people should not yet respect promising intellectuals and put their confidence in them by charging them with the administration of the country. In England the system of local government is far more advanced than in our country and local officers are popularly elected. In this way even if there is a change of cabinet the local administrations are not affected. But in Japan prefectural governors and local officers are selected by ministerial appointment. So in case of a change of cabinet, the local administrations are affected too. Moreover if cabinets are changed frequently, they cannot have the time to devote themselves to their jobs, and the people worry being left without leadership. England experienced these same troubles before. The English system was not built in a day, but was evolved through long experiments and slow progress. In Japan modernization is just at the beginning and traditional aspects still remain.

If the diet is established, whenever the people have some grudge against the government they might be tempted to change the cabinet. This will cause serious crises, so we must be prudent in this matter.

In Prussia according to the constitution, the emperor has the right to appoint and dismiss the prime minister, whose tenure of office is determined by the emperor's will not by the votes of parliament. So also the prime minister cannot quit without an imperial order. I think this is desirable for our country.

As far as the right of imposing taxes is concerned, we should not leave it to the diet. Here again I refer to the history of England. As previously stated, the English parliament has the right of confidence or no confidence in the prime minister and also the right of taxation. Once a bill was presented. Parliament told the king that taxes would not be collected unless the king approved the bill. Another example can be cited: the king appointed a prime minister not liked by parliament. Parliament used the same means to force the king to submit to the will of parliament. The English king can do nothing about taxation as it is determined by parliament. An English proverb says: Nothing is impossible to parliament, but to change men into women and women into men. The English king has neither legislative power nor administrative power as laws are passed and carried out by parliament. As the king is just a nominal ruler, I feel that England should be called rather a republic than a kingdom.

In Prussia the emperor has determined through the constitution that if the government and parliament do not agree on some tax bill, the government has the right to collect the same amount of taxes as in the previous year without the consent of parliament. Therefore the emperor has administrative power limiting the excessive rights of parliament.

As Japan's parliamentary system is still in the initial stages, I fear that it does not have enough influential power that it can concede tax collecting rights to the prefectural assemblies. If the diet causes trouble and the prefectural assemblies also follow suit, who is going to collect taxes? Or if the diet decides to impose upon the people a heavy tax, it may not be possible to force the people to pay it.

Now, I am sure you understand how important it is to write into the constitution clear rules about taxation, and I suggest that the preparation for the constitution should start as soon as possible, so also the diet should be convoked as soon as possible. But if the constitution were made by some other people without provisions on the said matters [Inoue was alluding to Ōkuma], we had better have neither constitution nor diet. The drafting of a constutition is one of the most serious things for a nation. I really do hope that you will do what you think best for the country and the people.

I hope that you will forgive my boldness in expressing my opinions so frankly.[36]

In a second letter on July 2, 1881, Inoue Kowashi insisted that Itō Hirobumi had to take upon himself the responsibility of preparing the constitution. Inoue once again declared himself in favor of a Prussian-style constitution with a strong executive branch.

> To put into effect a Prussian-style constitution is an extremely difficult task under existing conditions, but at the present time it is possible to carry it out and win over the majority and thus succeed. This is because the English-style constitution has not become firmly fixed in the minds of the people. Among the samurai in the countryside more than one-half, no doubt, have a lingering desire to uphold the Imperial House.
>
> But if we lose this opportunity and vacillate, within two or three years the people will become confident that they can succeed and no matter how much oratory we may use, it will be difficult to win them back. Most of the political parties will be on the other side, not ours; public opinion will cast aside the draft of a constitution presented by the government, and the private drafts of the constitution will win out in the end.[37]

Inoue continued by suggesting that if Itō wanted to give up his position in the government and build up a system like that of England —a monarchy in name but in reality a democratic republic—the only thing to do was to accept Ōkuma's plans and the Kōjunsha (a political club) draft prepared by Fukuzawa Yukichi[38] and to set up a party cabinet. But, Inoue insinuated that if Itō wanted to build a real monarchy like that of Prussia, then he must hurry and frame a constitution based on the principle of a strong and independent executive.

The political crisis became even more accentuated when to the constitutional debate the economic scandal of the disposal of government property in Hokkaido was added. The scandal erupted when the people learned that the newly formed Kansai Trading Company had been assured that the government properties would be sold to them for the ridiculous price of 387,082 yen. Even the *Nichi nichi shimbun*,[39] generally inclined though it was to defend the official line, in this case came out strongly against the corruption of the government officials. Inoue Kowashi in a clear memorandum to Itō said that the government had to back down if they wanted to save what was of greater importance, that is, the monarchical principle in the future constitution. Inoue warned that if the government alienated the people in this open scandal, it would be more difficult to overcome the popular movement aiming at the establishment of a parliament and a constitution along British lines.

1. Usually when a government issues a law or decree it should stick to it even if the law turns out to be undesirable in order to show that the government is stable. So I think that you should not be afraid of this kind of small problem whatever public opinion says about it. But today the government is also confronted with another kind of important problem, so it seems better that the government submit to the pressure of public opinion in the small items and get its way in the important matter. Besides, though this problem might appear a trifle to the government, it appears as a most important issue to the people. . . . I am afraid that the intellectuals might be convinced that the government cannot be trusted because of this small incident even if they appreciate other good policies. A very small mistake may destroy the good results accomplished through the serious work of one hundred years.

2. You may fear that it is a sign of weakness if the decree of sale is resinded at this late date. But if the director of the Colonization Bureau for the development of Hokkaido explains the situation to the emperor when he returns to Tokyo from his inspection tour and the revocation is declared in the emperor's ngme, it would build up the sacredness of the emperor and would greatly help the realization of the task you plan to carry out.

   I wrote this letter because I am anxious about the present political situation. I would be very happy if you would let Kuroda and Saigō read this letter. I hope you understand that I don't have any ambition to win fame because of this plan of mine.[40]

Inoue suggested cleverly the use of the stick and carrot. He wanted to appease the people through the revocation of the sale of the government property which had been attacked from all quarters by public opinion. This should be done in the name of the emperor to show that the emperor cared for the good of the people and so it would enhance the chances of a constitution based on the monarchical principle as interpreted by Roesler and Inoue himself. At the same time he was all for the expulsion of Ōkuma from the government and for the rejection of the

Kōjunsha plan of constitution. He wanted to gain the essentials by sacrificing accidentals. This was the plan which finally was approved and executed.

Inoue also authored the imperial rescript announcing the date for the establishment of the diet and the promise of a constitution. Here, too, the policy of the soft touch combined with a strong admonition was very cleverly used by Inoue Kowashi. After enumerating the various provisions already taken in order to establish a constitutional form of government, the rescript continues, "Systems of government differ in different countries, but sudden and unusual changes cannot be made without great inconvenience. . . . We perceive that the tendency of Our people is to advance with excessively rapid strides, and without that thought and consideration which alone can make progress enduring and We warn our subjects, high and low, to be mindful of Our will, and that those who may advocate sudden and violent changes, thus disturbing the peace of Our realm, will fall under Our displeasure."[41]

As the final result of the political crisis of 1881 the government won a free hand in the preparation and formulation of the Meiji Constitution and the re-organization of the administrative set-up.

II. THE MAKING OF THE MEIJI CONSTITUTION

THE imperial rescript promising the establishment of the diet and constitution was promulgated on October 12, 1881. On October 21, a special bureau was established in the Council of State to assist in the drafting of the constitution. Itō Hirobumi was selected as chairman with Tanaka Fujimaro as his deputy. The members of the committee included Saionji Kimmochi, Inoue Kowashi, Itō Miyoji, Hirata Tōsuke and Kiyoura Keigo.[42] In March of 1882, the emperor ordered Itō to lead a mission to Europe to investigate different constitutional systems in order to collect material for the formulation of the Japanese constitution.[43]

While Itō was abroad studying under Gneist and Stein, Inoue was left in Japan to examine the Japanese national traditions so that the future constitution would not be contrary to the fundamental national polity. In this research he was greatly assisted by Konakamura Seitan and Ikebe Yoshitaka,[44] the adopted son of Konakamura. Both Konakamura and Ikebe were students of the Japanese classics and Japanese ancient legislation. They made research on the Taihō Code and the related changes, and especially the nature of the Japanese political community as it appears in the Japanese classics. Ikebe presented to Inoue the result of his investigation on the meaning of the two words: *shiroshimesu* (reign and govern) and *ushihaku* (occupy), which became the foundation for upholding the principle of indivisible sovereignty in the emperor.[45]

Professor Siemes has already shown beyond all doubt the great indebtedness of Inoue Kowashi and Itō Hirobumi to Roesler's constitutional and social ideas. Similarly Inoue's political ideas leaned heavily on Ikebe's research into the Japanese classics.[46] Inoue expressed his fundamental attitude on constitutional matters in a *haiku*:

> *Totsu kuni no chigusa no ito wo kasegi agete*
> *Yamato nishiki ni ori nasamashi wo.*

> Spinning thread from thousands of foreign herbs
> to weave it into a fine Yamato dress.[47]

For Inoue constitutionalism never meant a mere imitation of Prussian political ideas and institutions, but it meant accepting modern ideas without, however, changing the historical *kokutai*, which was unique and based on a tradition of 2,500 years. Inoue wanted to build not only a system of government but a form of government based on the history of Japan.

The preparatory work of the constitution started officially with the Itō mission to Europe. Actually, however, Itō and his collaborators were engaged in the drafting of the constitution only from 1886 to the spring of 1888. Before reaching the final draft known as the "Emperor's Advisory Draft Constitution" (*Goshijun-an*), over ten drafts were prepared. Among them the most important were "Draft A" and "Draft B" by inoue.[48] In Draft A the comments of Roseler and Mosse were appended and in Draft B the pertinent clauses from foreign constitutions were appended to each article. These drafts were prepared and presented to Itō around May of 1887.

These two drafts are very close to the final document that we know as the Meiji Constitution; there are, however, a few important differences. Inoue's drafts do not have any special article concerning the sacredness and inviolability of the emperor. The consent of the diet is made necessary not only in legislative matters, but also for the ratification of special treaties. The people are designated "citizens," not "subjects." The equality before the law, regardless of birth and status, is expressly stated. Free enterprise and freedom of education are recognized and defended. However, the right of the diet to initiate legislation is not found in Inoue's drafts. In general it can be said that Inoue's documents are much more liberal than the Meiji Constitution and, for that matter, Roseler's draft.

In June 1887, Itō Hirobumi and his most trusted collaborators withdrew to the little island of Natusuhima, between Yokohama and Yokosuka. There Itō Hirobumi, Inoue Kowashi, Itō Miyoji, Kaneko Kentarō and Roeler discussed in great secrecy the constitutional problems. Itō Hirobumi using Inoue's Draft A as a model wrote revised draft, known as the *Natsushima sōan* (Natsushima Draft) after the name of the island where it was prepared.[49] This draft represented a combination of Roesler's and Inoue's drafts; its general tendency, however, is more conservative than the documents on which it was based.

As soon as the Natsuhima Draft was completed, Inoue appended his commentary to each article (*Chikujō iken*) and proposed some revisions. Roesler, too, suggested some changes in his *Kempō sōan shūsei iken* (Opinion on the Revision of the Draft Constitution).[50] Inoue objected to the description of the emperor's person as "sacred and inviolable." He argued that the concept of sacredness did not belong to constitutional law. Moreover, he said, the word "inviolable" was very difficult to translate into Japanese. Inoue preferred that these concepts be expressed in the preamble of the constitution, not in the document itself. He insisted that it was absolutely necessary to give broad powers to the diet. The right to censure the ministers, present petitions, investigate the administration and propose legislative drafts were necessary for the perfection of the constitution, the happiness of the people and the stability of the political system. Without these powers there would arise instability leading to unrest and strong demands for a revision of the constitution. The following "October Draft" accepted many of Inoue's suggestions and gave a greater role to the diet, weakening somewhat the strong insistence by Roesler on executive independence.

After the completion of the October Draft, Itō Hirobumi and Itō Miyoji departed for a tour of inspection of the defense fortification in Kyushu and Okinawa. They were absent from November 8 to December 17, 1887. During this period Inoue continued his research on the constitution and submitted a long series of questions to Roesler and

Mosse. These questions dealt with a broad range of constitutional problems especially with the powers of the emperor and the diet. Roesler again and again repeated his arguments in favour of a strong monarchical system. The diet, according to Roesler, was not a parallel organ of the monarch, nor was it an organ having sovereign powers. The diet was subordinate to the monarch and, within the limits determined by the constitution, it had the right to help the emperor in the exercise of his sovereign powers. The constitution did not involve any separation or division of powers as did the English or French models but only a limitation in the exercise of these powers.[51]

Following these discussions Inoue prepared his *Shūsei iken* (Opinion on the Revision).[52] On his return Itō Hirobumi examined Inoue's opinion, and in January 1888, he called together his collaborators and they prepared the February Draft. This draft is very similar to the October Draft, the only difference being a somewhat more precise and appropriate formulation. The February Draft was revised in a few places and a commentary was appended to each article. This became the final draft and was presented to the emperor in April 1888. The draft was later closely examined and discussed in the Sūmitsuin or privy Council.[53] Itō Hirobumi was appointed President and Inoue Chief Secretary of the Sūmitsuin. Once the work of the drafting of the constitution was finished, Itō spoke of Inoue's role in the following terms:

> Because he was second to none in knowledge and trustworthiness and especially because of his grasp of political affairs, from 1875 on he has served faithfully the two leaders Iwakura Tomomi and Ōkubo Toshimichi. There were no matters of state which he did not deal with, for more than ten years .... sphere. After the death of these leaders, I inherited their plans and was able to carry on their programs only due to Inoue's help especially in the process of drafting the constitution.[54]

Even more strongly in a speech made in Kumamoto in April 1900, Itō Hirobumi pointed out Inoue's contribution to the making of the Meiji Constitution.

> About twenty-four years ago after the establishment of the prefectures the people's rights movement became very strong,

receiving great impetus from the ideas and conditions in Europe. After the war of 1877, most of the people were in favour of the civil rights theory and believed that a constitutional form of government had to be established immediately so as to put in practice the ideals of the people's rights movement.

There were various opinions on how to implement a constitutional form of government but in general there was the fundamental consensus about constitutionalism itself. The principle was accepted that Japan had to become a constitutional state along the lines of European countries, but there was no deep research on how to reach such a goal. The government and the Genrōin received draft after draft asking for the immediate establishment of a popular assembly and a constitution.

I was convinced that in such an important matter as determining the form of the fundamental structure of the state there could be no place for temporary measures. Of course, it was also clear that it was useless to defend a narrow form of conservatism: human affairs change and nations rise and fall. However, the existence of a nation is a historical phenomenon and a reform of the fundamental structure should be based on the national history. As long as the reforms are based on the historical background, the nation cannot be destroyed. So I thought that Japan's constitutional government should be brought about along the lines of the fundamental structure blending together change and continuity.

But at the time there were very few people with whom I could take council. The only person I could consult with great confidence was Inoue Kowashi of Kumamoto. . . . I feel that the constitution could not have been brought to a conclusion without his help. During our long relationship, we had a lot of discussions and disagreements, and sometimes we almost parted, because each of us was trying to uphold till the last his own position. But we were always reconciled after explaining and understanding each other's point of view. I am sure that I could not have performed my duty in drafting the constitution without Inoue's help.[55]

Inoue was also given the task of preparing the text of the imperial oath to be taken on the day of the promulgation of the Meiji Constitution, February 11, 1889. In this document Inoue summarized the two fundamental principles which had guided him in the framing of the constitution: continuity and progress; continuity in not changing the fundamental *kokutai* and in stressing that all the new things were but a development of things already existing in Japan since the founding of the nation; progress in recognizing the new tendencies and the advance of civilization. Keeping abreast of the times and the advance of civilization was for the strength of the country, but at the same time the constitution was established "in order to give clearness and distinctness to the instructions bequeathed by the Imperial Founder."[56]

III. INOUE KOWASHI AND THE MEIJI EDUCATIONAL SYSTEM

IF THE Meiji Constitution fixed the framework of the political system of modern Japan, the Imperial Rescript on Education gave the country its moral foundation and fixed the norms and ideals for the generations to come. Inoue Kowashi took an active part in the formulation of both important documents. However, his role in education was not restricted to the imperial rescript but extended itself to many fields.[57]

Already in 1878 at the request of Itō, Inoue Kowashi had written his *Kyōiku-gi* (Opinion on Education).[58] It was an answer and criticism of *Kyōgaku taihi*[59] (Fundamental Purpose of Education), a document written by Motoda Eifu, which purported to be the emperor's own sentiments and ideas on education. Motoda severely criticized the western-style ethics texts as responsible for the decline of public morals. The Japanese family system and loyalty to the state were being destroyed; students were being taught high-sounding academic theories and empty arguments. Motoda advocated a return to the teaching of the Chinese classics and the Confucian virtues.

Inoue accepted the descriptions of the evil customs of the day, but he stated that the evils in the educational system were more apparent than real. Educational methods stressing scientific and technical education were not invalid; adduced educational abuses were simply a reflection of the rapid changes stemming from the restoration itself. The changes had been too rapid, and the sphere of liberty in speech and action had been greatly increased. The former samurai found their new status not to their liking and were criticizing the new regime. To this discontent was added the new extreme ideological movement coming from Europe and spreading itself all over the nation.

It was too early to criticize the new system, said Inoue. This system had been established for the welfare of the country, and it would be a tragedy if it were changed without trial and were replaced by the old educational system. Inoue warned that if radical methods were used to try to extirpate these fleeting ills, the country might easily fall into the errors that had plagued Tokugawa Japan. Political moralizing and speeches were certainly not the need of the day.

Inoue did not deny the value of Confucianism in education, but he was also concerned with new technical knowledge and new educational methods. The western methods were to be adopted or condemned not out of prejudice, but according to the criterion of national utility. Inoue's Confucianism was closely tied to Yokoi's real and practical learning. While Inoue was one mind with Motoda in upholding Confucianism, he was also very close to Mori Arinori who advocated strong nationalistic principles of predominantly utilitarian trend. From the manuscripts preserved in Goin Bunko of Kokugakuin University, it is clear that Inoue prepared drafts for the educational ordinances and reforms promulgated by Mori Arinori, then the Minister of Education.

The fundamental principle of the new ordinances and reforms was this, that education should serve purposes of state. What was done in the administration of all schools was not for the sake of pupils but for the sake of the country. The regulations creating the new university opened with an article stating that the purpose of the university was to teach the arts and sciences essential to the state, and the educational system was conceived throughout not in a spirit of free inquiry but in conformity with nationalistic ideals. Mori's educational reforms expanded the Meiji educational system and succeeded in taking firm root. But on the other hand, they were also responsible for an ultranationalistic tendency in education. In a speech delivered by Mori Arinori we find the nationalistic tendency at the base of Meiji education.

> If we want to maintain the prestige of Japan among the powers and achieve everlasting greatness, we must cultivate and develop our national spirit and morale. This is possible only through education. Now, in the wake of civilization, our daily life is improving in many ways. But is the spirit of our people well trained, so that it can stand hardships and carry out the heavy responsibility in the future? Has the progress of these twenty years taken true and firm roots in the people's mind so as to stabilize the foundation of the country? Besides, since the feudal period, the *shizoku* (ex-samurai) have monopolized the civil and

military affairs, taking all responsibility themselves in an emergency. But at present, it is only a small portion of the population that supports and promotes the campaign for enlightenment and progress, while the majority stand in a daze without being able to understand the significance of the founding of the country. . . . The spirit of defense of the motherland by the people and the custom of loyalty, courage and obedience, which have been cultivated and handed down by our ancestors, still exist among us. This is a priceless capital and the most precious treasure for enriching and strengthening the country. . . .

If people learn and take into their heart loyalty and patriotism, have stability and purity of character, are ashamed of cowardice and have hatred toward insult, they will be able to withstand any hardships, cooperate with others and launch an enterprise, make efforts to learn without being urged and promote civilization in this spirit and energy. It is this spirit that cultivates wealth in industry. It removes all of the obstacles and promotes the fast development of the nation's power. When the elders teach this spirit to the young, parents impart it to children, people inherit it, families assimilate it, then the spirit of the nation is stabilized forever, and she will firmly establish herself as a strong power.[60]

According to Mori Arinori the most important point of education lay neither in mastering piecemeal the crust of western civilization, nor in regulating the educational system and provisions, but in pointing the direction toward which the whole nation should march. This was the goal of education. This reform was executed on the assumption that education at that time lacked this most important point. Inoue agreed completely with Mori Arinori's educational aims. He closely worked with Mori for the establishment of the system of previous inspection of textbooks, determining in this way the official line of thought and morality for the whole nation. After Mori's assassination, Inoue described Mori's principles which were also his own:

The fundamental principle of Mori's educational policy was education based on the *kokutai*. Education does not mean merely to collect and explain the materials of textbooks. The most important thing in education is to build up the character and give orientation to the students by showing them the spiritual way.

This is an extremely difficult task. The education which was practiced 2,000 years ago in the reign of Shun cannot be used today. In Europe there is a religion which serves to confirm the spirit of the young. There is no such creed in our country. I think that it is very difficult to achieve a sense of unity among the people through education. Fortunately in our country we have one beautiful treasure which is incomparable with that of any other country. This is the *kokutai* based on the imperial line unbroken for ages eternal. Nothing but the *kokutai* can be the keynote of education. No other country has a history like ours: our people have been loyal to the emperors of an unbroken line from the beginning of the country and they will be loyal to all future emperors as long as the national land continues to exist. Therefore we should make the *kokutai* the first principle of our education. Nothing else can be the basis of our educational system, and this was the first principle of the late Mori.[61]

As in the constitution the cornerstone had to be the *kokutai* because Japan did not have a religion which could unite the hearts and minds of the people, so also in education Inoue was convinced that the only principle to give unity and orientation to the pupils was to be found in the *kokutai*. Loyalty to the emperor as the living symbol of the *kokutai* was supposed to be instilled into the minds of the children as the first value. The main purpose of education was to foment the spirit of nationalism. Thus the state became the only absolute in education as well as in politics.

It was precisely on this point that Inoue and Yamagata both made their stand when the time came for the formulation of the *Kyōiku chokugo*[62] (Imperial Rescript on Education.) Yamagata Aritomo was Prime Minister when the First Diet convened in 1890. In a famous speech about the need for military preparedness, Yamagata used the two concepts of "sphere of sovereignty" and "sphere of national interest," saying that though the sphere of sovereignty was restricted to Japan proper, the sphere of national interest extended itself also to Korea and other Asian territories. This famous speech had been drafted by Inoue Kowashi as can be proved by the existing manuscripts. The title of this draft is "Plan to Defend the Sphere of National Interest." In it Inoue writes:

There are two indispensable elements in the field of foreign policy: the armed forces first and education second. If the Japanese people are not imbued with patriotic spirit, the nation cannot be strong, no matter how many laws are issued. . . . Patriotism can be instilled only through education. Every powerful nation in Europe strives to foster through compulsory education a deep sense of patriotism together with the knowledge of the national language, history, and other subjects. Patriotism becomes a second nature. Because of such an education the minds of the people become one in the defense of the national interest even if they have different opinions in other matters. Therefore I think it is of vital importance to improve the patriotic spirit among the Japanese people, because the very survival of the nation depends on it. The two things mentioned above are indispensable to make a nation fully independent.

I feel it is unfortunate that Japan should be isolated by the sea, because there is the danger that the people might feel over-confident caring only about territorial sovereignty without thinking of the sphere of national interest. If people make patient efforts to protect the line of national interest and make Japan a fully independent nation, in about twenty years our policy will reach splendid successes.[63]

Inoue wrote this draft when he was already aware of possible military confrontations between Japan and other Far Eastern countries, especially Korea. He supported a positive diplomacy backed by a strong military force, and at the same time he considered education an indispensable condition for Japan's full independence.

In May 1890 Yoshikawa Akimasa (1841–1920) became Minister of Education. Immediately after his appointment, Yoshikawa was told by the emperor to stress moral training as the fundamental policy and to edit proverbs suitable as a basis of moral education. The drafting process of the rescript on education started almost immediately. The people directly involved in this process were Yamagata Aritomo, Prime Minister, Yoshikawa Akimasa, Minister of Education, Nakamura Masanao, Professor at the Imperial University in Tokyo and advisor at the Ministry of Education, Motoda Eifu, advisor to the emperor, and Inoue Kowashi, then director of the Legislation Bureau.[64]

The first draft was prepared by Nakamura Masanao and was submitted to Yamagata by Yoshikawa in June 1890. Nakamura's thought was essentially based on Confucianism, but there were also strong western elements derived from Christianity and the English utilitarians. In a letter to Yamagata dated June 20, 1890, Inoue strongly criticized Nakamura's draft inasmuch as it was based on philosophical and theological principles. According to Inoue, philosophical and theological reasoning should be avoided, because this kind of thing was not subject to the ruler's decree and somehow aroused violent reactions among the people.[65] Inoue attacked especially the statement by Nakamura that loyalty and filial piety derived from a religious attitude of respect to the teachings of the Lord of Heaven. Inoue, however, later used a few points from Nakamura's document when making his own draft.[66]

Motoda prepared three different private drafts, in which a very narrow exposition of traditional Confucianism accompanied the explanation of *kokutai*. The five relations (rulersubject, parent-child, elder brother—younger brother, husband-wife, friend-friend) and the three virtues (wisdom, benevolence, courage) are made the base of all education. While Motoda was preparing his drafts, Inoue was asked by Yamagata to prepare an official draft for the imperial rescript. On June 20, 1890, Inoue submitted his plan to Yamagata. On June 28, Inoue visited Motoda and asked for his opinion on the draft. After this visit he revised his draft and resubmitted it to Yamagata on July 23. This draft was examined and somewhat revised in the cabinet and in the Ministry of Education and later it became the text of the Imperial Rescript on Education. From this summary exposition of the vicissitudes of the drafting process of the rescript it is clear that Inoue played an important role, and probably the most important, in determining the educational and moral policies of the Japanese school system up to 1945.

In the preparation of the rescript we find the manifold trends of thought which influenced the emergence of modern Japan. Assembled in an attempt to achieve a synthesis these trends were mainly three: that represented by Yamagata who wanted to base the national unity and progress mainly on military strength. The second was represented by Motoda who wanted to go back to traditional Confucianism and identify ethics and politics. And finally the trend urged by Inoue, who though accepting both Yamagata's principle of military strength and

Motoda's respect for Confucian principles, was convinced that Japan would prosper only through modern constitutionalism.

Inoue was opposed to Motoda's idea of making Confucianism both the moral basis of education and the state religion in the sense that it would be the unique aim of political life. According to Motoda, Confucian morality was above politics: politics and politicians should be judged according to Confucian ethics. Moreover, Motoda wanted to uphold a feudalistic Confucianism with anticapitalistic and antiutilitarian tendencies, which were in clear opposition to the new trends of modernization and industrialization in Meiji Japan. Inoue accepted Confucianism without, however, rejecting modernization.

During the political crisis of 1881 Inoue had written that after the Meiji Restoration a revolutionary atmosphere had been brought about by English and French literature. Inoue suggested that the only possible way to redirect such a trend was to promote the study of the Chinese classics in which loyalty and the traditional virtues were taught.

This common attitude toward Confucianism made it possible for Motoda and Inoue to collaborate in the preparation of the Imperial Rescript on Education. Motoda's traditional Confucianism and Yamagata's militaristic nationalism were blended together with Inoue's constitutionalism and other modern elements. Therefore, the character of the imperial rescript can be defined as the sum of Yamagata-Inoue militaristic nationalism (education and military power are the elements of national strength), Motoda-Inoue Confucianism (the traditional virtues are the center of instruction), and Inoue's modern elements of constitutional government, of utilitarianism and practical learning to improve society.

Inoue accepted the ideas of both Yamagata and Motoda, but in order to give the rescript as much universality as possible he opposed both Yamagata and Motoda on a few points. He objected to Yamagata's plan to have the rescript published as a political ordinance of the government; he said group politics ought not interfere with the content and promulgation of the rescript. Inoue stated that the rescript should be always considered as a document above politics making it the universal principle of morality in the nation. He also mitigated Motoda's literal and narrow approach to Confucianism by the insertion of new principles.

Against Motoda's attempt to remove the phrase "respect the constitution and observe the laws," as an undesirable element weakening allegiance to the person of the emperor, Inoue insisted that the constitutional principle had to be inculcated in the hearts of the young students. In the end the words "respect the constitution" were left in the rescript through the direct intervention of the emperor.[67] The final result of the imperial rescript was the inculcation of the three principles represented by Yamagata, Motoda, and Inoue. Inoue's main contribution was in bringing into the rescript the constitutional principle which was certainly not thoroughly understood either by Yamagata or Motoda. Inoue was able to collaborate with both Yamagata and Motoda because he had something in common with both of them: the idea of a militaristic and Confucian nationalism. Thus the three ideas: militaristic nationalism, Confucianism, and constitutionalism can be found in the imperial rescript.

> Our Imperial Ancestors have founded Our Empire on a basis broad and everlasting, and have deeply and firmly implanted virtue. Our subjects ever united in loyalty and filial piety have from generation to generation illustrated the beauty thereof. This is the glory of the fundamental character of Our Empire, and herein also lies the source of Our education. Ye, our subjects, be filial to your parents, affectionate to your brothers and sisters; as husbands and wives be harmonious, as friends true; bear yourself in modesty and moderation; extend your benevolence to all; pursue learning and cultivate arts, and thereby develop intellectual faculties and perfect moral powers; furthermore, advance public good and promote common interests; always respect the Constitution and observe the laws; should emergency arise, offer yourselves courageously to the State; and thus guard and maintain the prosperity of Our Imperial Throne coeval with heaven and earth. So shall ye not only be Our good and faithful subjects, but render illustrious the best traditions of your forefathers. . . . [68]

The traditional Confucian virtues of loyalty and filial piety are clearly stated, so also the respect for the constitution and the military service in a courageous dedication to the state. The moral code of the "Admonition to Soldiers" became in a certain way also the code of civil society. The draft for the Admonition to Soldiers had been prepared by Nishi Amane at the request of Yamagata.[69] Inoue, too, had participated in the writing of this important document. The admonition enjoined soldiers to be guided by the ideals of loyalty, bravery and obedience and warned against criticizing regulations or any government policy, insulting the emperor or even expressing private opinions on important laws. If the admonition defined the ideals of the modern soldier, the rescript on education defined the ideals of both civil and military society. In this way the dualism between civil and military society which appeared in Nishi's thought was destroyed by the unity of the rescript on education.

IV. INOUE KOWASHI AS MINISTER OF EDUCATION

IN 1893, Inoue was appointed Minister of Education in the second Itō Cabinet. He was Minister for only one year and five months but his influence on the educational system of Japan was greater than the short term of his service would suggest. His influence reached all fields, and his drafts of laws, speeches, memos, and other papers of the period when he was in office show his deep knowledge and thoroughness in approaching educational problems. These documents are now preserved in the Goin Bunko of Kokugakuin University in Tokyo.

Inoue was all in favor of Confucian moral education. In this he was at one with Motoda Eifu, but this aspect was only one side of his educational program. Besides this, he was in favor of an education that would help the development of industry and the modernization of Japan. His Confucianism was intimately connected with practical learning. Inoue's fundamental contributions in educational matters can be summed up in two principles: offer equal educational opportunities to all and foment technical industrial education.[70]

The reforms he induced into the primary school system, in the middle schools and girls' schools stem from the first principle. From this standpoint, too, he was strongly opposed to an over-centralization of educational facilities in Tokyo, a phenomenon emerging already in Meiji Japan. He wanted the diffusion not only of primary schools but also of high schools and universities all over the country. In order to give all children the opportunity to attend school Inoue strongly backed the plan for establishing an "Elementary Education Fund" out of the government budget. However, because of his conviction that education was merely one of several ways to enrich and strengthen the country, he felt that this establishment of the fund had to be balanced with other expenditures, especially in view of military needs for the Sino-Japanese war of 1894–95.

Diffusion of education was not enough for Inoue; he also insisted on the contents of education. He wanted *practical* learning. Education was intended not as an end in itself, but as a means toward the ultimate value of the state. The educational system was supposed to prepare the future soldiers and the future leaders of business and industry in Japan. From this conviction arose his eagerness to make people aware of technical and industrial subjects. He was also responsible for the establishment of the Institute for Technical School Teachers.

Inoue saw a changing world in which technology and industrialization were going to play the leading role in the shaping of political affairs. In this he was probably one of the most influential leaders in the building of the new Japan. To Inoue is due a large share of the credit for constructing the base which enabled the newly emerging nation to achieve such phenomenal progress in industry, technology and science.

During his short term as Minister of Education Inoue issued a series of orders concerning industrial, technical and agricultural education. While modern industry was rapidly developing, Inoue thought that the four years of compulsory education were not sufficient for the new needs. What Inoue planned was a system of education adequate to the daily needs of young workers and to the needs of modern industry. He defined the aims and curricula of the already existing industrial and technical schools and apprentices' schools which had nothing technical or vacational about them except their name. The regulations issued on November 20, 1893, for industrial continuation schools and related instructions of November 22 were decided by Inoue as well as the regulations for apprentices' schools (July 1894), the enactment of the Government Subsidy Act for Industrial Education (1894) and many other directives. Vocational training and knowledge which lead to improved methods of production and help the modernization of the country were to be at the center of the technical and industrial education. In a revealing passage Inoue wrote:

> The national strength and wealth of all countries in the world are growing larger year after year. This is simply because, in these countries, scientific study is encouraged, new inventions are

applied to practical purposes and the production is greatly increased by their insistent effort in improving technical schools. Japan has not become fully civilized yet and scientific knowledge and the ability of the nation has not improved. Education and labor have no influence upon each other. . . . Under these circumstances, it is earnestly desired that for national prosperity we should establish the scientific and technical education which is most necessary for the industrial development of Japan.[71]

Inoue considered education the foundation of independence and prosperity; hence it was incumbent on teachers to develop the spirit of patriotism among the students. Vocational training and guidance were considered all important. For this Inoue wanted specialization in courses and curricula. Teachers must be skilled and equipped to meet the demands of various regions and situations.

Inoue makes mention of Okinawa: teachers going there should know about the cultivation and production methods of the sugar industry.[72] Teachers working in other regions should study the best ways to improve the peculiar products of their special area. Inoue insisted also on physical education and the last ordinance he signed before resigning might be called "the ordinance about physical fitness."[73]

Never in good health himself, Inoue had to resign his post as the Minister of Education because of sickness on August 29, 1894. He then retired to his villa in Hayama but he never recovered.

The title of Viscount was conferred on Inoue in January of 1895. He died on March 15, 1895.

V. INOUE KOWASHI'S THOUGHT

SO FAR we have examined Inoue's contributions in the framing of the Meiji Constitution and the organization of the Meiji educational system. Now we want to attempt a general description of Inoue's ideological principles. It is hard, though, to find a system in Inoue's thought. His published books and writings are very few. Many of his manuscripts are political, legal or educational opinions prepared as answers to particular questions from Iwakura or Itō or Mori; these answers emerged from concrete, well defined situations. Although these documents may not express the whole range of his thought, yet they give us an outline.

A very important document is the letter he wrote to Ikebe Yoshitaka on September 28, 1886, entitled *Jukyō wo sonsu* (To Preserve Confucianism).[74] This letter is extremely important because it was written when Inoue was already working on the drafting of the constitution. It has been often stated that Inoue's thought was in opposition to that of Motoda Eifu and that the principles stressed in the Meiji Constitution were very different from the principles of the *Kyōiku chokugo*. An analysis of the *Jukyō wo sonsu* will help us to decide whether these oppositions were as deep as some authors have described or whether they were minor differences which did not destroy the fundamental identity.[75]

From *Jukyō wo sonsu*, it is evident that Confucianism was an essential element of Inoue's thought. This long letter starts with a general description of the origin of both the western and eastern civilizations. In the West, Egyptian culture constituted the basis of Judaism and Christianity. In China the moral ideas of Yao and Shun were transmitted from generation to generation through the teachings of Confucius and Mencius. While the doctrines of Judaism and Christianity were artificial and based on supernatural notions and myths, the moral ideas of the East were based on nature and on common sense.

Inoue found the reasons for the decline of Chinese power not in Confucianism itself but in the ritualistic and formalistic approach to the Confucian doctrines of the Chinese scholars. The Chinese had adhered to the letter without grasping the spirit of Confucianism. The West on the other hand had tried with great success to develop mechanical civilization, raise the standard of living and increase the wealth of their countries. At first, the reason for this contrast between China's decline and the West's progress might appear to be in that the West had accepted Christianity whereas China was non-Christian. But on deeper analysis of the Bible and the life of Christ, Inoue said, one comes to realize that Christianity was not the source of the West's progress. Christianity, on the contrary, was very inimical to the well-being of the political community, especially because Christian dogma believed in one God above all human authority, a God who gives reward and punishment after this world. Thus Christians were inclined to obey divine laws and respect the judgment of the next world rather than obey the human laws and respect the judgment of the political authorities. Christians considered the propagation of their doctrine an obligation, and death for their faith was esteemed as the supreme act of loyalty and a great honor. Christianity had been the cause of many a revolt against the political authorities and the origin of many a war and many a tyranny.

Religion which proclaimed itself as based on a revelation from God had in most cases led only to bloodshed and aggression. Confucius and Mencius, on the contrary, based their doctrines not on some theological principle or divination but on moral principles common to the whole world. In Confucianism there was neither dualism which separated politics from religion nor a clergy which imposed its authority in opposition to the political powers. Confucianism was the best ethical system because it did not base its teachings on revelation but on nature. Thus Japan ought to adopt from the West the ideas of civil law, the techniques of agriculture and industry, but in ethical problems it should follow the Chinese teachings and the Chinese classics.

Inoue's strong objection against Christianity was mainly due to the Christian dualism in the principle of loyalty: a Christian, he understood, is supposed to be loyal first and foremost to God and the Church; only a secondary obedience is due to political rulers and leaders as the recipients of limited powers from God. Moreover Inoue thought that Christianity dealt only with the relation between the individual and God; it did not care, according to his interpretation, about the social relations among men. These ideas expressed by Inoue were close to those upheld by Motoda Eifu.

The difference between the two was in this, that Motoda advocated the idea of the unity of religion and politics; thus he wanted the emperor to be both the political ruler and the high priest of the Japanese nation. Motoda's political and religious system was essentially Ōdōron[76] (imperial way), involving the direct participation of the emperor in the determination of moral ideals and political decisions. The emperor and the court advisers were supposed to join the cabinet in the decision-making process in order to carry out the realization of a system of moral politics. Inoue, on the contrary, accepted constitutionalism as the first principle of a modern form of government; he wanted a clear separation of the fields of thought and politics. Government could not be involved in the determination of moral principles deriving from a religious point of view. There was also another fundamental difference between the Confucianism of Motoda and that of Inoue. For Motoda the Confucian principles were eternal, not susceptible to change, and the Chinese classics were the only source of moral education and political behavior.

Inoue's Confucianism, however, was never so narrow. If Confucianism was the "teacher," the Japanese classics and the *kokutai* were the "father."[77] Motoda thought that Confucianism represented a universal morality with unique absoluteness and that the Japanese political and social system had to be adapted to such a universal norm. Inoue considered the Japanese *kokutai* as unique and absolute, and Confucianism was just a means to maintain the *kokutai* in its purity. The *kokutai* was for Inoue the only absolute: Confucianism and western civilization—legal system, technology and general culture—were the supporting elements of the wealth and power of the Japanese nation. Practical learning, in Inoue's scheme, was combined with the study of the Japanese language and literature and the Chinese classics. Motoda, in a word, was a moral scholar; Inoue was mainly concerned with problems of political power. Motoda was more of a Chinese Confucianist, whereas Inoue was primarily an advocate of the principle of *kokutai*.

Thus although Confucianism was a very important element of Inoue's ideological system, it cannot be considered the main characteristic of his thought. Foremost in his system was the principle of the *kokutai*. This principle gave unity to his whole career, especially to his work in the framing of the Meiji Constitution and in the drafting of the Imperial Rescript on Education. Both the preamble to the constitution and the rescript began with the fundamental statement of the uniqueness of the Japanese nation based on the imperial line unbroken for ages eternal. The same principle was stated also in the rescript promising the establishment of the diet in 1881 and in the imperial oath at the proclamation of the Meiji Constitution.[78] The notion of the *kokutai* applied to political thought, implied the absolute sovereignty of the emperor. The emperor became the only repository of sovereign power, and this power apparently came from the divine ancestors.

One might ask the question why Inoue accepted such mythological notions. The answer is probably found in an important speech by Itō Hirobumi on June 18, 1888, at the first meeting of the Privy Council before starting the discussions on the draft constitution. On this occasion Itō spoke about the principles that had guided the framers of the constitution. Itō said that every system of government, especially a constitutional form of government, required the rationalization of a set of fundamental beliefs of religious or quasi-religious character into a political way of life. According to Itō and also according to Inoue, in Japan there was no religion nor tradition of responsible participation

112

of the people in the affairs of state. Only the Imperial House and the ideology of the *kokutai* could become the foundation of the new constitutional system.[79]

The third principle of Inoue's system was transcendentalism, that is, the conviction that the cabinet should be above political parties and free from the interference of the diet in executive matters. This principle was stated openly in the documents Inoue wrote during the political crisis of 1881. In these documents Inoue strongly attacked the English form of constitutional government. Also, because he was under the influence of Roesler, Inoue defended the principle of monarchic constitutionalism with strong conservative implications. The adminstration had to be above all political division and struggle. The cabinet could not be a party cabinet, because by definition a party cabinet would represent only the interests of one part of the state.

Behind this theory of political transcendentalism was the Hegelian ideology of the role of the state. This ideology had influenced Lorenz von Stein and through Stein had been accepted by Roesler and Inoue. Society was essentially class society, and class struggle was the true content of society. The general and inalterable condition of society was the struggle between a dominant and a dependent class. The social order was necessarily a class order; its prime feature was self-seeking, that is, the general inclination of each to acquire the means for his own independence and the means for making others dependent. In contrast to the principle of society, the principle of the state was the development, progress, wealth, power and intelligence of all the individuals without distinction, positing all individuals as free and equal. The state preserved the common interest, impartiality, and freedom from the conflicting private interests of society. Only the state could give a superior spiritual and moral sense.

Inoue's opposition to the party-cabinet principle was based on this ideology. He asked Roesler what the basis of a true of constitutional government had to be.[80] Roesler turned in a long and detailed description of his sociopolitical system. Roesler saw that the development of society would lead necessarily to a democratic form of government. He predicted that the bourgeoisie would become the dominant class in Japan. It should be checked lest it undermine the security of other classes: both the landowners and the proletariat. Roesler said that the state's most urgent task was a harmonious social balance through social legislation and an active administrative policy that worked for the physical and cultural welfare of the lower classes. To overcome class conflict and to maintain an ethical political attitude that placed the welfare of the whole above class interest, the institution of hereditary monarchy was necessary. This monarchy, possessing the loyal allegiance of the people, would care for the common welfare and would become the custodian of the weak. Inoue applied this theory to the Imperial House and to the cabinet. The cabinet as the executive branch of government had to be independent in carrying out the policy of the common welfare.

The last but one the least element of Inoue's thought was adaptation to modern trends. This adaptation started from his formative days in Kumamoto: *jitsugaku* or practical learning meant matters of taxation, judicial administration, irrigation, land reclamation, welfare policy and so on. Adaptation led Inoue to study modern languages and the legal and political system of other countries. He was not a narrow minded *laudator temporis acti*. If the *kokutai* remained his fundamental principle, and Confucianism gave him the mental attitude to solve moral political problems, he also saw that many techniques and principles had to be adopted from western contries. Constitutionalism was among these modern elements. Inoue again and again stressed the point that the constitution had to be a *modern* one, according to the principles of western tradition. This was of essential importance. The aim of a modern constitution was to limit the powers of the monarch and to defend the rights of the citizens. This modern element appears also in Inoue's insistence on technical instruction in his educational policies.

Inoue Kowashi in his ambivalent attitudes and principles represents the ambiguous commitments and solutions of the early Meiji period. The leaders of Meiji Japan firmly believed that they had achieved a synthesis between traditional Japanese elements and modern western aspects. They thought that *kokutai*, transcendentalism, constitutionalism, freedom of thought, Confucianism, scientific spirit and traditional ethics could be mingled into one system always preserving the equilibrium among these conflicting aspects. History proved them wrong; but the historical result does not alter the fact that theirs was a serious attempt to achieve for Japan a suitable compromise between the modern and traditional aspects, between continuity and change.

1. One of the first references to Inoue Kowashi 井上毅 in a western language was the article by Suzuki Yasuzō (translated by Johannes Siemes), "Hermann Roesler und die japanische Verfassung," *Monumenta Nipponica*, IV (1941) 54–55. In western works dealing with Meiji Japan there are only passing remarks on Inoue Kowashi. In Japanese there is as yet no critical monographic study on Inoue's life and thought. The two published biographies, though rich in detailed biographical data, are panegryrical and uncritical: Hirata Shinji 平田信治 ed., *Motoda—Inoue ryō sensei jiseki kōen roku* 元田。井上両先生事蹟講演録 (Collection Speeches on the Achievements of Motoda and Inoue) Kumamoto, 1913; and Morimoto Yonekazu 森本米一 ed., *Inoue Kowashi sensei* 井上毅先生 Kumamoto, 1932.

2. 藩

3. 飯田権五兵衛

4. *Hyakunin isshu* 百人一首 is a collection of one hundred famous poems. There are different collections. Hirata, *Motoda–Inoue*, pp. 1–4.

5. 長岡監物

6. 木下犀潭

7. 横井小楠　元田永孚

8. 時習館

9. Quoted in Uno Tetsujin 宇野哲人, *Hosokawa reikan kō to jishūkan* 細川霊感公と時習館, (Hosokawa Reikan and the Jishūkan) Tokyo, 1942, pp. 29.

10. 朱子学、徂徠学、実学 See Donald H. Shively, "Motoda Eifu: Confucian Lecturer to the Meiji Emperor," in David S. Nivison and Arthur F. Wright, eds., *Confucianism in Action*, Stanford, 1959, pp. 305–306. Also for curriculum in the Bakumatsu period see, R. P. Dore, *Education in Tokugawa Japan*, Berkeley & Los Angeles, 1965, pp. 124–175.

11. Umetani Noboru 梅溪昇, *Meiji zenki seiji shi no kenkyū*, 明治前期政治史の研究 (Studies in the Political History of Early Meiji Japan), Tokyo, 1963, pp. 319–320. Umetani's book is the best work on the ideological system of Inoue, and I have used it frequently in the preparation of this essay.

12. 三計塾

13. Yasui Sokken 安井息軒 (1799–1876) was a great educator of the Bakumatsu period. After the visit of American warships he published the book *Kaibō shigi* 海防私議 (On Coastal Defense) (1863). He was an advocate of practical learning, but at the same time a strong defender of Confucian thought.

14. The text of *Bemmō* 辨妄 published with an interpretation is found in *Meiji bunka zenshū* 明治文化全集, XV (1929) pp. 209–221.

15. For the life and ideas of Motoda see Shively, "Motoda Eifu," pp. 302–333.

16. Etō Shimpei 江藤新平, then Minister of Justice, prepared the mission, but at the last moment he was forced to remain in Japan abandoning his plan to lead the mission. The mission itself, however, was not canceled. Ōkubo Toshiaki 大久保利謙 erroneously states that the mission did not take place and that Inoue lost his chance of visiting Europe. Ōkubo Toshiaki, "Meiji 14 nen seihen to Inoue Kowashi" 明治十四年政変と井上毅 (The Political Crisis of 1881 and Inoue Kowashi), in *Meiji bunka shi ronshū* 明治文化史論集 (Studies in the Cultural History of Meiji Japan), Tokyo, 1952, p. 614. See Inada

Masatsugu 稲田正次, *Meiji kempō seiritsu shi* 明治憲法成立史 (History of the Framing of the Meiji Contitution), 2 vols., Tokyo, 1960, 1962, 1, 190.

17 Kamishima Jirō 神島二郎, "Inoue Kowashi: kokka kikō no seisaku" 井上毅　国家機構の制作(Inoue Kowashi: The Formation of the State Structure), Asahi Janaru, ed., *Nihon no shisōka* 日本の思想家 (Thinkers of Japan), 3 vols., Tokyo, 1962–63, 1, 156.

18. The French original was Laferrière et Batlie, *Les Constitutions d'Europe et d'Amérique*, Paris, 1869. Inoue's translation *Ōkoku kenkoku hō* 王国建国法 is found among Inoue's papers in the Goin Bunko, No. 291, of Kokugakuin University in Tokyo. "Goin" was another name used by Inoue instead of Kowashi.

19. 大久保利通　木戸孝允　岩倉具視

20. On the Formosan Incident see Masukazu Iwata, *Ōkubo Toshimichi: The Bismarck of Japan*, Berkeley and los Angeles, 1964, pp. 184–224.

21. 西郷従道

22. Morimoto, *Inoue Kowashi sensei*, pp. 5–6.

23. 伊藤博文

24. 岸良賢養

25. Quoted in *ibid.*, p. 38. At the end of his career, Inoue Kowashi told one of his best friends, Adachi Kenzō 安達謙藏, "I have made a failure of my life in the service of Itō." There might be different meanings of the words *isshō wo ayamarareta* 一生を誤まられた; anyway the relationship between Itō and Inoue was a very deep and lasting one. Ōkubo, "Meiji 14 nen seihen," p. 627.

26. 森有礼

27. 西郷隆盛

28. The constitutional movement in early Meiji Japan is described by George Akita, "Development of Parliamentary Government in Meiji Japan," Ph. D. thesis, Harvard, 1960.

29. 元老院、日本国憲案

30. George Beckmann, *The Making of the Meiji Constitution*, Lawrence, Kansas, 1957, pp. 120–125, gives a translation of the Genrōin's draft. For a lengthy analysis of this draft see Asai Kiyoshi 浅井清. *Genrōin no kempō hensan temmatsu* 元老院の憲法編纂顛末(An Account of the Draft Constitution of the Genrōin), Tokyo, 1946.

31. In a letter to Hirobumi, written on December 21, 1880, Iwakura deplored the fact that the Genrōin's draft was but an imitation of foreign constitutions, without any consideration for the Japanese *kokutai* 国体 (national polity) and the peculiar circumstances of the Japanese nation. Inada, *Meiji kempō*, 1, 335–336.

32. 山県有朋　黒田清隆、山田顕義、井上馨、伊藤博文、大木喬任、大隈重信

The various opinions of the junior councilors are examined in detail by Inada. *Ibid.*, pp. 426–507. A translation of the opinions of Yamagata, Ōkuma, Itō and Iwakura is found in Beckmann, *The Making of the Meiji Constitution*, pp. 126–148. Not only Iwakura's opinion, but also Itō's were written by Inoue as it is evident from the manuscripts in the Goin Bunko.

33. Suzuki Yasuzō 鈴木安藏, *Kempō seitei to Roesler* 憲法制定とロエスレル (The Making of the Constitution and Roesler), Tokyo, 1942, pp. 141–152; Inada, *Meiji kempō*, I, 465–491.

34. Translation from Beckmann, *The Making of the Meiji Constitution*, p. 59.

35. For the political crisis of 1881 see Joyce C. Lebra, "Ōkuma Shigenobu and the Political Crisis of 1881," *Journal of Asian Studies*, XVIII, 475–487 (1959); Akita, "Development of Parliamentary Government," pp. 68–105; Ōkubo, "Meiji 14 nen seihen," pp. 613–652.

36. The text of this letter is found in Ōkubo, "Meiji 14 nen seihen," pp. 630–632.

37. *Ibid.*, p. 634.

38. 交詢社、福沢諭吉

39. 日日新聞

40. Tanaka Sōgorō 田中惣五郎, "Inoue Kowashi" 井上毅、in Konishi Shirō 小西四郎 ed., *Nihon jimbutsushi taikei* 日本人物史大系 (Biographies of Japanese Personalities), 7 vols., Tokyo, 1959–1960, V, 233.

41. Walter W. McLaren, ed., *Japanese Government Documents, 1867–1889*, vol. XLII, Pt. I, *Transactions of the Asiatic Society of Japan*, Tokyo, 1914, pp. 86–87.

42. 田中不二麿、西園寺公望、伊東巳代治、平田東助、清浦奎吾 Osatake Takeki 尾佐竹猛, *Nihon kenseishi taikō* 日本憲政史大綱 (An Outline of Japanese Constitutional History), 2 vols., Tokyo, 1938–1939, II, 655.

43. Itō's mission to Europe is covered by Shimizu Shin 清水伸, *Dokuō ni okeru Itō Hirobumi no kempō torishirabe to Nihon kempō* 独墺における伊藤博文の憲法取調と日本憲法 (Itō Hirobumi's Constitutional Investigation in Germany and Austria and the Japanese Constitution), Tokyo, 1939.

44. 小中村清矩、池辺義象

45. Umetani, *Meiji zenki*, pp. 313–316. *Shiroshimesu* 知ろし食す (reign over and govern) was applied only to the emperor, who through the unbroken line of his ancestors received the supreme power by a divine command. *Ushihaku* 領く means occupy, possess and was used to describe the relationship between the tutelary gods and the Japanese people.

46. Johannes Siemes, "Hermann Roesler no kempō riron ni okeru shakai hatten to rikkenshugi no kankei" ヘルマン・ロエスレルの憲法理論に於ける社会発展と立憲主義の関係 (Social Progress and Constitutionalism in Hermann Roesler's Constitutional Theory), *Kokka gakkai zasshi* 国家学会雑誌, 1–41, LXXV, 181–202, 306–330, 418–424, 1962. Siemes has also published an article in German, "Hermann Roesler und die Einführung des deutschen Staatsrechts in Japan," *Der Staat*, II, 181–196, 1963, See also Siemes's introductory article to "Hermann Roesler's Commentaries on the Meiji Constitution," *Monumenta Nipponica*, XVII, 1–66, 1962; XIX, 37–65, 1964. Siemes's contribution to the understanding of the German influence on Meiji thought and institutions is very important especially because he gives the philosophical and social background of Roesler's work. Ikebe (1864–1923) was born in Kumamoto *han* to which also Inoue belonged. In 1882 Ikebe entered the University of Tokyo in the department of classic literature. In the late Meiji period and during the Taishō era he was a famous scholar of Japanese classics

and poetry.

47. とつ国の千草の糸をかせぎあげて やまと錦に 織りなさましを
Morimoto, *Inoue Kowashi sensei*, p. 35. See also Umetani, *Meiji zenki*, p. 314.

48. 御諮詢案 The text of both drafts is found in Inada, *Meiji kempō*, II, 68–82.

49. 夏島草案 *Ibid.*, pp. 197–213. This draft is also called the "August Draft."

50. 逐条意見、憲法草案修正意見 *Ibid.*, pp. 213–247.

51. *Ibid.*, p. 288.

52. 修正意見 *Ibid.*, pp. 311–329.

53. 枢密院

54. Morimoto, *Inoue Kowashi sensei*, pp. 35–36.

55. *Ibid.*, pp. 36–39.

56. Itō Hirobumi, *Commentaries on the Constitution of the Empire of Japan*, tr. Miyoji Itō, 3rd ed., Tokyo, 1931, pp. 153–154.

57. For Inoue's role in education see Kimura Kyō 木村匡, ed., *Inoue Kowashi kun kyōiku jigyō shōshi* 井上毅君教育事業小史 (A Brief History of Inoue Kowashi's Achievements in Education), Tokyo, 1895; Nihon kindai kyōikushi kenkyūkai 日本近代教育史研究会, ed., *Inoue Kowashi no kyōiku seisaku* 井上毅の教育政策 (Educational Policies of Inoue Kowashi), Tokyo, 1963; Kaigo Tokiomi 海後宗臣, "Kyōiku chokugo to Inoue Kowashi" 教育勅語と井上毅 (The Imperial Rescript on Education and Inoue Kowashi), *Nippon* 日本, VIII, 88–93, April, 1965. In *Inoue Kowashi no kyōiku seisaku* there is also a very helpful bibliographical note of the most important works on Inoue Kowashi.

58. 教育議 Murakami Shunsuke and Sakata Yoshio 村上俊亮、坂田吉雄, eds., *Meiji bunka shi: kyōiku dōtoku hen* 明治文化史、教育道徳編 (History of Meiji Culture: Education and Morals), Tokyo, 1955, pp. 147–155. See also Watanabe Ikujirō 渡辺幾治郎, *Nihon kempō seitei shikō* 日本憲法制定史講 (Studies in the Making of the Japanese Constitution), Tokyo, 1937, pp. 161–184.

59. 教学大旨

60. Translation adapted from Tatsuo Morito, *Prospect and Retrospect of Japanese Education*, Tokyo, 1961, pp. 17–18.

61. Umetani, *Meiji zenki*, p. 315.

62. 教育勅語

63. *Ibid.*, pp. 293–294.

64. 芳川顕正、中村正直 The various drafts of Nakamura, Motoda, and Inoue are given in *Ibid.*, pp. 368–399.

65. Ōkubo Toshiaki, "Meiji 14 nen seihen," in *Meiji seiken no kakuritsu katei* 明治政権の確立過程 (The Emergence of the Meiji Political Power), Tokyo, 1957, pp. 149–153.

66. Umetani, *Meiji zenki*, p. 371.

67. Shively, "Motoda Eifu," p. 331.

68. Hugh Keenleyside and A. F. Thomas, *History of Japanese Education*, Tokyo, 1937, p. 100.

69. 西周 For the history of the Admonition to Soldiers see Umetani, *Meiji zenki*, pp. 196–240.

70. Nihon kindai kyōikushi kenkyūkai, *Inoue Kowashi no kyōiku seisaku*, pp. 144–147.

71. Japanese National Commission for Unesco, ed., *History of Industrial Education*, Tokyo, 1959, p. 162. See also pp. 146–173.

72. Morimoto, *Inoue Kowashi sensei*, pp. 52–55.

73. *Ibid*., p. 69.

74. 儒教を存す Umetani, *Meiji zenki*, pp. 309–324.

75. For instance Ienaga Saburō 家永三郎, "Kyōiku chokugo seiritsu no shisōteki kōsatsu" 教育勅語成立の思想史的考察 (An Ideological Historical Consideration on the Making of the Imperial Rescript on Education), *Shigaku zasshi* 史学雑誌, LVI, 1173–1191 (December 1946), overstresses the differences between Inoue and Motoda and almost makes Inoue a champion of liberal thought.

76. 王道論

77. Umetani, *Meiji zenki*, p. 323.

78. Itō, *Commentaries on the Constitution*, pp. 156–157.

79. Shimizu Shin 清水伸、*Teikoku kempō seitei kaigi* 帝国憲法制定会議 (The Council for the Enactment of the Imperial Constitution), Tokyo, 1940, pp. 87–89.

80. Inada, *Meiji kempō*, II 142–150.

WILBUR M. FRIDELL

GOVERNMENT ETHICS TEXTBOOKS
IN LATE MEIJI JAPAN

From early in the Meiji period (1868–1912) until the end of the
Pacific War in 1945, Japanese government authorities attached considerable importance to ethics (*shūshin*) instruction in the schools as a
means of uniting the people behind the throne. There were, of course,
other channels through which ideological propagation was effected,
such as imperial rescripts, the military forces, Shinto shrines, and
miscellaneous community organizations (Youth Association, Hōtoku
Society, etc.). Still, over the decades the Japanese schools served as
important agencies for the propagation of national-imperial values, and
in the total school curriculum ethics training played a key ideological
role.[1]

In this article I will deal with government ethics textbooks in the
latter part of the Meiji period. For one thing, the late Meiji story is less
well known than the earlier period.[2] Also, from around the turn of the
century the government assumed much more direct supervision over

Wilbur M. Fridell is Associate Professor of Religious Studies at the University of California,
Santa Barbara.

Reprinted from *Journal of Asian Studies*, XXIV, 4 (August, 1970), pp. 823–833, with
permission of the author and publisher.

the writing of ethics textbooks, so that they came to reflect even more accurately the national values which state ideologues sought to promote.

Two momentous documents, the Meiji Constitution (1889) and the Imperial Rescript on Education (1890), enshrined the chief traditional elements of an emerging educational ideology. The Education Rescript exalted filial piety and loyalty (ruler- or emperor-loyalty), both associated with the Confucian tradition, and called upon all Japanese subjects to observe familial virtues in daily life, while holding themselves ready to serve state and throne at any time. Here we find the themes of familism, emperor-loyalty, and patriotic devotion, which would increasingly characterize public educational ideology. Perhaps the chief contribution of the constitution was to declare the emperor "sacred and inviolable" (Chapter I, Article III), and to reserve for him the rights of sovereignty by virtue of his descent from the glorious "Ancestors," going back to the highest Shinto *kami* (Preamble).[3] Here was final religious sanction for an imperial figure who could command the reverent loyalty and obedience of his people.

Building on these old principles, revised ethics instruction came to stress three main themes: (1) A new kind of emperor. With increasing clarity, the official image of the emperor was that of a ruling monarch who was not simply the repository of sacred authority, but who *was* that authority in his own person. With the declaration that the emperor was sacred, we already have the beginning of the apotheosis of the Meiji emperor. This process, which reached culmination after the turn of the century, fixed the pattern for the rest of the modern authoritarian era. (2) Familization of nation and throne. By linking filial piety and emperor-loyalty, mid-Meiji ideologues were able to make a super family of the nation, and a super father figure of the emperor. That is, they began by idealizing the warm devotion that is due one's parents (filial piety), then affirmed that this principle found its highest fulfillment in filial devotion, or absolute loyalty, to the "national family" and its revered head. This familial notion of nation and emperor would reach a high point in the government-produced ethics texts of 1910, and subsequently wane. (3) Universalization of the old elite ethic. Absolute lord-loyalty, above loyalty even to one's parents, was the distinguishing mark of the samurai ethic in the Bushidō tradition. By the end of the Tokugawa period, samurai loyalists had focused supreme allegiance on the emperor. Now government ideologues undertook to universalize this elite ethic, in a somewhat modified form, so that it would serve as the norm for the whole mass of the Japanese population. As Kawashima Takeyoshi has said, "the ethic of the old authoritarian samurai class (was) revamped to serve as the tool of the new power control."[4] This effort to extend the samurai ethic to all Japanese continued throughout the whole modern period, up to 1945.

The above themes find concrete expression in Higashikuze Michitomi's *Shūshin Kyōkasho* (Morals Textbook), which was based on the Imperial Rescript on Education and approved by the Ministry of Education for use in elementary schools from 1890. Higashikuze's books (actually a series of texts) were long considered models in their field, and may be taken as representative of the maturing ideological formulation of ethics textbooks in the post-Rescript years.

Higashikuze first took up behavior in the home, emphasizing family loyalty and filial piety. Then he extended to the emperor those warm familial feelings which naturally attach to parents. ". . . The ties which bind ruler and subjects," he wrote, "are exactly the same as the intimate relationship between a father and his children . . ." Therefore, ". . . we should always obey the Emperor, thinking of him as our distant Father." The emperor is the father of the nation because the imperor family is the "national Head Family" (*kokumin sōka*), in a relationship of *honke* (head family) to all other Japanese families, which are *bunke* (branch families). The imperial family is the "national Head Family" because it derives from the topmost *kami* in the Shinto tradition: ". . . The Imperial Line originated in the ancestors of the Head Family . . . The emperor possesses the legitimacy of Jimmu Tennō, and transmits the Sacred Treasures. . . . (He) derives from the . . . heavenly *kami*."[5]

Here are ancient elements of the Japanese tradition: Shinto *kami* beliefs sanctifying the imperial lineage, Confucian filial piety, ruler-loyalty, even the *honke-bunke* family structure. Yet new features are clearly discernable. Higashikuze is quite explicit, for example, on the familization of nation and throne, in his extension of loyalty and filial devotion from local family and parents to "national family" and patriarchal emperor. It is also evident that he exalts the "new kind of emperor," who possesses in himself the sacred credentials to rule. There is no question, moreover, but what Higashikuze's teachings are set forth as the norm for all Japanese, as members of the "national family." The whole approach is couched in remarkably warm language. Although the emperor's awesome authority is plainly enunciated, the call is not so much to duty as to voluntary allegiance. In presenting the old samurai ethic to the common man, a softer tone emerges.

With the basic principles of moral instruction fixed by the promulgation of the Rescript on Education in 1890, there appeared a rash of ethics texts similar to Higashikuze's. Between 1892 and 1894, some eighty texts were privately produced.[6] Not all were of high quality, and some departed from the officially approved interpretations of the Education Rescript. In order to exercise greater control over the content of these books, the Ministry of Education set up machinery for examining and approving texts before they could be released for use in the schools. In December 1891, the Ministry established official standards for ethics texts, based on the Rescript. In 1893 it warned that some texts were still unsatisfactory and that they must hew more closely to the official line.

Before long, criticism in the House of Representatives was directed against privately produced schoolbooks of all types. Finally, in 1897, both houses of the Diet ruled that at least the ethics texts, of such crucial importance to the morale of the nation, should be produced by the government. Katō Hiroyuki was appointed chairman of a committee in the Ministry of Education to compile an official set of ethics textbooks. By 1903 his committee had written books for all elementary grades, and from that time until the close of the Pacific War the production of materials for ethics education in the public schools remained in the hands of the state.

Government-produced ethics textbooks appeared in five separate editions: the original edition of 1903, and revised editions in 1910, 1918, 1933, and 1941. Here only the first two of the five will be discussed; and special attention will be given to the 1910 texts, for with these official ethical instruction rose to a kind of plateau. While each subsequent edition responded uniquely to the political climate and educational needs of its time, the 1910 texts nevertheless set a tone, and developed certain basic themes, which greatly influenced later revisions.

The 1903 texts had incorporated a certain progressive emphasis, described by Miyata Takeo as the "ethics of a modern citizens' so-

123

ciety."[7] Instruction in basic social conduct went beyond the traditional five relationships[8] to such things as kindness to animals, the dangers of excessive drinking, public charity, and how to behave on crowded trains.[9] It is the opinion of Karasawa Tomitarō that, in their modernity, these teachings were not unlike those taught today in postwar Japan.[10] National and imperial values did not, of course, disappear, but the whole seemed progressive, at points even Western. In regard to vocational ethics, for example, children were encouraged to look forward to a job in which they could work for their own happiness, as well as for the happiness of others and the welfare of the state.

Behind this modernity lay a certain confidence about the domestic scene: earlier uncertainty about the unity and loyalty of the people had been swept aside by a powerful wave of patriotic enthusiasm (e.g., "Japanism") associated with Japan's victory over China and mounting rivalry with Russia over Korea. By 1903 there was no urgent need to arouse national loyalty, for it was a living reality among most of the people.

Almost from the beginning, however, the 1903 texts were criticized by some for their lack of emphasis on national values. Three members of the nobility addressed a statement to the Ministry on Education in which they denounced the books as mere "handbooks on good manners," deficient in teachings on ancestor reverence, respect for the imperial family, patriotism, and the loyalty-filial piety (chūkō) principle.[11] In like manner, the Nihon Kōdōkai (Society for Expanding the Japanese Way) published "An Opinion on the State Ethics Texts" in 1905, calling for greater stress on ruler-loyalty (chūkun), patriotism, reverence, and familial ethics.[12]

Educational authorities were further encouraged to revise ethics by the social unrest which followed the Russo-Japanese War of 1904–5. Japanese leaders and people had been remarkably unified during the latter half of the 1890's and the first years of the new century, as they fought first China and then Russia. With the end of the Russian war, however, the spirit which had sustained the prolonged national effort seemed now to wane, and dissent flared into the open with a shocking series of strikes and riots by socialists and anarchists. As another facet of the late Meiji ferment, many intellectuals attracted by a Western type of individualism became critical of traditional values. The government's deep concern over the mounting restlessness led to the proclamation of a special imperial rescript (Boshin Rescript of October

Years

1903 VERSION   1910 REVISION

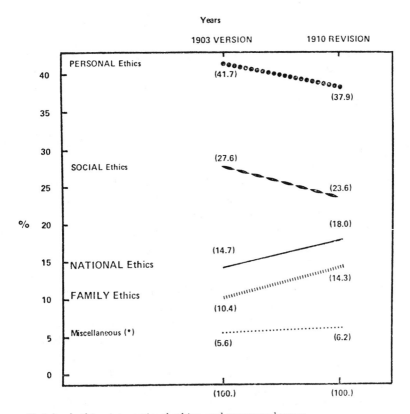

(*) School ethics, international ethics, and summary lessons.

Figure 1. Teachings in State Ethics Textbooks, 1903 and 1910.[14]

1908) in which the emperor appealed directly to the people for social harmony and self-sacrificial toil for the good of the nation. In this setting, ethics textbooks were seen as weapons for combating the new social and intellectual discord.

In 1908 a top-flight committee was established under the personal direction of the Minister of Education himself, and instructed to "rectify and review elementary school ethics, history and language texts," as well as any other textbooks the Minister might wish to include. The First Division of this committee worked exclusively on the revision of ethics textbooks, under the chairmanship of Hozumi Yatsuka, Dean of the Tokyo University Law School and a staunch conservative. By the end of 1910 the new series was essentially completed.

In contrasting the 1903 and 1910 ethics texts, Karasawa comments as follows about the shift of ethical instruction from the relatively progressive tone of the 1903 texts to the more conservative emphasis of the 1910 version:

> In the 1910 revision the modern ethics of the 1903 texts were eliminated, and in their place a feudal family ethic was stressed. All lessons such as "Others' Freedoms," "Social Progress," and "Rivalry" were removed, and new lessons like "Ise Shrine," "The Founding of the Nation," "The National Essence (*kokutai*)," "Guard the Prosperity of the Imperial Throne," ... and "The Dying Instructions of our Imperial Ancestors" were added in their place.[13]

Karasawa's findings as to the percentage of lessons devoted to different types of ethical instruction in each of the two series are revealing. Of the categories delineated by Karasawa, four are of particular significance: (1) personal ethics, typically on hygiene, personal character, and deportment; (2) social ethics, primarily on immediate relations with friends, neighbors and teachers; (3) family ethics, emphasizing filial piety in home relationships; and (4) national ethics, designed to produce patriotic, self-sacrificing subjects of the emperor. In the 1903 texts by far the largest number of lessons was devoted to personal ethics (41.7 percent) and social ethics (27.6 percent), perhaps justifying the earlier criticism that they were little more than "handbooks on good manners." National ethics claimed only 14.7 percent of the lessons, and family ethics 10.4 percent. In the 1910 texts the greatest number of lessons was still devoted to personal and social ethics, but the percentage in these two categories had declined (to 37.9 and 23.6 percent, respectively), while the percentage in the national and family categories had risen (to 18.0 percent and 14.3 percent, respectively). Schematically, this may be represented as shown in figure 1. From Karasawa's analysis it is clear that the 1910 revision, when compared with the 1903 texts, constituted a reversion to a Higashikuze type of family and national ethics. Contemporary intellectuals referred to the 1910 ethical formulation as "national morals" (*kokumin dōtoku*), but modern scholars tend to describe it as a "family state" (*kazoku kokka*) ideology.[15]

The family state idea was entirely new to the late Meiji period. It appeared in rudimentary form in Higashikuze's texts of 1890, and Inoue Tetsujirō incorporated elements of it in his *Chokugo Engi* (Commentary on the Rescript), which appeared in the same year.[16] In 1898, Hozumi Yatsuka began an annual series of summer lectures to secondary school teachers on the constitution and national ethics, in which he developed the familial state theme.[17] The 1903 government ethics texts, moreover, contained some teachings along this line. It was not until the years following the Russo-Japanese War, however, that the family state concept emerged in full, definitive form.[18]

The family state ideology had three parts: (1) a German "state organism" (*kokka yūkitai*) theory of state sovereignty—the intellectual superstructure; (2) a Confucian-like familyism (*kazoku-shugi*)—the ethical base[19]; and (3) ancient Shinto beliefs—the religious sanction.

"State organism" had been used by conservative Japanese thinkers to counteract liberal doctrines associated with the *Jiyū Minken* (Freedom and People's Rights) movement of early Meiji years, and now it was revived for opposing such notions as socialism and individualism. According to this theory, the state or nation was one great living, eternally evolving organism, of which transitory individual subjects comprised the component cells. As cells, individuals were subordinate to the whole and found their meaning in service to the total organism. The cells did not contract to participate in the organism: it was an arrangement given by nature, and marked by inescapable necessity. The purpose of this doctrine was to unite all Japanese in one harmonious "organism," so as to minimize social discord and intellectual fragmentation.[20]

As in mid-Meiji years, the base of political ideology was the Confucian, familistic ethic focused on filial piety and emperor-loyalty. In late Meiji, Japanese leaders and ideologues referred to the nation more and more as an "extended family," not by way of analogy, but as a historical fact. The nation was not *like* a family, it *was* a family, by virtue of the fact that the distant ancestors of ordinary Japanese households were offshoots of the main imperial family line. Inoue Tetsujirō, distinguished professor of philosophy at Tokyo University, systematically developed the "national family" concept in a series of writings between 1908 and 1912. Thus, in his *Kokumin Dōtoku Gairon* (Outline of National Morals, 1912), he delineated the "individual family system"

127

(*kobetsu kazoku seido*) and the "comprehensive (i.e., national) family system" (*sōgō kazoku seido*). Filial piety practiced in the individual family became, without change, loyalty to the comprehensive or national family. The traditional patterns and values of the individual family must be strengthened and maintained, insisted Inoue; for it was the individual family system which supported the comprehensive (nationsl) family system and thereby preserved *kokutai*.[21]

If the national family (or family state) was supported from below by the socioethical patterns of individual households, it was sanctified from above by Shinto beliefs which rendered it sacred. In a word, the national family was sacred because the imperial family, from which all other families of the nation derived, stood in a direct line of succession from the chief *kami* of the Shinto tradition. Since ordinary Japanese families were related to the imperial family, they all shared in its sanctity.

Not only was the national family sacred, but increasingly the great, imperial father figure of the nation came to be regared as sacrosanct in his own person. The 1889 Constitution had declared the emperor "sacred and inviolable." Hozumi Yatsuka traced this high view of the emperor to its Shinto source when he said in 1900,

> The Imperial Scion is holy, by virtue of the divinity of the Imperial Progenitor [Amaterasu Ōmikami]. By virtue of the august spirit of the Imperial Progenitor, the authority of the extant Emperor is inviolate.[22]

With the sanctification of the national family and the apotheosis of the emperor, the state acquired a certain mystical absoluteness which greatly enhanced its power. Writing of the late Meiji years, Kōsaka Masaaki has said,

> A change had taken place from the earlier period when the State had been observed, studied and criticized. Now, by law, by myth, and by the revival of ancient ethics the State was to be revered; it had become something to be obeyed submissively. One no longer explained the State, one *believed* in it![23]

The family state ideology, propagated through the public school system in the form of "national morals," found particular expression in the 1910 ethics textbooks. The texts did not employ such sophisticated expressions as "national morals" or "state organism," for these books were written in simple language for elementary school children. The basic themes of the official ideology are nevertheless clearly evident.

"State organism" thinking appears to stand behind the persistent stress on the duty of subjects to obey the state. For instance, a ninth grade lesson reads,

> The state protects the subjects. But if the subjects do not completely obey the state, the state cannot completely protect the subjects. It is the first duty of subjects to obey and protect the state.[24]

There is also the following interesting passage, which seems to be based on the "state organism" concept of individual cells finding their fulfillment in the welfare of the total organism:

> Subjects are particles which together comprise the whole nation. The prosperity of the subjects is tied to the prosperity of the state. Subjects and state are one body.[25]

The influence of "state organism" thinking is also reflected in the exaltation of the demands of the eternal state over the private (selfish) wishes of transitory individuals, as in this passage:

> The state exists independently forever, but the individual for only a time, and compared with the state his life is very brief. It is only natural that the people must conform to the purposes of the eternal state, and give no heed to personal interests.[26]

By far the most fundamental support for state authority in the 1910 ethics texts is not, however, to be found in the foreign notion of "state organism," but in a sharpened and updated presentation of familiar Confucian and Shinto ideals: essentially a much fuller elaboration of Higashikuze's "familization of nation and throne," in which local loyalties are extended to the national level and sanctified by Shinto *kami* beliefs. Following is a brief analysis of these modified traditional elements in the 1910 texts. It should be made clear that the texts themselves are not organized according to the categories here described.

1. *Filial piety in the home.* These teachings cover such points as the need to express gratitude and obligation to ancestors as the founders of one's house, the duty to love and obey parents and work for the prosperity of one's family, the common virtues of family harmony and solidarity, and so on. The chief emphasis is on filial piety, with stress on love and obedience to parents.

2. *Filial piety = emperor-loyalty.* Having begun in the home, the writers of the texts next attempt to extend familial loyalties and affections to the emperor, as father of the "national family." Even more than in earlier texts, (emperor-) loyalty and filial piety are closely identified, to the point where one is equal to the other. Not only does filial piety find its perfect fulfillment in emperor-loyalty, the two are *actually one and the same.* As a ninth grade lesson says, " . . . loyalty and filial piety are one and inseparable."[27] A favorite expression in these texts is *chūkō no taigi,* or the "great loyalty-filial piety principle," in which the two are fused into a single concept. An official Ministry Education document now refers to *chūkō* (loyalty-filial piety) as the "pivot (*sujiku*) of our national morals," and says that while it had received emphasis in earlier texts, "in this revision we have worked even harder to train the children in this principle."[28]

The upward extension of loyalty from home to emperor may be illustrated by the following passage from a lesson on "Loyalty and Filial Piety":

> It is only natural for children to love and respect their parents, and the great loyalty-filial piety principle springs from this natural feeling. . . . Our country is based on the family system. The whole country is one great family, and the Imperial House is the Head Family (*sōka*). *It is with the feeling of filial love and respect for parents that we Japanese people express our reverence toward the Throne of unbroken imperial line.*[29]

3. *Emperor-loyalty = patriotism.* To make certain that emperor-loyalty would benefit the state, emperor-loyalty is next fused with patriotism. This is a new development in the 1910 texts, and is accomplished by equating the two terms *chūkun* (lord-, or emperor-loyalty) and *aikoku* (patriotism, love of country). Now the two words become one expression, *chūkun-aikoku,* perhaps best rendered into English as "patriotic emperor-loyalty." In the 1910 texts numerous lessons are

devoted to *chūkun-aikoku,* and heroic stories are related by way of illustration. Thus Kōno Michiari, who fought bravely against the Mongolian invaders in the 13th century, "had a deep spirit of patriotic emperor-loyalty (*chūkun-aikoku*)," as did Kusunoki Masashige in defending Emperor Go-Daigo against the intrigues of Hōjō Takatoki in the 14th century. As a more up-to-date example, the children are told that Japan won the Russo-Japanese War because the nation rallied sacrificially in the spirit of patriotic emperor-loyalty (*chūkun-aikoku*).[30]

4. *State authority sanctified by Shinto beliefs.* Finally, it is Shinto beliefs which infuse emperor-loyalty and patriotism with a quality of sacred absoluteness. The 1910 ethics texts are saturated with Shinto assumptions and teachings. In addition to lessons continued from the 1903 series (such as "The Imperial Throne," "The Emperor," and "Revere the Imperial Family"), new lessons are added to give even greater weight to Shinto and imperial themes. In lessons on Ise and Yasukuni Shrines, for instance, it is related how the emperor visited them periodically to pay his respects to the spirits enshrined there—at Yasukuni, the spirits of those who had died for their country, at Ise the spirit of Amaterasu Ōmikami, the nation's chief ancestral *kami.*

The last lesson in most of the ethics texts is entitled "The Good Japanese," and serves as a kind of encapsulation of national values. In the following excerpt from the Ordinary Elementary School fourth year text we find elements which are clearly Shinto in import (italics mine):

> *Remembering our deep obligation to the Emperor for his favors,* we should strive to become good Japanese by devoting ourselves to ruler-loyalty and patriotism, *revering the Imperial Family,* respecting the law, honoring the flag, and *bearing in mind the origin of festival days.*[31]

The admonition in the above passage to remember the emperor's favors with "deep obligation" is illustrative of the new manner in which the 1910 texts refer to members of the imperial family. In the 1903 Teachers Commentary for the first year lesson on the emperor, Mutsuhito's accomplishments were simply recounted in a straightforward, factual way. The 1910 commentary on the same lesson, however, is written so as to impress upon the children's minds the imperial blessings they enjoy. Much the same is true of material on the empress.[32]

The sanctity of the emperor does not seem to be stated explicitly, but is inferred from his sacred lineage and authority. From an examination of some forty ethics lessons distributed over five grades, the only two instances in which the word "sacred" (*shinsei*) is used are in connection with the imperial household. The references are to the "sacred Imperial Ancestors" (*shinsei naru kōsō*),[33] and to the "sacred Throne" (*shinsei naru kōi*).[34] The imperial ancestors are sacred because they go back to and include the chief Shinto *kami,* and the throne is sacred because the imperial family was authorized to occupy it by Amaterasu herself.

More emphatically than before, the 1910 ethics textbooks present Shinto mythology as believable historical fact, with much stress on Amaterasu's commission to her grandson Ninigi-no-Mikoto to "govern the land." A sample statement from a fifth grade lesson on "The Japanese Empire" reads,

> In ancient times Amaterasu Ōmikami sent down Ninigi-no-Mikoto and had him govern the land. His (Ninigi's) great grandson was Jimmu Tennō. It has been over 2,570 years since he acceded to the Throne, and his descendants have followed him on the Throne generation after generation.[35]

Again, this sentence from a ninth grade lesson on "The Imperial Throne":

> The *kōi* is the Emperor's Throne, and ever since Amaterasu Ōmikami sent down the Heavenly Grandson Ninigi-no-Mikoto, his descendants have occupied the Throne and presided over the sovereign power of state rule.[36]

In such manner the 1910 ethics textbooks sanctified the political authority of the state by an appeal to transcendent religious symbols. Daniel Holtom, writing of these texts as a contemporary observer, concluded that the Japanese government was "very plainly seeking to surround a doctrine of political absolutism with the final sanctions of religious belief."[37]

The crucial service of the 1910 texts in support of family statism was their absolute identification of filial piety and emperor-loyalty.

There were some, however, who saw these two ideals not in terms of identity, nor even necessarily in terms of harmony. Indeed, when it came to military service, they even seemed to clash. According to the elite samurai code, lord-loyalty clearly superseded filial duty to parents, and one must be ready at every moment to die for one's lord. Though the common people honored this ideal (now directed toward the emperor), it was hard for them to follow such a severe standard. They inclined more to follow the Confucian principle that a son should protect his life so he could live to care for his parents, both during their lifetime and through memorial services after their death. But how could one fulfill this natural filial obligation if he died for the emperor? This had become a problem for many persons during the Russo-Japanese War, and the authorities sought to deal with it through ethical instruction. By fusing filial piety and emperor-loyalty, they hoped to erase any conflict between the two. In actual practice, however, many Japanese faced with military service remained torn by their dual obligations.

It seems that the authorities themselves recognized the difficulty of promoting national loyalty by way of familism. At any rate, after 1910 family ethics received less emphasis in subsequent revisions of ethics textbooks, while indoctrination in national ethics steadily rose. This shift is dramatic in the 1941 revision, which was published at a time when many young men were dying on the Asiatic mainland.[38] Japanese educators seem to have downgraded the familial approach to national loyalty in favor of a direct national-imperial appeal.

The late Meiji program of government ethical training rounded out earlier experimental decades, pulling together diverse values and concepts into a scheme of "national morals" which was more comprehensive and systematic than previous formulations. Updated traditional Shinto and Confucian elements were combined with German statist thinking to forge in ideological instrument for strengthening the authoritarian Meiji order. From 1910 the official indoctrination program had a greater sophistication of content, was related to a more massive bureaucratic implementation, and expressed an increasingly aggressive concern with national-imperial interests. As ideological propagation assumed an even more important role over succeeding decades, Japan's leaders had only to expand on foundations already laid.

1. Especially in the 1930's and '40's, ethics increasingly shared this role with history, geography, and language. In the Meiji period, however, ethics instruction was still central as the vehicle of value-indoctrination in the school system.

2. On government ethics texts in early and mid-Meiji, see especially G. B. Sansom, *The Western World and Japan*, (New York: A. A. Knopf, 1958) chap. 15; Herbert Passim, *Society and Education in Japan*, (New York: Teachers College Press, Columbia University, 1965) chap. 4; W. W. Smith, *Confucianism in Modern Japan*, (Tokyo: Hokuseido Press, 1959) pp. 68–88; and two articles by Donald H. Shively: "Motoda Eifu—Confucian Lecturer to the Meiji Emperor," in D. S. Niveson and A. F. Wright (eds.), *Confucianism in Action*, (Stanford: Stanford University Press, 1959); and "Nishimura Shigeki, A Confucian View of Modernization," in M. B. Jansen (ed.), *Changing Japanese Attitudes Toward Modernization*, (Princeton: Princeton University Press, 1965).

3. *Kami* are spirits, or deities, in the Shinto tradition.

4. Kawashima Takeyoshi, *Ideorogii toshite no Kazoku Seido* (The Family System as an Ideology), (Tokyo: Iwanami, 1963) p. 44.

5. Quotations in this paragraph are from Kawashima Takeyoshi, *ibid.*, p. 43. Jimmu Tennō: first mythical emperor and ancestor of the imperial family. Sacred Treasures: the three imperial regalia (sword, mirror, and jewel).

6. Kaigo Tokiomi and Yoshida Kumaji, *Kyōiku Chokugo Kanpatsu igo ni okeru Shōgakkō Shūshin Kyōju no Hensen* (Changes in the Teaching of Ethics in Elementary Schools after the Promulgation of the Rescript on Education), (Tokyo: Nihon Bunka Kyōkai, 1935) pp. 1–2, and chap. 2, *passim*.

7. Miyata Takeo (ed.), *Dōtoku Kyōiku Shiryō Shūsei* (Compilation of Moral Education Materials), (Tokyo: Daiichi Hōki, 1959) vol. I, p. 9.

8. The Confucian doctrine regarding relations between father-son, husband-wife, older brother-younger brother, friend-friend, and ruler subject.

9. Karasawa Tomitarō, *Kyōkasho no Rekishi* (A History of Textbooks), (Tokyo: Sōbunsha, 1960) pp. 232–33.

10. *Ibid.*, p. 231.

11. Kaigo and Yoshida, *op. cit.*, chap. 7.

12. Miyata, *op. cit.*, vol. I, p. 12.

13. Karasawa, *op. cit.*, p. 286.

14. Adapted from Karasawa, p. 228. The percentage of lessons devoted to national ethics in the 1910 texts, given by Karasawa as 18 percent, would be even larger if he had included all elementary grades in his calculations for that year. As he indicates in a note on p. 227, he based his 1903 figures on ethics texts for all grades of both Ordinary and Higher Elementary School, but his 1910 figures only on Ordinary Elementary School materials. That is, for 1910 he did not include the ethics texts for the important three years of Higher Elementary. From my own study of both texts and commentaries, however, it is clear that the third year ethics text of Higher Elementary School, as the last in the entire series, contained an especially high concentration of national ethical teachings. The inclusion of this material would raise Karasawa's figures comewhat above 18 percent.

15. *Kazoku kokka* can be translated "family state," or again "family nation"

in the sense of "national family." I prefer "family state," as it more adequately reflects the strong statist dimension of the ideology.

16. Ishida Takeshi, *Meiji Seiji Shisō-shi Kenkyū* (Studies in the History of Meiji Political Thought), (Tokyo: Miraisha, 1961) pp. 6–7.

17. Miller, Frank O., *Minobe Tatsukichi, Interpreter of Constitutionalism in Japan*, (Berkeley: University of California Press, 1965) p. 30.

18. No attempt will be made in this article to set the family state formulation within the broader context of *kokutai* (national essence, or entity), that grandiose ideological catchall which goes back as far as Kitabatake Chikafusa's 14th century *Jinnō Shōtōki* (Record of the Legitimate Line of the Divine Emperors), but was more explicitly developed in the 19th and 20th centuries. The fact that the Japanese could never really explain *kokutai*, even to themselves, undoubtedly contributed to its mystic appeal. It did, however, include such elements as Shinto-based reverence for the imperial family, the union of myth and history, the Confucian-type ethic of loyalty and filial piety, and selfless Bushidō devotion to one's lord. To one extent or another, all of these themes entered into the notion of the family state, as well.

19. On these two elements, I am much indebted to Ishida's history (see footnote 16), especially pp. 8–16, 73–80 and 105–39.

20. Both this "organism" concept of state sovereignty and Minobe Taksukichi's "organ theory" (*kikan-setsu*) regarding the emperor's role in the state derive from similar German sources of political thought, but Minobe's formulation was considerably more liberal. Although Minobe assigned the emperor the position of "highest organ" (*saikō kikan*) of the state, he saw him as but one organ among others, including the Diet. The state organism theory, on the other hand, especially as propounded by Katō Hiroyuki, insisted upon an absolute distinction between the emperor and the rest of the state organism. Katō criticized Minobe's treatment of the emperor as an organ of state, holding that he was a sovereign ruler in a much more absolutist sense. For Katō, the emperor was in a transcendent position as the "thinking center" (*shii chūsū*) of the state or national organism. On Minobe's views, see Frank O. Miller, *Minobe Tatsukichi, Interpreter of Constitutionalism in Japan*, especially chaps. 1 and 4; also Ishida Takeshi, *op. cit.*, especially pp. 127–28.

21. Ishida, *op. cit.*, pp. 107–09; also Kōsaka Masaaki (ed.), *Japanese Thought in the Meiji Era*, (Tokyo: Pan-Pacific Press, 1958) pp. 390–91.

22. Kōsaka, *op. cit.*, p. 384.

23. *Ibid.*, p. 364.

24. Miyata, *op. cit.*, vol. II, p. 494 (lesson on "Subjects").

25. *Ibid.*, vol. II, p. 494 (same lesson).

26. *Ibid.*, vol. II, p. 494 (lesson on "The Nation").

27. *Ibid.*, vol. II, p. 499 (lesson on "Lyalty and Filial Piety").

28. *Ibid.*, vol. II, pp. 177–78.

29. *Ibid.*, vol. II, p. 499. Italics mine.

30. *Ibid.*, vol. II, p. 259 (lesson on "Patriotic Emperor-loyalty").

31. *Ibid.*, vol. II, p. 240. These festivals (*shukusai*) were closely associated with Shinto and the imperial family.

32. Karasawa, *op. cit.*, pp. 282–83.

33. Miyata *op. cit.*, vol. II, p. 508 (lesson on "Boshin Rescript").

34. *Ibid.*, Vol. II, p. 494 (lesson on "Subjects").

35. *Ibid.*, Vol. II, p. 243.

36. *Ibid.*, Vol. II, p. 493.

37. Holtom, Daniel C., "The Political Philosophy of Modern Shinto," in *Transactions of Asiatic Society of Japan*, series II, vol. XLIX, (London: Kegan Paul, 1922) p. 236.

38. The percentages of family and national ethics in the ethics textbooks from 1910 are as follows:

	1910	1918	1933	1941
Family ethics	14.3	12.0	10.5	5.8
National ethics	18.0	18.4	19.8	37.5

(From Karasawa, *op. cit.*, p. 228)

RICHARD J. SMETHURST

THE ARMY,
YOUTH, AND WOMEN

1916 was the beginning of the era of national crisis in Japan. It is not an exaggeration to say that from 1919 until the time of the Manchurian Incident in 1931, Japan fell into the abyss of spiritual darkness. . . . Individualism, liberalism, and democratic thought flowed freely and the muddied waters of materialism, utilitarianism, and the worship of the almight yen (*kinkenshugi*) seeped in at every level. Socialism, communism and anarchistic thought spread like contagious diseases among students and young workers. Intellectually discriminating persons who thought of their country truthfully could not bear to see this.

Teikoku zaigō gunjinkai sanjūnenshi (Tokyo, 1944), p. 112

Three years ago [in 1921–1922], spitting at the Italian flag, cursing the army, and despising soldiers was advocated as progressive thought, and it was said to be all right to reduce the term of military service to six months. However, after Mussolini formed his cabinet,

Richard J. Smethurst is Associate Professor of History at the University of Pittsburgh.
    Reprinted from Smethurst, Richard J., *A Social Basis for Prewar Japanese Militarism; the Army and the Rural Community.* (Berkeley: University of California Press, 1974), pp. 22–49, copyright © 1974 by the Regents of the University of California, with permission of the author and the University of California Press.

the spirit of the general populace made a basic change and today they no longer spit at the flag. . . . In 1921–1922, Italy had 643 labor disputes, but in 1925, only 154. Moreover, farm disputes fell in number from 46 to 2. These disputes were related to economic and political conditions, but most of them occurred because of dangerous ideas spread by socialists. Hence, as a result of the victory of fascism over socialism, disputes gradually disappeared and production became prosperous. We too must pay special attention to this point. . . . The main force in saving the Japanese people from this kind of national crisis is the army and the reservist association.

> Tanaka Giichi, quoted in Kawatani Yorio,
> *Tanaka Giichi den* (Tokyo, 1929), pp. 198–199

The fear of domestic unrest in the first quarter of the twentieth century had a tremendous impact on the thinking of Tanaka Giichi, Ugaki Kazushige, and other officers who followed in Yamagata's [Yamagata Aritomo] footsteps. Although these officers exaggerated the actual threats to national unity, Japanese society had in fact become more diverse and harder to control by the time World War I erupted in 1914. Universal education and wider university opportunities, expanding contacts with the outside world, urbanization, the increasing impersonality of the modernizing society, and industrialization unleashed forces that challenged Yamagata's dictum of "rich country and strong army." Most of the newly educated, imbued with the patriotic values of the *Imperial Rescript on Education*, enthusiastically followed the government's lead, but some did not. Even before 1910, a few intellectuals, inspired by foreign ideologies and conditions at home, had joined the miniscule Russo-Japanese War peace movement and the even tinier postwar socialist party, and had impelled Katsura Tarō's government to suppress them. It is not surprising that Tanaka and Ugaki cast a jaundiced eye on the larger antimilitary socialist and communist movements which coalesced after the successful October Revolution. At the same time as these winds from Europe fanned the radical blaze, labor disputes and rural antilandlord unrest added to the military leaders' sense of national disunity. Only 107 strikes occurred between 1903 and 1907. But as the industrial labor force and urban population increased, the frequency of strikes did also, to 497 in 1919, and 1202 in 1927. And the rural, antilandlord discontent of the same decade must have terrified Tanaka and Ugaki even more than labor and urban radical organizations since the generals modelled their ideal Japanese society on the "traditional" village. The rural unrest was most intense in those areas where the local elite abandoned paternalism for impersonal, modern contractual relationships with their tenants; and reservist planners felt compelled to build barriers to prevent further erosion of the traditional.[1]

Labor-farmer unrest, progressive party organization, and antimilitary feeling may have been moderate by European standards, but Yamagata's successors interpreted them as a major threat to the unity of Japanese society. Tanaka's speeches and articles, for example, contain many expressions of such fears. The following is one from a speech to reservist leaders in January, 1924:

> Today there are Japanese who think that mankind should know no national boundaries. They plead for a so-called internationalism and a world without national distinctions. They think war cannot occur again, and that we can limit or even ignore military preparedness. But while they talk of worldwide international cooperation, these Japanese also incite labor conflict and class struggles at home. Accordingly, they constantly create friction and antagonism among the people. Thus, people neglect their work. And tenant, antilandlord disputes are rife in agricultural areas. And patriotism is thought to be suitable only for old-fashioned bigots. These trends lead youths astray and some even dare the fiendishness of high treason. Last December's attempt on the life of the Crown Prince [The Toranomon Incident of December, 1923] originated from this kind of misguided subversive thought.... If we want protect the national welfare, public order, and honor, we must destroy all of these 'isms' [internationalism, pacifism, socialism, etc.].[2]

At the same time that Tanaka feared these threats to Japanese national cohesion, the world's armies entered the era of total war (sōryokusen). Warfare became more sophisticated and called not only for the army's, but for the whole nation's participation. As early as the Napoleonic Wars, and especially after the American Civil War and Franco-Prussian War, Western observers had begun to see that the days of battles between rival kings, each with his own mercenary army, were over and that those of "national wars" had arrived. New technology leading to increased firepower and better transportation and communications, the tendency toward greater mass involvement in national affairs, the need to mobilize larger armies through conscription, and the necessity of industrial support for fighting machines compelled the populace to participate in military affairs. Tanaka and Ugaki realized this clearly after the outbreak of World War I. Tanaka believed, moreover, that national mobilization for cohesion had benefits even in defeat. He thought that revolution failed in postwar Germany because the German people respected, and had been trained to respect, law and order. Japan too needed to be immunized against disunity.[3] Time and time again Tanaka stated that future wars (and peace) would demand total national mobilization, but never more clearly than in this speech to reservist officials in Tokyo in 1915:

> The outcome of future wars will not be determined by the strongest army, but by the strongest populace. A strong populace is one which has physical strength and spiritual health, one which is richly imbued with loyalty and patriotism, and one which respects cooperation, rules, and discipline. The populace which has this kind of education will not merely have a strong army, but will also be successful in conducting agricultural, manufacturing, commercial, and other industrial efforts. The reservists must achieve the reality of becoming good soldiers and good citizens exert their influence (for these goals) in their home community.[4]

It was against this background of fear of increased disunity and belief in a greater need for national cohesion that Tanaka nurtured the reserve association, and that he and Ugaki looked for additional ways to crush opposition and create popular support for the military. They were not above suppression as one way of eliminating unorthodoxy and recreating unity; but this was only a temporary palliative. Real unity came through education.

TANAKA AND THE FORMATION OF A
NATIONAL YOUTH ASSOCIATION

With the rapid growth in the numbers of reservist local branches after 1910 and factory branches after 1914, Tanaka saw grow to fruition his military education network for physically fit twenty- to forty-year-old men (and to some extent for their neighbors, for whom reservists were to become models of civic propriety). Yet the army still did not have the means to influence all civilians. It is true that the school system trained all children, male and female, fit and unfit, in the ideals of Yamagata's *Imperial Rescript on Education* which were not unlike those of the soldier's ethos. But primary education was compulsory for only six years (although many students received an extra two years of schooling in upper elementary schools), and only 20 percent of the graduates advanced to middle school. Formal education and nationalistic indoctrination ended for most at age fourteen or fifteen. Because of this five-year gap between the completion of primary school and entrance into the army or reserve association for the 60 to 70 percent of the male population that passed the conscription physical examination, Tanaka decided in 1915 to fill this educational lacuna by creating a unified, reservist-dominated, national youth association from the thousands of existing young men's groups. This centralized organization would recruit the unfit 30 to 40 percent as well.[5]

Organizing the unified national youth association was no easy task. Tanaka could centralize the reserve association with the backing of Yamagata and Terauchi alone, for the army had no problem justifying an organization of ex-servicemen (in the early years it played down the role of those who had not served). The same justification was not valid for unifying local youth groups, however, because the Education and Home Ministries had jurisdiction over youth education and regional organizations. The creation of a military-influenced youth association called for delicate negotiations between the army and these two ministries as well as an ability to deal with the Diet members and the newspapermen who might object. Tanaka showed himself capable of this kind of diplomacy.

When Tanaka returned from Europe in 1914 convinced not only of the need for reservist factory branches, but also for a centralized youth association oriented toward nationalistic and physical education, he contacted two civil bureaucrat acquaintances with similar ideas. These two men, Yamamoto Takinosuke, a long-time youth organizer and official, and Tadokoro Miharu, a division chief in the Education Ministry and reservist association adviser, also believed that a youth association could complement the educational system if it were used to propagate patriotic ideals and increase the health and physical conditioning of teenagers. These two men in turn acted as intermediaries between Tanaka and the appropriate cabinet ministers in the Ōkuma Shigenobu government of the time. These ministers, Home Minister Ōura Kane-take, and Education Minister Ichiki Kitokurō, both of whom were among Yamagata's closest civilian followers, agreed with Tanaka's ideas about youth groups. A fifth figure, Takada Sanae, joined the group in August, 1915, when Ōura was forced to resign because of allegations of election irregularities.[6]

A description of how Tanaka and these five civil bureaucrats joined forces is beyond the scope of this chapter, but Yamagata's shadow and Tanaka's skills as a "political general" must have influenced the development of the 1914–1915 plans. Even before his trip abroad, Tanaka had persuaded party politician Ōkuma, famed as an adversary of the army (*rikugun girai*), to speak to army and reservist gatherings about reservist association matters on at least six occasions. Tanaka may also have played a role in helping Ōkuma become Prime Minister and in winning from him the two divisions refused to the army in 1912. Finally, Tanaka persuaded Tadokoro, who soon became Vice Minister of Education, to serve as a *zaigō gunjinkai* adviser and fre-quent contributor to *Comrades in Arms,* the reservist monthly, and Ichiki to write in that magazine on youth group-reservist relations.[7] This civil-military cooperation resulted in the Home and Education Ministries' publication in September, 1915, of a joint order to establish a national youth group headquarters.

This government order and the explanatory letter from the Home and Education Vice Ministers which followed indicated that the founders conceived of the national youth association'a local role as both similar and complementary to the reservists'. These bureaucrats and officers hoped that the *seinendan*, like the reservist branches, would popularize patriotic values and serve national goals through local acceptance and mutual cooperation with other community groups and leaders. The letter established four primary guidelines: (1) the youth association branch was to be both a work and community service organization, as it had been in the past, and an ideological and educa-tional one; (2) it was to be organized with city, town, and village branches and hamlet subdivisions; (3) it was to seek the active support of village and school officials, the police, the reservists, and local religious leaders; (4) it was to maintain a maximum age of twenty for membership.[8] Tanaka and the other founders viewed each of these four guidelines as crucial to attaining their goals.

According to the first guideline, Tanaka and his Education and

Home Ministry colleagues forced the existing local groups to add three new functions: patriotic and ethical education, physical training, and military drill under reservist leadership. The patriotic and ethical education was easily acceptable to villagers because it was an extension of one of the main functions of the existing groups. Youth clubs (*wakamono-gumi, wakashū-ren*), dating back at least to the Tokugawa era, traditionally performed both labor tasks such as festival preparations, policing, and communal road and canal repairs, as well as moral education. Young men's groups in all of the seventeen, pre-1915 hamlets and hamlet clusters in Anjō, one of our case study communities, for example, carried out extensive labor and festival activities and enforced strict codes of ethical behavior. Such behavioral rules as those of the Yamazaki village (after 1906, part of Anjō) youth group, published in 1891, were reminiscent of parts of Tanaka's soldier's ethos.[9] They were as follows:

1. When one gambles in violation of the rules:
    a. if he lives in the hamlet or has his permanent address in the hamlet, he will be fined thirty sen.
    b. if he gambles where he lives, he will be fined fifty sen.
    c. anyone who reports gambling will be rewarded with ten sen.
2. All members will observe a ten o'clock curfew.
3. Bothering others by arguing and making excessive noise on the streets is strictly forbidden.
4. Taking a high position when entering or leaving, and lying around the house bothering others is strictly forbidden.
5. Trafficking with prostitutes, hanging around restaurants, or going to evil places (*aku basho*) is strictly forbidden.
6. Becoming infatuated with girls and maid servants and bothering them by saying or doing anything untoward is strictly forbidden.
7. Making uncalled for remarks when a bride (or adopted son-in-law) is moving to her husband's (or wife's) home is strictly forbidden.
8. Arguing or fighting during Shinto shrine festivals or when on sightseeing trips is forbidden and the transgressor will be sent home immediately.
9. Extraordinary behavior when going to or at the Buddhist temple is forbidden.
10. One must be careful to avoid damaging crops.
11. One must use the proper salutation when greeting others.
12. One must not spread rumors of events in Yamazaki to other hamlets.

13. One must honor superiors, show compassion to inferiors, revere his parents, maintain a harmonious family, be humane in dealing with other people, and always act with propriety.[10]

Local rules like these were aimed at maintaining the existing hamlet social hierarchy, at reinforcing such values as frugality and hard work, and at ensuring the conformity of all youths to community standards of behavior. Patriotic training actually helped the hamlet achieve these goals because it added the imperial and national sanction to community values. And, conversely, the members' commitment to community traditions, as we shall see in Chapter V, reinforced feelings of loyalty to the emperor and to the army. Even physical training and military drill helped hamlet leaders to strengthen the community's order; from 1915 on, Anjō reservists led youth group members in calisthenics and military drill on an average of one or two times a week at daybreak. As Tanaka himself pointed out, teenagers' participation in "early risers' clubs" helped to prevent frivolity in the evenings, kept the youths out of bars and restaurants, and forced them to save money —they were too tired after an hour and a half of early morning drill to cause trouble in the evening.[11] Tanaka's successful "character building" *seinendan* branches combined the new patriotic, athletic, and military training with the old ethical and work functions, and the result was mutually beneficial to both hamlet and national leadership.

The planners organized the youth association with its lowest official rural headquarters at the administrative village or town level, but the second guideline also allowed for the maintenance of hamlet subdivisions because the planners realized that such subunits were essential to educational success. Although after 1868, the amalgamation of Tokugawa hamlets into new larger administrative villages, migration to the cities, education, and military service began to break down particularistic local identity, hamlet allegiance remained important well into the postwar era. The 1915–1945 period under study here was, as Satō Mamoru points out, a transitional one between the Tokugawa era when a farmer's whole world was his hamlet and the post-World War II epoch when land reform, the amalgamation of villages into larger communities, and out-migration destroyed local identity to a large extent. In 1850, a young man joined the *wakamono-gumi* out of loyalty to his family and hamlet; in 1935 he enrolled out of loyalty to family, hamlet, and nation; in 1970, he joined to fulfill his own individual needs. In transitional 1915, Tanaka probably felt compelled

144

to maintain hamlet subunits to use the still important hamlet cohesiveness and sanctions against nonparticipation (i.e., against nonconformity) to ensure widespread enlistment and functional success, but at the same time to establish village and town level branches. In Anjō, for example, the *seinendan* was part of the national chain of command, had a town office headquarters and leadership, but also hamlet leaders. All of the members belonged to the hamlet subunits and performed most of their functions—military, physical training, and social as well as the older labor and religious ones there. By functioning in this way, the village or town youth branch benefited from hamlet cohesiveness, community office financing, and from government, school official, and reservist leadership and support.[12]

Tanaka, Ichiki, and Takada also urged youth group members to cooperate closely with leaders of other nationally centralized, but local organizations—the mayor, his community office subordinates, police (Home Ministry), school officials (Education Ministry), reservists (Army Ministry), and local Shinto and Buddhist priests. This clause of the national leaders' order caused no problems at all. It was natural and not new for the youth group to cooperate with the village office, which financed the youth group, with the school officials, who taught the members for six to eight years of their young lives, and with the local priests especially from Shinto shrines where most hamlet festivals took place. Cooperation with the *zaigō gunjinkai* presented no dilemma either. Reservists commanded respect because they were the community's fittest men in their prime work years and the leaders of other village organizations. Even if the reservists had not been charged with many youth group leadership roles, the hamlet's young men would have followed and respected these men. The new youth association regulations simply added three new types of activity—patriotic, athletic, and military—to the ones youths already carried out under the direction of these same elders. In Anjō, the reservist branch members drilled, led exercises, and taught the soldier's ethos to youth group members. In a different guise, reservists directed the young men in the volunteer fire department, road repairs, and other community services.[13] The two age groups added new functions after 1910–1915, but they did not develop new relationships.

The two ministers included in the youth association's regulations Tanaka's demand that the maximum age for youth group membership be twenty, and this turned out to be his only miscalculation. Tanaka

145

insisted on this limit because he envisioned a system in which young men left the *seinendan* at the age when they became eligible for military service and reserve association membership. The former was to be a pipeline for the latter, and all males from the age of six to forty would receive patriotic and military training. The school system indoctrinated children from six to fourteen, the youth association teenagers from fourteen to twenty, and the army and reserve association from twenty to forty.[14]

Tanaka's insistence on an age limit of twenty ran counter to hamlet tradition and, for the ultimate success of the centralized youth association, was revised upward. This was because in the older *wakamono-gumi*, which lacked national leadership, age requirements varied from hamlet to hamlet. Some considered a man a youth until he married or even until he assumed the family headship and required that he belong to the youth group well after he passed the age of thirty. Thus, although the Home and Education Ministry officials accepted Tanaka's proposal, some local leaders were recalcitrant. For the organization to perform as both a community service and a national educational one, some compromise had to be reached. In 1920, the central leadership raised the age limit to twenty-five, and in some communities eventually as high as forty-two.[15]

Several scholars, following the interpretation of Tazawa Yoshiharu, Tanaka's more liberal rival in youth affairs, interpret the 1920 regulations as a move toward greater local autonomy and a defeat for Tanaka. Since local *seinendan* members from this time on were allowed to determine their own maximum age and to choose their own leaders, Tazawa and later scholars believe that 1920 marked the end of military influence over the youth association at least until the wartime years. Actually, the new age limit benefited the army and the reserve association. After 1920, men between the ages of twenty and twenty-five normally functioned in both the community's youth and reservist branch. Because they were the oldest and ablest of the youth branch members, reservists became leaders and exerted strong influence over local *seinendan* affairs. The Japanese scholars go astray by basing their interpretations on Tazawa's democratic intentions when he proposed the rules' changes, rather than on a study of the local level of the system where the new regulations had their actual impact.[16]

Reservists influenced the two and one-half million member youth association even when they did not provide the organization's official leadership. Available evidence from local youth group and community histories, from reservist publications and Anjō documents, and from interviews and questionnaires, reveals that in the communities covered, youth branches conducted many functions in cooperation with and under the direction of the local reservist branch. The two organizations cooperated locally to perform such joint educational and service enterprises as military drill, patriotic ceremonies, disaster relief, public works, physical training, and athletic meets in Anjō, in its Hekikai County in general, in Isurugi Town and Higashi Nojiri Village in Toyama Prefecture, in Utsunomiya City just north of the capital, in Fuchū City and Tsubota Village in Tokyo Prefecture and throughout Nagano and Yamanashi Prefectures. Actually, every available local *seinendan* history except the one for Nagoya City refers frequently to reservist-youth group cooperation and to the leadership the former provided the latter. Even the Nagoya history indicates a strong army influence in that city's youth affairs. And Satō Mamoru, in his study of local youth organization in three widespread regions, specifically reports close reservist-youth cooperation in several of the communities he researched. He concludes that both organizations played important roles in educating young men in patriotic values.[17] We shall deal with local youth and reservist branch leadership, cooperation, and mutual community service and nationally oriented activities in Chapters IV and V. The evidence to be presented there indicates that the two organizations complemented each other in winning local acceptance for national, nationalistic, and military values and institutions.

THE NEED TO SUPPLEMENT
THE YOUTH ASSOCIATION

In spite of the youth association's success in helping the army spread its values to teenage Japanese males, in a little more than a decade the army established the parallel youth training center system. If the *seinendan* functioned so well for army purposes, the question we must raise is why did Tanaka and Ugaki, who became the prime mover of the army's system for civilian education after 1924, conclude so soon that they needed another organization? I think we can discern the answer fairly easily. They wanted to supplement the already existing youth branches with a related and complementary organization because they recognized a lack of nationwide uniformity in military education from branch to branch. These variations, while not large enough or extensive enough to threaten seriously the youth association's overall military endeavors, did impress Tanaka and Ugaki, officers obsessed with order and standardization. The problem arose from the inability of the army and the national reservist leaders to control securely enough the youth association's central headquarters and from their difficulties in obtaining and maintaining cooperation in a few local communities.

The first problem, the inability of the army to dictate to the nationally unified *seinendan,* resulted from civilian fear of excessive military influence. Many civilians in the Home and Education Ministries, but particularly in the press and the lower house of the Diet, believed Tanaka's goal was the militarization of Japanese youth. Their evidence was the twenty-year-old age limit which seemed to make the *seinendan* a reservist association auxiliary. Tanaka answered this criticism with the following statement to the press in 1915:

> We have no intention of making youths into soldiers or giving them military preparatory training as in Russia or in France. The order clearly states that our goal is to make youths into healthy future citizens. According to the order ... the *seinendan* is not a work organization, not a research organization, not an organization to aid in production, but an association for building character.[18]

Tanaka's statement did not confront squarely the issue raised by the civilian criticism because the training of soldiers which he mentioned and the militarization of youth which his critics feared were two related, but still different matters. Events proved that Tanaka had every intention of encouraging youth association military drill, not apparently with the short-range purpose of training recruits for the army, but rather to produce physically and spiritually fit citizens. Since Tanaka believed that good citizens are good soldiers, and good soldiers are good citizens, his long range youth association goal was the militarization of Japanese youth, that is of Japanese society. If by achieving this goal the army also gained pretrained recruits as a by-product, it was all well and good. But Tanaka's ideal youth association would have a broad, not a narrow goal; and, as his critics contented, it was a military goal.

Tanaka's disclaimers rightly fell on skeptical ears, and criticism continued after 1915. The two civilian ministers were questioned repeatedly during the next decade about the justification for Tanaka's twenty-year-old age limit and about his and the army's influence in youth association affairs.[19] This criticism undoubtedly helped motivate them to change the maximum age limit in 1920 but, as we have seen, neither criticism nor the regulation revisions ended the army's influence on the youth association.

To ameliorate the impact of the criticism over army influence on the youth association, the planners decided from the beginning to minimize the military's role in the central headquarters. When the Home and Education Ministers proclaimed the establishment of a national youth headquarters in 1915, they abandoned the original plan to have the Army Minister join. No soldier except Tanaka served on the organization's board of directors, and even he resigned and became an adviser in 1919. Tanaka was the only officer to serve in any official capacity until after the China War began in 1937.[20]

Although the Army Ministry had no official control over the *seinendan's* central headquarters, this was an insufficient reason for Tanaka and Ugaki to think they needed a new, army-directed organization. Tanaka himself was able to exert military influence on the youth association at the highest levels, and he also knew that Takada, Ichiki, Yamamoto, Tadokoro and most of their colleagues and successors were committed to ideological values similar to his. He saw no need to bring the youth association under military supervision because his civilian colleagues had made the *seinendan* the character training organization he desired it to be.

Furthermore, the army could dominate the local youth branches without controlling the Tokyo headquarters. Taisho democracy, the liberal atmosphere which surrounded it, and the fear of militarism was primarily a condition of the cities. At the village level, this influence did not have the impact it had in Tokyo or Osaka. Thus, the youth branches after 1915, as before, operated under the leadership of the older members (although for the first five years they were not actually members because of the twenty-year-old age limit); most of them were simultaneously reservists, the army's rural representatives. Villagers did not perceive these reservists, approximately two-thirds of the 20 to 40-year-old age group in the community, to be militarists infiltrating the local *seinendan*. They saw them rather as the healthiest men in the

149

community, men in their prime, asserting their leadership over their natural followers, the local teenagers.

Tanaka recognized the rural opportunity the army had because villagers accepted *zaigō gunjinkai* branches as integral parts of their communities. Therefore, between 1914 and 1925, he devoted himself to educating reservists about youth leadership so that they would utilize this potential and lead teenagers in the "right" direction. He ground out numerous articles in the issues of *Comrades in Arms* and presented frequent speeches which were then published in his collected writings on the subject of reservist youth guidance. Tanaka also wrote an important pamphlet on the subject, *The Social Education of the Public* (*Shakaiteki kokumin kyōiku*), which, according to the youth association's official historian, Kumagai Tatsujirō, reached a circulation of 700,000 copies, including one to every reservist branch and elementary school in the country. In all of these articles and pamphlets, Tanaka urged reservist and local school and civil officials to cooperate in the essential enterprise of strengthening young people's characters through rigorous patriotic, military, physical, moral, and vocational training. The evidence to be presented in Chapter V indicates that Tanaka's efforts at indoctrination without central control by the military worked well in the communities studied.[21]

There were, nevertheless, minor exceptions to this pattern of sucess which may have influenced Ugaki and Tanaka to build a new organization. The 1915 youth association organizers met scattered and temporary "traditional" resistance to their centralization efforts, resistance which was overcome, but which led to a lack of total uniformity of practice nationwide. Several Japanese scholars report cases, for example, of villages in which each household sent only one son to the pre-1915 *wakamono-gumi*. This presented problems in centralization because the ministers' orders required that all young males between the ages of thirteen or fourteen and twenty join the *seinendan*. The Oikata hamlet in Akita Prefecture met this problem by maintaining two youth organizations, one to perform "national," and one to conduct "local" functions. This in turn jeopardized the use of local practices to spread military ideals since the new imposed organization remained a bureaucratic one without profiting from the benefits of hamlet cohesion. Luckily for the national leaders' success, the two Oikata groups gradually merged and helped fulfill the central officials' goal.[22] Although we have no idea whether or not this type of local problem was widespread, and although this one seems to have been shortlived, it and others like it may have provided and incentive to the military's formation of a more tightly controlled and standardized supplementary young men's organization.

Tanaka and Ugaki seem also to have searched for a way to supplement youth association military education because of radical activity which prevented the army and the reservist association from dominating certain branches. In a few areas in the nation, "proletarian" leaders seized control of local youth association organs. A carefully documented case of this was in Shimo-ina County in southern Nagano Prefecture. Here in the 1920s the local youth association leaders, many of whom were Communist Party members, successfully withdrew the county organization from the national and prefectural organization and fought to a draw local government and reservist efforts to create a conservative, rival youth association. They even blocked the development of the county's youth training centers for a few years after 1926 by refusing to allow their *seinendan* members to attend. The movement collapsed in the early Showa period largely because in 1928 the Tanaka government jailed hundreds of Communist Party members, and in doing so decimated the Shimo-ina radical leadership. The increased parochialism and chauvinism of the early 1930s destroyed the radical movement's remaining popular support. It is difficult to determine the national incidence of radical youth activity in rural Japan during the 1920s— Hirayama Kazuhiko, a student of the Shimo-ina case and sympathetic to the radical movement, thinks this southern Nagano situation was a rate example. Nevertheless, Tanaka, a staunch anti-Communist with nostalgic memories of his student years in imperial Russia, and Ugaki must have been impressed.[23] Shimo-ina County presented, from the military's point of view, a chaotic and unacceptable youth association situation. It provided an incentive for the establishment of a more highly controlled youth training system in 1926 to supplement the officers' earlier attempts to create patriotism, military popularity, and national unity out of hamlet particularism.

TANAKA, UGAKI AND THE
YOUTH TRAINING CENTERS

General Ugaki, Tanaka's successor as Army Minister in 1924, was the officer most involved in the creation of the youth training center system. Ugaki, who served as the army's cabinet representative when the Education Ministry issued the order in 1926, established centers as part of his "readjustment of the army" (*gumbi seiri*). Under strong public and political pressure for disarmament, the minister eliminated four army divisions, but he used the funds saved to mechanize the army and to add to the national mobilization structure. The keys to this addition were the youth training centers and the assignment of active duty officers to middle schools as military instructors.

Ugaki, echoing Yamagata and Tanaka, wrote that he believed military drill for teenagers was vital for producing better individual citizens, for bringing young men into intimate contact with the army, and for fulfilling his desire of unifying the entire society as a disciplined national power under the emperor. He stated that only the army, by training soldiers, reservists, youths, and women, could produce citizens who worked cooperatively to increase Japan's wealth and military strength. The army could do this because it served the whole nation, not special interests as the political parties did, and it "touched" most of the populace, not just a few members as the navy did. Ugaki considered the establishment of youth centers to be one of his most important contributions to Japan.[24]

Without question, Tanaka's intellectual influence, support, and patronage made Ugaki's training centers possible. Although General Ugaki did not credit anyone else with helping him establish the youth drill system and although he was extremely critical of Tanaka in his famous diary, Ugaki clearly worked in the Yamagata-Tanaka tradition of building national unity, and he rose to high military position, including even that of Army Minister, because of Tanaka's very real support.[25]

Tanaka was willing to patronize Ugaki, a non-Choshu officer, because they shared similar views on national mobilization. To both, a strong army depended on modern armaments, rational organization, and strict discipline founded on a solid basis of national popular support, unity, and wealth. Tanaka's influence and role in creating the youth training certers must not be overlooked.

One Japanese scholar has pointed out that the fundamental idea that supported the need for the centers, the necessity for educating young men in national and military values, was essentially Tanaka's. Ugaki believed in the same ideas and spoke of them with as much intensity as the Choshu general, but Ugaki was a Tanaka follower and absorbed the ideas from his mentor. Moreover, shortly after Tanaka became president of the *Seiyūkai* opposition party, he took the unprecedented political step of having his party publicly urge the Katō Kōmei cabinet to adopt Ugaki's December, 1925 proposal for military training centers for youths. It was the Katō government which promulgated the order establishing the centers in 1926. At the high-water mark of "Taisho democracy," the leadership of both major political parties supported the creation of one of the army's major institutions in its efforts to militarize.Japanese society.[26]

General Ugaki received help in establishing youth training centers from his colleague, Education Minister Okada Ryōhei, in the two Katō and Wakatsuki Cabinets in 1924–1926, as well as from Tanaka and the two major political parties. The centers, after all, came under the jurisdiction of the Education, not the Army, Ministry, and could not exist without Okada's approval. Ugaki and Okada, a youth association adviser along with Tanaka, had first cooperated in early 1925 when the two men assigned army officers to middle schools as drill instructors. The plan not only rescued the army from the necessity of retiring the officers displaced by the elimination of four divisions, but also required the ministry to recruit more to fill all of the educational needs. It also brought the 20 percent of the teenage population which went into secondary education under military influence. Okada backed Ugaki's plan because the Education Minister believed systematic military drill helped build physically and morally strong, patriotic citizens. Later in the year, Ugaki and Okada presented the second part of their military socialization plan for teenagers. On December 18, they presented the youth training center proposal to the second Katō Cabinet's Educational Deliberations Committee. This committee quickly accepted the proposal and within months the Diet, dominated by Katō's government party and Tanaka Giichi's opposition party, passed the necessary budget bill to fund the centers. In July, 1926, Ugaki's and Okada's centers, made possible by Army, Education Ministry, and political party cooperation, were in operation.[27]

According to the April 20, 1926 order establishing the centers, and several subsequent Education and Army Ministry orders, local communities were required to set up and finance four year schools for the 80 percent of the Japanese male youths who did not continue with higher education after completing compulsory education. These young people between the ages of fifteen and twenty, the majority of whom simultaneously held jobs or labored on their families' farms, received eight hundred hours of education, including four hundred of military drill and one hundred of ethical education, over a period of four years in the new centers. Although the Education Ministry alone had official jurisdiction over the youth training centers, the army's influence was inescapable. Reservists directed the 400 hours of drill, provided 40,000 of the 110,000 teachers, and the army's regimental area commanders had the duty to inspect annually the state of the student's military proficiency. From 1926 on, the army worked through both organizations. It used the centers for military drill and patriotic training and the youth association branches for broader military, physical, and patriotic training, to maintain army-community ties, and thus to recruit students for the youth training centers. In some communities, the youth association relinquished its drill responsibilities to the new centers, although in others, Anjō for example, young men drilled in both.[28]

Several Japanese historians have written that the centers met immediate and widespread opposition in 1926. These scholars, however, support their contention with only two examples of opposition: that of a Tokyo newspaper, expressed in an editorial, which tells us nothing about rural acceptance of youth centers, and that of the Japan Peasant's Association. This association, it must be admitted, was the most important of the prewar, antilandlord organizations, but one must remember that all of the farmers' unions, at their peak membership, enrolled only 6 percent of the agricultural families in the nation. Moreover, the Japan Peasants' Association splintered before 1926 into four separate organizations, only two of which by any stretch of the imagination could be considered "proletarian." Thus when one of the authors states that the union opposed the centers because they were classless and broke down class distinctions by giving military drill to the rural "proletariat" as well as to the more affluent people, we can surmise that his reference did not point to all four parts of the union. The reference was rather to its radical wing, representing at most 2 percent of the rural population. The army's ability to recruit students for its centers and members for its other organizations depended on the farmers' perceptions of themselves as members of a corporative and cohesive vertical hamlet, not as part of a horizontal social class. A prewar Japanese peasant union that based its chances of success on farmers' class consciousness was doomed never to recruit a large membership.[29]

Reports in the *Asahi shimbun,* Tokyo's leading newspaper, and enrollment figures also belie these scholar's claims. The newspaper published a series of articles between July, 1926 and July, 1927 which reported continued success for Ugaki's training centers, and when they opened their doors in 1926, the centers enrolled the significant number of 800,000 male teenagers. The number grew steadily thereafter. By 1934, 915,000, or over one-third of the nation's young men in the appropriate age bracket—about 40 percent of those who were eligible (students who entered middle school did not enroll in youth training centers)—studied in the 15,000 centers. The percentages ranged from less than 10 percent in Tokyo, to over 50 percent in highly agricultural Yamagata Prefecture.[30] The basic reason for the difference in urban and rural matriculation is clear and has been mentioned several times before in discussing the army's other local organizations. Hamlet cohesion and emphasis on conformity resulted in high enrollment and attendance rates. Although the Education Ministry organized the training centers by "artificial" school districts and not by "natural" hamlets, this did not lessen the impact of community pressure. The students usually belonged simultaneously to the *seinendan* with its hamlet subdivisions, and received drill instruction from neighborhood reservists. The pressures from their youth association peers and reservist elders were potent in the case of the centers as well as in that of the other organizations. The young villagers' commitment to their hamlet enforced participation in a curriculum which emphasized military drill and nationalistic ideals. This is another example of local particularism which helped the army mold national villagers. The number of students would have been even higher if the curriculum had not duplicated youth association functions in some communities and if many youths had not studied concurrently in similar but partly competitive vocational schools. The latter problem was solved in 1935, as we shall see, by the merger of the centers and vocational schools into militaristic youth schools.

YOUTH SCHOOLS AND THE EXTENSION OF
MILITARY DRILL FOR TEENAGERS

The year 1935 saw a major expansion of the prewar military socialization system for male Japanese; in that year, the youth training centers merged with the nationwide system of supplementary technical schools (*jitsugyō hoshū gakkō*) and became the basis of a broader network of military indoctrination. In 1893–94, the government created a series of vocational schools at different educational levels to give secondary and higher education to many of the primary and middle school graduates who did not go on to study in colleges and universities. The system included three types of practical schools: higher technical schools for middle school graduates which turned out such skilled technicians as doctors, veterinarians, and agronomists; technical schools in which elementary school graduates studied full time for two to five years, depending on their educational background; and supplementary technical schools in which graduates of compulsory elementary education studied part-time while they held jobs or worked on their families' farms. The students in the last type of vocational schools, which had by far the largest enrollment—in 1927, the higher schools educated 21,000, the technical schools 250,000, and the supplementary schools almost one million students—studied ethics, Japanese language, arithmetic, and the type of technical education appropriate to the school's geographical area. About 75 percent of the 7,000 schools specialized in agriculture, and only about 400 in commerce and industrial technology. In other words, a very high percentage of the schools was located in rural areas. It was the supplementary schools which overlapped and competed with the youth training centers. By 1935, the schools played important roles in the educational life of their communities and had become the focus of intense civic pride. The author of the history of the town of Nambu, just west of Kofu, for example, bragged that the Mutsuzawa Village (one of the villages amalgamated into Nambu after the war) Vocational School was of such high quality that it was as good as a second-rate middle school. Because of their local prestige, large enrollment, competition, and wide distribution in rural Japan, it is easy to understand why the army cast a covetous eye on the schools.[31]

The merger had an important benefit for the army; it allowed the military to increase its indoctrination network considerably. In 1935, 915,000 students studied in the youth training centers, but another 944,000 males and 470,000 females enrolled in the supplementary technical schools. Although a half million male students attended both types of schools concurrently, another half million did not. Thus the army concluded that if the two systems merged, it could reach 50 percent more young men as well as a large number of girls. The Education Ministry also probably favored the amalgamation as a means of avoiding the extra expense of maintaining two school systems, each with overlapping functions and students.

In 1935, therefore, the Army and the Education Ministries created youth schools, and enrollment increased immediately to almost two million students, including 500,000 young women. The schools continued, as the centers had, to give military, patriotic, and ethical training, but added more extensive academic and vocational education than before. From 1926 until 1936, center students spent half of their two hundred hours of education per year in drill training; after 1935, drill consumed only 70 to 90 of 210 annual school hours. Girls did not receive military drill. Instead they undertook 30 hours of physical education and 40 hours of "housewife" training, mostly sewing.[32]

After the merger, well over 50 percent of the nation's teenage males participated in the youth schools and received military drill training. In this case, as in that of all the army's educational organizations, more rural and fewer urban youths enrolled. In a number of agricultural prefectures, the power of the hamlet insured that 75 to 80 percent of the eligibles matriculated. The army, with its rural foundations secure, began to search for ways to expand city enrollment, particularly when surveys showed that youth school graduates achieved better results both on the conscription examination and on active duty. In wartime 1939, therefore, the Army and the Education Ministry made attendance compulsory. Their aim was to enforce attendance with each new class and achieve full enrollment by 1943. By that year, three million boys and girls, almost 80 percent of Japan's sixteen- to twenty-year-olds, participated in the youth schools. The other 20 percent were either young men on active duty in the military or teenagers (mostly urban?) who somehow still managed to evade enrollment. The youth school students provided a large part of the labor in Japan's factories in the closing two years of the war.[33]

THE NATIONAL DEFENSE WOMEN'S ASSOCIATION

Women were the last group the army attempted to educate in military values. Before the "crisis" decade of the 1930s, officers made only two sporadic efforts to reach women. One was through the army's influence on the existing women's groups, particularly the Patriotic Women's Association (*aikoku fujinkai*); the other was through the reservist association's publication of a magazine for women, *Our*

Family (*Wagaie*).[34] Tanaka, Ugaki, and their associates had seen no need to recruit women because, given the family-oriented and male-dominated nature of Japanese society, organizing men automatically involved organizing women. Even before the 1930s, women aided reservists and youth group members in many of their community services and other activities. When hamlet reservists, for example, helped the families of men on active duty farm, the reservists' women joined in. If the aid included rice transplanting, a female duty, mothers and wives did the work. Hamlet women were unofficially part of the army's local system before they became defense women.

The army first decided to organize women officially after the events of the early 1930s led to increased foreign pressure against Japanese emigration, development of military armaments, and expansionist policies. In the "crisis" era of the 1930s, Japanese military men felt that their nation needed to strengthen its internal unity in an increasingly hostile international milieu and to prepare for total national mobilization in case of what they believed was almost inevitable war. This atmosphere led to the creation of the Greater Japan National Defense Women's Association in 1932 and to its expansion to gigantic proportions by the end of the decade.[35]

The original founders of the defense women's association were Osaka women, most of whom were army wives, and military police officers. This regional beginning led army authorities to boast later that the organization had grass roots origins in the patriotism of the rank and file of Japanese women. To the extent that a group of officers' wives and the *kempeitai* commander represented grass roots, they were right. The Tokyo authorities, including the Army Minister of the day, Araki Sadao, showed immediate interest, and by 1938 the famed "white apron" organization grew to nationwide dimensions with almost eight million members. By the time war broke out in China in 1937, the army controlled a women's organization which had branches in every city, town, and village in the nation.[36]

The army dominated the new women's association to a much greater degree than it did the youth association and schools, and it shared only minimal influence with the Home, Education, and even Navy Ministries. The army alone created the defense women's group, and in its bylaws gave to the Army and Navy Ministers "supervisory leadership" (*kantoku shidō*) over the organization, but to the two civil ministers only "leadership" (*shidō*). Moreover, an active duty army major or lieutenant general always served as the general manager (*sōmu buchō*), the person who actually directed the *fujinkai*; six of the nine bureaucratic advisors to the new organization were drawn from the two military ministries so that officers could outvote civilians six to three; and the organization located its headquarters from 1932 until 1936 within the Army Ministry itself. Finally, the top positions, which were actually held by women, reflected the army's domination. The chairwoman of the organization was the wife of a prominent general, Mutō Akira, and the list of the names of women who served as vice chairmen, directors, advisors, and councillors reads like a roster of the army's Showa leadership—Suzuki, Minami, Araki, Hayashi, Sugiyama, Hata, Tōjō, etc. Only a few famous navy names such as Yonai and Nagano and civilian names such as Tokutomi and Kiyoura punctuate the list.[37] The army controlled the *kokubō fujinkai* throughout its history and shared some of its power only with the navy.

The army's dominance was even stronger at the intermediate and local than at the central level. The army asserted its power by structuring the organization according to the format of the reserve association and establishing defense women's headquarters at divisional, regimental, administrative community, and hamlet levels. At the division and regimental levels, active duty officers supervised and directed women's association affairs. Their wives, or the wives of prefectural governors or locally prestigious families—the wives of former feudal ruling families, like the Hosokawa in Kumamoto and the Tsugaru in Hirosaki—held the titular posts, but real power lay in the military headquarters. This structure bypassed the Home and Education Ministries, and the navy could claim authority only in the areas of their Yokosuka, Sasebo, and Kure bases, where they already held responsibility for *zaigō gunjinkai* affairs.[88]

At the lowest levels, even in the navy districts, army influence was absolute. This was because the reservist branches, the army's local appendages, dominated their communities' women's associations. Not only did the *kokubō fujinkai* structure exactly parallel that of the reservists, but, more important, the local *zaigō gunjinkai* units, under army direction, took the initiative in enlisting the women in their communities into the new organization and in providing guidance and leadership for women's activities. Jointly sponsored lectures, patriotic ceremonies, funerals for the war dead, aid to active duty families, and reservist-directed rifle training, drill, and maneuvers were carried out all over the country between 1932 and 1945. Reservists even led women in the famed "bamboo spear" units, organized to prepare for the American invasion of Japan in the closing year of the Pacific War. In a sense, the National Defense Women's Association became the women's arm of the *zaigō gunjinkai* and thus, at the local level, responded to the same kind of army control as the reservists.[39]

This spectacular army-reservist success in organizing women also led to the major obstacle to the new organization's development. The preexisting national women's organization, the Patriotic Women's Association, resented the new organization's competition and tried, albeit unsuccessfully, to block its development. The reasons for the resistance and for the failure to halt the army's efforts call for a short description of the older organization and its inability to sink roots into the rural hamlet.

The Patriotic Women's Association dated back to 1901, when a group of socially prestigious women with the support of a field marshal from Satsuma and the Speaker of the House of Peers, who was also the scion of the most illustrious princely house in Japan, established the organization primarily to conduct war relief for soldiers. The army praised it highly for its efforts to comfort soldiers in the 1904–1905 Russo-Japanese War. The association's leaders from its inception envisaged it as a primarily national, not a local organization, tended to recruit members from the well-to-do—one had to pay substantial dues to join—and made no effort to set up local branches. It gained the reputation of being "an upper class women's club," never built a solid local base, and thus did not carry out systematic organizational and educational activities on the hamlet level. The Patriotic Women's Association, under Home Ministry patronage, began to organize local branches and carry out policies to win rural support only after it first felt threatened by the army's group.[40]

By late 1937, the *aikoku fujinkai* had grown to almost three million members, but its membership was still only a little more than one-third its rivals. The Patriotic Women's Association, despite its prestigious history, Home Ministry support, and post-1931 efforts, could not successfully compete with the new organization because it lacked the local advantages of its rival. Home Ministry patronage guaranteed the patriotic women the assistance of prefectural and even of community governmental officials—the wife of the chief executive at each level usually served as *aikoku fujinkai* leader for that jurisdiction—but this local backing was strictly bureaucratic. The defense women's organization, on the other hand, had its own preexisting parallel structure on which to build. It maintained subdivisions like the *zaigō gunjinkai* at the hamlet level, and most potential members were the mothers, wives, and daughters of reservists and youth branch members. Family and community pressure enforced enrollment. It is no wonder that the membership grew to eight million in five years.[41]

The army-dominated organization also performed a much wider range of activities than the older, "upper class" group, despite *aikoku fujinkai* claims to the contrary. The defense women's association branches, usually in conjunction with community youth and reservists, provided labor for the families of men on active duty, helped prepare and perform the funerals of war dead, sponsored lectures and movies to disseminate military ideas, conducted all manner of savings, frugality, and antiluxury campaigns, helped at the army's annual draft examination and inspection of youths and reservists, sent off and greeted soldiers to and from the barracks, and performed war relief. Even the war relief efforts of the new organization differed from those of the old. When the Patriotic Women's Association members raised money from their dues to buy and send newspapers, cigarettes, and comfort packages to soldiers at the front, they did so on an impersonal level because of their lack of a local base. When the defense women performed the same function, they did it for men from their own communities. Thus, they could include pictures, letters, and other personal items. Even in the area of the older group's greatest success, the new group outperformed them. The army easily countered the *aikoku fujinkai's* claim that its efforts were duplicated by the new organization; officers said that the military's association carried out a much wider range of activities. The older group's recognition of this and its efforts to compete after 1937 came too late.[42]

The final reason for the army association's triumph was the most damaging to the older group's efforts at competition—the army successfully claimed its organization had a "spiritual" mission which made it both superior and more Japanese than its rival. To paraphrase Colonel Nakamura Akihito, Army Ministry officer responsible for Defense Women's Association affairs, the older group's leaders completely misunderstood the true situation if they thought the purposes of the two organizations overlapped at all. The National Defense Women's Association, he wrote, aimed not only at fulfilling its activi-

161

ties—better run funerals, greater savings for investment in national projects, etc., it also aimed at spreading and deepening among women a belief in the uniquely Japanese "way of women," and in Japanese military values like "familism," the soldier's ethos, and the concepts of "good citizens are good soldiers" and "all the citizens are soldiers." A woman, by joining the army-dominated women's club, he concluded, fulfilled her military obligation as a citizen, served as a "home front soldier," and performed a spiritual mission for her people. How could a "materialistic" organization like the Patriotic Women's Association, with its better educated and more cosmopolitan membership, counter this kind of attack in the crisis and "spiritualistic" atmosphere of Japan in the 1930s?[43]

CONCLUSION

Between 1890 and 1935, the Choshu clique's leaders and their successors built a machine to mobilize the rural populace for total war in the face of growing threats to Japan's national unity. These army officers established four nationally centralized organizations with local village and hamlet branches and subdivisions for teenagers, adult men, and women. The purpose of these groups—the reservist, youth and defense women's associations, and the youth schools—was to use the members' commitment to their agricultural hamlet and its values to mold patriotic "national villagers" who supported the army and its "rural" and military ideals. By 1935, the four organizations were in full operation and enrolled eleven to twelve million people.

1. Kishimoto Eitarō, *Nihon rōdō undōshi* [Japanese Labor Movement History] (Tokyo, 1950), p. 38; Ōkubo Toshiaki, *Nihon zenshi* [A Complete History of Japan], *Kindai* III [Modern Vol. 3] (Tokyo, 1964), pp. 218–234; Shiota Shōbē, *Shōwashi no shunkan* (Tokyo, 1966) I, pp. 78, 118, 122; Barbara Ann Waswo, *Landlords and Social Change in Prewar Japan* (Ann Arbor, 1970), pp. 198–199; Tanaka Giichi, *Taisho kōsho yori* (Tokyo, 1925), appendix, pp. 76–78.

2. "Akushisō o korobose" [Crush Subversive Thought], Kawatani Yorio, *Tanaka Giichi den* (Tokyo, 1929), pp. 201–202.

3. Tanaka, "Osorubeki shisō no appaku" [The Frightening Ideological Pressure], *Senyū*, 93 (1918), pp. 9–12; Tanaka, "Otazune ni kotau" [Answering an Inquiry], *Senyū*, 92 (1918), p. 7; Ugaki Kazushige, *Ugaki Kazushige nikki* (Tokyo, 1968–1971), I, pp. 482–483, 519, 523; Fujiwara Akira, *Gunjishi* (Tokyo, 1961), pp. 134–138; Tanaka, *Taisho kōshoyori*, p. 45.

4. *Tanaka Giichi denki* (Tokyo, 1960), I, pp. 421–422.

5. Tokiomi Kaigo, *Japanese Education: Its Past and Present* (Tokyo, 1968), p. 89; Kumagai Tatsujirō, *Dainihon seinendanshi* [The History of the Greater Japan Youth Association] (Tokyo, 1942), pp. 113–114; Tanaka, "Seinendan no igi" [The Meaning of the Youth Association], *Tanaka chūjō kōenshū* (Tokyo, 1916), pp. 252, 256–257.

6. Matsumura Ken'ichi, "Shakai kyōiku ni okeru kokumin kyōka no tenkai" [The Development of National Enlightenment Through Social Education], in Waseda daigaku shakai kagaku kenkyujo, *Nihon no fashizumu: keiseiki no kenkyū* [Japanese Fascism: Studies in the Formative Period] (Tokyo, 1970), pp. 216–219; Oka Yoshitake, *Yamagata Aritomo* (Tokyo, 1958), p. 134; Roger F. Hackett, *Yamagata Aritomo in the Rise of Modern Japan, 1838–1922* (Tokyo, 1971), pp. 146, 242, 256, 268, 279, 295–296; Kumagai, *Seinendanshi*, pp. 113–120; *Tanaka Giichi denki*, I, p. 608.

7. See *Senyū*, 9 (1911), pp. 1–2; 13 (1911), pp. 6–14; 16 (1912), pp. 1–10; 17 (1912), pp. 49–51; 20 (1912), pp. 2–10; 21 (1912), pp. 1, 90–91; 22 (1912), pp. 8–15; 29 (1913), pp. iii, 10–15 for Ōkuma speeches or reports of Ōkuma speeches to reservists; *Teikoku zaigo gunjinkai sanjūnenshi* (Tokyo, 1944), p. 77; Hosokawa Ryūgen, *Tanaka Giichi* (Tokyo, 1958), pp. 77–86; *Tanaka Giichi denki*, I, pp. 451–453; Tadokoro Miharu, "Kokumin no shūyō" [Training the People], *Senyū*, 27 (1913), pp. 6–15; Ichiki Kitokurō, "Zaigo gunjinkai to seinendan" [The Reservist Association and the Youth Group], *Senyū*, 96 (1918), pp. 7–9. Ichiki ironically was attacked as a "Minobe-ite" by radical reservists in 1935.

8. Tanaka Giichi, *Shakaiteki kokumin kyōiku* [The Social Education of the Public] (Tokyo, 1915), p. 123; Kumagai, *Seinendanshi*, pp. 199–200.

9. *Anjō-machi seinendanshi* [A History of the Youth Association of Anjō Town] (Anjō, 1936), I, pp. 11–67.

10. *Anjō-machi seinendanshi*, I, 60–62.

11. *Anjō-machi seinendanshi*, I, pp. 126–129; *Tanaka chūjō kōenshū*, p. 246.

12. Satō Mamoru, *Kindai Nihon seinen shūdanshi kenkyū* [Studies in the History of Modern Japanese Youth Organization] (Tokyo, 1970), pp. 64–65, 539–540; *Anjō machi seinendanshi*, I, *passim*; *Anjō-shi seinendanshi* [A History of the Youth Association of Anjō City] II (Anjō, 1962), pp. 1–269.

13. *Anjō-machi seinendanshi*, I, pp. 124–138, 221–455; II, pp. 50–264; see also *Toyama-ken Nishi Tonami-gun Isurugi seinendanshi* [A History of the Toyama Prefecture Nishi Tonami County Isurugi Youth Association] (Kanazawa, 1937); *Toyama-ken Higashi Tonami-gun Higashi Nojiri-mura seinendanshi* [A History of the Toyama Prefecture Higashi Tonami County Higashi Nojiri Village Youth Association] (Kanazawa, 1935).

14. Kumagai, *Seinendanshi*, p. 116; *Tanaka Giichi denki*, I, pp. 615–619; Hori Shika, *Saishō to naru made Tanaka Giichi* (Tokyo, 1928), p. 133.

15. Kumagai, *Seinendanshi*, p. 116, 119–120; *Tanaka Giichi denki*, I, pp. 615, 620; Satō Mamoru, *Seinen shūdanshi kenkyū*, pp. 55, 226–228; Fukutake Tadashi, *Japanese Rural Society* (London and New York, 1967), pp. 103–104; *Asahi nenkan* [Asahi Yearbook], 1936, pp. 571–572. In 1936, 2 prefectures placed the age limit at forty-two, 19 at between thirty and forty, and 26 at twenty-five. The prefectures with the highest age limits tended to be the most agricultural ones.

16. In 1930, 99.6% of 53,210 youth association leaders were 20 years old or older. *Zenkoku seinendan kihon chōsa* [A Basic Survey of the Youth Association Nationwide] (Tokyo, 1934), p. 5. Matsumura, "Shakai kyōiku ni okeru kyōka no tenkai," *Nihon no fashizumu*, pp. 222–223; Tazawa Yoshiharu, *Seinendan no shimei* [The Mission of the Youth Association] (Tokyo, 1930), p. 308; Inoue Kiyoshi, "Taishōki no seiji to gumbu," in Inoue Kiyoshi, ed., *Taishōki no seiji to shakai* (Tokyo, 1969), p. 401; *Isurugi seinendanshi*, p. 67; *Higashi Nojiri-mura seinendanshi*, p. 74; *Anjōmachi seinendanshi*, I, pp. 190–215; II, pp. 35–49.

17. See Smethurst, A *Social Basis for Prewar Japanese Militarism*, Chapter V, footnote one.

18. Kumagai, *Seinendanshi*, p. 116.

19. Kumagai, *Seinendanshi*, pp. 114–120, 219–223.

20. Kumagai, *Seinendanshi*, p. 114, Appendix VI, pp. 181–193; Hori, *Saishō to naru made Tanaka Giichi*, p. 133.

21. See Matsumura, "Shakai kyōiku ni okeru kokumin kyōka no tenkai," *Nihon no fashizumu*, pp. 209–219, for a discussion of Tanaka and Yamamoto's views on the functions of the youth association. Kumagai, *Seinendanshi*, p. 114; Tanaka, *Shakaiteki kokumin kyōiku* especially pp. 119–127; *Tanaka chūjō kōenshū*, pp. 170–182, 197–230, 236–264; *Senyū*, 90 (1917), pp. 6–7. The 43 issues of *Imperial Youth*, 1916–1923, housed in the library of the Japan Youth Hall (*Nihon seinenkan*) include 25 articles and advertisements for four books by Tanaka.

22. Satō Mamoru, *Seinen shūdanshi kenkyū*, p. 55.

23. Hirayama Kazuhiko, "Chihō seinen undō no tenkai" [The Development of the Regional Youth Movement], in Furushima Toshio et. al., *Meiji Taishō kyōdoshi kenkyūhō* [Research Methods in Meiji and Taishō Local History] (Tokyo, 1970), pp. 248–250; *Nagano-ken seinen hattalsushi* [A History of the Development of Nagano Prefecture Youth] (Nagano, 1935), pp. 156–163, 250–251.

24. *Ugaki nikki*, I, pp. 482–483, 497–498, 519–521, 523, 528, 547–550; Yabe Teiji, *Konoe Fumimaro* (Tokyo, 1952), I, p. 301. The novelist, Takeda Taijun, in a series of essays on politicians' writing styles, points out sarcastically that "to touch" (*sesshoku suru*) was clearly a euphemism for "to manage" (*shihai suru*) or "to mobilize" (*dōin suru*). *Seijika no bunshō* [The Writings of Politicians] (Tokyo, 1960), p. 6.

25. See Matsushita Yoshio, *Nihon no gumbatsuzō* [A Portrait of the Japanese Military Clique] (Tokyo, 1969), pp. 221–222, for a discussion of Tanaka's crucial role in making Ugaki Army Minister in 1924. *Tanaka Giichi denki*, II, pp. 329–336.

26. Kubo Yoshizō, *Nihon fashizumu kyōiku seisakushi* [A History of the Educational Policies of Japanese Fascism] (Tokyo, 1969), pp. 113–114; *Tanaka Giichi denki*, II, p. 398.

27. Kubo, *Nihon fashizumu kyōiku seisakushi*, pp. 117, 121–123.

28. Okabe Tomio, ed., *Dainihon kyōikushi* [The History of Education in Greater Japan] (Tokyo, 1939), pp. 1237–1242; Ishikawa Ken, ed., *Kindai Nihon kyōiku seidō shiryō* [Materials on the Modern Japanese Educational System] (Tokyo, 1956), III, pp. 553–555; Mombushō, *Gakusei hachijūnenshi* [The Eighty Year History of the Educational System] (Tokyo, 1954), pp. 290, 348–350; *Anjō-machi seinendanshi*, I, pp. 453–454.

29. Kubo, *Nihon fashizumu kyōiku seisakushi*, pp. 123–125; Ōtsuka Shigakkai, *Shimpon kyōdoshi jiten* (Tokyo, 1969), p. 454; Ronald P. Dore, *Land Reform in Japan* (London, 1959), pp. 75–80; Tokinoya Katsu, ed., *Nihon kindaishi jiten* (Tokyo, 1960), p. 141.

30. See Table II in Chapter Three. The *Asahi shimbun* articles not only reported the centers' success, but welcomed it as well. See especially July 2, 1926, p. 1; July 4, p. 6; July 8, p. 2; August 14, p. 3; October 5, p. 4; October 20, p. 3; July 9, 1927, p. 7; July 10, p. 7.

31. *Shimpan kyōdoshi jiten*, p. 253; *Gakusei hachijūnenshi*, p. 348; *Nambuchōshi* [The History of Nambu Town] (Kofu, 1964), pp. 639–641; See also *Kawai-mura kyōdoshi* [The Local History of Kawai Village] (Morioka, 1962), I, 1092–1095.

32. *Gakusei hachijūnenshi*, pp. 289–291, 348–351; *Kindai Nihon kyōiku seidō shiryō*, III, pp. 554–557; Gonda Morinosuke, *Nihon kyōiku tōkei* [Japanese Educational Statistics] (Tokyo, 1938), p. 213.

33. *Shimpan kyōdoshi jiten*, pp. 310–311.

34. A typical example of *Our Family* is the November, 1935 edition. The cover featured a picture of a mother in formal black kimono with two children visiting Yasukuni Shrine, the shrine dedicated to Japan's war dead, on the day of a childrens' festival (*shichi-go-san*). The issue contained articles on the imperial family, on educating natives in Japanese territories, on brave Ethiopian women fighting next to their men for their country, on the mother of Oishi Yoshio, the hero of the 47 Ronin, on Basho, a seventeenth-century poet, on heroines of the Meiji Restoration and Russo-Japanese War, on recipes, on growing bean sprouts, and on diaper covers. There were also pictures of Atsuta Shrine, the location of one of the three imperial regalia, of defense women helping fire victims, of girls receiving rifle training, and of reservist and defense women's association leaders and a Shintō priest at the time of a local ceremony to commemorate the fourth anniversary of the Manchurian Incident. Advertisements included those for life insurance, a midwifery school, defense bonds, perfume, seals, patent medicine, and a book on Taiwan. In other words, the contents included a combination of patriotic, military, romantic and practical material.

35. The major source of information on the defense womens' association is the *Dainihon kokubō fujinkai jūnenshi* [The Ten Year History of the Greater Japan National Defense Women's Association] (Tokyo, 1943). In 1938, the organization enrolled 7,929,684 members (p. 159).

36. *Kokubō fujinkai jūnenshi*, pp. 26, 159, 236, 285.

37. *Kokubō fujinkai jūnenshi*, pp. 12, 109, 114, 265–266, 322–323, 619–623.

38. *Kokubō fujinkai jūnenshi*, pp. 109–114, 265, 630–635.

39. *Kokubō fujinkai jūnenshi*, pp. 26, 288–289, 345–346, 429, 448, 454–455, 492–498, 541; *Tokushima nichinichi shimpō* [The Tokushima Daily News] included thirty-two articles between February 15 and July 8, 1935 which revealed reservist-defense women's cooperation. See especially February 15, p. 3; February 19, p. 2; March 3, p. 2; March 11, p. 1; March 26, p. 2; April 27, p. 2.

40. *Kindaishi jiten*, p. 4; *Shimpan kyōdoshi jiten*, p. 1; Shimonaka Yasaburō, ed., *Yokusan kokumin undōshi* [The History of the National Imperial Rule Movement] (Tokyo, 1954), p. 1058; *Aikoku fujinkai yonjūnenshi* [The Forty Year History of the Patriotic Women's Association] (Tokyo, 1941), I, 478–484, 506–537; II, 67. Several interview respondents expressed the same feeling as three of the published sources, that the Patriotic Women's Association was an elitist organization.

41. *Aikoku fujinkai yonjūnenshi*, I, pp. 506–537, 830; *Kokubō fujinkai jūnenshi*, p. 159.

42. *Aikoku fujinkai yonjūnenshi*, I, pp. 481, 831–832; *Kokubō fujinkai jūnenshi*, pp. 287–289, 345–346, 543–544.

43. *Aikoku fujinkai yonjūnenshi*, I, p. 830; *Kokubō fujinkai jūnenshi*, pp. 542–547.

TSURUMI KAZUKO

THE PROCESSES OF ARMY
SOCIALIZATION

Emptying the Self: The Socialization of Negative Affects

"The army quarters is a space of 120 square yards enclosed by a palisade and code books. It is an abstract society built under strong compulsion. Within that society, human beings, being deprived of their humanity, become soldiers."[1] This definition appears in Hiroshi Noma's novel about the Japanese army in World War II entitled *Shinkū Chitai (Zone of Emptiness)*. In an army barracks "even the air is expelled by force," leaving only emptiness. Army socialization, in Noma's probing analysis, is a process of dehumanization, or emptying of the self as the center of distinctively individual feeling, thinking, and acting.

As Erik Erikson points out, isolation is the *sine qua non* of indoctrination.[2] Thus isolation from the ordinary world and the destruction of privacy were the initial steps of army socialization. The new recruits were detached both physically and symbolically from civilian society.

Reprinted from Tsurumi Kazuko, *Social Change and the Individual: Japan Before and After Defeat in World War II*, copyright © 1970 by Princeton University Press, pp. 114–126, with permission of the author and the publisher.

First they had to dress in a particular style, with close-cropped hair, khaki uniforms, field-service caps, gaiters, and boots. They were disciplined to speak in the manner befitting a soldier. When referring to "I," the soldier was to use *watakushi* in addressing his superiors and *ore* in speaking to his equals; all other ways of expressing "I" in ordinary language—such as *boku, watashi,* and *washi*—were to be eliminated. To refer to money, "one meter" should be used to mean one *yen,* and "one centimeter" one *sen.*[3] Not only were the vocabularies different from ordinary Japanese, but so also were the acceptable endings of the sentences. It was one of the sources of agony for new recruits to learn the new conventions of speech, since any mistake meant a punishment of several blows on the face.[4] The suppression of the ordinary conventions of speech and the substitution of the army jargon did, however, give the new recruits a compensatory sense of superiority over the civilian population.[5] The surrogate tongue fulfilled another function as well. Since recruits came from various provinces with different dialects and it was difficult for them to communicate with one another, the army language served as a substitute for standard Japanese.

The second step in army socialization was the destruction of privacy. The conscripts were placed under twenty-four hours' surveillance; they were under the strict control of the training officers during the day, and they were watched by their squad commanders during the night.

> For instance, when we tried to go to the toilet at midnight, we had to pass by a guard standing at the door. A new conscript had to report: "So and so is going to the bathroom." If his voice was too loud, he was admonished that he should not speak so loudly while his fighting companions were asleep. But if his voice was low, he was also chastised. Thus we had to live under circumstances which made us feel that we were always tied up with invisible hands.[6]

The third technique of army socialization was the use of violence. Every evening before bedtime there was a roll call, when each soldier's arms and belongings were checked. The field-service cap, overcoat, uniform, underwear, knapsack, boots, gun, and sword of each soldier were examined by his superiors to confirm that nothing was missing and everything had been properly attended to. If the belongings of any soldier were missing or dirty, his superior would shout at him: "How is it that you have time to eat but no time to clean your gun!" or "How could you dare find time to sleep while you have no time to do your laundry properly!"[7] The shouting was usually followed by a shower of fist blows or kicks administered by the superior officer. New recruits called the evening roll call "the hour of terror."[8]

An ex-officer relates his experience of disciplining his new conscripts.

> [The purpose of discipline is] to give new conscripts shock treatments. When they first come into the army, they look sloppy and too relaxed. It is hard to explain exactly what is wrong with them. But we somehow feel that way about them. Whenever we find any impropriety in their attitudes, behavior, or speech, we chastise them while keeping them standing at attention. Usually soldiers do not understand what is wrong with them, while they are being punished. The ultimate purpose of shouting at them and hitting them is to make them feel miserable, and thus to hammer it into them that absolute obedience is imperative in the army and that neither criticism nor protest is allowed. When superiors chastise conscripts, the former may ask why the recruits committed this or that blunder. If the conscripts begin to give reasons for their deeds, they are hit for having tried to answer. If they keep silent, they are also hit. Either way there is no escape from being beaten. The best they can do is to reply "Yes, sir" to whatever is said to them.[9]

It is important to note that the disciplining of new conscripts was not based on any consistent system of abstract rules but only on the whim of their superiors. More often than not, when new recruits were hit or humiliated by their superiors, there were no reasons for the acts other than the need to drive home the necessity of unquestioning obedience. The relentless destruction of privacy and the extensive use of violence were methods of negative affect socialization; by these means anger and contempt were maximized in the socializing agents, while distress, fear, and humiliation were maximized in the persons socialized. Whenever new recruits attempted to think, write, say, or do anything of their own accord, they met with punishment through admonition or violence. After constant repetition of this treatment, the fear of encountering humiliation and violence became so ingrained within the personalities of the conscripts that they were inhibited from thinking, doing, or feeling anything of their own volition.

> One year's army life has drained the humanity out of everyone. Second-year privates treat us first-year privates as though we were their slaves or rather machines. They have no other job than hazing and torturing us. . . . Every night we are strapped with slippers. One of us was beaten with the sheath of a sword and was hospitalized with a wound that required four stitches. Even a corporal acts like a god toward us. . . . Were a second-year private to discover that I have written a letter like this in the toilet, I would probably be murdered.[10]

A student marine wrote two months after joining the Marine Corps:

> The two things that made me suffer most after I entered the armed forces were the alternate attacks of physical and mental pain. Physical pain was the result of cold and extreme muscular fatigue, and the mental pain arose from being deprived of books. Hunger and a hankering for food occupied a great part of one's daily thought. . . .
>
> Even when I read the news of heavy fighting, I feel differently from what I did when I was a civilian. When I was a civilian, I felt some determination to cope with a war situation growing ever more serious. But since I entered the Marine Corps, I have lost the freedom and composure necessary to have a will of my own, being enslaved physically and mentally from morning till night. . . .
>
> When I began to feel some relief from the sense of oppression, toward the end of the second month as a sailor, I realized that my integrity in coping with problems had been gradually paralyzed. . . .
>
> First I wished I could become spiritually nothing. I thought I had to put an end to the life and thought of a civilian.[11]

Eight months after he had entered the Marine Corps, the same marine noted in his diary:

The head sailor was giving "spiritual education" to the sailors in his charge, with on oak stick at his waist. . . . He told his men to step forward one by one, and then he began to strike with his full strength at the hips of each man. . . . Each sailor stood with his back turned towards the head sailor, with his hands held up and legs open. I heard the dull sounds of bang, bang, hitting the pelvic bones of the sailors. I felt I was witnessing a disgusting scene; indeed it was more than merely disgusting.

On Sunday some weeks ago, I also saw the same head sailor hitting another sailor, because he had returned to the barracks only ten minutes before the deadline. . . . The sailor fell on the gravel, groaning. Another sailor tried to help him stand up, but . . . he fell on the ground again. I saw a streak of blood running down the back of his head onto the collar of his uniform.

Both the tyrant and the victim will eventually be my subordinates. What should I make of this fact? Anyway, it is useless to think. It is completely nonsensical to think seriously.[12]

There were various forms of punishment other than verbal reproach and hazing. Among them were the postponement of meals or the suspension of holidays. A more severe form of punishment was confinement to the barracks jail. The decision to inflict this penalty was mainly at the discretion of a subofficer and a company commander. Sometimes the unfavored "sons" of the subofficer and the company commander were sent to the front as punishment. Demotion was yet another penalty. The most serious punishment was court-martial and imprisonment in the army prison. The army prison was under the jurisdiction of the gendarmerie and was distinct from a barracks prison, which was under the control of regular army officers. Although they were usually justified, each of these forms of punishment was sometimes applied out of animosity, rivalry, and hatred. The accused had no way of protesting against such injustices.[13] Protest was a form of disobedience—a capital crime in the army.

Isolation from ordinary life, the relentless invasion of privacy, constant reproach and hazing, and imprisonment constituted the apparatus of negative affect socialization. Owing to the changes wrought in their personalities by this socialization, men ceased to act voluntarily and, instead, acted out of fear and terror. New conscripts were humiliated until they felt less worthy than their horses. Some squad leaders publicly announced that horses were more precious than men, since men could easily be recruited whereas horses could not be replaced overnight. Thus horses were treated with meticulous care. On the occasion of a horse inspection, the soldiers assigned to stop galloping horses suddenly were often kicked and injured by the horses, but they preferred to risk this danger rather than be reprimanded by their superiors.[14] It was not, then, only fear that motivated soldiers; it was also the hierarchy of fears and terrors that determined their conduct, and, in this hierarchy of fears, first place was assigned to fear of the consequences of disobeying one's superiors.

Indoctrination: Socialization for Death

Indoctrination in the army included the word-for-word citation of the basic code books. The qualifying examinations for cadets were drawn from these code books, and the new conscript memorized them during his first year of training.[15] A graduate of the Law School of Tokyo University wrote about his first examination in the army:

On the second day after my entrance into the army, the first qualifying examination took place. The first question was "Deferentially write the part on loyalty in the *Imperial Precepts*." An examination on the *Imperial Precepts* is extremely hard. The *Imperial Precepts to Soldiers and Sailors* is a long piece, and it takes twenty minutes to recite it. The language [especially the Chinese characters used] is so difficult that we cannot read it accurately unless parallel readings are given in the alphabet. In the examination, we are required to write exactly in the same manner as the original texts, using the archaic alphabet, wherever it is used in the texts. In the texts, sometimes *koto* [the fact that] is written in phonetics and sometimes in Chinese characters. The same applies to *mono* [those who]. We are expected to remember where *mono* is written in phonetics, and where *koto* is written in characters. . . .

The second question was "What is military discipline?" I thought about this problem on my own and wrote: "Military discipline is a system of norms, observance of which is essential for the maintenance of the various activities of the armed forces."

This answer was rated as close to zero. The right answer was to write out the fourth article of the *Infantry Drill Book*: "Military discipline is the lifeline of the army. It is military discipline that makes the whole army, from generals to rank-and-file soldiers stationed in various places and assigned with various duties in the battlefield, consistently obedient and creates the unified policy necessary for concerted action. The destiny of the army hinges on the firmness or looseness of this military discipline." All the other examinations followed a similar pattern. In the army there is no room for what you think yourself. (We call our own thoughts "private code books.") We are expected to learn the military code books by heart, word for word. It is different from the kind of education we have received at the university, in which emphasis was placed on our own ideas. But considering the fact that the language in the military code books is the most exact and concise expression of certain ideas, it is only natural that word-for-word memorization is required of us.[16]

There was a continuity between military indoctrination and compulsory moral education at primary schools. The common denominator was the fetishism of words as words. In schools in the regular class in compulsory moral education, as well as on ceremonial occasions such as the Emperor's Birthday or the National Foundation Day (called *Kigensetsu*, the day when, according to tradition, the Japanese Empire was founded by the first Emperor Jinmu), the *Imperial Rescript on Education* was recited. Whenever any part of the *Imperial Rescript* was read loud, the reader was expected first to raise the book of sacred teachings above his head and bow deferentially to it before beginning his recitation. Not only was the Emperor sacred, but so were the words issued in his name. The fetishism of words was applied to the language of the military code books. As the passage quoted above shows, the language of these documents was difficult for a law school graduate to learn. It was even more so for those who had had only elementary schooling. Army indoctrination was a strictly one-way communication, in which only the socializer spoke and the socializee was expected to accept silently whatever was told him. It was an imperfect communication, since the socializee was not expected to understand precisely what these words meant but only to grasp vaguely what they were about. Their ambiguity created a halo of sanctity around the words of the Imperial dicta. The inexplicable was taken for profound thought, something to be held in awe and revered. Perfect communication, or at least an attempt at perfect communication through free discussion, was tabooed, since in discussion the veil of euphemisms might be torn aside to reveal the actual motivations of the designers of the ideology and the socializee might be encouraged to think about the possible consequences of following the precepts he was taught.[17] On the other hand, if the socializee failed completely to understand the meaning of the *Imperial Precepts* and other code books, then socialization through words was impossible.

Thus imperfect communication, instead of complete discommunication or perfect communication, was functional for the military elites as a method of indoctrinating soldiers in the ideology of death. The use of imperfect communication as a vehicle of army socialization was related to the functional diffuseness of its ideological content. Perfect cognitive communications defines and delineates precisely what one is expected to do. Imperfect communication, in contrast, expands the range of duties and obligations that can be demanded of the socializee almost without limits, at the discretion of the socializer.

Yanagida has pointed out that there is a sharp distinction between the formal or ceremonial (*hare*-clear) and the informal or everyday (*ke*-cloudy) languages in Japanese colloquial conventions. In learning ceremonial language, students were taught "to recite meticulously word for word, without paying any attention to misunderstandings of the meaning."[18] Yanagida regretted that in prewar schools only the stereotypes of ceremonial language, with its inhibition of invention and creativity, were inculcated, to the utter neglect of everyday language.[19] Following Levy, we have already distinguished between actual and ideal patterns of action. Ceremonial language is the linguistic form of expressing ideal patterns of thought and action, whereas everyday language is the linguistic form of expressing actual patterns of thought and action. This distinction leads to the hypothesis that, if we compare what a person expresses in ceremonial language with what the same person says in everyday language, we may be able to gauge the distance between his ideal and actual patterns of thought and action.

The *Imperial Precepts to Soldiers and Sailors*, the basic text of army socialization, was written in the most ceremonial of ceremonial languages. After first examining the ideological content of the *Precepts*, we shall analyze how this army socialization was accepted or rejected by the soldiers as shown in their diaries and letters. Unfortunately from the sociologist's point of view, the writers of these letters knew that their communications faced censorship, and probably some of the letters were for that reason written in more ceremonial language than they otherwise would have been.

The *Imperial Precepts* prescribed five primary virtues for soldiers: loyalty, propriety, valor, fidelity, and simplicity. Among these five virtues, loyalty ranked first:

> Soldiers and sailors, We are your Commander-in-Chief. Our relations with you will be most intimate when we rely upon you as Our limbs and you look up to Us as your head. . . .
>
> Remember that, as the protection of the state and the maintenance of its power depend upon the strength of its arms, the growth or decline of this strength must affect the nation's destiny for good or for evil; therefore, neither be led astray by current opinions nor meddle in politics, but with single heart fulfill your essential duty of loyalty, and bear in mind that duty is weightier than a mountain, while death is lighter than a feather. Never by failing in moral principle fall into disgrace and bring dishonor upon your name.[20]

This glorification of death was an ideology that provided incentives for dying for the sake of the Emperor. Four main elements constituted this glorification of death: a taboo on the discussion of politics, an organismic concept of the state, familism, and the prestige to be gained by dying.

The phrase "neither be led astray by current opinions nor meddle in politics" has a historical significance. The *Imperial Precepts* was promulgated in the heyday of the Freedom and Popular Rights Movement. The leaders of the movement tried to win the soldiers over to the cause of popular rights. They defined the primary duty of soldiers as the defense of the people's rights against their oppressors. The movement's leaders declared:

> Soldiers should always be aware of public opinion. Who are the internal enemies? Since a country's policy should be guided by public opinion, those who threaten and interfere with public opinion are the internal enemies. . . . If the government interferes

175

with public opinion, it should be denounced as an enemy. Soldiers must understand this.[21]

The popular rightists not only published these appeals to soldiers but organized public meetings for men eligible for conscription.[22] They also advocated vigorously the creation of a revolutionary army in the true spirit of the *levée en masse*. One of the immediate purposes of the *Imperial Precepts* was to isolate the soldiers from these agitators. In opposition to the ideology of engagement, the *Precepts* sternly prescribed an ideology of detachment. This counsel in favor of detachment from politics failed to prevent the military magnates from dictating the political course of the nation up until Japan's defeat in World War II. But it did succeed in establishing a taboo among the rank-and-file soldiers against the discussion of politics or war and, in effect, said: Shut your mouth and die quietly. This strong taboo against political discussion in the army accounts in part for the absence of criticism of the war policy by soldiers and, indeed, by the entire male population who had received military training. They could not even think of any criticism.

Second, the official presentation in the *Precepts* of the relationship between the Emperor and the army as one organism of which the Emperor is the head and the soldiers are the limbs embodies the organismic concept of the state. Just as in the *Imperial Rescript on Education*, the organismic analogy was used in the *Precepts* to make identification of the soldiers with the father-image of the Emperor effective.

Third, loyalty to the Emperor was justified on the basis of traditional familism, as in the *Imperial Rescript on Education* examined earlier. Yet the Emperor-soldier relationship was, according to the *Precepts*, more "intimate" than the Emperor-civilian relationship. Soldiers were told that they were the Emperor's favorite sons. They were, then, even more deeply burdened with the Emperor's *on* than civilians and, consequently, were more heavily obliged to repay his *on* by demonstrating greater willingness to die for him than civilians.

There was another aspect of familism applied to the army. The treatment of new conscripts as "children" in the "family" of soldiers in the barracks was an important socializing device to make the ideology of death acceptable. Tomkins points out:

Earlier affective response can be readily activated if another adult fails to treat us as an adult. So long as we are treated like adults, we act and feel like adults, but many adults can be made to feel like ashamed children by an overly authoritarian police officer who speaks to them as they might have been spoken to by their parents when they transgressed. It is always possible to activate earlier feelings by acting toward the adult as though one were his parent and he was the child.[23]

Even adults who in their civilian capacities were expected to act as independent and rational persons, such as university students or heads of families, had their childhood roles of dependence and obedience activated under the treatment accorded them as army recruits. The absence of privacy and the subjection to humiliation, terror, and anxiety also helped to evoke childhood roles of dependence and obedience. Since the new recruits were treated as "children," they began to act like children and became more submissive to the ideology of death than they would have been if they had been allowed to sustain their adult roles.

Fourth, soldiers were provided with positive incentives for death, in the form of prestige. They were told that they would become gods of the fatherland and would be worshiped in the Yasukuni Shrine in Kudan, Tokyo. It is a folk belief that any dead member of a family becomes a god and protects the surviving members of the family.[24] To be made a Yasukuni god is a special honor bestowed only on national heroes. Whereas a family god protects just his own family, a Yasukuni god protects the entire fatherland. This mark of distinction ennobles not only the individual soldier but his whole family, since his family name is listed among the gods. According to the Confucian doctrine as expressed in *Hsiao-Chin*, the achievement of fame for one's family name is the ultimate stage of filial piety. Thus, in the act of dying for the sake of the Emperor, the unity of loyalty and filial piety was held to be fully realized. In contrast, to fail to die like a soldier and to allow oneself to captured by the enemy was to disgrace not only oneself but one's family and village community. This was the meaning of the passage "Never . . . fall into disgrace and bring dishonor upon your name."

How was this incentive to die according to the ideal pattern understood by the soldiers in interpreting their own motivation? A student-soldier noted in his diary while at the front:

> Soldiers believe with extreme naiveté that they are heroes in the defense of their country. They are proud to be the saviors of their fatherland. That is an easy sentimentalism. But that is the anchorage of their emotion. It is a kind of soldiers' mental masturbation for which they are willing to waste their youthful energy.... This is sad. They do not possess enough reason to be critical of their own state of mind. Moreover, *should they deny this belief, they would have nothing left to sustain them in their hardships.*[25]

To accept the nonrational belief that they would become a national god was actually, then, a defense mechanism for many soldiers. Without it they would have been unable to face the brutal fact that they were wasting their lives in a war over which they had no control.

In summary, prewar Japanese army socialization used imperfect communication as its method and was mainly negative in affect socialization. Its ideological content was predominantly nonrational, particularistic, dependently collective hierarchical, and detached.

1. Hiroshi Noma, *Shinkū Chitai*, Tokyo, Kawade Shobō, 1952. The English version is entitled *Zone of Emptiness*, tr. Bernard Frechtman, Cleveland, World, 1956. This quotation is translated by the author from *Gendai Bungaku Zenshū* (*Collected Works of Contemporary Literature*), Tokyo, Chikuma Shobō, 1958, LXXXII, 217.

2. Erik H. Erikson, *Young Man Luther*, New York, W. W. Norton, 1958, p. 135.

3. Kōji Iizuka, *Nihon no Guntai* (*The Japanese Army*), Tokyo, Tōdai Kyōdō-kumiai Shuppanbu, 1950, pp. 24–25. This work includes a series of symposia in which two former company commanders in the army related their World War II experiences. A vivid description of army language is found in Masaharu Fuji, *Teikoku Guntai ni okera Gakushū Jo* (*A Preface to Learning in the Imperial Army*), Tokyo, Miraisha, 1964, pp. 180–182.

4. "A student in my squad said 'boku' [I] by mistake and was hit with a fist by his squad commander. Being hit, that tall man, to my surprise, sank

and sat flat on the floor. It must have been very shocking to him." Wadat-sumi-kai, ed., *Senbotsu Gakusei no Isho ni Miru Jūgonensensō* (*The Fifteen Years' War Seen Through the Messages of the Students Who Died in the War*), Tokyo, Kōbun-sha, 1963, p. 210. This book consists of the letters and diaries of forty-seven student-soldiers.

5. Iizuka, *Nihon no Guntai*, p. 25.

6. *Ibid.*, p. 105.

7. *Ibid.*, p. 165.

8. *The Fifteen Years' War*, p. 74.

9. Iizuka, *Nihon no Guntai*, p. 165.

10. Nihon Senbotsu Gakusei Shuki Henshū Inkai (The Committee for the Compilation of the Letters of the Student-Soldiers Who Died in the War), ed., *Kike Wadatsumi no Koe* (*Listen, the Voice of the Sea*), Tokyo, Tokyo Daigaku Shuppankai, 1952. This book consists of letters by seventy-nine student-soldiers who died in the war.

11. *Ibid.*, pp. 177–178.

12. *Ibid.*, p. 184.

13. In his *Zone of Emptiness* Noma relates a story of a soldier who was demoted from superior private to first-class private because of a false charge against him. He was also imprisoned for two years. This soldier used to work in the accountant's office and knew that his superiors, noncommissioned officers, appropriated army money, food, and other goods for their private use. In order to cover up their illegal practices, the officers saw to it that the soldier was sent to prison, and that, when he got out, he was put on the list of soldiers to be sent to the front. In this novel, based on the author's own experiences, Noma tries to describe corruption within the army, personal animosities and hatreds arising from rivalry among officers for power and promotion.

14. *Listen, the Voice of the Sea*, pp. 55–61; Iizuka, *Nihon no Guntai*, p. 113.

15. Those who had finished higher education were allowed to take quali-fying examinations at the beginning of their first year as new conscripts. Those who had received secondary education were allowed to take such examinations at the end of their six-months' basic training. See *The Fifteen Years' War*, pp. 135n, 141n.

16. *Listen, the Voice of the Sea*, pp. 53–54.

17. Peirce defined the meaning of a symbol as follows: "The entire intel-lectual purport of any symbol consists in the total of all general modes of rational conduct which, conditionally upon all the possible different circum-stances and desires, would ensue upon the acceptance of the symbol." *Philo-sophical Writings of Peirce*, ed. Justus Buchler, New York, Dover, 1955, p. 290.

18. Yanagida, "Kokugo no Shōrai" ("The Future of the National Language"), *Yanagida Kunio Shū*, 1963, XIX, 31.

19. *Ibid.*, pp. 31–34.

20. De Bary, *Sources of Japanese Tradition*, II, 198–200; Tiedemann, *Modern Japan*, pp. 107–112.

21. Ienaga et al., eds., *Jiyūminken Shisō*, p. 104.

22. *Ibid.*, pp. 105, 176–177.

23. Tomkins, *Affect, Imagery, Consciousness*, Vol. II: *The Negative Affects*, New York, Springer, 1963.

24. Yanagida, "Tamashii no Yukue" ("Where the Spirit Goes"), *Yanagida Kunio Shū*, 1963, xv, 561.

25. *The Fifteen Years' War*, p. 139.

VICTOR N. KOBAYASHI

JAPAN: UNDER AMERICAN
OCCUPATION

Curriculum reform was only one component of a broader program to reconstruct the entire educational system of Japan during the Allied Occupation (September 2, 1945, to April 28, 1952). Moreover, educational reform was just one part of a grand blueprint to redirect the nation. The study of the Occupation therefore gives one an almost unique opportunity to see the interaction between curricular reform attempts and other major efforts that aimed at the same target, for the objectives of the curriculum reformers were broad, but clear, and identical to the entire Occupation's general aims of the demilitarization and democratization of Japan.[1]

As an observer of the Occupation has pointed out, the Occupation was not an ordinary military project merely limited to disarmament and reparations; it was a "saturation-type operation" intended to affect all aspects of Japanese culture, with consequences that would survive the eventual signing of a peace treaty.[2] Japan had threatened

Victor N. Kobayashi is Professor of Comparative Education at the University of Hawaii.
Reprinted from R. Murray Thomas, et al (eds), *Strategies for Curriculum Change: Cases from 13 Nations* (Scranton: International Textbook Co., 1968), pp. 93–115, with permission of the author and publisher.

other nations with her military might in a disastrous war; her militaristic tendencies were viewed as an expression of her authoritarian tradition. The Allies hoped that Japan would be transformed into not only a peace-loving nation, but also into a democratic state, for it was believed that a democratized Japan would contribute to international order. Thus the Occupation became one of the most enormous experiments in "social engineering" ever conducted in any nation.

A listing of some of the Occupation's activities would communicate the magnitude of the operation to demilitarize and democratize Japan. A new constitution was written, which in many respects was more liberal than the American Constitution. Article 23 simply read, "Academic freedom is guaranteed." Women were given the franchise, and were to have other rights equal to that of men. The Constitution drastically altered the position of the Emperor and created a new governmental system that was intended to be more responsive to the populace. War was renounced as an instrument of national policy and the creation of military forces was forbidden in the now controversial Article Nine.[3]

The Occupation also attempted to dissolve the monopolistic industrial combines—the *zaibatsu*. Strong labor unions were established to give workers a more powerful voice. An extensive land reform program involving thirty million land transfers was undertaken to minimize absentee landlordism and to provide farmers with a greater degree of autonomy.[4] The legal and judicial structure was transformed. Radio, movies, newspapers, books, were subject to censorship; the Occupation even paid attention to such details as assigning men to the Kabuki theatre so that plays that seemed to express militaristic and anti-democratic sentiments could be suppressed.[5] These were only some of the activities of the Occupation that penetrated the political, economic, social, and artistic sectors of Japanese life.

In the area of formal education, compulsory education was extended from six to nine years. An American style 6-3-3-4 school ladder was created, with six years of elementary schooling and three years of lower secondary schooling for everyone. A comprehensive three-year upper secondary school was created (as contrasted to the prewar differentiated type of upper schools) and university education was broadened to include a larger place for general education. Coeducation was promoted at all levels. Control of schools was decentralized, and elected local and prefectural boards of education were established.

Private schools and universities were given greater autonomy. Public-supported schools for the Imperial family and nobility were abolished. Provisions for public-supported facilities for handicapped children were extended. Teacher training was raised to university level. The growth of American style PTA's, teachers unions, and professional teachers organizations was fostered. Libraries that would be open to the people were encouraged. Attempts were made to simplify the Japanese written language, so that schooling for functional literacy could be facilitated. These were only some of the major efforts of the Occupation to democratize education in Japan.

A feature of the Occupation important in understanding its operation concerns the parties involved. Although it was an "Allied Occupation," it almost exclusively involved Americans and Japanese. Unlike the case of Germany, other Allies played a minor, peripheral role in planning and execution of the Occupation. The psychological state of the participants is another consideration. If disillusionment with previous ideals are preconditions for the formation of new commitments, then the Japanese, at least early in the Occupation, were open to change. They had suffered a disastrous defeat and were about to endure the first occupation by foreign troops in their long history. Many of their myths of race, nation, and destiny that had been built over the years were suddenly undermined. The state of shock appeared to make them accept, and even actively to participate in the Occupation.

Perhaps it was also the submissiveness of the Japanese that surprised the Americans. They had expected the worst, for the wartime propaganda had created in their minds a conception of Japanese personality that was hostile, militaristic, and rigid. The pleasant surprise of confronting cooperative and amicable people when they set foot on the islands may have contributed to making the Occupation one of the friendliest encounters between former enemies in the history of military occupations.[6]

Another important ingredient in any general assessment of the Occupation lies in the unique and controversial figure of General Douglas MacArthur, who, as Supreme Commander for the Allied Powers (SCAP), carried the entire weight of the responsibility for the Occupation. Holding this position for most of the duration of the Occupation,[7] he wielded almost absolute authority over Japan.[8]

His mandate became clear to the Japanese when the Emperor paid a visit to him on September 27, 1945, at the American Embassy in

Tokyo,[9] an unprecedented event, for never in Japan's history had an Emperor called upon a foreign diplomat at his office. The image of the Emperor, in formal dress, confronting the General, in casual summer uniform, with a hint of aloofness about him, remains in the minds of the Japanese as a symbol of a new era in their hectic modern history.

Educational Reform and
Strategies for Curriculum Change

The Administrative Strategy

The actual conduct of the Occupation at the local level was the responsibility of the Eighth Army, with headquarters in Yokohama, and directly responsible to MacArthur. It maintained Civil Affairs Teams,[10] which, among other duties, assisted and guided the Japanese in local areas in carrying out educational policies.

Separate from these teams, and working through a different channel of command, was the Civil Information and Education Section (CI & E) with an Education division which had the main responsibility for assisting in the formulation of national educational policies. The CI & E was one of several staff sections under General Headquarters, SCAP, in Tokyo. Officers in the Education Division had no direct access to the Civil Affairs Team education officers who worked at the local level; the Occupation drew a clear line between staff and field personnel. Although it often worked, this mode of organization frequently proved inefficient, for it created barriers to communication between education officers in SCAP and in the Civil Affairs Teams.[11]

A basic feature of the Occupation was that the Americans worked through the medium of the existing Japanese governmental machinery. Although the structure of the government itself, including the educational administration, was hopefully to be transformed later in the interests of democratization, the Occupation, partly out of necessity, depended heavily upon the basic institutions that had been created in Japan since the Meiji Restoration of 1868.

The Education Division of CI & E, SCAP, was organized so that each major bureau of the Japanese Ministry of Education had its counterpart in the Education Division. The Chief of CI & E roughly corresponded to the Minister of Education, while for every major position in the Ministry, there was a comparable American position.[12] In this way, the existing Japanese bureaucracy was retained, with controls upon it exerted through a parallel U.S. administrative arrangement.

In general, Americans in the Education Division initiated reforms by communicating policy "suggestions" to their counterparts in the Japanese government, The Japanese would in turn react to them, perhaps seek modifications in the proposed policy before agreeing to it. Americans retained the power to veto such modifications, and even to intervene at any time. The actual execution of the policy would be left as much as possible in Japanese hands, assisted by the Eighth Army Civil Affairs Teams in the field. This general operational policy of working in the background, according to material produced by the CI & E, was based upon the assumption that

> The reform of Japanese society should be accomplished by the Japanese people themselves; that SCAP should not impose a blueprint and that the function of General Headquarters and the Army of the Occupation was not to govern Japan, but to supervise the efforts of the Japanese people to reform themselves and their society. This policy rests upon the belief that within the Japanese people an honest desire exists to build a democratic society capable of directing itself in reconstruction and reform to create a Japan worthy of a position of dignity in the community of nations.[13]

However, a few lines later, the document included a qualification that illustrated the paradox of democratization through compulsion.

> Delegation of responsibility to Japanese agencies does not, however, preclude direct action by the Supreme Commander.[14]

However, SCAP initiated only a relatively few directives, and they came in the early months of the Occupation. These directives dealt with the negative goal of demilitarization, mostly with the elimination of militaristic educational materials, the screening of teachers, and the suspension of morals courses.[15] As the Occupation progressed, the reforms, at least officially, came from the Japanese government. The CI & E primarily worked in the background, advising, often in great detail.[16] Whether the Japanese viewed these "suggestions" at face value remains an open question but it was obvious that they were cooperative.[17] It should be kept in mind, also, that to some Japanese, full cooperation may have meant a prompt termination of the Occupation. But, then, too, many of the Japanese seemed genuinely interested in creating a democratic Japan.

Policies were spelled out in the form of national laws enacted by the Diet and various kinds of orders that emanated from the Ministry of Education. The most important of these were the Fundamental Law of Education (1947) and the School Education Law (1947).

An important device for the initiation of education policy was the use of professional consultants from the U.S. who were invited to make suggestions for specific reforms. A total of nine major educational missions visited Japan; there was one on medical education, for example, and another on engineering education. The most important was the First U. S. Education Mission, composed of twenty-seven eminent U. S. educators. Headed by George D. Stoddard, Commissioner of Education of New York State, and president-elect of the University of Illinois, the group of twenty-seven deliberately consisted of representatives of all important categories of American educational life: elementary education, secondary education, higher education, educational psychology, comparative education, philosophy of education, the National Education Association, Negro education, National Catholic Welfare Council, labor, and women's education.[18]

The Mission arrived in Tokyo in early March, 1946, and undertook a heavy schedule of visits, briefings, and conferences with both American and Japanese groups. A Japanese Education Committee, composed of Japanese educators who had been active in prewar liberal movements was created to work with the Mission in drawing up recommendations.[19] In less than a month after arrival in Tokyo, the Mission produced a report that touched upon nearly every phase of Japanese education.[20] One of the clearest and most concise expressions of what American educators of the period meant by "democratic education," it included statements on aims, school administration, curriculum, teacher education, adult education, and higher education. Although the Report of the United States Education Mission was in the form of recommendations, it was in general accepted and followed by American and Japanese educational workers. The Report, in retrospect, may be viewed as the prime source of SCAP's educational policies.[21]

In working through the existing Japanese Ministry of Education, the Americans were in one sense fortunate, for they had inherited a capable and dedicated bureaucratic machinery. The Ministry's efficiency had been demonstrated by its prewar success in building the first modern educational system in Asia. It had taken the initiative of instituting programs that met Occupation objectives even before the establishment of CI&E. It had, for example, begun a school textbook censorship program in which pictures and passages considered militaristic or ultranationalistic were deleted. The Ministry also had closed military academies and dispersed the students into civilian schools so that not more than ten percent of them would make up any school enrollment. When Japanese officials were later asked why they had performed such actions, they were reported to have smiled and answered, "Haven't you read the Potsdam Declaration?"[22] The ministry channels were also efficient: orders to lower levels of the educational bureaucracy reached Japanese officials long before Civil Affairs Team officers received the equivalent instructions from SCAP Headquarters.[23] It was not unusual for the Japanese in the field to know what had been decided at the National level before their American counterparts.

But the strength of the Ministry tended to make the Americans perhaps overly dependent upon its bureaucratic machinery. Eventually the Occupation attempted to emasculate the Ministry of control over the educational system for it was felt that one of the weaknesses of democratic education in Japan was the powerful hold of the Ministry upon school policies. The Ministry was clearly against the decentralization of the educational system, and came into conflict with the Occupation's aim to make elected local and prefectural school boards the main loci of policy making.[24] However, one of the first reforms to be modified significantly after the Occupation was the amendment of the Board of Education Law of 1956, when boards of education were made appointive and some of the powers were returned to the Ministry of Education. In the long run, therefore, the Ministry's vitality may have undermined CI&E's efforts to democratize educational administration.[25]

An attempt was made to control the situation by placing men with liberal backgrounds in key positions in the Ministry. Well-known scholars and educators with prewar anti-militarist postures were installed as ministers and vice-ministers of education, replacing the politicians and professional bureaucrats who traditionally had held these posts. But the Americans did not seem to appreciate the unwillingness of the Japanese intellectual to participate directly in governing. More so than their American counterparts, Japanese intellectuals felt uncomfortable in the bureaucracy, and did not remain in their posts too long. The position of Minister of Education, for example, was taken by a new person at least once a year. By the end of the Occupation, control of the Ministry returned to the politicians and professional bureaucrats. The last educator to be Education Minister was Amano, who was replaced by Okano. Because Amano's surname was written with the Chinese ideograph meaning "heaven," and because his successor wrote his with a character meaning "hill," the Japanese often referred to this transition as one of descent from "heaven to earth." The idealistic, rarified conception of education by intellectuals was replaced by the earthy, practical, realistic perspectives of professional bureaucrats and politicians.

Placing persons with liberal backgrounds in key bureaucratic positions was only one aspect of the policy to facilitate educational changes by altering the "mix" of educational personnel. The Occupation undertook an immense program of purging and screening teachers and education officials. On October 30, 1945, SCAP issued a directive to the Japanese government to remove immediately "All persons who are known to be militaristic, ultranationalistic, or antagonistic to the objectives and policies of the Occupation and who are at this time actively employed in the educational system of Japan. . . . "[26] The purge involved a half million educators. About twenty-two percent of them were affected as a result of the screening program. Between August 1945 and April 1947, persons who left the educational system totaled 119,768.[27] Most resigned rather than undergo official screening.

The attempts to create a new corps of educational personnel that would aid in the democratization of education were not limited to removing those deemed inappropriate. The Occupation instituted programs to reeducate teachers and school administrators. Many short term institutes were held to acquaint educators with new school curricula and teaching methods. The Institute for Engineering Education, for example, held twelve programs with 1300 teachers of engineering participating. But one of the best known programs was the Institute for Educational Leadership which held workshops and study sessions for teachers, administrators, and professors of education. Between 1948 and 1952, over nine thousand educators participated.[28] American specialists in such fields as curriculum, audio-visual education, vocational education, educational psychology, guidance, and library science, were brought by SCAP to act as consultants in courses that lasted from three days to several months. Participants were transported by SCAP and the Ministry of Education to the institutes, often held in major university centers, and the process of living together seemed to help make the study sessions effective. A highlight of many of the workshops was the organization of professional societies that would continue to encourage educationists to promote the study of special fields in education. Several of these societies continue to exist and to publish journals although some have become inactive. Graduates of the Institute were placed in influential positions in teacher education as well as in school administration and supervision.[29]

Japanese educators were also sent to the United States to visit schools and universities, as part of the reeducation program. A total of 261 educational leaders representing diverse fields spent two- to three-month tours in the United States. Participants were nominated by members of Japanese professional associations. Returning participants later held leadership positions in education, and were encouraged to share their experiences with their colleagues through conferences, publications, radio and other media.[30]

At the local level, education officers in Civil Affairs Teams also were encouraged to establish, with the cooperation of the Japanese, various kinds of in-service training programs for educators.[31] In the Kyoto-Osaka area, for example, a Try-Out School Association was formed by school-masters to promote the sharing of the results of experiments in democratic schooling. Several of the schools used "progressive," "experience-centered" approaches to school curriculum. The association continued to exist after the Occupation.[32] In the Shikoku area, the civil education officer not only produced guides for democratic procedures for the general citizenry as part of his adult education program, but also helped to reorganize Parent-Teacher Associations so that they would operate more in line with democratic principles.[33]

Strategies for Democratizing the Curriculum[34]

The negative goal of the Occupation, demilitarization, was relatively simple to define in curricular terms. It merely meant the elimination of militaristic material from the curriculum and it was therefore accomplished rapidly. Some of the earliest actions of SCAP were the suspension of courses which were suspected of including much militaristic and ultranationalistic content.[35] The Ministry of Education had earlier, at its own initiative, removed military training from the school, and had abolished military academies. The Americans also eliminated *judo* because it was considered a militaristic sport. This activity was returned to the physical education curriculum after the Occupation, and American educators who visit schools today probably would consider it curious that *judo* would have been considered undesirable by the Occupation.

The second goal—that of democratization—was more complicated and difficult to define in terms of curricular reform, partly because of the way in which the Americans conceived of the curriculum. The Occupation personnel viewed the curriculum in the broadest sense of the word:

> It no longer merely indicates a list of school subjects for teaching subject matter and skills, but includes all of the activities of a school day.[36]

Furthermore, the curriculum was to be viewed as promoting in the pupils a set of dispositions more general in scope than intellectual skills.

> The success of a school is no longer measured in terms of aptness in skills and knowledge of facts, but also in terms of attitudes, social habits, and spiritual qualities.[37]

The curriculum was not to base itself primarily upon traditional subject matter or conventional disciplines of knowledge but was to focus upon the individual pupil as the starting point. As stated in the *Report of the First U. S. Education Mission to Japan,*

> A good curriculum cannot be designed merely to impart a body of knowledge for its own sake. It must start with the interests of the pupils, enlarging and enriching those interests through content whose meaning is intelligible to the pupils. As in the statement of aims, so in the construction of the curricula and courses of study: the pupil in a particular environment must be the starting point.[38]

Starting with the pupil's interests was believed not only to be in keeping with sound psychological principles of teaching, but also in

190

keeping with democratic principles since it viewed each pupil as a starting point. No particular group of children, no matter how talented, was to have priority in the educational system. All children were to be viewed as ends, and consequently the meaning that the pupil obtained from what he experienced in school was to be what ultimately mattered. Thus competition for excellence in mastering an artistic technique was to be de-emphasized (but not neglected). Art and music were to be taught primarily in terms of "means of expressing thoughts and emotions; developing worthwhile hobbies as a means of wholesome recreation."[39] Any individual, the Occupation seemed at times to be saying, can be taught to find meaning in any educational activity in a democratically honest way.

A related emphasis was upon problem-solving as a mode of curriculum organization. A corollary approach was the emphasis upon interdisciplinary integrated courses, that focused upon problems, rather than upon specialized disciplines. General mathematics, social studies, general science, became the rule in the curriculum of the compulsory schools. SCAP report declared, for example, that

> The new General Science cannot be considered merely [sic] an amalgamation of specialized biology, physics, and chemistry subjects formerly taught at this level [grades 6 through 9]. The new courses have been built from the ground up, and are based upon defined pupil needs, more or less without reference to the former subject matter.
> The problem-unit method of organization is in almost universal use all over the nation. There is emphasis upon the problem-solving method of study and investigation and upon the utilization of science in improvement of everyday living.[40]

Another emphasis was upon cooperation and participation in the society. Democracy, to the curriculum reformers, meant full involvement of the individual in a society and his participation in the determination of social policy. Translated into curricular terms, this meant emphasis upon cooperative projects, upon the development of skills that helped individuals communicate with each other, and upon pupil-teacher planning of the curricular units. Thus, for example, the teaching of the national language would deemphasize calligraphy which was considered a "frill." Instead, efforts would be made to "develop those reading, speaking, listening, and writing skills which are essential to effective participation in social life."[41] There would be greater emphasis upon the teaching of the "social use of arithmetic."[42] The usual lecture approaches were to be replaced by greater dependence upon discussion methods, where the interaction of pupils with each other was maximized.

Thus, all school activities, all classes, all subjects, all student government activities were viewed as part of the curriculum that was subject to democratization. Coeducation was viewed as related to curricular concerns. The Occupation looked at each school activity and considered ways in which it, too, could be a medium through which democratic values could be fostered. The creation of student-body government, complete with elections, was encouraged to promote practices in applying democratic principles.

SCAP educational reformers took most of their cues as to what constituted a "democratic curriculum" from the literature of the progressive education movement in America in the twenties and thirties, and the Japanese specialists recognized this fact.[43] Common expressions heard during the Occupation were "child-centered curriculum," "project methods," and the "experience curriculum." A SCAP report on the progress of educational reforms criticized the elementary science curriculum in Japan in the following way; the statement also illustrates how much of what was introduced into Japan was the American version of "progressive education."

> Weaknesses still persist: too little pupil purposing, too little developing of concepts from experiences, and too much emphasis upon the need for a science room patterned after a science laboratory at the upper secondary or university level.[44]

"Social studies" was one of the important features of the new curriculum because it was not only to epitomize the democratic approach to teaching techniques, but also to foster in children an awareness of social problems that would make them responsible citizens in a democracy. Introduced in 1947, the social studies replaced the former courses of geography, history, civics, and ethics, which had been taught as separate subjects. It was to integrate various material around several topics, beginning with life at home and in the school and neighborhood at the first grade level and progressing and expanding into problems of society, life in an industrialized society, and the world community.[45] Principles of democracy would be explicitly and directly studied and celebrated in the social-studies classroom. Social studies was to be a required part and the "core" of the compulsory school programs (grades one through nine).

Because of this heavy emphasis upon the potential of every part of the curriculum to promote democratic values in pupils, and because democratic techniques were viewed as the key to the democratization of the curriculum, much of the teacher re-education and in-service training programs was devoted to the study of teaching methods.[46] As part of the workshop or conference activities, teachers often visited classrooms which were considered outstanding in the implementation of the new teaching approaches. In these sessions, Japanese educators learned a new vocabulary which reflected the influence of American educationist ideas. A handbook, the *Dictionary of the New Education*, published by the Japanese Ministry of Education in 1949, was an attempt to assist educators to understand Japanized versions of words like the "Winnetka Plan," "guidance," "panel discussion," "activity curriculum," "cumulative record," "sociogram," "group interview," "core curriculum," "scope and sequence," and "practical arts."[47]

The radio was also used to offer in-service teacher programs, beginning in 1947. Produced by the Ministry of Education with the aid of CI&E personnel, the programs placed great emphasis upon the new approaches to teaching and curriculum development.[48]

Another important aspect of the strategy to democratize the curriculum involved the creation of new curricular aids and materials. Guidebooks were published that emphasized democratic teaching techniques. New textbooks were compiled that would support the curriculum changes. On October 30, 1948, the first volume of the *Primer of Democracy* was published. Written jointly by Japanese scholars in such fields as economies, history, and political science, with the assistance of CI&E personnel, the book was an attempt to show that democracy was more than a method of formal government; it was also a way of life. It traced the development of democratic institutions in the West, and showed how democracy might help the Japanese to prevent themselves from being tricked by despots as they had been in World War II. A second volume, published on August 26, 1949, traced the history of democracy in Japan, pointed out the bases for many of the Occupation reforms, discussed the implications of democracy in the international context, and ended with a chapter on "The

Promise of Democracy." The final line of the chapter affirmed the faith in democracy.

> Where there is a will, there is a way. Let us seek the path by the will of all the people, cultivate the path with the strength of all the people, and build up the security, happiness and prosperity of all the people which is the promise of democracy.[49]

The Occupation policy of working through Japanese channels was also applied in the writing of the new textbooks and their related teachers' guides. Here again, the relationship between the Americans and the Japanese authors was a delicate one. There was the fact that Americans approved the members appointed to work on textbook committees and established some guidelines for the texts, *e.g.*, books would not support ultranationalism or the Shinto doctrine of absolute loyalty to the Emperor and state. Nevertheless, there was a surprising degree of freedom allowed the writers. Japanese history was entirely rewritten, so that traditional mythology would be treated as such and ultranationalism and militarism viewed with a cold eye.[50]

In addition to materials prepared by the Ministry of Education and professors in teacher-training institutions and universities with the help of Americans, professional books, textbooks, and other curricular materials were obtained from the United States and placed in various SCAP information centers, textbook and curriculum centers, and libraries throughout Japan so that they would be accessible to educators. Some of the materials were translated into Japanese and published,[51] although there were problems of gaining permission from copyright holders. By the end of the Occupation, twenty Textbook and Curriculum Centers were in operation in the major cities of Japan. Most of these Centers were attached to colleges of education. An average of six thousand persons visited the twenty Centers each month, according to SCAP statistics.[52]

The Course of Reforms

From the outset, SCAP had to meet the immediate problem of the economic reconstruction of Japan. The country was in ruin and was threatened by the possibility of a severe food shortage when the war

194

came to an end. But even as conditions improved as the Occupation progressed, economic concerns continued to dominate policies not only in the political realm but also in education. Although economic well-being may be a necessary condition for a healthy democracy to thrive, the emphasis upon economic development tended to place priority upon education for social efficiency, rather than upon education for the development of democratic attitudes in the people.[53]

American educators had been vigorous in their zeal to promote democracy in Japan in the early years of the Occupation, but as time progressed, their enthusiasm tended to be dampened. Their efforts, at times, seemed to produce restlessness among the youth, rather than a healthy commitment to the society. The removal of ultranationalists and militarists from public positions tended to encourage those with leftist leanings to resume open agitation that had been suppressed by the authorities during the war.

Although student dissatisfaction with adult institutions might be interpreted by some as a healthy sign of democracy taking root in Japan, it was perceived in many quarters as undermining the social solidarity required to hasten economic recovery and to build a democratic state. The Japan Communist Party re-emerged in Japanese political life, and the activities of student organizations, particularly the *Zengakuren*, formed in 1948, and the Japan Teachers Union, which the Occupation had helped to establish in 1947, began to worry both Occupation and Japanese government officials. They had hoped, for one thing, that education and politics would be kept separate.[54] Strikes and demonstrations by leftist groups embarrassingly led Occupation authorities to rethink their policies, and moved some to understand and sympathize with the thinking of their more conservative colleagues in the Ministry of Education. Then, too, many of the early Americans who had worked earnestly in trying to implant democratic ideals in education had begun to return to their homes in the U. S., leaving the job of maintaining the Occupation in the hands of professional administrators, who were not as optimistic about the possibility of rapid democratization of Japanese life.

By 1948, Americans working with Japanese educators were cautioned about the need to combat communism, the need to foster a healthy nationalism in Japan, and the need to promote political and economic stability.[55] Dr. Walter Crosby Eells of CI&E devoted much of his effort to attacking the Communist movement that seemed to be dominating the campus life of many universities and subverting the building of democratic institutions.

The increasing hostility between Russia and America led SCAP personnel to work more closely with Japan as an ally, rather than as a former enemy. With the success of the communist takeover of mainland China in 1949, and the onset of the Korean War the next year, American interest in Asia tended to concentrate less upon Japan. Efforts in Japan focused upon assisting her into becoming a strong ally in the Cold War. By the time the Peace Treaty was signed in San Francisco in 1951, Japan was well on the road to becoming an economically rehabilitated nation. In the meantime, however, American efforts in democratizing teaching techniques, although still present, had declined considerably, and the responsibility for the reconstruction of the school curriculum was left almost completely in the hands of the Japanese, many of whom were still bewildered about how to go about handling an "experience curriculum" or were still doubtful as to the educational merits of the innovations.

However, on August 27, 1950, the Second United States Education Mission to Japan, composed of five members who had been on the first Mission, arrived in Tokyo to spend a month in studying the progress in educational reforms in terms of the recommendations the First Mission had made in 1946. They were impressed. Their short report, which was submitted to General MacArthur by Chairman Willard E. Givens, stated that significant democratic progress had been achieved in Japan in the past five years. It also emphasized that there was need to review the curriculum constantly and that a democratic educational system was necessarily dynamic.

> Many things remain to be done that will insure the real substance of a democratic educational program. There will never be a time when the people and educators of Japan can sit down and say that the task is finished. It should be stressed that a democratic educational system continually reviews research, evaluates experience, improves techniques, and modifies procedures. This keeps the structure and the curriculum dynamic and geared to the present rather than merely a reflection of the past.[56]

Since the termination of the Occupation, many significant modifications have indeed been made in the curriculum as well as in other aspects of the educational system. Although some of these changes may be viewed as a necessary trend in Japanizing the basically American character of the Occupation reforms, it is questionable whether these changes have been in keeping with the ideals of democratic education, as defined by the Occupation. Americans had assumed that democracy had principles which were grounded in humanitarianism, and which therefore transcended national cultural biases. The bases for these assumptions were in such documents as the Charter of the United Nations and in the draft constitution of the United Nations Educational, Scientific, and Cultural Organization. The First United States Education Mission to Japan assumed also that democratic elements existed in every human community, and that these took different forms, and Japanese life, also, had democratic tendencies.[57]

Yet many of the reforms were modeled after American precedents.

The Strategies: Success or Failure?[58]

If one considers the massive resources that were expended to change a nation's schools during the Occupation, the results observed in the Japanese educational institutions of today might seem meager, in comparison to the effort. Along with some other Occupation reforms, such as the decentralization of control or the comprehensive senior high school, curricular changes have met the same fate of being "reversed" by the Japanese.[59] The separate course in ethics has been re-instated. The concept of the social studies envisioned by CI&E only lingers in the classrooms, where "subject-matter" approachers dominate. Teaching methods have become more "teacher-centered," "essentialistic," except for the lower grades of the elementary school. A new nationalistic emphasis has appeared in the social studies and ethics curriculum.

Some of these changes were portended in the latter part of the Occupation; the development of a course in moral education is a case in point. A special note was made concerning moral and spiritual education in the 1950 report of the Second U. S. Education Mission. The Mission noted that many Japanese had expressed to the members that the new education had failed to provide Japan with the "moral and spiritual stamina which is essential to its all-around development."[60] Japanese were concerned about the post-war attitudes of youth towards the values and institutions of Japan. The Mission, however, basically reaffirmed the policies and principles of the SCAP educational reforms.

It pointed out again that the building of moral values was an important function of schools, but that all parts of the curriculum should take responsibility for cultivating these values. Moral education, it claimed, could not take place effectively through direct instruction in morals. Furthmore, it was "indeed vain to think that moral education can come from the social studies alone."[61] The Mission also emphasized that the cultivation of morality in youth could not be separated from the influences of other agencies in society like the home or religious institutions. Here, the group had made the same assumption as did the First Mission which nearly five years earlier had said that "If Japan goes democratic in fact, democratic ethics will get taught."[62] The Second Mission had had the opportunity to re-investigate the problem of moral education which clearly was of great concern to the Japanese but left the matter to them. The Americans seemed to feel that the basic work of the Occupation was completed; it remained for the Japanese to take full responsibility for their educational system.

A concern for the clarification of moral education continued to plague the minds of Japanese educators. As early as 1951, the Ministry of Education published several teacher's manuals on moral education. There were rumors that the government planned a return to the practice of a special course in morals in the curriculum. In fall of the same year, the Minister of Education, Teiyu Amano, leaked to the press a draft outline of ethical practice for the Japanese, which he planned to publish and distribute to schools as a guide for teachers to use within the existing curriculum. The draft received such hostile reactions that the Minister withdrew plans for its publication. Although the outline affirmed democratic principles, there was strong emphasis upon the Emperor as a symbol of the state and as the focus of morality and patriotism.[63] Many critics viewed the outline as a replacement for the Imperial Rescript on Education which had been the ideological basis of the ultranationalistic morals textbooks used in the thirties and early forties. The Rescript had been rescinded by the Occupation.

Thus there were signs of modifications of the Occupation's moral education curriculum policies before the termination of the Occupation on April 28, 1958, the Ministry of Education was able to include in its revised course of study for the compulsory schools an optional, weekly, one-hour class in moral education. Prefectures and local school units were given the option to choose whether or not to include it in the curriculum of the six-year elementary school and the three-year lower secondary school. Despite criticisms from many quarters, this plan became mandatory in 1962. The one-hour course became required of all compulsory schools. The outline of the course provided by the Ministry was general, and left a great degree of freedom for the teacher's own imagination. However, the Ministry soon published a guide for teachers for use in the course beginning in the 1964 academic year. The manual included essays, articles, and stories that emphasized various moral qualities, including patriotism. Although it was described as a guide as a collection of suggestions, many intellectuals and leftists, and especially the Japan Teachers Union viewed the events with alarm, and criticized the move of the Ministry as another step backwards into Japan's ultra-right past when morals was a course that aimed to indoctrinate youth into chauvinistic and authoritarian values.[64]

Most Japanese, however, did not share the fear, and on the contrary appeared to feel that Japanese youth needed greater aid from the schools in developing stronger characters. They also saw the need for the schools to aid in reversing the rising trend in juvenile delinquency and irresponsible action by youth. As late as 1965 and 1966, several Ministry reports on "The Ideal Japanese" appeared which added to the suspicion among liberals and left-wingers that educational policies were continuing to move further right.

The events leading to the re-instatement of a separate course in morals do demonstrate withdrawal from some of the basic curricular principles that were laid down during the Occupation. On the other hand, if one looks at the total society of Japan today, there are signs of significant transformations that show the acceptance of new democratic values and institutions.[65] The new Constitution, for example, remains in effect. The position of women has changed in an irreversible way, the outcome of which is still in process. Japan is the most prosperous nation in Asia, and the new wealth has raised the standard of living for most of her people. She has close and friendly relationships with the United States despite the bitter war. The emphasis on reconstruction, rather than upon punishment of a former enemy, and the general policy of working through the Japanese and letting them have as much freedom as possible in executing the details of the Occupation programs were important factors here. There has been a steady growth in the scientific study of society in Japan which should have an impact upon educational thought and practice. Up to the end of World War II, the study of history, sociology, and psychology was dominated by German philosophical and non-empirical approaches; under the influence of the Americans during the Occupation, the social sciences have blossomed in Japan. They have become more empirical, less ideological, and more varied in terms of approaches and subject matter. The development of new social scientists in Japan since the end of the war, with their interests in such problems as the relationship between schooling and socioeconomic class, may have important implications for educational policies as well as to the treatment of the study of society and history in the school curriculum.[66]

The determination of how these and other changes are related to specific curricular reforms conducted during the Occupation is a difficult knot to disentangle, but it can at least be said that the Occupation, taken as a whole, did foster important changes that are positively related to the democratization of society.

However, some of the Occupation's reforms did have effects that have undermined its curricular reforms. The policy of extending mass education to higher levels, of opening greater opportunities for youth to continue education, together with the new affluence have led to a phenomenal number of youths seeking admittance into noncompulsory higher schools. This pressure for entrance has in turn helped to make the curricular programs in schools more subject-matter oriented in order to meet the demands of the entrance examinations of the upper schools. The emphasis on cramming for examinations that had disturbed Americans during the Occupation years is one of the biggest headaches as far as present Japanese are concerned.

Another relevant point is that curriculum changes in Japan to this day have tended to follow, or at least be responsive to trends in the United States. Many of the ideas of curriculum advocated in Japan during the Occupation have gone out of style in the United States. The general disillusionment with the curricular approaches of "progressive education" that came to Americans after World War II has spread to Japan. Japanese educators today talk in terms of programmed learning and the "new math." Terms like "experience unit" or "core curriculum" have become passé. The steady stream of Japanese students into American graduate schools and of American books and journals into Japanese bookstores have helped to keep Japanese educators attuned to educational developments in the United States.

There are amazing similarities between the present curricula of Japan and the U.S.; furthermore, there are significant differences between the curricula of prewar Japan and that of today. Although there is legitimate concern among the younger Japanese liberals over the emphasis upon nationalism appearing in official statements concerning education, the new patriotism with its emphasis upon the Emperor as a symbol of the state is not as extreme nor of the same category as that found in the preware educational documents. In the controversial fall, 1966, final report on the "Image of an Ideal Japanese," to the Central Education Council, for example, love of country is emphasized along with respect for freedom of the individual, for the international community, and for the promotion of peace.[67]

One must bear in mind, too, that the Occupation believed in the creation of an independent Japan. The Occupation itself was based upon the premise that Japan would regain her national entity when the peace treaty was signed. There was hope that Japan would continue to develop a democracy in her own way, and retain a unique national identity. The First U.S. Education Mission itself did not intend that the schools destroy national loyalties in order to promote the broadest conception of democracy possible. "It is not that loyalty and patriotism are not desirable in every nation; it is a question of how to assure them at a reasonable price."[68] One must also bear in mind that the Occupation retained the Emperor, although it reduced his position to the symbolic head of state.

Furthermore, although cosmopolitanism is a worthy ideal, the actual world within which the Japanese educational system operates, rightly or wrongly, is based upon national units. There is no national school system today that does not attempt to foster patriotism of some sort, implicitly or explicitly. In a country like Japan, where youth tend to look outside of her borders to find models of behavior, the curriculum, in the view of most educators, necessarily must be more explicitly nationalistic.[69] When viewed in this way, it is significant that Japan is so open to communications with the West; it is also significant that she, more than any other country, has the largest mass program of teaching English as a foreign language.[70]

In the curriculum of Japan today, democracy is at least celebrated, although it may only occasionally be practiced; it had never been a value that was eulogized in the official textbooks and curricular materials before the Occupation. And if one were to accept the observations of such contemporary writers as Edgar Friedenberg, Paul Goodman, Jules Henry, John Holt, or Earl Kelley, American classrooms seldom manifest in behavioral terms ideals associated with democracy such as "freedom," "creativity," or "treating individuals as ends, never as means." The significance of the Occupation's impact on education in Japan may lie more in the fact that an ideal—that of democratic education—was implanted in Japanese *thinking* about curriculum than in the fact that the curriculum has returned to a more traditional form. There is healthy criticism of the educational system too in Japan.

The problem of what constitutes a curriculum appropriate to the high ideals of democracy and how to implement such a curriculum remains an elusive one today both in Japan and in America. In evaluating any effort to "democratize" the curriculum, one perhaps ought to be pleased with (but not content with) even modest successes.[71]

1. Two of the earliest documents that spell out the Occupation's aims were the Potsdam Declaration of July 26, 1945, proclaimed by U.S., U.K., and China, and the "United States Initial Post-Surrender Policy for Japan," a more detailed statement which was approved by the U.S. President on September 6, 1945, and transmitted to the commander of the Occupation. These and other relevant documents are included in Supreme Commander for Allied Powers (henceforth abbreviated SCAP), Government Section, *Political Reorientation of Japan, September 1945 to September 1948*. Washington, D.C.: U.S. Government Printing Office, 1949, pp. 411–441.

2. Robert E. Ward, "The Legacy of the Occupation," in Herbert Passin, ed., *The United State and Japan*. Englewood Cliffs, N.J.: Prentice-Hall, Inc., 1966, p. 35.

3. A convenient text of both the prewar and the 1946 Japanese constitutions is appended to Hugh Borton. *Japan's Modern Century*. New York: Ronald Press, 1955, pp. 490–507.

4. John D. Evre, "Post-Occupation Conditions in Rural Japan," *Annals of the American Academy of Political and Social Science, Japan Since Recovery of Independence*, Vol. 308 (November 1956), p. 114.

5. An interesting discussion of the Occupation and its approach to drama is found in Earle Ernst, *The Kabuki Theatre*. New York: Grove Press, 1956, pp. 258, *et. passim.*

6. The psychological state of either the Americans or the Japanese as a factor is frequently mentioned by authors who participated in the Occupation. See, for example: Robert King Hall, *Education for a New Japan*. New Haven, Conn.: Yale University Press, 1949, pp. 1–2. Edwin O. Reischauer, *The United States and*

Japan. New York: Viking Press, 1957, pp. 217–218. Borton, *op. cit.*, pp. 399–400. Ward, *op. cit.*, pp. 33–34. Kazuo Kawai, *Japan's American interlude.* Chicago: University of Chicago Press, 1960, pp. 4–6.

7. He was removed by President Harry S. Truman on April 11, 1951, and the last thirteen months of SCAP were served by General Matthew Ridgeway.

8. According to the statement approved by the U.S. President on Sept. 6, 1945, sent to General MacArthur, "The authority of the Emperor and the Japanese Government to rule the state is subordinate to you as Supreme Commander for the Allied Powers." See "Authority of General MacArthur as Supreme Commander for the Allied Powers," in SCAP, *Political Reorientation of Japan,* p. 427.

9. See "Emperor Recalls Meeting M'Arthur," *Japan Times,* August 26, 1965, p. 4.

10. These were at first called Military Government Teams; in 1948 they were renamed Civil Affairs Teams. In July 1949, the Eighth Army was relieved of responsibility and the teams were placed under the Civil Affairs Section of SCAP.

11. Frederick Nichols Kerlinger, "The Development of Democratic Control in Japanese Education: A Study of Attitude Change in Shikoku, 1948–1949," unpublished Ph.D. dissertation, University of Michigan, Ann Arbor, Mich., 1953, pp. 72–73.

12. This parallel of American and Japanese bureaucratic arrangements is beautifully diagrammed in James I. Doi, "Educational Reform in Occupied Japan: A Study of Acceptance of and Resistance to Institutional Change," unpublished Ph.D. dissertation, University of Chicago, Chicago, 1953, fig. 1, p. 51.

13. *Education in New Japan,* Vol. I. Tokyo: SCAP, 1948, p. 136.

14. *Ibid.*

15. SCAP directives to the Japanese on educational matters are reproduced in *ibid.,* Vol. II, pp. 26–57. The first to appear is dated October 22, 1945; the last, October 12, 1946.

16. See Doi, *op. cit.* Doi was a clerk in the CI & E. An American of Japanese descent, he was able to communicate with Japanese officials in their own language. Kerlinger in his dissertation, *op. cit.,* p. 67, points out a similar tradition of "indirect rule" where a power group operates behind the formal authorities. This tradition helped the Japanese to work effectively with the Americans.

17. Professor Tatsuo Morito, who was Minister of Education, June 1947 to October 1948, has pointed out that all reforms initiated by the Japanese had to be approved by SCAP. Lecture at International Christian University, Tokyo, July 28, 1962. Professor Daishiro Hidaka, who was Vice Minister of Education, March 1951 to August 1952, has said that most Japanese in the Ministry of Education during the Occupation tended to be obedient and submissive to CI & E, and accepted suggestions without question. Lecture at International Christian University, Tokyo, July 12, 1962.

18. See the discussion of this group in Robert King Hall, *Education for a New Japan, op. cit.,* pp. 76–77. The members are listed by the author, who as a

CI & E officer, conceived the idea of the Mission.

19. Later called the Japanese Education Reform Committee, the Occupation officials made it become an advisory and quasi-policy-making body throughout the Occupation. It operated at the cabinet level, and made recommendations directly to the Prime Minister.

20. *Report of the United States Education Mission to Japan, Submitted to the Supreme Commander for the Allied Powers, Tokyo, March 30, 1946.* Washington, D.C.: U.S. Government Printing Office, 1946. This edition includes statements by General MacArthur praising the work of the Mission.

21. The impact of the *Report* is clearly revealed in the Ministry of Education's *Progress of Education Reform in Japan.* Tokyo: Ministry of Education 1950. See especially Appendix 5, pp. 181–194, where a progress report is outlined in terms of each of the *Report's* recommendations.

22. Quoted in Doi, p. 60.

23. Paul S. Anderson, "The Reorientation Activities of the Civil Education Section of the Osaka Civil Affairs Team: A Case Study in Educational Change," unpublished Ph.D. dissertation, University of Wisconsin, Madison Wisconsin, 1954, p. 121. Frederick Kerlinger, who was a field officer on Shikoku island, notes the relative slowness of the American machinery as compared to that of the Japanese. See his dissertation, *op. cit.,* p. 76.

24. Mark T. Orr. "Education Reform Policy in Occupied Japan," unpublished Ph.D. dissertation, University of North Carolina, Chapel Hill, North Carolina, 1954, pp. 230–231.

25. It can be questioned, of course, (and it often has been by the Japanese themselves) as to whether a centralized system of education is necessarily less "democratic" than a decentralized one.

26. SCAP Directive AG 350, 30 Oct 45, CIE, in SCAP, *Education in the New Japan,* Vol. II, *op. cit.,* pp. 29–30.

27. SCAP, *Education in the New Japan,* Vol. I, pp. 157–158.

28. *Post-War Developments in Japanese Education.* Tokyo: SCAP, 1952, p. 389.

29. *Ibid.,* pp. 386–392; see also: Ministry of Education, *A Brief History of Institute for Educational Leadership in Japan.* Tokyo: The Ministry, 1953. Ronald S. Anderson, *Japan: Three Epochs of Modern Education.* Washington, D.C.: U.S. Dept. of Health, Education and Welfare, 1959, pp. 165–168.

30. SCAP, *Post-War Developments in Japanese Education,* pp. 382–383.

31. Headquarters, Eighth Army, "Operational Directive No. 19, Civil Education Program," February 29, 1947, as reproduced in Appendix IV of Kerlinger's dissertation, *op. cit.,* pp. 218–221.

32. This writer attended one of its meetings as late as July 23, 1962, in Kyoto. A history of the association is published in Japanese: Shitahodo Yukichi, ed., *Shin kyoiku ju-nen* [Ten *Years of the New Education*]. Nagoya, Japan: Reimei shobo, 1957. Ronald S. Anderson, who worked with the group during the Occupation, has written on the Association in his *Japan: Three Epochs, op. cit.,* pp. 160–161.

33. See, besides Kerlinger's dissertation, *op. cit.,* his articles, "Decision-Making in Japan," *Social Forces,* 30, No. 1 (October 1951), pp. 36–41; "Local

Associations in Shikoku," *Occasional Papers*, No. 2, University of Michigan Center for Japanese Studies, 1952, pp. 59–72. As Civil Education Officer in Shikoku, Kerlinger produced for the Japanese a *Techniques of Democracy: A Guide to Procedure for Japanese Organizations*. Takamatsu, Japan: Shikoku Military Government Region, 1948. This was published in Japanese as *Minshushugi no gijutsu*. Hiroshima, Japan: Hiroshima Tosho, 1949.

34. This discussion primarily refers to the curriculum in the first nine years of schooling. However it also generally applies to the Occupation's strategy in approaching the three-year non-compulsory upper secondary school curriculum, and also, although not as thoroughly, to the university curriculum. A detailed discussion and evaluation of the Occupation's influence on an aspect of the university curriculum may be found in the following. Tetsuya Kobayashi, *General Education for Scientists and Engineers in the United States of America and Japan*. University of Michigan Comparative Education Dissertation Series, No. 6. Ann Arbor, Michigan: School of Education, University of Michigan, 1965. The author points out that the Japanese had a specialist training approach to the education of scientists and engineers until the Occupation, when ideas about broadening the university curriculum to include "general education" were introduced.

35. SCAP Directive AG 000.8, 31 Dec 45, CIE, in SCAP, *Education in the New Japan*, Vol. II, op. cit., pp. 36–37.

36. SCAP, *Post-War Developments*, Vol. I, op. cit., p. 12.

37. *Ibid.*

38. *Report of the United States Education Mission*, p. 11.

39. SCAP, *Post-War Developments*, Vol. I, pp. 20–21.

40. *Ibid.*, pp. 18–19.

41. *Ibid.*, p. 19.

42. *Ibid.*, p. 14.

43. For a discussion of how the Japanese tended to interpret the Occupation's policies in curriculum as based not only on "progressive education," but also on the philosophy of John Dewey, see: Victor N. Kobayashi, *John Dewey in Japanese Educational Thought*. University of Michigan Comparative Education Dissertation Series, No. 2. Ann Arbor, Michigan: School of Education, 1964, pp. 112–136.

44. SCAP, *Post-War Developments in Japanese Education*, Vol. I, p. 13.

45. See Ministry of Education. *Progress of Education Reform in Japan*, pp. 17–18.

46. See, for example, the reports of conferences and workshops described in SCAP, *Post-War Developments in Japanese Education*, Vol. I, pp. 213–225.

47. Mombusho [Ministry of Education], *Shin kyoiku yogo jiten*. Tokyo: Mombusho, 1949.

48. SCAP, *Post-War Developments*, Vol. I, pp. 243–244.

49. *Primer of Democracy*, Vol. II, English translation, mimeographed, p. 58. Vol. I was also translated into English in a mineographed edition. Both volumes were available at the East-West Center Library, University of Hawaii, Honolulu. The Japanese volumes, published by the Ministry of Education, are entitled *Minshushugi* [Democracy]. Names of authors do not appear in the volumes.

50. See Herbert John Wunderlich, "The Japanese Textbook Problem and Solution, 1945–1946," unpublished Ed.D. dissertation, Stanford University, Standford, California, 1952. SCAP, *Education in the New Japan*, Vol. I, pp. 249–252. Ministry of Education, Hatsu kyo no. 118, "Instruction in Japanese History," November 9, 1946, in *ibid.*, Vol. II, pp. 178–180. The author is indebt also to John Caiger, graduate student at the Australian National University, for the opportunity to read his unpublished paper, "The First Post-War History Book in Japan—Japanese or American," where he shows that the first history textbook was, despite Occupation controls, basically a Japanese creation. For an indea of the kind of history taught in schools during World War II, see the English translation of an official Ministry of Education book, *Kokutai no Hongi, Cardinal Principles of the National Entity of Japan*. Robert King Hall, (ed.). Cambridge, Mass.: Harvard University Press, 1949.

51. Lists showing the kinds of materials are found in SCAP, *Post-War Developments*, Vol. I, pp. 228–234.

52. *Ibid.*, p. 371.

53. Economic development continues to this day to be a central concern that influences policies of the Ministry of Education today. An important factor in this situation is the relatively high degree of dependence of the Japanese upon outside resources and markets.

54. This attitude is reflected in various documents. See, for example, Article VIII, of the Fundamental Law of Education, 1947; a copy of the Law appears in SCAP, *Education in the New Japan*, Vol. II, pp. 109–111.

55. See Lawrence H. Battistini, *The Postwar Student Struggle in Japan*. Tokyo: Charles E. Tuttle Co., 1956, pp. 56–84. Interview with Professor Ronald S. Anderson, University of Hawaii, March 13, 1967, who worked with the Occupation as an education specialist.

56. *Report of the Second United States Education Mission to Japan, Submitted to the Supreme Commander for the Allied Powers, Tokyo, September 22, 1950*. Tokyo: Nippon Hoso shuppan kyokai, 1950, p. 3 (in English and Japanese).

57. *Report of the U.S. Education Mission*, pp. 4–6, 8–11, *et passim*.

58. For some Japanese assessments in English of the Occupation's educational reforms see the following. Kazuo Kawai, *Japan's American Interlude*. Chicago: University of Chicago Press, 1960. Daishiro Hidaka, "The Aftermath of Educational Reform," *Annals of the American Academy of Political Science, op. cit.*, pp. 140–155. Mamoru Oshiba with Don Adams, "Japanese Education—After the Americans Left," in Oshiba, *Four Articles on Japanese Education*. Kobe, Japan: Maruzen, 1963, pp. 14–24. *Journal of Social and Political Ideals in Japan, Education in Japan: 1945–1963*. Vol. I, No. 3 (December 1963).

59. See note 25; in all probability, Americans would not look as horrified about a centralized educational system today as did the Occupation educational reformers.

60. *Report of the Second U. S. Education Mission.* p. 27.

61. *Ibid.*, p. 28.

62. *Report of the U. S. Education Mission to Japan*, p. 14.

63. An English translation of the draft appears in R. P. Dore, "The Ethics of the New Japan," *Pacific Affairs*, 25 (June 1952), 147–159.

64. A sample of the Guide is provided in English translation in Benjamin C. Duke, "The New Guide for Teaching Moral Education in Japan," *Comparative Education Review*, vol. 8, No. 2 (October 1964), pp. 186–190. See also essays on the "revival" of the course in morals by Japanese intellectuals in *Journal of Social and Political Ideas in Japan, Education in Japan, op. cit.*

65. A recent study of democratic values among Japanese high school children indicates that the Japanese were more "authoritarian," on Christie's version of the F Scale, than the Americans, but scored higher on "democratic" items compared to the Americans. See Agnes M. Niyekawa, "Authoritarianism in an Authoritarian Culture: The Case of Japan," *International Journal of Social Psychiatry*, 1966, pp. 283–288.

66. See: Tatsumi Makino, "Educational Sociology in Japan," *Journal of Educational Sociology*, Vol. 26, No. I, 1952, pp. 37–42; Yasumasa Tomoda, "Recent Trends in Educational Sociology in Japan," *Sociology of Education*. Fall, 1966, pp. 397–496.

67. A summary outline of this report is provided in English in *Japan Times*, September 20, 1966, p. 12.

68. *Report of the U.S. Education Mission*, p. 7.

69. A study of Japanese children in 1961 indicates that a foreign nation (the U.S., for children in elementary school, and Switzerland, for children in lower secondary school) had the most responses in answer to the question, "Which nation do you like most?" Japan came in second, for the elementary group, and third, after the U.S., for the lower secondary school students. See Michiya Shimbori and Hideo Ikeda, "An attempt to Construct a National Prestige Index," *Indian Journal of Social Research*, III, No. 1, pp. 25–36.

70. See John A. Brownell, *Japan's Second Language: A Critical Study of the English Language Program in the Japanese Secondary Schools in the 1960's.* Champaign, Ill.: National Council of Teachers of English, 1967.

71. The author is grateful to the following individuals for help in preparing this chapter: Professors Ronald S. Anderson and Ann Marie Keppel of the University of Hawaii; Cleo, Mary Ann, and Peter Kobayashi; former colleagues at the University of Michigan, particularly Prof. James I. Doi, who was a CI & E clerk, Prof. William Clark Trow, a member of the First U.S. Education Mission to Japan, and Prof. Robert E. Ward, Director of the Center for Japanese Studies, helped the author to understand the Occupation.

Part II

Selected Dimensions
of Contemporary Japanese Education

Since the end of the Occupation period, Japan's steadily expanding economy has been virtually without parallel in modern history. She has, despite her military defeat, achieved almost all of the economic objectives for which she went to war in 1937. Her literacy rate stands at an impressive 99.9 percent her secondary school graduates rate close to the top in many international achievement tests; her colleges and universities are bulging with students and, in the eyes of some scholars, she among all of the world's nations, has best combined quality education with mass education. On almost any criteria one chooses, Japan is one of the most successful nations in today's world, and her educational system is one in which she can take pride.

This does not mean to imply, however, that there are no blemishes on this record or that everything is running smoothly. On the contrary, there are a number of very serious educational problems facing Japan, and in many instances she is nowhere near solving them. None are more serious than the so-called *shiken jigoku* or "examination hell" which plagues students from an early age through their entrance into higher education. Professor Ezra Vogel suggests that "No single event, with the possible exception of marriage, determines the course of a young man's life as much as entrance examinations, and nothing, including marriage, requires as many years planning and hard work." The human debris resulting from this often cruel system can best be seen in the startling rise in suicide rates among young people following the announcement of the examination results in the early spring of each year, and in the "dead-end" jobs that are the legacy of others who fail the examinations. Professor Vogel provides many insights into the examination system, its workings, and its effects not only upon students but also on family, friends, and teachers.

A topic that has been the focus of often bitter controversy in postwar Japan has been that of the textbooks used in schools. As we have seen in Professor Fridell's article, government control over school textbooks is not new, and, indeed, dates from 1886, but it has been only in the postwar period that this power has been seriously challenged. The person best known for his insistence that the *Mombusho* (Ministry of Education) cannot legally "censor" textbooks is the widely respected leftist historian, Ienaga Saburo. Professor Benjamin C. Duke, a long-time faculty member at International Christian University in Tokyo and a close observer of the Japanese educational scene, provides us with a useful survey of the textbook authorization system in general, and the Ienaga Case in particular. The heart of this case lies in the Ministry's refusal to allow Ienaga's interpretations of such topics as the mythological origins of Japan, the Japan-Soviet Neutrality Treaty, the Meiji Constitution, etc. At this time thoughtful Japanese are waiting for the Supreme Court to issue a definitive decision in this case.

An element of Japanese education that is rarely discussed in English-language studies is the subject of Professor Fred C. C. Peng's discussion of the "Ainu problem" in Japan. Japan's indigenous people, the Ainu, are a proto-Caucasian race whose origins are shrouded in the misty origins of Japan. Today, the Ainu, found almost exclusively in the northern island of Hokkaido, face daily discrimination, and it has only been in the last several years that they have become politically active in an attempt to better their lot in society.

Professor Peng examines the traditional education of the Ainu, describes the government's historical attempts to deal with the problem of Ainu education and its role in breaking down traditional Ainu culture. This article reminds one of similarities found in the education of minorities in other countries, especially in the United States.

As in most of the world, the Japanese student movement reached its peak during the decade of the 1960s and early 1970s, forcing the cancellation of President Eisenhower's proposed visit to Japan, destroying political careers and toppling prime ministers, wreaking unprecedented violence across the educational landscape, and causing some of Japan's oldest and most prestigious institutions to shut down for extended periods of time.

Shimbori Michiya, a distinguished sociologist of education at Hiroshima University, helps us to understand the context within which the Japanese student movement flourished and provides a brief history of the *Zengakuren* and a useful typology of Japanese student movements in his contribution which focuses on the famous "Waseda Struggle" of 1965. Although more than a decade in the past, this event is not untypical of the larger movement, strands of which are still obvious in today's Japan.

Professor William Cummings, on the other hand, looks at reform measures in Japan's higher education, beginning with the Meiji Restoration, within the framework of the traditional Japanese propensity of conservatives carrying out radical innovation. Professor Cummings sees two earlier university reform periods: in mid-Taisho (1912–1926) and during the American Occupation (1945–1952). A third reform era, he suggests, may be ushered in with the establishment of the new and innovative Tsukuba University. He traces the rough passage of the legislation authorizing this new university, and sketches the issues which fueled the ten-year controversy over its establishment. Professor Cummings's piece is revealing not only for his comments on reform of higher education, but also for helping us to peer behind the scenes to witness some of the drama of Japan's academic politics.

In a perceptive article, originally written for *The Japan Interpreter*, and brought up-to-date for this collection of readings, Professor Thomas Havens discusses the growth of Japan's university system from its modest beginnings a century ago to its current status as one of the most extensive in the world. It comes close, for example, to achieving mass higher education with one out of every four people in the 19–23 age bracket attending a university or junior college. Havens sees the main changes in higher education since 1960 as democratization, diversification, and dispersal and concludes that, on balance, these developments are healthy ones.

Edward Beauchamp's "Report from Japan" provides a brief survey of recent educational controversies facing the Japanese. They include the ever-present ideological rivalry between the conservative Ministry of Education and the leftist-oriented Japan Teachers Union; the newly instituted shūnin system which critics charge is designed to increase the conservative's hold on the schools; recent developments in the "Ienaga Textbook Case" described earlier by Professor Benjamin Duke; the bleak unemployment outlook for graduates of Japanese higher education and its implications for the small, but growing, Japanese women's movement; and the increasingly violent quarrels among student factions over ideological purity.

EZRA F. VOGEL

THE GATEWAY TO SALARY: INFERNAL ENTRANCE EXAMINATIONS

No single event, with the possible exception of marriage, determines the course of a young man's life as much as entrance examinations, and nothing, including marriage, requires as many years of planning and hard work. Because all colleges and high schools, and many private junior high schools, grade schools, and even kindergartens use entrance examinations to select only a small proportion of the applicants, and because examinations are open to all,[1] the competition is fierce. Passing examinations to a good school seems as difficult to the Mamachi resident as for a camel to pass through the eye of a needle. There is virtually no limit to how much one can prepare for examinations. The average child studies so hard that Japanese educators speak of the tragedy of their school system which requires students to sacrifice their pleasures, spontaneity, and sparkle for examination success. These arduous preparations constitute a kind of *rite de passage* whereby a young man

Ezra F. Vogel is Director of the East Asian Research Center at Harvard University.

Reprinted from Ezra F. Vogel, *Japan's New Middle Class: The Salary Man and His Family in a Tokyo Suburb* (Berkeley: University of California Press, 1967), copyright © 1963 by the Regents of the University of California, with permission of the author and publisher.

213

proves that he has the qualities of ability and endurance necessary for becoming a salary man. The Japanese commonly refer to entrance examinations as *shiken jigoku* which literally means "examination hell."

The Mamachi youth is willing to endure these tortures because if successful he will be able to join a large successful firm where he can remain for life.[2] To be admitted to such a firm, one must attend a good university, and to attend a good university one must pass the entrance examination. To pass the entrance examination for a good university one must have good training, and to acquire the good training one must pass the entrance examination to a good high school. In the final analysis, success is determined not by intelligence tests, nor by the school record, nor by the teacher's recommendations but by entrance examinations.

Although it seems a tragedy to the participants, there is a certain logic in how the examination system works. Because the firm commits itself to a young man for life and because business in contemporary Japan is highly competitive, the firm must be careful to select men of unusual promise and ability. The number of men a large firm takes in each year is so large and the number of personal connections of company officials so great that it would be impossible to use personal evaluations as the primary basis to select applicants. One need only imagine the problems of large numbers of company employees each urging the company to support his favorite candidate, to understand the convenience and value of a more universalistic basis of judgment. Because there is such wide agreement in Japanese society as to which universities are most desirable, firms consider the university attended as important or even more important than their own examinations for selecting salary men. Not only the university's relative standing, but even its style of life, has considerable stability over time, because of the practice of inbreeding. Nearly all professors at a major university have received their training at the same institution, and it is almost unthinkable for a professor to move from one major university to another.[3] Organizations add to this stability by selecting applicants according to the university's reputation. Young applicants know which universities the firms prefer and choose their university accordingly, thus perpetuating the emphasis on the university attended as a basis for selecting competent young men.

A large company ordinarily hires older workers only when absolutely necessary and even then gives more security and more rapid pay increases to younger employees. Here again, there is a self-fulfilling accuracy to the company's predictions. People who do change companies tend to be opportunistic and less devoted to the company's interests, and the company feels justified in hiring workers directly from college making work experience irrelevant as a criterion.

From the view of the outside observer entrance examinations involve an intensity of affect which cannot be explained only by the desire to obtain a good job. Although the search for security has rational components, as mentioned before, it has been heightened by the many upheavals in the lifetime of the average adult and by the difficulty which the contemporary urban parent had in finding a long-term livelihood when he was young. For the urban resident, a job in a large corporation is as close as one can come to the security that country relatives have by belonging to a household firmly attached to land and the local community. Just as obtaining land is thought to secure the future of a family even in the next generation, so does a job in a large corporation provide long-range security and insure that one's children can be given a proper position in life.

There are now opportunities in Japanese society for adventurous and talented young men, especially in new fields like electronics, advertising, entertainment, and foreign trade. New small companies in these fields can offer higher salaries than larger organizations, but most young men are unwilling to take this risk of less security; however, those who do not pass the entrance examinations to a good university may have no other choice.

But even if one wants to work in a smaller company, attending a good university makes it easier to get a good job and even to change jobs at a later time.[4] Once a student has passed an entrance examination to a first-rate university, he has no worry about graduating because the university is committed to his success and would dismiss him only for extreme misbehavior or incompetence. Compared to American state universities, which dismiss a large proportion of first-year students, the number of students failed from Japanese universities is negligible. Moreover, students do not transfer from one university to another. Being admitted to a given university becomes, in effect, a basis of ascription which provides fairly clear limits to one's later mobility.

Although students in a good university may still be concerned about being accepted by the best possible organization, the range of differences in status between the corporations or government bureaus they will join is relatively narrow. The room for achievement within the company is also relatively minor compared to whether one attended an outstanding university and whether one was admitted to a large reputable organization. To a large extent advancement within the firm depends simply on the date of entry into the organization. All new members of a company are admitted on the same day each year, go through the same general training program, and are treated as equals in most matters, such as salary and position. Even when employees begin to get different functional assignments, seniority remains relatively more important than skill and ability in determining rank and salary. An employee's standing vis-à-vis outsiders is determined when he enters the firm, and is little affected by the minor differentiations of status within the firm.

Even if some students from a lesser university are admitted to a good company or government office, they still may be at a disadvantage compared to those who attended the better universities. While some say that cliques of graduates of a given high school or university are weaker than before the war, fellow alumni of the same university are known to show preferences for their fellow graduates. It is assumed that those who attended a certain university (and sometimes even a certain department within a university) will feel mutual loyalty and share similar attitudes, making it possible for them to work together harmoniously despite differences of opinion and temperament. Especially in large government bureaus, acceptance in informal circles and even rate of advancement may be affected by the university one attended.

This analysis has focused on the boy and his problem of entering a large organization, but similar considerations apply to girls even though their career is marriage. Girls generally worry less about examinations than boys. Some people even question whether a girl who has attended the most competitive coeducational universities will make a good wife, and many girls prefer not to go to a coeducational school where they would have to study harder to keep up with the boys. But the better girls' schools are regarded as highly desirable, and these schools also require entrance examinations. Marital choice even in urban Japan is still decided in large part on the basis of objective criteria rather than simply on the diffuse relationship between a young man and a young lady, and the university or school attended has become an even more important criterion than ascriptive considerations like family background. Indeed, a boy's family proudly speaks of marrying a girl who attended a well-known girls' school just as her family will speak proudly of a young man who attended a good university. Thus, examinations are crucial to the girl's as well as to the boy's career.

In the view of the Mamachi resident, one's station in life is not predetermined by birth, but it is determined by the time one has his first job. For those who aspire to the new middle class, the opportunities for mobility are highly compressed into one period of life, late adolescence. The intense concentration of pressure for finding one's position in life during this brief time is undoubtedly related to the fact that Japan is the one country in the world where the suicide rate is high in the late teens and early twenties and declines during middle age.[5] Success or failure in finding the right opening at the time of college admission is considered permanent, and failure or fear of failure is disturbing even to the most talented.

Preparing for and Taking Examinations

Mamachi residents are careful in their selection of schools, and the range and variety of possible choices are enormous. At the apex of educational life are the great national universities, such as Tokyo University, and the well-known public high schools, such as Hibiya and Shinjuku, which students of all social classes can afford to enter if they pass the examinations. Next are the good private universities and the attached private elementary, junior, and senior high schools. Entrance examinations for these schools are almost as difficult as those for the best public institutions but tuition is higher, so that only well-to-do students can attend. Thirdly, there are public and private schools of lesser quality ranging from expensive schools which few salary men can afford, to public and less expensive private schools widely attended by children of salary men. At the bottom of the scale are the local public elementary and junior high schools, the only schools which do not require entrance examinations.

All students are required by law to complete junior high school, but any student who wishes to go beyond must take examinations. (The length of compulsory education is not determined by age but by number of years [nine] of schooling. No student is failed. One might speculate that failing students would arouse the same kind of threat to group solidarity as discharging a man from a firm.) It is assumed that once a student has been admitted to a junior or senior high school or college, he will remain in the same school until he graduates, but it is possible to change school systems at the time of each graduation. Although normally a student takes examinations in order to continue after each successive graduation, certain school systems, known as *escareetaa* (escalator) schools since students can move up within the same system from kindergarten to college, have only nominal examinations for students within the same system. When a child is admitted to an outstanding kindergarten such as those associated with Keio University (private) and Ochanomizu Women's University (public), he is thought to be on the *escareetaa* and established for life. Thus, a heavy premium is placed on getting into the kindergarten of the *escareetaa* schools, and the schools charge higher tuition for kindergarten than for the upper levels. The applicants to the best kindergartens are so numerous that difficult examinations cannot sort out the applicants adequately, and a lottery also is required to select the favored few. Recently, special schools have been opened in Tokyo to prepare three- and four-year-olds for the kindergarten entrance examinations.

Occasionally a Mamachi child takes these difficult kindergarten examinations, but the chance of passing is so slight, private-school costs are so high, and the daily commuting to Tokyo on public transportation is so taxing for mother and child that nearly all Mamachi children go to the local kindergartens and elementary schools. Mamachi families then concentrate on preparing their children for entrance examinations for the better junior and senior high schools and colleges, which are, by and large, in Tokyo.

Junior and senior high-school entrance examinations are not thought to be important for their own sake, but because they permit a child to get the better training that makes it easier to pass an examination to a difficult college. Because college entrance is considered so crucial, many students who fail the examination the first time may choose to wait a year and try the examination again. These students, not attached to any school or university, are called *ronin*, the name formerly used for the lordless samurai. Some persistent young people who have their hopes set on a certain school and whose families can afford to continue supporting them, may attempt the examinations several years before being admitted, in the meantime attending special preparatory schools.

Examinations, by and large, measure educational achievement. Because they must be given to large numbers, they consist mostly of objective factual questions of the multiple-choice variety. At the kindergarten level they may test the child's knowledge of the Japanese syllabary, perhaps a few characters, and elementary arithmetic. Junior-high and high-school examinations generally test science, Japanese language and literature, mathematics, history, and English. College examinations are similar but require more technical and specialized knowledge, especially in foreign languages.

A student ordinarily begins to prepare seriously about a year or two before the examinations that take place in January or February before the new school year begins in April. He studies several hours after school every day, and in the summer vacation preceding the February exams, he spends most of the day and sometimes part of the night in study. He often gives up movies, hobbies, and other recreation during this year of preparation. Athletes usually are advised to drop their sports activities, and music and dance lessons ordinarily are suspended.

In the year preceding the examination the mother spends much time investigating expenses, entrance requirements, and the schools' records in successfully placing their graduates. She visits schools, reads advice columns and books, and gathers information from friends. In addition, she spends much time consulting with her child's teacher and other parents in order to assess her own child's abilities. Naturally she wants her child to get into the best possible school, but this requires strategy and risk-taking. A child can take as many as three or four examinations if they are not offered on the same date, but it is seldom possible to take more. If a child fails all these, he may be out of luck. In addition, the process of taking examinations is tiring for the student and his mother, and they frequently require money payments. If a student tries to take three or four examinations during the same season, he may be so exhausted and discouraged from the first ones that he will not perform well on the later ones. Hence it is important for the mother to assess her child's abilities accurately and have the child take the most appropriate examinations.

The mother does most of the ground work but she must make sure that the father and the child approve her choices. The child's veto of a school is usually final, for while the mother often persuades a child to accept her choice, without his co-operation and hard work, the mother can have little hope of success. The mother does not want to risk being solely responsible for the choice of schools in case the child fails, and she is likely to consult with the father. Indeed, the family is likely to have frequent and sometimes heated discussions during the period of decision-making.

By late January these initial decisions are made, and the process of application begins. A candidate can apply only during an allotted two or three days. The mother applies in person, taking health certificates, school records, and the entrance fees. At almost every school on the first day of applications, there will be a few mothers who have waited in line overnight with their small snack and cushions, so that they will be among the first to apply. These mothers know that schools state that arrival time makes no difference. But apparently they hope that they may impress the school administration with their seriousness of purpose, that the low number on the application blank may be lucky, or that their child may be called for the examination early in the day and hence be somewhat fresher in taking the examinations. Their early arrival simply may reflect anxiety and excitement and a desire to get the application process over with. While most Mamachi mothers think it somewhat foolish to wait overnight, nevertheless many start out on the first train leaving Mamachi, at about four o'clock in the morning, on the day when applications are due. Even then, there may be a long line when they arrive, and those who have enough courage to come later in the day may have a wait of several hours before filling out the application. A mother who is going through the application procedure for the first time or who is applying for her only son is more likely to be among the first in line. If a woman is a "beteran" (veteran) she may be confident enough to come much later.[6] Sometimes it is necessary for the children to go along with the mother for applications, but for a college application the child probably will go by himself. This same standing in line may be done three or four times, depending on the number of applications a person is making.

If a personal interview is required at the elementary and junior high school age, the mother and child will be concerned about the impressions they make. It may be desirable to bring along letters of introduction from people who have important positions or some personal connection with the faculty, administration, or Parent-Teachers Association. Although a mother and child carefully plan what to say during this interview, it is not uncommon for the child to be frightened and to have difficulty expressing himself in the interview. Even if the mother and child consider the examination more crucial than the interview, they approach the interview as if it were of the greatest importance.

The month or so before and during examinations is commonly known as "examination season." The child studies very long hours, and if the family can afford it, a tutor comes to the house regularly. The child's household responsibilities are taken over by his brothers and sisters who are warned not to interrupt his study. In extreme cases the mother may bring him meals on a tray, sharpen his pencils, and stand ready to serve his every need. His father may come home from work early to help with the studying if the tutor is not available. The family is collectively on tiptoe for fear of disturbing the young scholar. They become almost hypochondriacal, and the slightest sign of a cold is taken seriously as a possible hindrance to examination success. Community activities and social visiting come to a complete halt, so absorbed are the families in their children's preparation. On street corners, at the neighborhood shops, in business offices, and at the dinner table, conversation revolves about the one topic of most immediate concern to all—examinations.

During the weeks around examinations, mothers of applicants try to avoid meeting other mothers and friends. Usually they leave their homes only for necessary shopping or to make arrangements for school applications. If they should meet an acquaintance accidentally, they attempt to steer conversation away from the delicate question of their child's examinations. Since a family will be embarrassed if it becomes known that their child has been refused by a school, the mothers usually do not identify the schools to which they are applying. If it is obvious to the other party, they explain that they do not expect to succeed for they have not prepared properly and they really are trying to get into another school (to which they are almost certain to be admitted). Sometimes a family denies that their child is taking a certain examination only to be discovered on the scene of the exam by the very friend who questioned them. Children also watch closely to see who is missing from school on an examination day to ascertain which schoolmates are taking which exams. On the whole, children are more open and direct in talking about examination plans than their parents, and they often report their findings to their mothers.

Mothers accompany children to all but the college examinations to give them moral support. If the father can take off from work or if the examination is early enough in the day, he may accompany the child in place of the mother. There is a waiting room close to the examination room where parents can sit while the children are taking the examination. A number of mothers reported that they were unable to sleep on the night before the examination. By the end of a series of two or three examinations over a period of eight to ten days, mothers as well as children are so exhausted that they often have to go to bed for a few days.

There is a hiatus of several days before the results of the examinations are announced. If a child takes examinations for two or three different schools, he may hear the results of the first examination before he takes the last. Since the report of the first examination is the first real indication for the family of the child's standing, the results have an exaggerated importance. The mother whose child has passed the first examination generally is jubilant. Conversely families with a failure are extremely gloomy and pessimistic. Tensions increase as families await the results. Most people will not telephone or communicate with examination families until after the results have been announced. A few mothers and children cannot resist talking about the examinations, and worries are at least shared and discussed within the family and among some friends and relatives. Some mothers have said that there is such an ominous weighty feeling during this time that they would almost prefer to hear negative results rather than continue the uncertainty.

The dramatic climax comes with the announcement of the results. Usually grades are not mailed, but the names or code names of successful candidates are posted at the school. Sometimes the names of successful candidates for well-known schools and universities are announced on the radio. Even if a family has heard the results on the radio they also check the posted list to assure themselves that there has not been an error.

The date the list is posted usually is known long in advance, but the time of day often is indefinite. Crowds gather as much as twenty-four hours before the auspicious hour. Frequently parents will go because children might have difficulty controlling their emotions in public. Even the father may take off a day or two from work at this time to check the examination results or to be of moral support to the mother and children. People concerned about controlling their emotions go to see the bulletin board during the night. Some, attempting to be casual, wait several hours after posting to check the results.

If a child has succeeded, he and his parents are only too glad to tell the results, although they will attempt to show the proper reserve. They may whisper the result saying "please don't tell anybody else," but their smiles are irrepressible and there can be no doubt about their satisfaction. If a mother looks troubled, friends do not ask the results. Indeed, the mother of an unsuccessful candidate may cry and sleep for several days before going out to face friends. Although to my knowledge there has been no suicide in Mamachi in recent years as a result of examinations, stories of juvenile suicide as a result of examination failure are widely publicized in the mass media and well known by all those taking examinations.

Because there are so many schools in the Tokyo area and because suburban children attend so many different schools, it is rare for more than two or three students from the same grade school to continue to pass examinations for the same junior high school, high school, and college. Even if two friends should intend to take examinations for the same school in order to continue together in junior high school or high school, if one passes and the other fails, the one who succeeds will not let friendship stand in the way of attending the better school. While at first they may attempt to keep up the friendships while attending different schools, the difference in status leads to embarrassment, and the ties generally become less meaningful.

Since a large portion of Japanese universities is in Tokyo, many ambitious children from all over the country come to stay with relatives in Tokyo and Mamachi or other suburbs while taking the examinations. Although it may take forty-five minutes or an hour to commute from Mamachi to Tokyo for the examinations, inn houses are expensive and relatives in Mamachi can take the responsibility for comforting the child and seeing that he gets sufficient food and rest. The niece, nephew, or cousin probably will come to Mamachi a few days before the examination to get accustomed to the new environment and to have a good rest for a night or two before taking the examination. He may also stay on a few days after until he learns the result, but he usually is encouraged to return to his parents immediately after the examination to comfort him in case of failure. Some of the universities, at the request and expense of the student, are willing to send a telegram, indicating whether he has passed or failed. This telegram usually does not state the examination result directly, but in code. For example, a telegram indicating failure might read something like "The cherry blossoms are falling." Despite the attempt to state the result in as nice a way as possible, failure is none the less hard to bear. In other cases, the suburban family will find out the result and then telephone the rural relatives. Several families have indicated the sorrow they felt when they telephoned to pass on the news of failure, and found the phone answered by the applicant who had been waiting beside the phone.

Even families whose children are not taking the examinations cannot avoid the excitement of examination season. Notices of examinations appear everywhere in the newspapers and the weekly magazines. News reels show pictures of applicants waiting in line or taking examinations. Experts appear on television to give advice to parents or to evaluate the implications of the examination system for Japanese society. Desks, study supplies, and guides to examination success are widely advertised. Statistical reports in newspapers and in magazines indicate precisely how many students from which high schools enter which colleges. Any middle-class parent can rank the first few high schools by the number of their graduates admitted to Tokyo University, and also the leading junior high schools by the number of graduates who enter the best senior high schools. Advice columns for mothers of younger children give hints ranging from ideas for room arrangements to suggestions for motivating the child to study and for dealing with the accompanying tensions. Some people cut out these articles and save them.

Even when no child in a family is taking examinations, the parents may be called upon by relatives, friends, and even acquaintances for assistance in getting a child admitted to a good school. Because of their influence, friends of school-board members, principals, prominent school teachers, PTA officers, and alumni of a particular school, employers or superiors at work are particularly likely to receive such requests. Usually they try to be helpful to close friends and to others for whom they feel some fondness or obligation, and even if they refuse a request, they usually make at least a token effort to help. Knowing the difficult problem of gaining admission, they generally want to be as helpful as possible although they resent requests from some people who never feel the obligation to return favors.

Families with means may employ students from the most famous universities to tutor their children for examinations. Tutoring younger children provides college students with their best and most common opportunities for *arubaito* (part-time work, from the German word

"Arbeit"). Students at lesser universities are less in demand and may have to be content with smaller fees. Wealthy families may use several students as tutors, each in his special field, while the ordinary salary-man family at best is able to afford a tutor only one or two nights a week. Nevertheless, even the middle-class family tries to find a tutor specializing in the subject in which their child plans to major. The tutor is generally of the same sex as the student and often provides a kind of role model, but the focus of their discussion is on preparation for examinations. Families which cannot afford a private tutor for a year or two before examinations will try to hire a tutor just before examinations or at least to join with other families in hiring a tutor for a small group of children preparing for the same examination. College students in need of money are pleased to find work as tutors since it is related to their field of study, and they generally have more free time once they themselves have been admitted to college.

When confronted with the question of why examination pressure is so intense, many Japanese respondents answered that it is because Japan is a small crowded country with few opportunities for success. This answer unquestionably highlights a factor of crucial importance, but it does not explain everything. There are many universities in Japan which are not difficult to enter, and there are opportunities for success aside from examinations. There are other crowded countries where opportunity is limited but examination pressure much less severe. Implicit in this response is the feeling that one's opportunity to achieve security and social mobility is highly compressed into one brief period of life, and many explicitly recognize that the best way for a commoner to rise on the social ladder is to enter a famous university. At least two other social systems, the family and the school, seem important for understanding the full force of this pressure. The importance of these two systems, like the life-time commitment to a firm, are further manifestations of a striking characteristic pervading Japanese social structure: the high degree of integration and solidarity within a given group.

The Family's Contribution: Maternal Involvement

Success or failure on examinations is not only the success or failure of an individual but of his family. The self-sacrifice, anxiety, excitement, and happiness or sorrow that attend examinations are fully shared by the parents and siblings. It is assumed that a child is successful in large part because of his parents' help, and community recognition for success or failure is accorded to the parents as much as to the child himself. But beside the applicant himself, the most involved person is the mother. In listening to a mother describe examinations, one almost has the feeling that it is she rather than the child who is being tested.

Beginning in first grade a child brings a book bag home every day so that he can get his mother's help with the daily homework assignments. Even if a tutor is hired for brief periods, the ultimate responsibility for helping with (or, from the child's view, hounding about) the homework is the mother's. The work usually is sufficiently difficult so that the child cannot do it without his mother's assistance, and the typical mother cannot do the work without some preparation on her own. Because most Mamachi mothers have completed only elementary school, or at most the prewar "girls' school" (equivalent to eleven grades under the new system), and because postwar educational reforms brought great changes in course content and methods, it is not easy for mothers to help children with homework, even in elementary school. Many mothers read their children's books and study other books while the children are in school, and others consult with tutors or school teachers to keep up with their children's work. It is a challenge for the mother to keep one step ahead of the child—a challenge these mothers take seriously.

The mother wants the child to succeed not only for his sake, but for her own sake. At school meetings, in front of an entire group of mothers, a teacher often will praise or criticize a mother for her child's performance. On certain occasions a mother is expected to stand behind the child while her child performs and other children and mothers look on, and the comments about performance are as likely to be directed to the mother as to the child since it is expected that the mother will see that the child follows the teacher's instruction when practicing at home.

In formal and informal gatherings of mothers, children's performance often becomes the focus of attention. Most children wear uniforms of their school, which signify status as clearly as military uniforms. Some schools post on a bulletin board the class position of all students or seat students according to rank. But even if schools make no such announcement, most parents have a good idea of the relative standing of their children. When mothers of classmates get together, they generally

226

know roughly the academic standing of each other's children, and mothers whose children are doing poorly are likely to listen carefully to mothers whose children are doing well. Mothers of successful children, even when discreet, indirect, and modest, have difficulty refraining from bragging about their children's successes. They may, for example, mention casually that their child is planning to specialize in a certain field since his teacher has praised him; or they may describe some technique in dealing with the child which seems to have worked since the child is doing so well; or they may encourage another mother, describing how their child once reacted negatively to mother's pressure but then suddenly began performing well.

The importance of the child's performance for determining the mother's status is reflected, for example, in the problems that schools have faced in trying to introduce special classes for retarded children. The parents have been resistant to sending their children to special classes because of the stigma attached. They have made special appeals for permission to allow their children to attend regular classes, because it would be so embarrassing to them to have their children attend special classes.

Even the families of high social standing are not immune from competition between mothers over children's success. In some ways it is even more difficult for upper-class mothers since they expect their children to do better than other children. Some have withdrawn their children from music lessons rather than face the wound to their pride when their children were not doing as well as some lower-status children.

While some status adjustments are required of mothers as a result of their children's examinations, these adjustments are usually minor since the family and community, through rank in class and practice examinations, already have a fairly good estimate of how a child will do in his examinations. Nevertheless there are always surprises, and mothers always entertain the hope that their child will be admitted to a difficult school, and that their community prestige will rise accordingly.[7]

So closely are mother and child identified that it is sometimes difficult to distinguish the child's success from the mother's success or even the child's work from the mother's work. During summer vacation grade-school children are required to do daily assignments and given optional projects to hand in when school reopens. It is common knowledge that good projects praised by teachers are done in part or almost entirely by the mothers. Although most mothers are critical of "mother's projects," still they feel they must keep up with the Gombeis (Joneses) by helping their children. The danger, clearly recognized by many mothers, is that the mother may exert herself so much that education may be more for the mother than for the child. Many thoughtful mothers are concerned lest their children become too dependent on them for assistance with homework and lose their own initiative. However, most mothers do not think that helping the child with homework interferes with the child's learning. They feel, rather, that the child needs guidance and that their assistance makes it possible for the child to learn more adequately and rapidly.

While the conscientious mother is very ambitious for the child, she is aware that if she pushes too hard, the child will resist. Yet some mothers become so anxious to be praised before a group that they will drive their children in order to achieve rapid success. Even if the mother uses more subtle techniques and tries to strike a balance between her own ambitions and the child's ability, there is no question that her enormous involvement in examination success will get communicated to the child.

The School's Contribution: Teacher Involvement

The Japanese Ministry of Education contributes indirectly to examination anxieties by pressing schools to raise their standards, and the schools in turn pass the pressure on to the families. At least since the Meiji Restoration, the Japanese government has stressed the importance of education in the development of a modern nation. The Ministry of Education continually compares Japan's level of educational achievement with that of other countries and has set high standards in an effort to make her students' achievements as high as those of any in the world. Thus, all students are expected to study a foreign language (generally English) in junior high school; a mathematics student is expected to complete calculus in high school.

One of the most lively public issues in recent years has been the question of whether there should be teacher-rating systems. Although the origins of and interest in the issue are partly in the realm of politics, its supporters have been arguing that in order to raise the standards of education, it is necessary to rate each teacher's competence. Many teachers have complained that this would permit school authorities to evaluate teachers by their political attitudes under the guise of efficiency ratings. Regardless of the political aspects of the question, this also reflects the seriousness with which the government considers the problems of raising the level of education.

In order to raise standards, many educators have encouraged the publication of materials evaluating each school's performance record, and newspapers and magazines diligently publish this information. Even educators who lament the enormous pressure placed on the children have recognized that posting of such results is useful in getting the schools to do the job more adequately.

Especially in private schools both teachers and students feel closely identified with their school. Since the students in the urban areas can choose between a number of junior and senior high schools and colleges, there is intense competition, especially among private schools, for better students. Schools enjoy a feeling of importance derived from people clamoring to gain admission, and a school without large numbers of applicants standing in lines would be regarded as a school of little consequence. This competition between schools tends to be more open than in the United States, and competition on the athletic field pales in comparison with the competition in placing graduates. Indeed, just as the American football coach is judged on the basis of the number of games his team wins, so the Japanese high-school principal is judged by the proportion of graduates who go on to the better universities; he in turn judges the teachers by the same standards.

The Japanese teacher does not make a sharp distinction between specific classroom duties and a general responsibility for his pupils. In a sense, he is required to take his troubles home with him. School teachers are expected to be available during vacations, and the school principal has the right to require them to report for work at any time. Even during summer vacation, a teacher will be expected to come to school at least two or three times to evaluate the progress of children's homework, and to take his turn supervising children's play activities.

The teacher to some extent is held responsible even for the safety and behavior of a child outside school. For example, one school principal said that a major share of his time is spent in handling children who get in trouble in the community. In the mind of Mamachi residents, the parents are partly to blame for a delinquent child, but the school is also responsible for not having provided better moral training. Although most parents are opposed to the reintroduction of formal moral training, the school does have a responsibility for inculcating basic moral virtues. For example, the teacher must see that girls do not wear make-up, that they have simple hair-dos and no permanents, that they wear proper uniforms, and, at some private schools, that they do not walk with boys. The teacher sends memos to parents, particularly at vacation times, outlining the procedures the parents should follow to insure that their child has a healthful vacation and listing places considered inadvisable for the child to visit. It is only natural that the teacher's responsibility extends to cover examination success.

On the numerous occasions when the mother goes to visit the school, she shows respect for the teacher and takes his advice seriously. Many a mother, relatively calm before going to a PTA meeting, returned concerned about whether she was doing enough to help the child and resolved to follow the teacher's advice more closely. She will, of course, show deference to the men teachers, who comprise as much as one-half of the elementary-school staff and an even larger proportion of the coeducational junior and senior high school staffs. But in addition, because the mother's own education is often inadequate, she must look to the teacher for guidance in helping her child. While mothers collectively may complain that certain teachers are not giving their children adequate training, by and large they feel grateful for the teachers' help, especially for the many teachers who provide extra tutoring in preparation for examinations. Mothers express their appreciation often, sometimes by means of presents. Knowing how much they depend on him and how important examination success is to a child's career, a teacher cannot help but feel a keen sense of responsibility to the mothers and children he advises.

When we asked families about the importance of teachers' recommendations for university admissions, we were told that they carry almost no weight since it is assumed that the teacher will be trying to push his own pupil ahead. His recommendation is more likely to be an exercise in flattery than an objective appraisal. It would be almost like asking a parent to write a recommendation for his own child.

The school teacher who wants to please his superiors and who takes seriously his responsibility for his pupils' futures will want to do everything he can to insure the child's success. This inevitably means that he will advise the mother to have the child study harder and to sacrifice other activities that might interfere with studying.

230

Mitigating The Harshness

The cause of examination worry is not only the finality of the results but the fact that examinations are impersonal and therefore unpredictable. The generation which came to the city from rural areas relied on personal contacts as a basis of finding positions, and Mamachi parents still consider personal contacts a much safer way to find a good job. By having properly placed friends and keeping up a good relationship with them, one previously could be virtually assured of success. But there is no such assurance when one is evaluated on the basis of competency by some impersonal authority. Examination questions might be different from what one had anticipated, or one might not feel well, or one's nervousness might inhibit performance.

Some families, unwilling to take this risk, try to find other paths to success. Genuine alternatives to examinations are, however, extremely few. One alternative is enrolling a child in a private "escalator" school permitting him to advance from kindergarten or elementary school through a reputable university with only nominal examinations. But these private "escalator" schools are so expensive and require close family connections with such prominent people that virtually no Mamachi salaried family has given this possibility serious consideration.

Another alternative is for a family to arrange for their son to be taken directly into a large organization regardless of educational background. Most schools leave a few openings for students who do not pass the examinations, and the selection of these students is generally made by a committee of prominent people in the school; and this permits a few students to be admitted on the basis of particularistic claims on the school, either because the parent is an alumnus, has contributed financially to the school, or has a friend influential in school affairs. However, there is considerable competition for these openings. The family's strategy is to get the person most powerful in the selection committee to make the most forceful appeal for the admission of their child. To do this the family tries to do anything it can to increase the influential person's personal motivation, because of personal liking or feeling of obligation, so he will make this vigorous appeal to the committee. A standard way to establish such a *kone* (connection) is to get one's friends who know such influential people to try and persuade them to help out. Often parents bring presents to influential school officials. Some junior

231

and senior high-school principals receive two or three presents for every opening, and even if they announce that they accept no presents, they often find it difficult to refuse. Parents are thoughtful in selecting unique, appropriate, carefully wrapped gifts and presenting them in a polite way. School officials try to avoid any feeling of obligation to these families, but they do honor some obligations, especially if the applicant also is relatively competent. While principals and important teachers or school officials sometimes derive substantial economic gain from such presents, there were no indications of their misusing their position for purposes of personal gain. The responsibility they incur as a result of receiving presents causes considerable discomfort, and there is undoubtedly a large measure of truth when they say they prefer not to receive them.

The foresighted mother sometimes begins courting potentially influential people years in advance, offering generous presents and a variety of personal services. If such a friend later gives assistance in getting a child admitted, the mother feels an obligation and expresses appreciation for many years afterward.

To be really influential these claims on particularistic relations must be more than simple introductions because any salary man can get some kind of introduction. But even with the most influential friends who will exert themselves most forcefully, one cannot entirely escape the importance of examinations. The lower the examination score, the more difficult for an influential person to get his favorite candidate accepted by the rest of the committee, and if the examination score is too low, no introduction will help. Furthermore, the child who enters with a low examination score is often at a disadvantage vis-à-vis his classmates, and some children who could use connections prefer to study hard and take the examinations so they will not be accused of succeeding because of their family's wealth or influence.

Money, like introductions, can be used to supplement examination results, and within a limited range may be used instead of examination scores. A student who did fairly well on examinations can attend a private school which has a high entrance fee and tuition and is comparable in quality to a public institution which has slightly more difficult examinations.

Some wealthy parents who wish to avoid possible embarrassment by open competition with ordinary families often plan to use private schools and connections from the beginning. But salaried families cultivate these ties only as an alternative in case the child does not pass the more difficult examinations at a public school.

If a family cannot afford the better private schools, there is still the possibility of sending the child to a local public school which happens to have an unusually good reputation. Since a local public school is open only to children living in that particular school district, sending a child to a school in another district is, strictly speaking, illegal. Yet this practice is so common that principals from different school districts occasionally meet to discuss the problem of some school districts bearing the burden of financing the education of children in other districts. Various informal estimates suggest that in certain school districts, one-tenth or more of the students actually reside in another school district.

It happens that Mamachi's elementary school is known as a fairly good school so that some parents in nearby school districts enroll their children in the Mamachi elementary school, but some Mamachi mothers similarly enroll their children in such a public junior high school in Tokyo. Even though the differences between these local schools may be minor, they are treated as if they were major since just such small differences may determine whether a student passes or fails a later examination. It is rare for a family to move to one of these school districts, but it is common for the mother and child to register as living at the home of some friend, relative, or acquaintance in that school district.

Many school officials and teachers feel sympathy for the earnest young children desiring to get ahead and are reluctant to raise objection to illegal crossing of school districts. In contrast to the city officials, school officials may be pleased about the desirability of their school and willing to take these ambitious children, so long as city officials raise no objections. At times, city officials concerned about the heavy school expenditures will carry out an investigation and ungraciously send the child back to his own school district.

Although most people are aware of the problem of crossing of school districts, and although high registration rates of mothers and children of certain ages in well-known school districts are sufficient evidence of the problem, investigations are relatively rare. If there were to be a search, the mother would probably explain that due to domestic quarrels or illness, she and her child have in fact taken up residence apart from the husband in that particular school district. The family will have left clothing, a school uniform, and some school supplies with friends and relatives whose address they are using in case a law officer came to investigate. While this practice makes it more difficult to prove violations, many potential violators are caught at the time of registration, and many run the risk of being thrown out and then having difficulty entering another school.

At the college level the only alternative for a student who fails his examinations is to become a *ronin* for a year or so. It is not especially embarrassing to be a *ronin* for one year, and many famous universities have stories of students who entered on their fifth, sixth, or even tenth attempt. But because the typical salary-man family has difficulty supporting the student for the extra year while studying for examinations, some *ronin* must compromise by working part-time while preparing for examinations. The status of a *ronin* is filled with anxiety. The student who has already failed one entrance examination generally feels somewhat more desperate, and doubt about success overshadows the entire period of *roninship*. Many families will take a second failure as clear indication that a child will not make a first-rate university, so that a first-year *ronin* may feel that he has only one more try. As a consequence, few families are able to tolerate and afford more than one year of *roninship*, and a student reluctantly may enroll in the university which was his second or third choice rather than become a second-year *ronin*.

It should be clear, then, that it is difficult for a salaried family to escape entirely from judgment by examination. A higher-status family, by wealth and community prestige, can often manage to pave the way to success for a child who does not perform well on examinations. But the typical salaried family lacks the resources to command these alternatives. At best it can use its savings and personal contacts to enable the child to attend an institution slightly better than he would by relying solely on examinations. The salaried family is more likely to concentrate its most valuable resources, the mother's time and the family's savings on helping to prepare the child more adequately for examinations.

The Hypertrophy of Examinations

From an analysis of the various institutions and practices associated with entrance examinations, it is possible to understand why entrance examinations should receive such emphasis. Yet Mamachi residents feel that it has gone entirely too far and that they have become enslaved to the system. They feel sorry for the child who is forced to lead a restricted life deprived of jovial fellowship, music appreciation, sports, hobbies, movies, television, and pleasure reading. One girl, for example, a year before taking a college entrance examination, said that her leisure time activities consisted of occasionally stopping off at a department store for a few minutes on the way home from school. This asceticism, so closely associated with the traditional peasant's outlook, is endured because of the hope of living an easier life later. Preparation for examinations is painful not only because one must make such sacrifices but also because until one has finally passed entrance examinations there is always the anxiety and fear that one may not make the grade.

There is no question that during this period of asceticism these students absorb an amazing amount of facts. Not only do they master their own language, literature, and history, but they also learn to read English and become familiar with the history and culture of Europe and America. Course requirements in mathematics and science are at a higher level than those of comparable American schools.

But at the same time, students must sacrifice types of scholarship not measured by entrance examinations. For example, since the examination is written and not oral, a pupil studying English does not practice ordinary conversation, but concentrates on reading, on fine points of grammar, and, in some cases, on pedantic expressions which likely to appear on the examination. High-school teachers complain that they cannot get students interested in laboratory work connected with science because the examinations measure only what can be read and answered. Since examinations cover a full range of subjects, a child who begins to show a strong interest in one field usually will be encouraged by his teacher and his parents to broaden his interests so that he can get fully prepared also in other subjects. Since multiple-choice examinations cannot measure original and creative thought, the emphasis is placed on memorization.

Even if the students who do not take entrance examinations imitate the study patterns of examinees, they feel relatively deprived—falling behind their peers in preparation for success in life and neglected by the teachers at school. Since no students are failed, poorer students are supposed to be given special supplementary classes. The poor students often complain that, instead, supplementary classes are given to good students preparing for difficult examinations. While the schools are supposed to help students who wish to get part-time jobs and to

help them find employment after the ninth grade, those students likewise feel that they are slighted because the school is more interested
in placing the continuing students. Even those who do not complain
are distressed that their children will not have such good chances of
becoming salary men.

In most modern societies, the task of educating the youth is performed not in the home but in the school system. For these salaried
families, however, education is performed by the school *and* the home.
In a sense, parents become assistant teachers, checking frequently
with the regular teachers about the work the parents should be doing
to help educate and train their children. Therefore to a large extent
the parent-child relationship is the relationship of teacher and student.
The mother must supervise her child, give him assignments, check the
work, and impose necessary sanctions to see that he performs the work
adequately. Whereas, in some industrialized societies, the mother-child
relationship is more strictly limited to primary socialization and to
providing affection, among these salaried families it must also take on
in addition a task orientation in which the mother and the child prepare
for examinations.

Achievement without Rivalry

The prominence of examinations in the life of Mamachi salaried
families reflects an acceptance of the principle that success should be
determined by competence as judged by a universal standard. The path
of success is not determined primarily by birth or connections but by
superior capacity as demonstrated by performance. While Japan is
sometimes described as a particularistic society, at the time of examinations particularistic relations clearly give way to these universalistic
standards. One of the dangers of open competition, however, is that
rivalry may prove disruptive to groups.

Yet the extent of disruption is very limited in groups to which
Mamachi residents belong because within the group competition is
carefully controlled. Once a child is admitted to a school, grades are
not given great importance, and there is a strong feeling of group
solidarity which serves to inhibit competitiveness between the students.[8] Once in the firm, one's success has been assured, and rivalry is
kept in bounds by the primacy of seniority which is non-competitive
and the common interest in the success of the firm. Since schools and

236

firms do not drop members for poor achievement records, there is no feeling that one's remaining in the group depends on another's leaving.

Even in taking entrance examinations, a person plays down competition with friends. A person ordinarily hopes that all in his group of friends will be among those who pass. Even if friends are separated and pursue different paths as a result of examinations, there usually is no feeling of acrimony. In a sense, the one who did not get in feels that the position he hoped for was filled not by his friend but by a stranger.

Achievement patterns also do not disrupt family solidarity. In the United States, for example, where achievement is defined as an individual matter, the child who goes beyond his parents in achievement level often feels that his parents have difficulty understanding the kind of world in which he lives. Among the Mamachi families, however, the child's success is more directly a family success. The mother continually keeps close to the child and his work. Even if the child does not need his family's introductions, he will require the family's help in preparing for the examinations. While disparities between achievement of siblings may create some problems, brothers and sisters are also so involved in each other's success and share in the community respect awarded to a family that examinations serve usually to unite siblings as well as other members of the nuclear family.

Under conditions of competing with strangers the achievement pressures are least controlled. Just as considerations of politeness do not prevent the shoving of strangers getting on a subway, so competitiveness is accepted as natural at the time of entrance examinations. In this way, the entrance-examination system operates to preserve the distinction between friends and strangers because blatant competition is concentrated at the time of admission when one competes with strangers. Once admitted, competition is subordinated to loyalty and friendship within the group. Thus the phenomenon of entrance examinations operates to maintain universalistic standards in such a way that it minimizes the threat to group solidarity. The cost to the individual is the anxiety and pressure which he must endure at the crucial point of admission.

1. This is in contrast to many developing countries where for reason of race, language, ethics discrimination, or financial requirements, the opportunities are limited to certain groups in the population.

2. Abegglan argues that the key differences between Japanese and American factories is the Japanese factory's life-long commitment to the employee. James C. Abegglan, *The Japanese Factory: Aspects of its Social Organization*, Clencoe, Ill.: The Free Press, 1958.

Recent evidence indicates that there is in fact considerable mobility, even of people working in large firms, but it has greatly declined since the war. Kenichi Tominaga, "Occupational Mobility in Japanese Society: Analysis of the Labor Market in Japan" (mimeographed, 1962). Also, Koji Taira, "Characteristics of Japanese Labor Markets," *Economic Development and Cultural Change*, 1962, X: 150–168.

Even if there is mobility, however, it may be to a company affiliated with the original company or through arrangements made by people within this company.

Even new or expanding firms prefer young people. One Mamachi industrialist opening a new plant kept expanding for three years before the plant reached full size. The new employees were admitted annually, immediately following graduation from high school or junior high school. He felt, like most Japanese employers, that he would have a greater likelihood of getting competent employees this way than by recruiting older people from elsewhere.

The age of Japanese farmers at time of entering a master's service was historically important in determining whether they would be granted highly desired semi-independent status. Those who entered service at a younger age were more likely to be awarded with such status. Cf. Thomas C. Smith, *The Agrarian Origins of Modern Japan*, Stanford, California: Stanford University Press, 1959.

3. They may, however, move from this major institution to smaller institutions, and then from there to better universities or back to this major university. It is unlikely, however, that they would ever move to a major university other than the one they attended.

4. The importance of the university attended is clearly greater for a salary man than for independent professionals or independent businessmen. The success of the young man who takes over his father's practice or business is determined not by the school attended but the size of his father's enterprise and his own ability. However, if family prestige or tradition is tied with a given university, it may be important for prestige purposes to attend that university regardless of economic significance.

5. It is not claimed that pressure to find the proper job or marriage opening is the only cause of the high suicide rate, but in the minds of Mamachi residents and in the popular press, there is a large connection between the two. On the basis of projective tests. Professor George De Vos has suggested that suicide in Japan is also closely related to the feeling of loneliness as a result of breaking the intense parent-childhood at the same age.

6. One is struck by the similarities between the mother's attitudes about giving birth and about having her child take an examination. In both, there

exists a great amount of folklore and advice constituting a special subculture passed down from veteran to newcomer. In the examination, however, one's odds for success are much lower, and the amount of effort required is much greater.

7. It may be argued that because the mother's status depends so much on the success of the child, the status gap between the mother and the child is never permitted to become large. The problem sometimes found in the United States, where the status gap between a lower-status mother and a higher-status child has created serious strains in the mother-child relationship, would seem to be less likely to lead to a break in Japan where the mother usually continues to adjust to the child's new position and keeps in close contact with his associates.

8. This pattern appears to begin at an early age. Miss Kazuko Yoshinaga who taught in middle-class kindergartens in both Japan and the United States reported that in kindergartens American children are much more openly competitive than Japanese children. Even about matters of age and size, Japanese kindergarten children rarely engage in comparisons and are less interested in who is bigger and older.

BENJAMIN C. DUKE

THE TEXTBOOK CONTROVERSY

During the summer of 1970, one of the most provocative judicial decisions affecting Japanese education was delivered by the Tokyo District Court. Inaugurating a new stage in the interminable controversy over the Ministry of Education's textbook authorization system, the District Judge declared the Ministry, in its rejection of a history text-book, in violation of the postwar Constitution and the Fundamental Law of Education. In response, the Ministry immediately notified local and prefectural school boards that the verdict would not affect the present authorization procedure unless a higher court denies an appeal. Simultaneously, the powerful Japan Teachers Union interpreted the decision as a vindication of its implacable opposition to reactionary governmental control over education, heralding the verdict as a monumental step in wresting postwar education from government domination.

The textbook case involved litigation brought by Ienaga Saburō,

Benjamin C. Duke is Professor of Comparative Education at International Christian University in Tokyo.

Reprinted from *Japan Quarterly*, XIX, 3 (July–Sept. 1972), pp. 337–352, with permission of the author and publisher.

240

well-known progressive scholar from Tokyo University of Education. Professor Ienaga, a prewar graduate of Tokyo Imperial University and a recognized historian, filed suit against the Ministry of Education in 1965 and again in 1966 following a protracted series of disputes over his Japanese history textbook for high school social studies. According to Ienaga, these court cases originate from his first manuscript designed for high school history courses written shortly after the war. However, because of the system then in existence whereby the Ministry of Education held exclusive rights for the preparation and compilation of textbooks, his manuscript could not be considered. Instead, it was published for the general public in 1947 by Sanseidō Press under the title of A New History of Japan (Shin Nihonshi).

After the textbook system, based on government compilation, was revised in 1949 to government authorization of manuscripts written by private authors, Ienaga applied through his publisher for textbook approval of a revised version of his Shin Nihonshi in 1951. It was initially rejected on minor points. The following year approval was granted without revisions, marking the author's first textbook success. In 1954 the publisher requested a complete revision for 1955. This edition was unacceptable to the Ministry of Education until 216 specified passages were revised. The author carried out a revision but 37 passages remained unacceptable since Ienaga refused to comply with every demand stipulated by the Ministry. This edition was predictably rejected.

In the midst of these negotiations, the Ministry's Course of Study was revised, requiring new textbooks for 1956. Ienaga undertook the third complete revision of his book for application in 1956. This edition was also rejected. In this instance the Ministry notified Ienaga that his text did not meet the aims of Japanese history textbooks defined by the Ministry accordingly: (1) to recognize the efforts of Japanese ancestors through the study of history, (2) to heighten the awareness of a student as a Japanese, (3) and to foster affection toward Japan. After this episode, the author contemplated abandoning efforts for gaining approval of his latest manuscript, but finally decided to make concessions for authorization. Although he objected to the Ministry's demands, he revised the text, which was rejected in 1957. Further revisions finally resulted in approval for use in 1959.

When the Ministry of Education implemented a mandatory high school curriculum in 1963, new textbooks were required. In anticipation, Ienaga completed the fourth major revision of his book. In March 1963 the Ministry rejected his new application on grounds that the manuscript did not comply with the revised social studies curriculum. The Ministry counted 320 defects in the manuscript. Since it was too late for revisions to be accomplished in time for the school year beginning in April 1963, the author revised portions of his draft and reapplied for authorization in September 1963 for the 1964 academic year. On this occasion the Ministry extended conditional approval, listing over 293 remaining conditions necessary for final authorization. Ienaga again reluctantly complied, completing a sufficient number of revisions for final approval from the Ministry effective for the 1965 academic year.

On June 12 1965 Ienaga filed suit against the Ministry of Education for ¥1,900,000 charging the Ministry with unconstitutional action in 1963 by refusing to approve his textbook manuscript. He claimed that compelling an author to revise his manuscript against his will and academic expertise, in order to secure governmental authorization, contravenes the Japanese Constitution. Then, in 1966, Ienaga submitted another version of his manuscript to the Ministry of Education for approval, even though his previously authorized edition was being widely used in districts where the Japan Teachers Union was strong. This was an obvious maneuver to strengthen the legal basis of his case, since the latest manuscript was based on the same version as the edition approved in 1963. The critical difference between the two editions involved 37 passages reinserted in the 1966 edition which were initially rejected in 1963. Ienaga claimed the unexpurgated version faithfully represented the fruits of his academic research.

In March 1966 the Ministry disapproved six of the 34 reinserted passages in the latest version, and accepted the remainder. In this instance, Ienaga refused to revise his manuscript to meet the Ministry's requirements. Instead, he immediately filed his second court case demanding that the Ministry be rejoined from rejecting his latest application. The basis for the charges was essentially the same as the first suit. The two companion cases then began their lengthy process through the Tokyo District Court, culminating in the momentous decision in Ienaga's favor in August of 1970.

Among the six passages consistently rejected by the Ministry, the most famous dispute concerns the first two chronicles of early Japan, the Ancient Chronicles (*Kojiki*) and the Chronicles of Japan (*Nihonshoki*). Ienaga wrote that:

Both the *Kojiki* and the *Nihonshoki* begin with the story of The Age of the Gods, followed by a description of several of the first emperors, including *Jimmu*. All of these stories were fabricated after the Imperial Family united Japan in order to justify sustained imperial rule. Nevertheless, included therein are popular myths and legends which teach us about ancient thought and are, therefore, important historical materials.

The Ministry of Education contended the two chronicles included the earliest known literature of Japan in the form of myths and legends, and could not be described merely as artificial devices to justify sustained imperial rule of Japan. Accordingly, the Ministry approved the following version:

> In *Kojiki* and *Nihonshoki*, myths and legends concerning the powerful families and people of early Japan are compiled, representing important historical materials which teach us about ancient Japanese thought.

The following passages are also drawn from the six disputed sections.

(Original—rejected)
> In April 1941 Japan signed the Japan-Soviet Union Treaty of Neutrality with the USSR in order to strengthen Japan's position for a southern advancement.

(Approved)
> In April 1941 Japan signed the Japan-Soviet Union Treaty of Neutrality with the USSR, in response to a proposal by the Soviet Union, in order to strengthen Japan's position for a southern advancement.

(Original—rejected)
> When Germany invaded the Soviet Union, Japan positioned a large military force near the Sino-Soviet border, under the pretext of the Kantō Army Grand Maneuvers, and prepared for an invasion into Siberia when the situation became advantageous.

(Approved)
> When Germany invaded the Soviet Union, Japan positioned a large military force near the Sino-Soviet border under the pretext of the Kantō Army Grand Maneuvers.

In another famous passage, originally rejected in the 1963 application, Ienaga wrote that:

> The Meiji Government established a national form of government through the 1889 Constitution with sovereignty vested in the Emperor. Shortly thereafter the Imperial Rescript was promulgated to secure the loyalty of the people to the new form of government. At this time there was a growing emphasis on respect toward the Emperor's picture and the Imperial Rescript in order to unite the nation. For example, the following year, Uchimura Kanzō, a famous Christian, was dismissed from his teaching post because he failed to pay proper respect to the ceremonial reading of the Imperial Rescript.

The Ministry rejected Ienaga's analysis of the Constitution and the Rescript claiming the author evaluated them purely from a negative and biased viewpoint. It was charged that Ienaga gave no consideration to the actual contents of the two controversial documents, nor to their positive aspects, but merely criticized their use. In addition, it was pointed out that he failed to recognize the fact that the Meiji Constitution represented the first constitution in Asia.

In the revised version, Ienaga reduced the descriptive material concerning the Constitution and the Rescript accordingly:

> The Imperial Rescript taught moral virtues including loyalty (chū) and filiel piety (kō). The people were exhorted to follow the dictates of the Rescript in the name of the Emperor.

The Ministry also rejected this revision. The criticism was made that Ienaga was negligent in failing to note that the Emperor himself obeyed the dictates of the Rescript, together with his people. The final version approved by the Ministry in Ienaga's 1964 textbook simply stated that:

> The Imperial Rescript taught moral virtues including loyalty and filial piety, which later became the standard of morals education in the schools.

Turning from the disputed passages to the controversial textbook authorization procedure itself, a rather intricate process has evolved.

Individual authors are free to prepare textbook manuscripts which they then submit to an officially approved textbook publisher. Upon acceptance, the publisher applies to the Ministry of Education for authorization. In practice, most textbooks are initiated by the approved publishing companies when teams of authors, or a single well-known author, are invited to prepare manuscripts in consultation with company specialists. The publisher, long before the text is officially screened, finances the writing expenses and prints in required textbook-like form sufficient copies for Ministry inspection. In the process substantial sums are committed to prepare a manuscript for review. Perforce, publishing companies conduct their own internal authorization procedure to assure insofar as possible that the final manuscript conforms to Ministry requirements in order to protect their initial heavy investment. Only an experienced and well-known author such as Ienaga can convince a publishing company to process a manuscript with content liable to invite rejection from the Ministry.

After the manuscript emerges from its rigorous initial screening conducted by the publishing company, a printed edition devoid of the names of the publisher and author, but conforming to specific regulations including the number of lines on a page, is submitted to the Ministry of Education. Copies are then turned over to a deliberative council called the Shingikai, consisting of 120 part-time members from the ranks of university faculties, experienced teachers, and other categories of educators, appointed by the Minister. Ninety members of the Shingikai are directly involved in textbook content analysis, forming the major unit of the larger body, herein simply called the Authorization Council. The Authorization Council of 90 is further divided into nine subcommittees according to subject matter areas.

The manuscript is initially distributed to members of the appropriate subcommittee who will each read the material and make an independent report for the main Authorization Council. Simultaneously two teachers and one university professor from an outside advisory committee called the Chōsakai, consisting of between 500 and 600 members, read the manuscript and submit independent reports to the Authorization Council. In addition, there are 41 full-time Ministry textbook inspectors called the Chōsakan, divided according to subject area. The appropriate Ministry inspectors read the manuscript and come to a single recommendation from the Chōsakan to the Authorization Council. The final step takes place when the Council arrives at a recommendation for the

Minister of Education, who invariably abides by the decision of the Council.

Criteria for authorizing a manuscript suitable for textbook use are contained in an official announcement (*kokuji*) published in 1958. The four broad stipulations concerning textbook content are: "(1) the material must conform to the purposes of the Fundamental Law of Education; (2) the material must conform to the purposes of the School Education Law; (3) the material must conform to the standards of the appropriate Course of Study published by the Ministry of Education; (4) the material must be fair and impartial (*kōsei*) regarding politics and religion. No propaganda or material biased toward or against a specific political party, religious sect, or ism may be included." The controversial passages in Ienaga's textbook were primarily rejected under category four, by failing to meet the test of impartiality and fairness (*kōsei*) as interpreted by the Authorization Council.

Professor Ienaga's textbook became the center of litigation which ultimately assumed epic proportions extending far beyond the textbook authorization procedure. It constituted an attack on the present uniformity of Japanese education in which a mandatory curriculum is standardized by the Ministry of Education and the textbooks require government authorization. Ienaga agreed that broad general standards are necessary but contended that national authorities have no right to determine the specifics of the content. According to him, only the free publication of textbooks fulfills the requirements of a democratic school system in which a variety of historical interpretations are made available to the student.

Specifically, Professor Ienaga argued that the authority of the Ministry's Textbook Authorization Council must be restricted to the correction of typographical and factual errors. For the Government to "correct" interpretations of history by competent authors constitutes state censorship. Furthermore, since the Council members are appointed by the Ministry of Education, there can be no way of assuring that fairness and objectivity are applied in the selection process.

Ienaga then goes to the very heart of the postwar political struggles between left-wing and conservative forces, in which education has become inextricably involved, when he charges that the Ministry exploits the textbook authorization system for invidious purposes. Not only is it designed to prevent a variety of historical presentations from reaching the student, but it is specifically employed to present a distorted view of Japanese history as interpreted by the Government. In effect, Ienaga is attacking the government for reviving a prewar policy of determining an official history of Japan.

The Government bases its right to demand revisions of textbook content on the School Education Law which states, "Textbooks used in the elementary school (and lower and upper secondary schools) must be those approved by the Ministry of Education's textbook authorization procedure." It is the application of this provision which became the immediate focus of the litigation in Professor Ienaga's suit. The Government contends that censorship is not involved since the book can be published for general use without Ministry approval, although it cannot be officially called a textbook and therefore may not be used in the classroom. Accordingly, the authorization procedure does not violate constitutional provisions, according to the Ministry.

The Ministry of Education interprets the authorization procedure as a means whereby acceptable national minimum standards can be established for textbooks. Under this system any author is eligible to prepare manuscripts which must meet basic qualifications so that a variety of textbooks at each level in each subject area receives the official stamp of approval. Local school boards, upon recommendation by teachers and administrators, can then choose from the approved list those textbooks which best meet local needs, with the assurance that all approved titles have met basic national minimum standards. To the Ministry of Education, the textbook system as it functions in Japan is appropriate for a democratic nation.

The Government has based its fundamental attitude toward an admittedly centralizing policy, in which the Ministry of Education sets the curriculum and approves the textbooks, on Article 26 of the Constitution. Former Minister of Education, Araki Masuo, one of the most powerful politicians within the ruling government party, summed up the Government's basic orientation accordingly:

> Article 26 of the Constitution states that "All people shall have the right to receive an equal education correspondent to their ability." Combining this with provisions in the School Education Law which state that "Matters concerning school subjects shall be decided by the competent authorities," which the Government interprets as the Ministry of Education, then the Ministry has a clear mandate. It must strive to provide equal educational opportunities for all children throughout the nation. In order to guarantee equal

educational opportunities, the Ministry must establish national minimum standards for the curriculum and the accompanying textbooks. Only through this method can the Government carry out its constitutional responsibility.

No one familiar with postwar Japanese education could deny that an additional motive underlies the Government's passage of legislation concentrating educational power at the central ministerial level. Araki Masuo himself, as Minister of Education from 1960 to 1963, clearly delineated the issues when he traveled around the country speaking to parents and educators, exhorting them to dissolve the powerful Japan Teachers Union. He estimates that in public speeches during 1961 he publicly branded activists within the Union as fools and outlaws approximately 150 times because they tried to brainwash their students with left-wing propaganda.

At a well publicized meeting with a national gathering of educational administrators, Minister Araki demanded that school officials shut out the nefarious Union because it aimed at a communist revolution. Citing statistics from the Public Security Agency that 3,000 of the 500,000 members of the Union belonged to the Japan Communist Party, he charged that:

> These communist members are trying to work up a revolution by brainwashing the good teachers and children. Rascals as members of the Union could not be trusted to educate Japanese youth. There is no choice but to get rid of the Union in order to pass on to the generations to come our culture and virtues developed through the efforts of our forefathers.

Viewed from the Government's position, the textbook authorization procedure, the mandatory curriculum, and all that attends a highly centralized system of education such as that existent in Japan, are methods employed by the Government to ensure political neutrality of education. The Ministry stands confidently on the provisions of Article 6 and 8 of the Fundamental Law of Education that "Teachers of the schools prescribed by law shall be servants of the whole community ..." and that "The schools prescribed by law shall refrain from political education or other political activities for or against any specific political party."

The issues are clearly defined in the textbook controversy. The Government claims its methods of administering national education, including the textbook authorization system, are based on laws duly passed by the Diet to implement the provisions of the Constitution and the Fundamental Law of Education. It contends that views and theories developed by authors must be officially reviewed in Japan, where conflicting interpretations of history confront each other from an ideological basis, because these views may be proven incorrect later. The opposition, including the Japan Teachers Union, the Socialist and Communist parties, a significant number of intellectuals, and virtually all other left-wing groups including the various student factions, vociferously disagree. They charge the Ministry with impinging upon constitutional rights through state censorship and improper control over education.

Even though the disparate positions are sharply defined in the Ienaga case, the significance of the contemporary textbook controversy cannot be fully understood without placing the authorization system in historical perspective. When the first national system of education was inaugurated in 1872, the Ministry of Education published a list of titles of books recommended for classroom use. The majority was drawn from books written by Western scholars. However, three of Fukuzawa Yukichi's works were on the list including *Gakumon no Susume* (The Advancement of Learning) and *Seiyō Jijō* (Situation in the West).

The Ministry of Education simultaneously began to compile material for textbook publication. In 1873, one of the first and most famous textbooks published and recommended by the Ministry was the *Shōgaku Tokuhon* (Elementary School Reader) which included chapters translated from an American school book, the *Wilson Reader*. Consequently, at the very beginning of the national school system in Japan, the free publication of textbooks was allowed, alongside those published by the Government.

Following the initial modernization period in which Western ideas were introduced into the schools through imported textbooks and teachers, a reaction set in by the 1880s. In that year a survey of textbooks was conducted by the Government which eventually led to the first textbook authorization system. Based on the survey, the Government published a list of prohibited titles, including one of Fukuzawa's books and even one of the Ministry's own publications, a translation in morals education.

The following year the Ministry implemented a textbook reporting system (*kaihō seido*) requiring each school to submit a list of all titles in use to the Ministry. The free selection of textbooks was still in modified operation, minus the proscribed books. Finally, in 1883, the first textbook approval system (*ninka*) was inaugurated in which titles for all books selected for textbook use by each school were sent to the government for approval. In practice, approval often came after the books were already in use, provoking increased criticism of the approval system.

Following Mori Arinori's appointment in 1885 as Minister of Education, national education became a tool of the Government for nation-building. Henceforth education was directly employed to meet the purposes of a government endeavoring to remain independent from Western colonial powers though adapting Western industrial and military techniques. In the process the Government revised the textbook regulations in 1886, instituting the first textbook authorization system (*kentei*) similar to the contemporary procedure, in which manuscripts written by private authors required Ministry authorization prior to publication. Although this method did not satisfy some critics, it survived into the twentieth century.

At the turn of the century Japanese society underwent a transitional period when the industrial revolution stimulated the growth of factories with increasing numbers of peoples moving into the cities for work. The growing ranks of workers became targets of a fledgling socialist movement. Confronted with the social challenge, marked by abortive political rights movements, the Government strengthened national control over education in 1900 by empowering the Ministry of Education to prescribe the curriculum. Previously, the Ministry published broad curriculum guidelines allowing prefectural governments to draw up the curriculum within the guidelines. A demand for government publication (*kokutei*) of compulsory education textbooks had already been recorded when the Diet passed various resolutions recommending to a somewhat reluctant Minister of Education the nationalization of textbooks in morals and Japanese language courses. The Ministry responded by preparing a model textbook in morals education.

In the midst of these events, the notorious textbook scandal erupted in 1902 when over 100 individuals including governors, mayors, school principals, and teachers were arrested and prosecuted for bribery, blackmail, and kickbacks. Under the authorization system (*kentei*), the

Government published a list of selected books in each subject. Officials within the individual prefecture then made the final selection from the authorized lists. When nearly all of the major textbook publishers were implicated in bribery with local government officials responsible for textbook selection, the defects of the authorization system were exposed. The scandal served to reinforce a movement already under way within the Diet and among prefectural governors for the nationalization of textbooks.

In 1903, the Minister of Education finally assumed responsibility for the preparation of textbooks (*kokutei*) when a law was passed by the Imperial Diet revising the Elementary School Code which granted textbook copyrights exclusively to the Ministry of Education. The first textbooks compiled by the Government in 1904 were those for Japanese language, morals, Japanese history, and geography. Others followed. From that time on until the end of World War II, Japanese textbooks for compulsory education were written, published, and distributed by the Ministry of Education, while textbooks for secondary education continued under the authorization system initiated from 1885.

At the very beginning of the American Occupation of Japan, textbooks came under immediate scrutiny. In one of the initial documents entitled Administration of the Educational System of Japan, October 22 1945, SCAP declared its basic policy accordingly:

> Existing curricula, textbooks, teaching materials, and instructional materials, the use of which is temporarily permitted on an emergency basis, will be examined as rapidly as possible and those portions designed to promote a militaristic or ultranationalistic ideology will be eliminated. New curricula, textbooks, teaching manuals, and instructional materials designed to produce an educated, peaceful, and responsible citizenry will be prepared and will be substituted for existing materials as rapidly as possible.

In the examination of the wartime textbooks in morals, Japanese history, and geography, SCAP officials discovered that "the objectionable doctrines were so inextricably interwoven throughout the whole of each book that they could not be used. For this reason the courses in morals, Japanese history, and geography were suspended by a SCAP Directive of December 31 1945 and the texts and manuals formerly used in these courses were banned." The texts used in other courses were censored with large portions blacked out or cut out which dealt with ultranationalism, militarism, and religious discrimination.

The responsibility for revising and compiling newly prescribed textbooks was empowered on January 8 1946 to a Textbook Committee with the Minister of Education as chairman. On January, 17, SCAP directed that all such publications be submitted to SCAP for review and approval before printing. In effect, the American Occupation was resuming the prewar and wartime system of *kokutei*, that is, government compilation.

With the arrival in Japan of the first United States Education Mission in March 1946 a new factor was introduced, initiating a series of proposals for revising the entire educational system. The Mission wrote that:

> Textbooks in Japanese education are virtually a monopoly of the Department of Education, which prepares and prescribes them for elementary schools, and has those for secondary schools prepared and submitted for approval . . . The preparation and publication of textbooks should be left to open competition . . . For economic reasons the selection of textbooks cannot be left wholly to the free choice of teachers. They should be selected by committees of teachers from a given area . . . The responsibility for the compilation of history and geography texts should not rest within the Ministry of Education. Councils of competent Japanese scholars should be established to develop authentical objective sources for the rewriting of Japanese history. Such materials should provide a basis for the preparation of textbooks . . . Powers at the National Level: Many present controls affecting curricula, methods, materials of instruction, and personnel should be transferred to prefectural and local school administrators . . . Powers at the Prefectural Level: Approval of textbooks recommended by the local school authorities.

Obviously, the Mission's recommendations concerning textbooks were designed for the future, since the American Occupation was then endeavoring to weed out militarism and nationalism permeating the wartime textbooks. SCAP was in no position to leave the preparation and publication of textbooks to "open competition." Rather, under SCAP direction, new "stopgap textbooks" were planned for 1946 to be compiled by the Bureau of Textbooks at the Ministry of Education, minus its former military advisor from the Japanese Army. Because of the shortage of time, wartime texts were used wherever possible with objectionable material being replaced by material acceptable to SCAP. All manuscripts prepared by the Ministry required translation into English for SCAP's review and approval before printing. The "stopgap" editions, necessarily shortened versions because of paper shortages, served the schools until more permanent texts could be prepared for the 1947–48 school year.

The Ministry of Education, with special advisory committees and SCAP advisors from relevant areas, compiled the new texts within criteria established by SCAP. Again, because of lack of time and shortage of materials, the new texts were based on the "stopgap" editions, which were essentially based on censored wartime texts. Completely new manuscripts were required for the banned Japanese history courses. New morals books were not required since the morals course remained proscribed from the curriculum.

The rewriting of Japanese history textbooks required special care for the resumption of the history course in September 1946. For several months the compilation section of the Ministry's Textbook Bureau had been preparing new history textbooks. However, responsibility was transferred from the Ministry to a committee of writers mostly from Tokyo Imperial University, apparently at the instigation of SCAP.

A major problem encountered with the history textbooks was the treatment of mythology, as distinct from historical truth, since the two were united in a prewar textbooks. Material drawn from the *Kojiki*, Japan's earliest collected writings, proved difficult to handle. Material supported from historical fact was approved. The rest was treated as pure mythology. The result was Japan's first postwar history textbook in two thin volumes entitled *Kuni no Ayumi* (The Footsteps of a Nation), authorized by SCAP. One of the major contributors among the committee of Japanese scholars was, ironically, no other than Ienaga Saburō, who wrote the first three chapters. It was from this material that Ienaga the following year prepared his own book called *A New History of Japan*, adapted for textbook use from 1953. This text eventually became the object of his legal case.

In October 1946, SCAP authorized the resumption of history teaching "with the proviso that only textbooks prepared by the Ministry of Education and approved by SCAP be used." Continuing the prewar nationalized textbook system now under Occupation control, the American authorities, obviously pleased with the *Kuni no Ayumi* publication, reported that "The textbooks which resulted from this project . . . were Japan's honest presentation of the story of the nation which was genuine and in proper historical perspective. The production of these textbooks has proved that there are competent historians in Japan and that they resent the corruption of their profession." Ienaga, as one of the major authors, was included in this category.

In March 1947 the Fundamental Law of Education and the School Education Law were promulgated, embodying most of the recommendations made by the United States Education Mission, except those concerning textbooks. Article 21 of the School Education Law stated that "the elementary school shall use the textbooks approved or those the use of which is authorized by the competent authorities or the textbooks published by the competent authorities. Books other than the above-mentioned textbooks and other teaching materials may be used, if they are good and suitable." Textbooks for the lower and upper secondary schools complied with this Article. In the Supplementary Provisions, "competent authorities" in Article 21 were specifically designated as the Minister of Education. Nevertheless, the American Occupation authorities continued as the ultimate body approving textbooks compiled under Ministry initiative.

In an effort to reduce the influence of the Ministry of Education, a new non-Ministry committee was established in December 1947 to succeed the Ministry's Textbook Committee. Included in the new Standing Textbook Committee were representatives from 27 prefectural education offices and ten publication specialists to advise the Ministry on the compilation, approval, and printing of textbooks. At the new committee's initial meeting in January 1948 a recommendation was approved to the effect that textbook compilation by the Ministry of Education should be supplanted by the free compilation by private authors for the 1948–49 academic year.

Based on this recommendation, the Ministry of Education established a Textbook Authorization Committee on May 12 1948 to supervise the examination of manuscripts submitted by independent authors for use from 1949. This marks the beginning of the present authorization system currently the center of the controversy, and a return to the procedure employed prior to 1903 before the Ministry was empowered to compile textbooks. Ironically, the present authorization system, under attack by opposition forces as a device strengthening the Ministry's centralized power, resulted from an effort over twenty years ago to reduce the Ministry's authority from compilation to authorization.

The new Textbook Authorization Committee included two elementary teachers, six secondary teachers, five university professors, and two representatives from the Japan Publishers' Association. The Committee appointed subject matter teachers to initially review manuscripts. Those receiving Ministry approval were ultimately forwarded to SCAP for final approval. All textbooks approved in this manner, plus those previously compiled by the Ministry, were then exhibited throughout the nation enabling local education authorities to choose from the authorized list beginning with the 1949–50 academic year.

Because the new authorization system was rather quickly implemented, private authors had insufficient time to prepare manuscripts for submission. The first results of the new system indicated that both lack of experience and time were important factors in the transitional period. Out of 584 manuscripts reviewed by the new Textbook Authorization Committee, 427 were passed. SCAP disapproved another 247. Finally, only 63 were printed in time for the 1949–50 year. SCAP reported that the major reasons for the high proportion of rejections were that many manuscripts were hasty revisions of old textbooks and others were haphazardly thrown together.

Even though the new authorization system was intended to reduce the role of the Ministry of Education, which formally held a monopoly on textbook compilation, the new system immediately received criticism from the growing ranks of the militant Japan Teachers Union. By this time the Union, founded in 1947, had become locked in internecine struggles with SCAP and the Ministry of Education over the Union's loss of the right to strike, as a result of General MacArthur's intervention in prohibiting civil servants this means of protest. In addition, the Union, coming under the pervading influence of the Japan Communist Party, had lost its recognition as the teachers' negotiating agent, previously contractually granted by the Ministry and unilaterally abrogated in 1948. Consequently, when the textbooks submitted by the Union were all rejected except one in music, the enmity between the Union and the Ministry was further exacerbated over the textbook authorization system. The Union's intractable opposition has plagued the Ministry of Education over since.

In the first postwar Ministry of Education Establishment Law of

1949, still under the American Occupation, a Textbook Authorization and Research Council was established "to examine textbooks under application for authorization, and to make research and deliberation on important matters concerning textbooks." This merely institutionalized the former Textbook Authorization Committee that had already screened the manuscripts for the 1949–50 school year.

By this time SCAP had revised its policy of approving manuscripts submitted by the Ministry for final review. Instead of blanket approval or disapproval, two new categories for acceptance were established. One category approved a text subject to specific recommended changes, and the other was to hold a disapproved book for further reworking by the author and reconsideration for the following year. Under this system, 412 books were approved and 159 disapproved by the Council in 1950–51. SCAP disapproved a further 75, approved 195 without change, and approved 142 subject to revisions.

When the American Occupation was terminated in 1952, the Japanese Government inherited an approval system from the Americans in which the Ministry of Education's authorization committee stipulated text-book revisions prior to acceptance. This procedure, in fact, represents the very point of contention in the 1970 Ienaga case. Required revisions prior to publication, a method employed by the American Occupation in its policy of screening Japanese textbooks, was declared in violation of the postwar Japanese Constitution.

The several years following the Occupation represent one of the most crucial periods in postwar Japanese education. During these years the textbook controversy became inextricably involved in a series of escalating events pitting the Ministry of Education against the Japan Teachers Union, culminating in the Government's major educational revisions of the American Occupation reforms. These, in turn, sparked an interlude of violent confrontation on the streets and in the school between the Government and organized teachers. During the eventful years of the 1950s, the textbook system underwent a significant evolution.

At the beginning of this momentus era, the number of textbooks receiving authorization for the 1952–53 school year attained a high level. For example, 459 different textbooks were approved for the three-year junior high school during that year. The rate of approval for all school levels reached 80 per cent, with 1,082 out of 1,339 manu-scripts receiving authorization. Obviously, authors had a rather wide margin of leeway in which to work.

At the same time, teachers were actively participating in the selection process by recommending titles from the rather extensive list of approved textbooks to the thousands of local school boards where the final decisions were made. In addition, teachers had gained an influential position on the school boards themselves through the regular elective process. For example, in the 1952 school board elections, candidates endorsed by the Japan Teachers Union conducting an avowed anti-Ministry campaign captured approximately 35 per cent of the influential prefectural school board posts, and an estimated 30 per cent at the city, town and village level. In the general elections held the same year, the Union's candidates won 38 seats in the Lower House and eight in the Upper House, for a bloc of 46 delegates in the nation's supreme legislative body.

The Government expressed unconcealed concern with what was interpreted as excessive political activities of teachers both in and out of the classroom. The Ministry was particularly provoked by a pamphlet distributed by the Teachers Union in 1953 entitled *To the New Teachers*. The Union went on record as opposing Japanese capitalists and the Government from the standpoint of a class struggle. Shortly thereafter, the educational world was rocked by the Yamaguchi Diary Case when it was revealed that the Japan Teachers Union through its branch affiliates compiled and published quasi-textbooks for classroom use in the form of workbooks and supplementary materials. Naturally, they were not processed through the Ministry of Education's textbook authorization procedure. In one of the most provocative passages in a workbook compiled by the Yamaguchi Teachers Union, a Japan Teachers Union affiliate, and widely used in the schools of Yamaguchi Prefecture, the following passage was included:

> The first aim of socialism is to obtain the happiness of laborers and farmers. It is diametrically opposite to capitalism. Capitalists who own the factories make their profits through exploiting laborers by paying them low salaries and paying low prices to farmers for their rice. Now, what is the difference between Russia, a socialist country, and Japan and the United States, capitalist countries?

Reacting to this case and others similar to it, the ruling Liberal Party published in 1955 a series of three important reports affecting the postwar textbook system. These publications, entitled *The Deplorable Textbooks* (Ureubeki Kyōkasho), mark the turning point in the textbook authorization procedure from a relatively free system in the early '50s to an increasingly rigid system by the end of the decade, ultimately leading to the Ienaga court case.

The ruling conservative party deplored the distorted textbooks and supplementary workbooks being recommended by the Japan Teachers Union. Evidence of distorted textbooks approved under the Ministry's authorization system were given as the social studies texts written by Munakata Seiya, Miyahara Seiichi, and Hidaka Rokurō, three famous left-wing antigovernment scholars at Tokyo University. All three had been instrumental in developing the antigovernment theoretical position of the Japan Teachers Union. For example, Miyahara was the leading member of the Union's special committee that wrote *A Code of Ethics for Teachers* which included the controversial slogan that *Teachers Are Laborers.*

The Government claimed that the increasingly biased books were supporting the political activities of the teachers' labor union movement, glorifying the Soviet Union and Communist China while criticizing Japan, and inculcating communist thought in the students. The charge was made that the Union had been applying increasing pressure on publishing companies to include more left-wing content in their textbooks in order to obtain teacher recommendation for purchase.

In particular, the Liberal Party attacked the supplementary workbooks published by local affiliates of the Teachers Union. Quoting the Yamaguchi Case, among others, the ruling party claimed that activist teachers within the Union required students to purchase the workbooks for summer study. Profits running into millions of yen were then employed to finance the Union's political campaigns. In certain instances, notably in Hokkaido, the Union published textbooks which passed what was criticized as the very loose authorization standards of the Ministry. With the Teachers Union writing and publishing textbooks, and teachers as Union members participating in the selection process, it was felt that the Union could gain a monopoly if this practice were allowed to spread. Finally, the charge was made that with so many books being processed each year through the Ministry's understaffed authorization committees, far too many factual and technical errors were passing undetected. The entire process had to be improved.

Apparently influenced by the ruling party's criticism, the Central Advisory Committee of the Ministry of Education in late 1955 drew up a report on *The Improvement of the Textbook System* which incorporated the following recommendations: (1) the Government should strictly enforce standards of the textbook authorization system by increasing the number of examiners to include full-time Ministry appointees on the committees, (2) the number of approved textbooks per subject area should be reduced, (3) textbook publishing companies should be registered and approved by the Ministry, (4) the cost of textbooks should be substantially lowered, (5) and the selection of textbooks should be conducted through larger geographical units than the local school board covers.

The year 1956 represents a pivotal year in Japanese education, with significant consequences affecting the textbook controversy. First of all, the Government submitted a bill in the Diet to revise the school board system from elective to an appointive method, and a textbook bill incorporating the major recommendations from the Central Advisory Committee on Education. During the ensuing confrontation in the Diet over the school board bill, the Government decided to withdraw the textbook bill in order to concentrate on the major administrative legislation. The school board bill was passed when police were called into the Diet chambers to stop the fighting among the representatives in order to restore order for a final vote.

Even though the textbook bill was withdrawn, the provisions, drawn originally from the recommendations contained in the Liberal Party's *Deplorable Textbook* reports, were subsequently implemented through Ministry of Education ordinances. To begin with, before the conflict over the school board law subsided, a highly controversial development was taking place within the Ministry later dubbed the "F Purge." To government critics the F Purge signals the implementation of a more rigid application of the textbook authorization system. In 1955 the Ministry's authorization committee (Shingikai) consisted of 54 members with five serving on the all-important subcommittee for social studies. Because the identity of the committee members was secret, the five social studies members indicated their approval or disapproval of textbooks under the code letters A to E. In 1956, when the Ministry increased the Shingikai membership from 54 to 100, and added full-time Ministry of Education appointees for the first time, a sixth member was added to the sensitive subcommittee on social studies textbooks.

With the addition of Mr. "F," later identified as a professor from Nihon University, the number of textbook rejections in social studies abruptly increased. Although the Ministry did not publish exact data about the rate of rejections, Ienaga claims that according to a personal survey of publishers involved in submitting manuscripts in social studies, the failure rate reached as high as 35 per cent following the expansion of the authorization committee. Ienaga's own manuscript was rejected by the newly expanded committee. The charge was made that a known conservative, Mr. F, whose expressed views included the opinion that the postwar consititution was imposed and did not originate from the Japanese people, was purposely added to the authorization committee in social studies to ferret out those manuscripts with views opposing those of the Government. Hence, the so-called F Purge.

The Ministry maintains that left-wing ideology was inexorably creeping into the manuscripts. Since the Government has the responsibility for maintaining political neutrality of public education, it was only natural the number of rejections would increase in proportion to the increase in manuscripts containing politically biased materials. According to the Ministry, the Government did not change its basic attitude at this time.

When the new school board system went into effect in 1957, conservative appointees replaced many of the activist teachers who were previously elected to serve on the boards. The new school boards were then exclusively authorized to select textbooks from the approved list. In addition, the Ministry of Education was empowered for the first time to veto the Superintendents of Education selected by the prefectural Boards of Education. Nevertheless, the Government was cognizant of the incongruity of a national textbook authorization system for a curriculum locally set. At that time the Ministry published curriculum guides enabling school boards to establish local curricula.

In 1958, the Government completed the series of major revisions of the earlier American Occupation reforms when a nationwide mandatory curriculum was promulgated by the Ministry of Education. Accordingly, the textbook authorization system assumed a new significance. With the mandatory curriculum, the government was finally in the position to stipulate course content and authorize only those textbooks which conformed to that curriculum. The new system marked one of the most crucial reforms of Japanese education since World War II.

With the principal of a compulsory curriculum established in 1958, the Ministry undertook to conclude the series of textbook measures for the implementation of the 1955 recommendations by the Central

Advisory Committee. For example, the number of approved textbooks per subject area continued to decline. The approved titles in junior high school history manifest the trend. From 30 titles in 1959, the number decreased to 14 by 1963. The final measures were implemented in 1964 when textbooks were made free, textbook publishing companies were required to register for approval, and the textbook selection procedure underwent revision.

The new selection procedure was designed to increase the geographical unit making the textbook selection. Under the 1957 law governing the new appointive school board system, each of the nearly 10,000 local boards was empowered to select textbooks for their local schools. From 1964, the thousands of local boards were grouped together under 467 Textbook Selection Districts, as determined by the prefectural Boards of Education. The prefectural boards established textbook guidelines for the local boards. Then the individual boards within each Textbook Selection District established a joint committee to make one textbook selection from the approved titles per subject at each grade level for every school in the district. One important effect of the new system was to increase the distance between classroom teachers, predominately members of the left-wing antigovernment Teachers Union, and the committees selecting the textbooks.

By the time Professor Ienaga filed his first textbook claim against the Ministry of Education in 1965, the Government had implemented its long-range plan for the reform of the textbook authorization and selection procedure. In a report from the Ministry around this time, entitled *Problems Concerning the Free Distribution of Textbooks*, it was stated that with a mandatory curriculum and the textbook authorization system, the result was essentially the same as a nationalized textbook system (*kokutei*). The 1970 verdict against this system represented the first reversal experienced by the Ministry of Education in the interminable textbook controversy.

In the highly heralded decision of 1970, the Tokyo District Court judge, Sugimoto Ryōkichi, in a rather long and rambling verdict, employed a variety of statutes to substantiate his decision. Following is a summary of the judgment:

> The birthright of every child is the right to learn. This is what we call freedom of education. The state's role should only be to encourage and support the child's right to learn. The state itself

has no educational rights. Authors are guaranteed by the Constitution the freedom to publish textbooks. The state thus has no right to evaluate the content. The actions by the Ministry of Education in this case represent censorship in violation of the Constitution and the Fundamental Law of Education.

Article 26 of the Constitution—"All people shall have the right to receive an equal education correspondent to their ability, as provided by law. All people shall be obligated to have all boys and girls under their protection receive ordinary education as provided by law. Such compulsory education shall be free." This means that education is the inalienable right of every child. Parents are obligated to fulfill this right, which can be termed the people's freedom of education (*kokumin no kyōiku no jiyū*). In contrast, the state's educational rights (*kokka kyōiku ken*) must be restricted. The state has a duty only to encourage the people's pursuit of their obligation, and to provide facilities and conditions which enable the people to foster education. The state is not allowed to intervene in the content of education.

Teachers have the direct responsibility to teach children at school. Thus the parents' obligation to educate their children is delegated to the teachers. Teachers must pursue truth in teaching, and provide an education which is suitable for the full development of the child. Education, therefore, is an academic endeavor.

Article 23 of the Constitution—"Academic freedom is guaranteed." This assures teachers the freedom to present academic viewpoints which they believe are legitimate. The state must devise means to offer guidance to teachers without restricting their rights. The state has no right to prohibit teachers from selecting textbooks, or to compel teachers to follow precise teaching instruction through mandatory teacher's manuals.

Article 21 of the Constitution—"Freedom of assembly and association as well as speech, press, and all other forms of expression are guaranteed. No censorship shall be maintained, nor shall the secrecy of any means of communication be violated." This guarantees the freedom of authors to publish their academic viewpoints through textbooks. Textbook authors thus have the freedom to prepare manuscripts in order to fulfill their obligation to educate children. Textbook authorization cannot be considered a patent which the state bestows. The present system represents censorship in which public authorities restrict the freedom of textbook publication by rendering judgment prior to publication. The authorization system is invalid if it evaluates textbook content.

Article 10 of the Fundamental Law of Education—"Education shall not be subject to improper control, but it shall be directly responsible to the whole people. School administration shall, on the basis of this realization, aim at the adjustment and establishment of the various conditions required for the pursuit of the aim of education." This can be interpreted as guaranteeing the autonomy of education. The administrative authority of the state in curriculum and teaching methods should be limited to guidance provisions and broad outlines of standards. The authorization of textbooks must be restricted to the correction of factual mistakes, publishing errors, and other objectively clear inaccuracies, and whether the content is in accordance with the broad outline of the curriculum guide. If the authorization system goes beyond this and judges the validity of the content, the system contravenes the intent of Article 10 of the Fundamental Law of Education.

Concerning the particular passages under dispute in this case, there are various interpretations of the descriptions in *Kojiki* and *Nihonshoki* as historical materials for educational purposes. In Professor Ienaga's interpretation concerning the Japan-USSR Treaty of Neutrality, the assertation by the Ministry of Education that the inclusion of one clause objectively renders the passage false, can be interpreted as the state's denial of the author's understanding of historical fact. On the contrary, since the author's analysis represents the product of his scholarly research, his interpretation must be recognized.

In conclusion, each passage rejected by the Ministry of Education represents prior judgment of the author's thought, herein interpreted as censorship according to Article 21 of the Constitution. In addition, since the passages cannot be objectively declared false, their rejection contravenes the provisions of Article 10 of the Fundamental Law of Education. Therefore, the textbook authorization system as applied by the Ministry of Education in this case is hereby declared unconstitutional and illegal.

The 1970 verdict marks the beginning of long and tedious litigation over the meaning, intent, and application of the provisions of the postwar Constitution, the Fundamental Law of Education, and the School Education Law. An appeal was filed in the Tokyo Higher Court in February 1971 from where that verdict will ultimately be appealed to the Supreme Court. The Government, in its appeal to the Higher Courts, intends to emphasize the legal and technical basis under-lying its position. According to the Ministry, Judge Sugimoto did not make his decision based on law, but rather on a philosophical interpretation of the role of the state, the parent, and the teacher in educational affairs. From a legal standpoint, the Ministry feels confident a Higher Court Judge, with more experience than a District Court Judge, will overrule the initial verdict.

The Ienaga case could prove to be one of the most critical landmarks in postwar education. If the higher courts uphold the lower court's verdict, the stage is then set for opposition forces to employ the precedent for an all-out judicial assault on the Government's entire educational policy. If the content of textbooks cannot be approved by the Ministry of Education, then it becomes problematic whether the Ministry has the right to set the specific contents of a mandatory curriculum. Without the authority to authorize textbooks and set the curriculum, an unprecedented era in Japanese education will emerge, a contingency the Government intends to exert maximum efforts to prevent. Until that ultimate decision by the Supreme Court is handed down, Professor Ienaga's latest revised textbook will remain banned under the Ministry's textbook authorization procedure, while his previously authorized and much revised textbook continues to receive wide use in high school history courses.

FRED C. C. PENG

EDUCATION: AN AGENT OF
SOCIAL CHANGE IN AINU
COMMUNITY LIFE

Introduction

Education is an interesting institution which more often than other
wise serves as an agent of social change that can either better organize
an aspiring community or help disorganize a politically, economically,
and linguistically threatened community. The latter case is evidenced
by the social change that has taken place in the Ainu community that
the author has investigated. For one of the factors contributing to the
rapid disorganization of traditional Ainu communities in the late
nineteenth and twentieth centuries was the program of compulsory
education begun for the Ainu at the turn of this century.

Although compulsory education helped pave the way for a new
existence, it destroyed the old way of teaching and learning.[1] And
education, like the economic sector,[2] has thus become an area where
the inferior status of the Ainu minority in Japanese society is most
evident. This is the area of seemingly paradoxical interests for which
the author proposes to account.

Fred C. C. Peng is Professor of Linguistics at International Christian University in Tokyo.
    Reprinted from Fred C. C. Peng and Peter Geiser, *The Ainu: The Past in the Present*
(Hiroshima: Bunka Hyoron Publishing Co., 1977), pp. 178–206, with permission of the
authors and publisher.

First, an attempt will be made to set forth some traditional patterns of learning and teaching by bringing into focus the social roles formerly played by Ainu men and women. These had a significant economical and linguistic bearing on their survival as a cohesive group. Second, a detailed account of the various policies of Japanese education that have affected the Ainu over the past few decades will be presented and posited as being a direct cause of the social transformation of the Ainu community. A concluding statement will show the consequences of such policies, indicating, so to speak the net result in its positive and negative terms.

.Traditional Mode of Ainu Education

The aim, in this section, is to present certain facts which pertain to the part of traditional Ainu social life called *learning*, consisting of the transmission of the technical know-how of a particular workmanship, the delicate skills required for the production of artifacts, and the sophisticated knowledge of verbal artistry. It is intended to present evidence of the process of learning that shaped the mode of Ainu education during the past few centuries. Once this traditional mode of Ainu education is explicated, one will be able to understand the changes which have been associated with modern education.

Fortunately, sufficient information has been made available of the hunting and gathering foundation of traditional Ainu economical life. Considerable information exists concerning the division of labor between men and women in their traditional community. For instance, men did the hunting and, in main, built the houses, officiated at religious ceremonies, manufactured weaponry, and made such items as *inaw* (whittled pieces of willow). Last but not least they cared for the young, the sick, and the weak.[3] Women, generally, did the gathering, farmed small plots of land, sought the inner bark of elm trees for purposes of making thread, wove cloth, made shoes, sewed clothes, and did the cooking.[4] However, there were areas of cooperation in which men helped women accomplish difficult tasks and vice versa. Both cooperated in the building of houses, farming the land, and cutting the inner bark from an elm tree.

When building a new house, men did the heavy-duty work, such as laying the pillars and constructing the roof,[5] while women sorted out the weeds and straw for the thatch. Although women ploughed the land, raked the grass, and sowed the seeds for farming, it was the men who helped them build a fence around the farm land—no more than ten to fifteen square meters—and who assisted in harvesting the crop. And when it was time to look for elm trees or oak trees, and the like, men and women went together; men cut the bark and peeled the lining while women tested the quality of the materials; they together pulled down the bark from the trees, and soaked it in a nearby pond or stream within a protected boundary set up by men.

The kind of work mentioned above, either carried out by men or women alone or shared by both, would have been forgotten a long time ago, had it not been transmitted (or taught, for that matter) from one generation to another. The fact that it had been passed intact from one generation to another proves the continued effectiveness of learning and teaching processes until the complete breakdown of the Ainu culture. The theory is that the young people, boys and girls, learned the knowledge and skills of those tasks both formally, i.e., through specific instructions, and informally, i.e., through observation without any specifically programmed instruction. Moreover, the author is of the opinion that boys and girls adopted their respective sex-models; boys learned their sex-related knowledges and skills from men, and girls learned theirs from women. The learning occurred in either an isolated situation, where only members of one sex were involved, or a mixed situation, where members of both sexes were involved.

Learning on the part of the Ainu youth was expected of them not only in the above mentioned economic domain but it was also expected in a domain which was linguistic in character. In this area of learning, a great deal of knowledge of the Ainu language was assumed. An Ainu youth had to be a full-fledged member of a speech community where Ainu speech was, first of all, a bona fide medium of instruction. It was only then that any instruction relevant to that domain could be given to him. It is in this domain that the author will be concerned with Ainu oral literature, more broadly, verbal artistry.

Traditionally, three areas of verbal artistry may be mentioned. They are labelled conveniently as (1) religiously-oriented, (2) morally-oriented, and (3) politically-oriented. The first two may be assigned to the realm of literature, in its broadest sense, concerned with definite aesthetic values, while the third one is more oratorical than aesthetic.

It is of interest to note that the Ainu religion[6] would not function in the absence of some kind of the religiously-oriented oral literature. In other words, at some point during a religious ceremony, oral literature in one form or another would have to be performed. The content and style is highly elaborate and the technique of performing it requires a certain amount of training. In one of his field trips, the author had an occasion to observe an old lady of 83 years of age and her daughter performing an interesting piece to him. The mother, after a few sips of Shōchū (an alcoholic beverage), chanted through a piece of oral literature with elegance and ease. The daughter, in her sixties, however, appeared to have great difficulty, even to the audience, for she made an obviously strenuous effort to mimic her mother without too much success.

One characteristic of religiously-oriented oral literature is that it is chanted with a melody of three or four notes, which is punctuated by a definite rhythm with certain embellishments and improvization. Another characteristic is that some could be performed only by men and some only by women, though many could be shared and performed by both. For example, to name but a few, *kamuy nomi itak* (prayers to gods) and a certain kind of *yukar* (epic poems), such as *kamuy yukar* (divine epic poems), could be performed only by a man, and *tusu sinotca* (witch's hymns) and a *yukar*, such as *menoko yukar* (female epic poems), could be performed only by a woman. But *rimse sinotca* (dancing hymns) could be done by both men and women together.

Of all religiously-oriented oral literature Ainu *yukar* (Ainu epic poetry), of whatever magnitude, is perhaps the most important. It is highly cherished and can be considered to be extremely stylized in that it was performed on special occasions, for instance, the Bear Ceremony. Each type of such oral literature is rhythmically chanted, and therefore requires a good deal of tutoring before one can master it. Youths making a mistake in their performances would be reprimanded by the elders, for such a mistake on a serious occasion could anger the supernatural to the detriment of the offender, resulting, for instance, in the loss of the next game upon which the whole *kotan* (village) might have to depend as a source of subsistence.

Morally-oriented oral literature, on the other hand, is characterized by the absence of a melody; it is said in the manner of a tale without any musical qualities. However, it has a blend of didactics in that each tale contains a lesson, e.g., sharing, unselfishness, the consequence of an aggressor (usually a *wajin*), etc., which was intended by its storyteller (usually an elder) to be learned by its listeners (usually young people). Examples are *uwepeker* (ancient tales) and *kamuy ucaskoma* (god's teaching).[7]

Politically-oriented oral literature is considerably limited in types but by no means in number. One characteristic is that it can be chanted or uttered, depending upon the occasion on which it is used; that is, the social role it plays is no less diversified. The best known type is perhaps what has been called *caranke* (debate).

Traditionally, whenever there was a dispute over an issue, be it marital, territorial, or otherwise, the Ainu solved their problem by holding a *caranke*. Certain *caranke* were chanted and others were uttered. The point is that if the problem was involved in more than one *kotan*, each *kotan* would send the best orator, who was considered expert in verbal artistry, to represent the *kotan*. The *caranke* was normally held at a predesignated place, where people from all *kotan*, more or less serving as referees, would come to hear the great event. The content might have little to do with the problem itself, for the content was supposed to be highly poetic and the style extremely elegant and flowery. The one *kotan*, whose representative had the sharper tongue, would be judged the winner, and the problem was settled at that. In the case of a marital problem, it usually, though not always, involved two different *kotan*, because of the *kut* exogamous restriction.[8] Thus, the man and the woman would seek representatives from their respective *kotan* to settle the problem over a *caranke* in which the families and relatives from both sides would then participate; sometimes, neighbors and friends would also be invited.

It seems clear that verbal artistry of whatever type in whatever area would need a high degree of training in the sense that each member of a language community had to acquire not only the ability of encoding, as in the case of story-telling, chanting, or debating, but also that of decoding, so as to be eligible to participate in normal social life. Moreover, the acquisition was most rudimentary, because without such skills and knowledge commonly possessed by the members of a community, the fabric of its social structure would simply fall into shatters. And it must be emphasized that although the skills and know-how in the economic domain mentioned earlier could be transmitted from one person to another without the use of the Ainu language, any kind of the verbal artistry described above could not be so transmitted. It is obvious that some sort of education, in its broad sense, was required to pass it down from one generation to another. It is this point that will be of major concern later.

Education Reforms in Hokkaidō

No more needs to be said for the traditional mode of Ainu education. In this section, care will be taken to examine the state of affairs in modern education at the time of its enunciation, by taking into account the educational policies and programs of the Japanese government from the Matsumae to the Taishō era regarding the Ainu in Hokkaidō. Attention will be called for to deal with the policies and programs together with their effect upon the education of the Ainu during the above mentioned period.

Under the Matsumae, in the seventeenth and the eighteenth centuries, education of any sort was strictly denied the Ainu in order to better exploit the trade relationship that had been established and upon which Matsumae fortunes depended. The contractors who gained control of the *basho* system after the rebellion of 1669 sometimes went to extremes to insure that the Ainu did not learn Japanese; "troublemakers" who realized they were being cheated and who could make it known in Japanese were sometimes simply done away with. All business between the merchants and those Ainu who traded with them was conducted through specially selected interpreters who came to occupy a position of great power and influence in Ainu affairs. After 1799, this policy was reversed under the Tokugawa. The Japanese language was encouraged and taught as well as simple arithmetic in an attempt to partially assimilate and win over the Ainu who were seen by some as potential allies of the Russians, should Japanese-Ainu relations continue to deteriorate.[9] The first blow, followed by others, was to all but make the Ainu's spoken language extinct.

In 1802, with encouragement from the Tokugawa Bakufu, three Buddhist Temples were established in Hokkaidō.[10] In addition to military instruction from Bakufu officials, priests gave moral instruction and lessons in reading and writing to the Ainu in their destricts, and in spite of orders to avoid changing Ainu customs, they did so with a good deal of success [Takakura 1960:71–3].

Before the Meiji Restoration in 1868, education in Japan was the prerogative of the privileged upper-classes. Realizing, however, the vital role education had played in modernizing western nations, the handful of scholars and statemen, who undertook the task of rapidly transforming a predominantly feudal society into a powerful modern one, seized upon the idea of universal education as a means to help achieve this transformation. As early as 1871 and eighteen years before Japan's first constitution was promulgated, a Department of Education was established, and in 1872, the Education System (Gakusei) was set up. In 1880, the Code of Education made education compulsory up to three years, and in 1886, education was standardized and the compulsory period was extended an extra year [Anderson 1959: 2–13, 217–17].

Education for Ainu as well as Japanese children was recognized as important to the national interest, and at first, Japanese and Ainu children attended school together. In 1892, elementary education was standardized in Hokkaidō, and schools were built in both Japanese and Ainu districts, but distances were great and Ainu attendance was minimal.

The integrated educational policy, which had been in effect since 1892 in Hokkaidō, was not working out well; Ainu children could speak little Japanese and Japanese children had little sympathy for the problems of their Ainu classmates and frequently provoked them. In 1901, a provision of the Protection Act, a ten-year plan, dealing with Ainu special education ruled that Ainu children should attend separate schools because of their different cultural background and the troubles they encountered under the integrated system. According to the plan, which was based on the Ainu Protection Act passed in 1899, twenty-one schools were to be built over the ten-year period, so as to carry out a special educational program for the Ainu. The plan was drafted in such a way that if there were thirty or more eligible children in a village, the government would spend part of its national budget to open up three schools every year. Thus, beginning with Biratori Elementary School in 1901, the projected twenty-one schools were completed by 1909.

Many Ainu balked at the idea of sending their children to Japanese-run schools where they were taught strange new ideas and an alien tongue. Ainu children were needed to work at home and often times schools were too far away to commute daily. Attendance, then, was low, and those Ainu who were on the move and who never stayed in one place very long received no education at all. Probably no more than one-third of the Ainu children eligible for school actually attended during the early part of this century.

In 1916, four years of elementary education were made obligatory for Ainu children, although Japanese children attended school for six years. Six years of schooling were available to outstanding Ainu. However, Ainu children, who attended school at all, usually went for four years and learned ethics, arithmetic, Japanese, physical education, sewing (for girls), and the rudiments of farming [Itō 1971:3–4]; no history, geography, nor science was taught in the Ainu schools, and many dropped out after only two or three years of attendance.

As can be observed from the above, the content of the special educational program, for the purpose of which the twenty-one Ainu schools had been built, was highly discriminatory in design, not to mention the segregated school system. The segregated school system itself was criticized by many Ainu as unfair and was seen as holding Ainu children back. Under attack from many quarters, all schools were then standardized in 1922, as far as the length of compulsory education and curricula were concerned, but not integrated until 1937.[11]

Although, on the surface, education was equalized, because Ainu children came from very different social and cultural backgrounds than did Japanese children, they had trouble adjusting to the integrated system, and even today discrimination in the schools has continued to cause much bitterness among the Ainu. As a matter of fact, discrimination has continued to persist and is manifested in various areas of social and educational life where *wajin* and Ainu have made any contact before and after the introduction of the integrated system. For one thing, the content of the special educational program, though well intended, was ill-formed; it was decided on the basis of the Educational Code for Hokkaidō Ainu[12] passed in 1901 by the Hokkaidō government. As was pointed out earlier, it included in the curriculum only ethics, Japanese arithmetic, physical education, sewing (for girls), and rudiments of farming, and deliberately cut off history, geography, and science. Although this Code was abolished in 1908, due to the fact that many of the teachers involved were opposed to the educational program with which it provided the Ainu. In 1916, the Educational Code for the Ainu[13] was reestablished, restricting the Ainu children from going to school before seven, even though the school age for Japanese children began at six. The reason is given in Article Three of the Code, which may be translated, in part, as follows:

That school age begins at seven or above for Ainu Children is because Ainu children of six years of age are not as mature as

272

wajin children of the same age bracket both emotionally and intellectually. Thus, to begin schooling at the age of six is too early for the Ainu. Based on experience it is deemed necessary that Ainu children should begin schooling at seven or more.

Again, due to protests from all quarters, the Code was abolished in 1922, leading eventually to the standardization mentioned above.

At this point, it may be well to ask why history, geography, and science were excluded from Ainu schools. Two related explanations are conceivable: The first may be regarded as a surface explanation, and the second, an underlying explanation.

First; as was mentioned earlier, compulsory education had been four years for Japanese and three years for Ainu between 1886 and 1916; after 1916, it was six years for Japanese and four years for Ainu, each difference corresponding to one Educational Code specifically designed to exclude the three subjects mentioned above. It can be said then that the Japanese government at that time used the differences in the school years as a justification to "excuse" the Ainu from the "burden" of learning history, geography, and science, because, it was considered not to be feasible for them to learn the three subjects as well within three years in the first place and within four years in the second place. In retrospect, this explanation amounts to nothing more than putting the cart before the horse.

Second, the Japanese government in establishing and modifying the Educational Code was motivated by the thought that the Ainu in the national interest would become better agrarian labors to cultivate the frontiers of Hokkaidō, already in the hand of *wajin* under the name of assimilation, if they did not study history, geography, and science.[14] Because history as a subject, in particular Japanese history, would more likely reveal their inferior status as a conquered people, geography, and especially world geography, might awaken the Ainu consciousness relative to other ethnic minority groups in the world, thereby touching off a sense of identity. Science could well strengthen the feeble mind of the Ainu. In other words, all three were considered too sensitive to be taught to the Ainu. This explanation is more plausible, because the Japanese government in both Meiji and Taishō periods reflected on the policies of the Matsumae, who had attempted to better exploit the Ainu by denying them the opportunity to learn things Japanese, and of the Tokugawa, who had tried to pacify the Ainu for fear of the Russians.

The objective of the Educational Code, established in both the Meiji era and the Taishō era, may become clearer, if the contents of three of the courses taught, as outlined in the syllabuses, are illustrative. The following is a translation from Itō [1971].

1. Ethics:[15] To cultivate well-behaved manners and habits in daily conducts by paying particular attention to such virtues as "being loyal to the Emperor and patriotic to the nation," "being diligent," "being obedient to law and order," and "being clean."
2. Japanese:[16] To pay attention to the pronunciation and exercises of Japanese so as to be able to express ideas intelligibly.
3. Arithmetic: To pay attention to elementary teaching, and to lower the level as much as possible, making sure that the important point gets across, and to drill simple calculation.

Education in Biratori Chō

The first school established in Biratori *chō* was built in the predominantly Ainu settlement of Nibutani in 1892, the year education was standardized in Hokkaidō. School attendance at first was minimal, and only the Ainu children living in the immediate area went regularly. Standardized, formal education was a new idea to most Ainu, and probably not more than one-third of the Ainu children attended school during these first years. Table 1 shows the Ainu school attendance in the Hidaka district from 1892 to 1898.

TABLE 1

AINU SCHOOL ATTENDANCE IN HIDAKA

Year	Eligible Children	Children in Attendance	Percent of Eligible attending
1892	1,294	80	6.2
1893	994	117	11.8
1894	155	205	21.5
1895	648	142	21.9
1896	631	127	20.1
1897	?	?	?
1898	375	149	37.1

Source: Bureau of Statistics [1924].
Note: No data are available for the year 1897.

274

It will be noted that the number of children attending remain more or less constant from 1893 on but that the number of eligible children decrease greatly from 1892 to 1898. This reflects the displacement of large groups of Ainu in the Hidaka district due to economic and social instability mentioned in the preceding section.

Under the ten-year plan launched in 1901, which was to provide classrooms to carry out the special educational program for Ainu children that ended in 1937 when Ainu and *wajin* were integrated, other schools were added. These were Biratori in 1901, Osachinai in 1902, Nukibetsu in 1903, and Nioi in 1909. When the segregated school system finally ended, on the surface at least, one area in Biratori and the community of Hon Nioi refused to send children to school, not so much out of an exaggerated sense of pride as the result of continued national educational policy of discrimination and exploitation. This policy was reflected sharply in the directives of the local board of education and seriously undermined the morale of many conscientious *wajin* teacher. Thus, many Ainu in this area received no education at all. The following is an account of such an incident:

During the Taishō era, around 1921, Ainu schools were not completely segregated, in spite of the Educational Code of 1916. In fact, the elementary school in Nibutani, an Ainu school, was also attended by a few *wajin* children, who were obviously in the minority. Even so, discrimination was inevitable, not so much from the *wajin* children, for they were outnumbered, as from the teacher. Kaizawa [1971], in his recollection of the Nibutani school years, reports thus:[17]

> In my class, although there were only a few *wajin* children, everyday when attendance was taken, the teacher always called their names first. In our class of about fifty, there were several sections (*kumi*) which separated the Ainu from the *wajin* children. The sections took turn to clean the classroom, the yard, and the rest room every afternoon. If the job was not done to the teacher's satisfaction, he had the power to punish the section in question to do it over again the next day. Our teacher thought that the Ainu children did not know how to sweep the floor, clean the rest room, and wipe the desks, so the Ainu sections were punished most of the time day after day. On the other hand, the teacher scolded the few *wajin* children, not infrequently, that they should be more studious or else they would lose ground even to the Ainu.

In most cases, classroom instruction was at a bare minimum limited mostly to "reading" (i.e. reciting Japanese) and to "writing" (i.e., learning *kana*) just to kill time. In the case of Nibutani, Kaizawa recalls that since the teacher was an old man, he came and left as he pleased, with no definite schedule set up for the class. "Though my textbooks on music, history, were bought for me," says he, "nothing was taught in them." When he graduated from the sixth grade, his class barely finished one half of the third grade's math book. Perhaps the teacher had no intention of teaching that school in the first place, though such was not the case in another Ainu school, as was reported by Akira Itō.[18] He cites the Directive of the Elementary School to which he belonged and blames in part the failure of education on the educational policy in general. The directive is translated as follows:

> Although the Educational Code has been abolished, that Code incorporates our fundamental principles which expect that we uphold the Imperial Rescript on Education (of 1908) as well as the essence of other Imperial edicts, related to the arousal of a national apirit, and that we obey the instruction of the educational policy, so as to train healthy citizens.

> School education does not mean just the teaching of educational materials; rather, it lies in the construction of a perfect character as well as in the creation of a perfect manhood. It is hoped that instead of pushing unwanted curricula on Ainu children, who would for sure be bored to death even if a 45-minute period is reduced to a 30-minute one, emphasis should be placed on the characterization of personality, thereby helping to promote those with high potentials.

As a result of this kind of directive, many creative-minded and sympathetic *wajin* teachers were blocked in their attempt to help Ainu students. On the other hand, certain outstanding *wajin* teachers have played an important role in helping Ainu children to adjust and relate to the realities of Japanese society and their ambiguous status in this society. One very well-known teacher at the elementary school in Nibutani was instrumental in organizing several young Ainu who emigrated to Manchuria in order to find a better life for themselves before the second world war. He and other teachers in Biratori *chō* have been involved in other movements and activities of *kotan* youth and have had a hand in shaping the attitudes of many Ainu youths to the world in which they live.

Roughly nine-tenths of those educated Ainu in the sample were educated under the old prewar system and about one-tenth under the new system (cf. FIGURE 1). The majority of those educated under the prewar system received four years of schooling (see Table 2). About a sixth of the sample of household heads and their spouses are over sixty years of age and received only three years of education. Of the 68 percent of those educated Ainu in the sample, who were educated after 1916 when six years of school became available to outstanding pupils, only 5 percent actually attended school for six years. Ten percent of educated Ainu in the sample received eight years of education but all of them attended school after 1941 when the Japanese government strongly encouraged students to complete the higher elementary school level (see Table 1). By way of contrast, 67 percent of Japanese students complete this level.[19] Although the data do not show it, it is likely that one-third or more of the Ainu in Biratori *chō* received no education at all. (This finding is implicit in Table 3.)

Table 2 shows the result of a survey done in the Hidaka district: 14.4 percent of this sample of 105 households did not graduate even from elementary school and only 1.8 percent (0.9 plus 0.9 in Table 2) went beyond the higher elementary level of eight years.

Educational reform was one of the major objectives of the postwar American Occupation which sought to destroy the roots of militarism and ultra-nationalism in Japan. Based upon recommendations from the

TABLE 2

PREWAR EDUCATION IN HIDAKA DISTRICT
PERCENT OF CHILDREN IN 105 HOUSEHOLDS

Level of Education	Total		Graduating Status	
	Entered	Not Entered	Graduated	Did Not Graduate
Higher Education				
Senior High	0.9	99.1	0.0	0.9
Junior High	1.8	98.2	0.9	0.9
Elementary Education				
Kōtōka	14.3	85.9	10.5	3.8
Regular	83.9	16.1	42.8	41.1

Source: Hidaka sub-prefecture [1965].

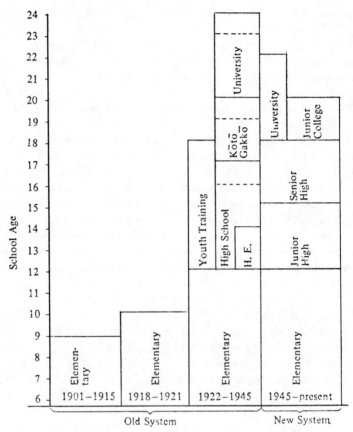

FIGURE 1. EDUCATION IN JAPAN

Source: Bureau of Statistics [1967].
Note: H.E. stands for Higher Elementary which is the translation for Kōtōka. Kōtō Gakkō may be equated to Junior College. During the war, High School was shortened to four years. Before that, a high school student in the fourth year could enter Kōtō Gakkō, if he passed the entrance examination in his own right. Hence the dotted lines.

U.S. Education Mission and the Japanese Educational Reform Council, the School Education Law was passed in 1947, providing for a system based on the American plan and making nine years of education compulsory[20] (cf. FIGURE 1). In the postwar period, Ainu-*wajin* relations have improved markedly; prejudice in the schools is no longer a major problem for most Ainu children, partly because their parents have a stronger voice in their community due to the awareness of democracy, compared with the prewar suppression the parents went through.

TABLE 3

SCHOLASTIC ATTAINMENTS OF RECIPIENTS
OF PROTECTION ACT AID

	System	A total of 4,601 expressed in percent of five categories
Attended High School	New	1.5
Finished Junior High	New	32.2
Finished Elementary	New & Old	45.2
No Education	Old	12.8
Other		8.3

Source: Hidaka sub-prefecture [1965].
Note: Other means drop-outs etc.

The postwar educational reforms and Japan's recent prosperity have thus made higher education, i.e., high school education and above, more accessible to the Ainu community, though academic attainment is still far below the norm for the Japanese community. Table 3 shows the results of a survey of 4,601 Ainu who, for the most part, have graduated from the new system: 12.8 percent received no schooling at all and only 1.5 percent went as far as high school. In contrast, about 45 percent of *wajin* in Hokkaidō go on to high school (which is implicit in Table 5).

About 90 percent of the children of the households in the author's survey have completed their education under the new system.[21] As shown in Table 4, slightly more than two-thirds of the sample have sent children through school. Of these only about two-thirds (or less than one-half of the sample) have sent their children on to middle school (i.e., Junior High) and about one-third (or less than one-quarter of the sample) have sent their children on to high school (i.e., Senior High). These figures, however, are most likely not representative of most Ainu districts around Hokkaidō. They reflect the bias of the sample, resulting from the fact that Biratori *chō* is probably economically better off than most areas of high Ainu concentration in Hokkaidō.

Free education is provided through middle school now. At the high school level, however, not only is tuition necessary, but in Biratori *chō* most students must travel a long distance, at their own expense, to the nearest high school. These are effective barriers for many Ainu children who are often needed at home as soon as possible after middle school to help support their families, especially if they are farmers. Most children, then, upon graduation from middle school, go to work in Biratori, get married, or find jobs out of the district.

279

TABLE 4

EDUCATED FAMILIES
OF BIRATORI AINU

| | Percentage | | Economic Index |
	of families of random sample who	of those who	
Send children to school	69	100	—
Send children to J. High	46	67	3.8
Send children to S. High	23	33	5.2

Source: Bureau of Statistics [1967].
Note: Socio-economic indices are presented in peng et al (1974).

A very small percentage (2 percent) graduate from night school and thus earn school diplomas. A few others go to technical or professional schools. Two Ainu students (not in the random sample) were attending college. There is also an economic factor at work as might be expected: families of children attending high school have an economic index of 5.2[22] which places them in the Ainu upper-class, while the remaining families have an average index of 3.8.[22]

As shown in Table 5, the percentage of children (over fifteen years of age) in the sample in Biratori chō is significantly lower than the average, for Hokkaidō might be expected of a predominantly rural area.[23] Only 18 percent of male Ainu children over fifteen years of age in the sample went on to high school after middle school, as compared to 31 percent for Biratori chō and 54 percent for Hokkaidō. However, due to the sensitive nature of the investigation, it was not possible to obtain interviews with many of the poorest families in the proposed random sample, and as mentioned earlier, there is a definite bias in the findings. It is also likely that, as suggested earlier, Biratori chō is not representative of Hokkaidō's Ainu and is perhaps more progressive economically than many other areas with large Ainu populations. One informed source estimates the percentage of Ainu receiving high school diplomas at little more than 4 percent for all of Hokkaidō, a figure quite below what is estimated here.[24] The number of Ainu receiving university education is probably not more than one to two percent. Table 6 shows the results of a survey done on Ainu children still attending school in Hidaka district. Only 1.7 percent have gone on to high school and college.

It is surprising and perhaps significant that while in both Biratori

TABLE 5

PERCENTAGE OF AINU STUDENTS
ATTENDING HIGH SCHOOL BY SELECTED CATEGORIES

Categories	Sex	
	Male	Female
I. Geographical Area		
(a) Resident in Hokkaidō	54	36
1. Resident in Biratori	31	18
II. Other Category		
(a) Random Sample	18	18

Source: Bureau of Statistics [1967].
Note: This table shows the percentage of Hokkaidō school children actually in high school as of 1966 and not the number that graduated.

TABLE 6

SCHOLASTIC ACHIEVEMENT OF RECIPIENTS
OF PROTECTION ACT AID STILL IN SCHOOL

	Percentage of a total of 2,256 students
In College	0.1
In Senior High	1.6
In Junior High	31.6
In Elementary School	66.7
Total	100

Source: Hidaka sub-prefecture [1965].

chō and Hokkaidō, the percentage of male Japanese students in high school is much higher than for girl students, about the same percentage of Ainu male and female students continue their education after middle school. Furthermore, of the two students attending college mentioned above, one was a girl. This points to the fact that in the Ainu community education is equally valued for males and females.

As might be expected, mobility is greatest for those with the best educations. About one-half of the male senior high graduates in the sample have left Biratori chō to find jobs, as compared to slightly more than one-third of the males with a junior high education. On the other hand, about half of the females leaving the district become brides. It follows that the relationship between education and mobility is not as important for females as for males.

Conclusion

If the traditional mode of Ainu education is compared with the system of formal education, which has been in force since the Meiji era in one form or another, it is not difficult to conclude that the system of formal education has had a great deal of impact on traditional Ainu culture. Several points, interdependent though they may be, are worthy of discussion here.

First, the system of formal education has helped break down the remnants of traditional Ainu culture in more than one way; in its earliest form it disrupted the traditional social economy, the foundation of which was the division of labor, on the one hand, and a tightly knit cooperation of group activities between the two sexes, on the other. It may be recalled that the Japanese government, in the early part of this century, was only interested in the education of the Ainu, insofar as they served the national interest of cultivating the frontiers of Hokkaidō. This attitude (or rather, motive) resulted in redistributing the Ainu population from their native areas of concentration, thereby disrupting their hunting territories and alienating them from their natural environments (i.e., familiar habitats). Natori [1940] reports that the Ainu in Okotsunai of the upper Saru River came from Shizunai, that one group of the Ainu in Penakore came from Tokachi, and that the Ainu in Kami Nukibetsu moved from Niikappu, while those in Memu moved from Mukawa and Shiberebe, some twenty years earlier.

Natori never mentions the migration (i.e., redistribution of Ainu populations) as the direct result of the Japanese government's policies. This is understandable since in 1940, at the height of Japanese militarism, he could not have been permitted to say so, even if he had been aware of it. But this is pointed out, with a strong feeling of bitterness, by Kaizawa [1971], now that there is no more fear of persecution. He mentions, as an example, that the Ainu living in Niikappu within the Imperial pasture were moved to Kami Nukibetsu, which was at that time still a forest, to cut trees and explore the jungle for further cultivation. There were many other similar cases throughout Hokkaidō. He even attributes the decrease in Ainu population[25] during that period to the "forced labor" by the Japanese government. As evidence, he cites several testimonial cases of hard labor, whereby children of early teens[26] were forced to work under extreme conditions of hardship. One of the severest of cases was that of forty-six out of 116 people, male and female,

282

of three former *kotan*, viz. Nibutani, Pipaushi, and Kankan, were forced out of their native places to work under strenuous conditions for the government. The old people and little children were left behind. All this was done under the name of assimilation within the pretext of education.

There is another interesting dimension to this point, which is worthy of mention here. The author has been unable to explain why so many Ainu in their sixties and above are actually older, by four or five or even six years, than their ages indicated in the government's registry (*koseki*). Kaizawa's report now furnishes a plausible explanation which is a quotation from Ainu elders as follows:

> In the old days, when a child was born, it had to be registered with the government as an Ainu. When the child reached a certain age, the child would be forced to work, along the coastal area of Hidaka, Kushiro, and other distant places, carrying heavy loads, from spring until late fall. The pay was insufficient and the Ainu suffered from want of food. It was because of these circumstances—for fear of losing one's children to forced labor—that most parents hid their children as long as they could from the government and raised them a few years before the children were finally registered with the government.

Second, it is of great importance to note that the system of formal education destroyed the psychological strength which any minority group, when threatened from without, would need to sustain their cohesion and solidarity in order to survive as a group, and which, had it persisted, might have protected the Ainu from increasing encroachment. As was mentioned above, formal education was given to the Ainu rather reluctantly and stingily and, more or less, as a convenience for administrative reasons. This was evidenced by the fact that the Ainu were given inferior materials in their curriculum and shorter period of schooling up to 1922. The Ainu knew this all along. Thus, formal education to them meant nothing more than another way of exploitation, of exposing their inferior status, and of building up self-hatred. They were caught in a dilemma of accepting new pattern of thinking, which would only transform them into second-rate citizens, or upholding their tradition, the foundation of which had already been undermined. In short, the system of formal education more or less forced them into accepting the former and thus eventually left them with no choice psychologically and socially.

Nothing could be more vivid than a passage from the memoir of a Japanese by the name of Iwano [1909][27] cited in Kaizawa [1971:12], to illustrate this point.

> On the whole, we have a misconception about the Ainu. In particular, the policy of the Hokkaidō government is wrong. Since the Ainu are living things, it is alright to give them a piece of land for a living. But why should anyone waste his effort on an inferior race whose extinction is marked? What is the purpose of educating them? Even though a few of them may achieve something, it is not desirable to have them mix with *wajin* to produce hybrids. In my opinion, it is sufficient to keep them alive like livestock. In exchange, however, we must preserve the things that the Ainu race needs to leave behind; these are by no means rotten bear skins and tools; rather, they are the language the Ainu speak and the literature the Ainu have. Greece and Rome perished, but their literature has been preserved permanently.

A third point, no less important than the previous ones, that needs to be raised is the fact that the system of formal education replaced the Ainu language, which had been so functionally important in Ainu culture in practically every aspect, with the Japanese language, that had very little to do with Ainu culture. Had the Ainu language been kept intact, like Hebrew among the Jews in Europe and the New World, some aspects of Ainu culture might have been preserved by the Ainu themselves. The difference is that Hebrew has a sophisticated writing system but Ainu does not (though a very primitive system is believed to have been developed).[28] Thus, as the Japanese language came to be learned and used along with new patterns and norms of social behavior, the foundation and basis for perpetuating traditional Ainu concepts were shaken; a whole new horizon, for better or worse, was opened to Ainu children that had been closed to their parents. It can be said then that the system of formal education helped to destroy the communication network that was so vital to the Ainu. Otherwise, this network would have been instrumental in preserving the remnants of traditional Ainu culture. The formal education policies established, among other things, a new network which conveyed no message to them about their historicity, an essential for any independent ethnic group. The disruption of the traditional learning system consequently led to the rapid disintegration of not only the Ainu's linguistic intuition but their traditional religious beliefs and practices as well. It was the new system of formal education, with its emphasis on new-Confucian ethics which in the early part of the Twentieth Century gave a final blow to the Ainu traditional concepts of the universe and the world view that was once reflected in the Ainu language.

In this sense, formal education was also instrumental in the destruction of traditional social patterns as well. In Ainu community life, there was a strict division between male and female children based on principles of kinship; the education of male children was the sole responsibility of male patrillineal kinsmen, and the education of females was the responsibility of the female matrillineal kin group. Compulsory education helped break down this pattern,[29] by throwing male and female children together and by taking a significant part of the socialization process out of the hands of Ainu parents.

Today, only less than a dozen Ainu can actually command the Ainu language in a conversation, though a good number of Ainu can still understand it, most of them being over seventy years of age. Most important, however, was the gradual change in outlook produced by formal Japanese education which caused many young Ainu to view the traditional way of life with increasing disdain and embarrassment. And today, formal education, while bringing many Ainu greater equality and opening many doors to them which were closed to their parents and grandparents, has also made them acutely aware that this equality is only relative and has only emphasized their minority status and dual identity.

One final point, which should not evade one's attention, is that the system of formal education has increased the mobility of many a young, aspiring Ainu. The general trend in the modern Ainu community is for upper-class families to send their children to high school and occasionally the university, while most lower-class Ainu are not able to afford education beyond middle school for their children. Even so, many young Ainu, with only a high school education, have moved to the Tōkyō and Yokohama areas where they apparently have greater opportunities. This is made feasible, because within the community itself the general educational level has risen due mainly to the postwar educational reforms. Nevertheless the overall percentage of Ainu children receiving higher education, as has been examined before, falls far below the norm for the Japanese community, both locally and nationally. In this sense, the policy of equal educational opportunities has led to greater social mobility for many Ainu. Eventually, more Ainu will disappear in the melting pot of urban areas where few people, if any, will pay much attention to them. Probably, this is the ultimate goal the Japanese government set out at the turn of the century and still hopes to achieve. But it may never be reached for the process of which formal education constitutes only a part is surely a long and painful one, and has yet to run its course.

1. See "The Ainu of Nisshin: Family Life and Social Residues" for an account of this aspect of the traditional Ainu way of life.

2. See "The Socio-economic Status of the Ainu" "the Past in the present." *American Ethnologist*, Peng *et al* [1974].

3. For a detailed documentation of these accounts, see a recent publication entitled *Ainu Minzoku Shi* (Ainu Ethnography) [1970] which has an excellent collection of articles related to these aspects of Ainu social life.

4. This information is available not only in the literature, new and old, including *Ainu Minzoku Shi*, but also in several documentary films made not long ago, which are (1) *Shinurappa*, (2) *Inaw and Nusa*, (3) *Ainu Clothes and Daily Life*, and (4) *Ainu Traditional Farming*.

5. This part of their cooperative activities is vividly documented in the films mentioned in fn. 4.

6. See "Religion: An Index of Social Change in Ainu Community Life" for a detailed account.

7. In his article [1956], Kubodera has classified Ainu oral literature into two kinds: (1) Chanson literature, and (2) Prosaic literature. The first kind has sixteen types, whereas the second kind, eleven. According to this class-ification, Ainu religiously-oriented oral literature would belong to the first kind, while Ainu morally-oriented oral literature, to the second. However, since Kubodera's classification makes no attempt to differentiate between regional dialects, e.g., Sakhalin and Hokkaidō, his classification contains over-lapping. The author, therefore, dissents from Kubodera's classification in the main text.

8. Munro has briefly alluded to this point. For a different interpretation, see "Kinship Systems and Marriage Patterns in the Ainu Community."

9. A well documented account of such deterioration is also available in Takakura [1958].

10. Cf. "Religion: An Index of Social Change in Ainu Community Life".

11. It is of relevance to mention in passing that the school system employed by the Japanese to their former colonials, e.g., in Korea and Taiwan, was a segregated one, whereby the nationals went to separate schools and the Japanese living in those places went to different schools in which only a very few elite nationals, no more than one percent, were permitted. The segregated school system, while it was abolished in 1937 with respect to the Ainu, ended in Japan's former colonies with the war.

12. This is intended to be the translation of *Hokkaidō Kyūdojin Kyōiku Kitei*.

13. This is the translation of *Kyūdojin Kyōiku Kitei*. Notice that it differs from the previous one in lacking the word Hokkaidō.

14. This will be fully accounted for in the final section in connection with "forced labor."

15. This is intended to be an approximate equivalence of the Japanese course title *Shūshin* (lit. to train one's body). In essence, this was a course designed to "brain-wash" children for ultra-nationalism. It was taught throughout the nation, including, later, in Japan's former colonies, until the end of World War II. Since then, it has been taken out of the elementary curriculum, but the subject-matter pertaining to the "Japanese moral code" have recently crept into the textbooks of such courses as "Japanese" and "History" in an increasing quantity. This may be regarded as a sign of the revival of what is known as Yamato Damashī (the Japanese spirit [exemplified à la Yukio Mishima's ritual suicide in 1970]).

16. This is an approximation of what is called in Japanese *Kokugo* (National Language).

17. Mr. Tadashi Kaizawa, himself an Ainu, is a leader in the Nibutani area and has been a strong proponent of Ainu human rights. He was one of the few Ainu who were sent to Manchuria before the end of the war to seek new opportunities. His health, however, prevented him from staying there throughout.

18. Mr. Itō is a *wajin* teacher who taught a number of Ainu schools during his youth. In one of the schools he met his wife who was an Ainu student. As a result, he was fired from the school.

19. Since the year 1944, 99.9 percent of the Japanese population have attended school [Anderson 1959:34–5].

20. For a detailed discussion, see Anderson [1959:22–3, 28].

21. See fn. 19.

22. For a detailed description of the index see Peng *et al* [1974].

23. Since 90 percent of the children of households in the survey have been entirely educated under the new system it is possible to assume that by using data for Hokkaidō, compiled since the new system went into effect in 1947, a fairly accurate comparison can be made. This is not possible for the prewar system.

24. This was taken from a twenty-minute documentary film presented on TBS Television on March 18, 1969 in which one of the best educated informants participated as narrator. The film is called *Furusato ni ikiru "Haru o Matsu Kotan"* (The *Kotan* that survives in the Homeland to await spring).

25. For some demographic changes of the Ainu in Hokkaidō, see Peter Geiser's "The Contemporary Ainu: A People in Search for Society."

26. One of the teenagers was Mr. Kayano's grandfather who, after much of the hardship, tried to get discharged by cutting his own finger but did not succeed. Not until eventually he painted his body with the gall juice of globe-fish, which made his skin yellow, was he discharged as a sick child to go home.

27. Mr. Iwano was some kind of a VIP who had travelled extensively in Hidaka and other districts, with the company of high ranking officials from the Hokkaidō government, before he wrote this notorious memoir.

28. A remnant of such a writing system is believed to be the *itokpa*.

29. This pattern, strictly speaking, had been breaking down long before the Meiji reforms were made. Agriculture, for one thing, threatened traditional male and female role patterns to some extent, but mixed education, for another, contributed to long-term historical changes being wrought in Ainu community.

SHIMBORI MICHIYA

THE SOCIOLOGY OF A STUDENT MOVEMENT—A JAPANESE CASE STUDY

WASEDA UNIVERSITY—a private institution founded in 1882 in Tokyo as Tokyo Semmon Gakko (Professional School)—is one of Japan's Ivy League universities. The University of Tokyo, the first national university, was established in 1869, and Keio University, a private institution, opened in the preceding year. Since the beginning of the Meiji era (1868–1911), these colleges have been among the major higher educational institutions in Japan. In contrast with the public universities, Waseda and Keio were founded by private individuals according to a clear ideal (Keio by Yukichi Fukuzawa, a leading democrat, and Waseda by Shigenobu Okuma, a liberal politician). Enlightened and inspired by Western ideas of democracy and liberalism in their study abroad, they took a lead in the movements for civil rights and liberty and called for constitutional government in the early Meiji period, when a substantial number of feudal elements remained, both in and out of the government. They founded their schools in opposition to the University of Tokyo, which was mainly aimed at educating high

Shimbori Michiya is Professor of Educational Sociology at Hiroshima University in Japan.

Reprinted from *Daedalus*, 97, no. 1 (Winter, 1968), pp. 204–228, with permission of the author and publisher.

government officials and stressed technology and science. Keio had a utilitarian slant and trained leaders in business, while Waseda was intended to be superior in political economics, journalism, and literature. Before Japan's rapid industrialization, the most prestigious positions available to university graduates were in the government and army. Thus, the divided market—training for government available primarily at Tokyo, business at Keio, and representative politics and journalism at Waseda—produced little conflict among the graduates of the three schools, although the Tokyo graduates had an advantage in the Japanese society as a whole. The government did not like the liberal, and therefore somewhat antigovernment, spirit of the private universities. Indeed, the government did not designate private colleges as formally equal to public universities until 1918. Waseda was suspected of being a training center for revolutionaries and from time to time was suppressed by the government. Among Waseda graduates there have been many liberal politicians, writers, and journalists who criticized the political elite and orthodox policies. Okuma, its founder, resigned his post as cabinet minister and became a leader of the Kaishinto (Progressive) Party.

During the prewar years, Waseda was the main center for student movements and within the past several years has again become the scene of student militancy. On December 20, 1965, the Board of Trustees decided to raise substantially the entrance fees and tuition. The student government opposed this increase and resorted to a strike, during which students refused to attend classes and to take examinations. After unsuccessful negotiations between the university authorities and the leaders of the student body, the students occupied the administration building on February 10, 1966. Alumni groups were unsuccessful in their attempts to mediate the dispute. Finally, at the request of the university, twenty-five hundred armed policemen invaded the campus on February 21, removing barricades the students had set up around the buildings. As soon as the policemen withdrew, the students reconstructed the barricades. In the meantime, the annual entrance examination, one of the main sources of income for private universities, approached, and the Waseda authorities were anxious to settle the dispute. Negotiations failed, but the arrest of 203 student leaders made it possible to hold the entrance examinations in a regular hall guarded by policemen. The struggle reopened after the examination, however, and the commencement and term examinations had to be postponed. The president resigned his office on April 23, to be followed by the members of the Board of Trustees. The new authorities made many concessions and showed a willingness to communicate with students. The students, in turn, voted to stop the strike, thus ending the six-month struggle.

Factors other than the traditional anti-establishment sentiment at Waseda were responsible for the general support this dispute evoked among the students. Private universities in Japan—supported neither by donations from corporate wealth and alumni, as in the United States, nor by the national budget, as in England—must depend almost completely upon student tuition. Fees and other expenses at private universities are, therefore, much higher than the standard expenses at national universities. According to a nation-wide survey by the Ministry of Education in 1961, 46.3 per cent of the total income of private universities came from tuition and entrance fees, 17.8 per cent from loans, and 21.7 per cent from university-owned enterprises, such as hospitals; subsidies from national budget contributed only 3.2 per cent and donations from outside agencies 5 per cent. As a result, tuition at a private university is about four times higher than at public institutions. In addition, there are other expenses, such as entrance fees and parents' donations, that do not exist in national universities.[1]

Concomitantly, the private universities must enroll the maximum number of students in order to survive. To attract more students, they have to provide such amenities as modern buildings and make examinations easier by eliminating certain required subjects (like the natural sciences) that are disliked by high-school graduates. Some private universities often enroll students who are rich, but not necessarily able, and emphasize the humanities and social sciences which require less elaborate facilities than the natural sciences and medicine.[2] In this manner, many "mass" and "mammoth" private universities have developed—Waseda among them with its 36,000 students, in comparison to the 15,000 enrolled at the University of Tokyo, the largest national university. Nippon University, the largest school in terms of enrollment, has 68,000 students and is called the "Department Store University" or "University Industry."

Private universities also tend to employ fewer teachers per student in order to meet their budget requirements. There are twenty-six students per professor in the private schools, in contrast to eight per professor in the public ones. In most private universities, the professors have little right to participate in administration and, thus, often have a negative attitude toward it. Like the students, they are, in a sense, the victims of poor financial conditions. They are poorly paid, have inadequate facilities, and suffer from heavy teaching loads. They give their lectures through microphones to a large audience, and there is little opportunity for teacher-student interaction.

Moreover, expenditure per student in private universities is less than one third of that in the United States, where—in contrast to Japan—the state universities, like Berkeley, Michigan, and Wisconsin, are mammoth, and the private institutions, like Harvard, Chicago, and Stanford, are small.

Greater financial burdens, poorer educational facilities, impersonal relations between students and faculty, the sentiment that students are treated as a source of income—all lead to resentment and antagonism against the university authorities as well as the governmental policies concerning higher education. This subconscious resentment can easily be brought into the open whenever there is an overt incident. Moreover, "professional" student leaders who are experts in agitation and organization co-operate in the search for issues around which to agitate.

At Waseda, the former president and the trustees underestimated both the students' resentment and their ability to organize a strong mass movement. They thought the student movement involved only outside "nonstudents" and a small group of campus radicals. Nor had the administration maintained good communication with the faculty, which generally has a more adequate understanding of the campus atmosphere. The professors had not even been informed of the plan to increase fees.

Before the beginning of the Waseda struggle, there was little communication among students, professors, and administrators. This evil may be inherent in the bureaucratization of the "mass" university, but the Waseda authorities had done little to improve communication or to know the general feeling among students and faculty. Because the campus is the traditional sanctuary of academic freedom, the administration's request for police intervention outraged many who had not previously been involved in the struggle over tuition. Once this occurred, the number of students supporting the strike and taking part in the demonstrations increased substantially. Given their initial point of view, the behavior of the Waseda authorities is understandable. They assumed that the opposition movement was run by a handful of politicized leaders, many of whom were "nonstudents," and that it was not supported by many students. Consequently, they felt that the only effective way to end the disturbances was to suppress this small minority decidedly and forcefully.

Since the so-called *Ampo-Toso* (Struggle Against the Revision of U.S.-Japan Security Treaty) in 1960, *Zengakuren* (All Japan Federation of Student Governments) had, in fact, been seriously weakened. It had split into a vast variety of factions, each claiming hegemony, competing with the others, and remaining aloof from the general body of students. This factional strife blunted the effectiveness of the movement, even though all groups oppose the present political regime and university administrations.

The names and ideologies of the various factions confuse the general public as well as the ordinary student. In general, most of the factions are far more radical than the Communist Party (except *Heimin-Gakuren* [Student Federation for Peace and Democracy]. which is under the control of the Party). They are against all the established, "bureau-cratized" political parties and opposed to every kind of power elite and source of authority. It is impossible to negotiate with them, since they refuse any compromise.[3] Shortly before the Waseda struggle of 1965, the student leaders demanded that the student union building be administered directly by a student committee. The Waseda administration assumed that this was an attempt by the militant student leadership to use the fee issue to mobilize and agitate the student population for broader purposes, and that, as such, it was a preparatory exercise for a struggle for a "student governed university." On the one hand were militant student leaders opposed to everything and, on the other, hard-headed administrators accustomed to deciding every-thing according to their assumptions. In between were the majority of students and faculty, generally uninformed, yet vaguely dissatisfied with their life at the university.

One can see that many issues were involved in the Waseda struggle— the poor financial situation of private universities, the inherently bureaucratized character of mass universities, and the radical objec-tives of the leaders of the student movements. The Japanese universities must solve these key problems if they are to function adequately as centers of scholarship and education.

A Typology of Student Movements

Was the Waseda struggle a student political movement in the strict sense? Seemingly, it was an outgrowth of such academic issues as fee increases and the dysfunctions of impersonal mass education. More-over, the agitation appears to have been confined to a particular campus, although some sympathizers and professional "nonstudent" leaders assisted the Waseda students. Nevertheless, the struggle must be called political, if radical leaders took up academic issues merely as a means to awaken a broader political consciousness and to unite the student body into an active anti-establishment organization.

Owing to the widespread system of higher education and the ideology of student leaders, a student movement can easily become political and national in scope in contemporary Japan. Any issue peculiar to a particular institution can be linked to broader political issues. Common in the national universities today are struggles for the right of student administration over dormitory and other facilities built with national funds. Students in private universities consider fee increases the result of governmental policy toward these institutions. Such university issues are thought to be products of the reactionary character of the capitalist system. A refusal of students' rights to con-trol dormitories is a result of the desire of the imperialist elite to hinder and weaken student power; poor support for private universities reflects the government's policy of promoting industrial capitalism while ignoring the educational needs of the poorer classes. According to this logic, any trivial issue must be interpreted in a broader context—from the perspective of an evaluation of the social and political order, or even the state of international politics. Since this logic is unfamiliar to and cannot be accepted by the majority of students, the leaders must use every issue that is clearly relevant to the campus situation as a starting point in the process of "educating" the majority into an "en-lightened and awakened" perspective. Accordingly, the student move-ment must continue to struggle until the present power structure comes to an end.

If one defines politics as a system or mechanism of power distribution, student political movements function along at least three dimensions: the intramural, national, and international. Student political movements or organizations can be classified into three categories as well: those, such as the Waseda struggle, that are confined to a particular university and within a campus; the national federations, like *Zengakuren*; and the international organizations, like the International Union of Students. In an age of organization and of close international interrela-tionships, intramural groups are easily absorbed by larger national or international federations. Thus, the ideology of local leaders tends to become influenced by national or international issues and ideas.

The impact of national and international ideologies on student movements was not great in their early history. The older universities of Europe were content to maintain their own freedom of inquiry. But the universities founded more recently in developed nations were established by secular powers, political or economic, in order to modernize the nation. Students at such institutions have been as concerned with secular matters as they have been with academic ones; they have been as much nationally-politically minded as intellectually-academically minded.

Whether student movements are intramural, national, or international in outlook is a function of the relationship of the academic community to the outside world. When universities are controlled largely by local boards of trustees with specific, particularistic educational orientations, the student struggles are often entirely intramural. When national issues—such as the unification of the country or constitutional and academic freedom—predominate, politically minded students do not show much interest in the struggles of students in other countries. The general concept of an international student movement did not arise much before World War II, except in a few cosmopolitan universities with students from many countries. Students, like workers, are more apt to respond to intramural sources of grievance, so that even where national and international organizations exist, student political leaders tend to seize upon local issues around which the less politicized students may be mobilized. Once students are drawn into the struggle against intramural "reactionaries," their horizons can be widened to include the nation, and even the world. Significantly, the largest continuous student movement, the University Reform of Latin America, began in Cordoba as a struggle over conditions in rooming houses.

In sum, student movements—whether intramural, national, or international—are essentially political in the sense that all the problems they tackle are, or are interpreted as, resulting from or related to the power structures of campus, nation, or world. At present, it is proper to say that international student movements do not exist—even though international student organizations have been formed, and many students are actually oriented to international politics—because a political movement must have a concrete object, and international issues have not yet provided such a clear focus. Thus, students movements can tentatively be classified into three categories—namely, intramural, intermural, and extramural—omitting the international aspect.[4]

The Waseda case was a typical intramural movement, although its leaders were professional and the ultimate concern of the leaders was political. As far as the form of the movement and the consciousness of the general participants were concerned, it was intramural. The movement was carried on within the campus, and it attacked the university administrators on the specific issues of raising fees and impersonal mass education. Although the Waseda struggle ended after six months of conflict, the problems inherent in the poor financial arrangements of private universities and in mass instruction cannot be said to have been settled. Thus, the Waseda solution may represent only a temporary armistice. As students have become aware of the similarity of their complaints, intramural or intermural movements have begun to appear. There are, however, enormous difficulties involved in building a national organization devoted to solving these problems.

National organizations are unlikely to retain the sympathy of the faculty and general public, who often tend to give stronger support to genuinely local intramural issues. Faculty grievances against administrators and the general support of adults for youthful idealism help to encourage intramural movements and thus to increase the possibility of their success. In contrast to an intramural movement, an intermural movement needs a bureaucratized organization like *Zengakuren*, with its liaison office and headquarters. Indirect democracy is a necessity, and representatives or delegates must be elected. Because these organizations are formed in order to solve the problems common to most universities, their dominant ideology tends to be political rather than academic. Thus, their leaders are professionals not only in organization and leadership, but also in political ideology. While an organization formed for the successful functioning of an intramural movement is easily dissolved once the initial objective is attained, an intermural organization, which is much more formal and bureaucratized, usually tries to survive the end of the given issue around which it was formed. It must create, invent, or discover, continuously and successively, new problems if it is to have a *raison d'être* and to attract the interest of ordinary students. Usually, "spontaneously formed" intramural movements precede intramural organizations. The reverse is true on the intermural level. In a national student organization in which political ideology is formed by professional leaders who are not always familiar with the sentiment of the wider student body, the more radical and more clear-cut ideologies are likely to be adopted. Principles that can guide movements on a nationwide scale must necessarily be more universal and general than those in a local movement.

The efforts to set up a national organization inevitably suffer because the distance grows between the leaders and their potential public as the ideology of the organization becomes more political, radical, and abstract and the leadership more professionalized and bureaucratized. In a circular process, the more unsuccessful the effort is at creating mass movements, the more radical and militant are the tactics adopted. When movements initiated by an intermural organization become purely political and not directly related to campus matters or to student life, the leaders tend to seek help from nonstudents, particularly the political parties and trade unions with ideologies similar to theirs. Since in most countries students are—not only in number, but also in organizability, mobilizability, and group identity—one of the largest politically conscious social groups, political parties and other organizations want to make full use of them. Hence, there is often close interdependence and co-operation between national student movements and other politically relevant organizations. Such joint efforts may be described as *extramural*.

Extramural movements have few standing organizations, because they are combinations of two independent groups, students and adults. They may be part of common federations and have common headquarters, but they do not have a unified organization. There always seem to be a struggle for hegemony and competition for power between students and their nonstudent allies. Sometimes a political party completely dominates a student organization; at other times, various party-linked factions in a student organization take over political movements. In many cases, the students become so much more radical, militant, and independent that the co-operating or sponsoring political parties cannot discipline them and are highly embarrassed by them.

In general, student movements in free societies are political and critical of the *status quo* and the present power structure, whether it be intramural or national. They are, therefore, against all university administrations, the ruling class, central government, and even leftist bureaucratic party organizations. Another type of movement is, however, not against the ruling powers, but allied with them. Proestablishment movements or organizations are often seen in a totalitarian state (for example, Hitler *Jugend* in Nazi Germany and *Hokokudan* [Patriot Student Body] in wartime Japan). They are quite often organized artifically and intentionally by the government or the university authorities in order to counteract the oppositionist sentiments and illegal student groups. Since they are manufactured from above, they are supported by power and not by ideological principle. The majority of the students are indifferent or even antagonistic to such organizations or their sponsors even though they hold compulsory membership. Teachers or official leaders often have the role of supervisor or spy, and are suspected by the membership, so that the distance between them is greater and less intimate than in intermural organizations. Anti-establishment groups, although forced underground, get the greatest share of the spiritual and moral support of the student populations.

The nation of Japan consciously opened the door to outside influences during the imperialistic world situation of a century ago. At that time, the Western powers were struggling with one another for the world market. It is not difficult to understand why nationalism became important in Japan in this situation. The fall of the Tokugawa Shogunate regime in the 1860's meant the defeat of conservative isolationism. Progressives who held. that Japan could survive only if it were modernized put through the Meiji Restoration in the name of the Emperor. Technology and material civilization could, however, not be assimilated independently of traditional Japanese ideology and philosophy. Soon after the new government was established, it founded Tokyo Imperial University (now the University of Tokyo), at which future leaders could assimilate Western technology and be trained. For some forty years after its establishment, this institution almost monopolized higher education. Because its graduates were relatively few in number, they could expect speedy upward mobility in government. Thus, as prospective national leaders, the majority of the students of Tokyo closely resembled the elite in their value system. They were politically minded, but did not question or oppose the ruling ideology. As indicated earlier, Waseda and other private institutions were established in opposition to the national university by leaders who were out of power and antagonistic to the government, or who wanted to expand the influence of Western ideology. An antagonism developed in this period between national and private universities, the latter becoming centers of an antigovernment movement, the so-called *Jiyuminken Undo* (Movement for Civil Rights and Liberty). *Aikokusha* (Patriot Party), the first national organization of this movement, was formed in 1875 with Fukuzawa and Okuma as its chief leaders. It prospered until 1890, the year of the first Diet. The government sought to suppress it by passing the Association Act (1880), the Meeting Act (1882), the Press Act (1883), and by prohibiting political discussions and gatherings of any kind. Many law schools, including that of Waseda, were founded during this period in order to train lawyers and journalists critical of the government. Under such circumstances, students, especially those in private schools, were ardently interested in politics and became proponents of the antigovernment movement. The first student strike occurred in 1879 at Keio University. Political lectures in schools and in the streets were in vogue, and many students were arrested for participating in political meetings.

Even at the national University of Tokyo, built on the model of Western universities and thus the ideal of academic freedom, students opposed the suppression of the antigovernment movement. A political study group called *Oto-kai* was organized at Tokyo, and some of its members became active in the *Kaishin-to* (Reform Party) of Okuma. In protest against the government's supervision of discussions, students of the University of Tokyo boycotted commencement exercises in 1883.[5]

The first phase of Japanese student movements lasted until the end of World War I and was characterized by the social atmosphere of Meiji nationalism. There had previously been no national federations nor organized student movements. The majority of students, especially those at the University of Tokyo, viewed themselves as a prospective elite and did not participate in any opposition movements, although a few were involved in such groups as a counter-elite. Student activism did not last long and was rather spasmodic. The concerned minority of students were nationalists and humanitarians, regardless of ideological differences.

The second stage in the history of Japanese student movements took place in the Taisho democracy. During this period, the opposition between national and private universities and the manifest psychological distance between students and workers disappeared or at least diminished. Activist students attempted to establish a common front with the masses. They were attracted to international revolutionary ideology, particularly Communism. World War I brought about a rapid development of industrialism, the growth of big business and urbanization, as well as a strengthening of the world-wide democratic current. Shortly after the war, the great Tokyo earthquake (1923) and depression (1926) resulted in social disorders that the party-based parliamentary government of Japan could not solve. The impetus for improving the working conditions of the laborers and for universal suffrage became greater.

In this chaotic atmosphere, higher education expanded greatly. The University Act of 1918 provided an important stimulus to university expansion. Four new universities were founded in 1917, sixteen in 1920, and thirty-one in 1923. According to Michio Nagai, the functional distinction between the national and private universities broke down as a result of this expansion. Both became training centers for the needed growth of the salaried white-collar classes. The private universities, formerly the champions of academic autonomy and counter-elite ideology, began to suffer serious financial problems. The national universities, more secure financially, took over the leadership in the struggle for academic freedom.[6]

During the same period, the growth of the labor movement accompanied industrial expansion. To illustrate, in 1912 there were 49 strikes involving 5736 laborers, while in 1919 there were 497 strikes in which 63,137 workers participated. Shortly before the formation in 1918 of the first national association of students, *Shinjin Kai* (New Man Society), *Rogaku Kai* (Laborer-Student Society) was created through federation between the workers in *Yuai Kai*, the first national organization of workers, and the students of various universities in Tokyo and in Kyoto. *Shinjin Kai* was an offspring of *Rogaku Kai*, and it acted as the intellectual leader of *Rogaku Kai*, publishing the periodical entitled *Democracy* and organizing many branches in other schools. The Russian words *V Narod!* (To the Masses!) were adopted as its slogan. Students tried to co-operate with workers for their emancipation, although the latter did not identify themselves with the students. *Minjin Domei* (Union of Common Men), a similar leftist organization founded in 1918 in Waseda, attracted various students who supported the goal of democracy by working for universal suffrage and in trade-union movements. Under the growing influence of syndicalist doctrines, its activities grew more radical, and some of its members were dismissed from the university. Accordingly, some of those ex-students formed in 1920 a new organization, *Gyomin Kai* (Society of Pioneers), which was based near the campus. While most of these societies were oriented to off-campus leftist social movements, *Sodai Bunka Kai* (Waseda Culture Society), organized under the influence of *Gyomin Kai* in 1921 with more than two hundred members, was concerned only with the campus matters. It advocated dismissing incompetent professors, boycotting lectures of reactionary and militarist teachers, improving educational techniques, and decreasing tuition.[7]

Most of these organizations were limited to the students of a particular institution. In 1922, *Gakusei Rengokai*, a federation of these independent organizations, appeared under the leadership of *Shinjin Kai*. It had forty-six member institutions (including the high schools) and an individual membership of 1600 (in 1924).[8] The federation initiated a campaign against three proposed laws—the Act Prohibiting Radical Social Movements, the Labor Union Law, and the Conciliation Act for Tenancy Disputes.

Both the ruling elite and many of the student body feared the student political organizations and their consolidated federation, with its radical leftist orientation. The ruling elite, alarmed that the Communist Revolution might spread to Japan, soon suppressed these organizations. Freedom for student political activities lasted under the Taisho democracy until 1925, when the notorious Law for Maintaining the Social Order (*Chian Iji Ho*) was promulgated, and *Gaku Ren* was declared an illegal organization. At the end of 1925 and in 1926, the so-called *Kyoto Gakuren Jiken* (Kyoto Gaku Ren Affair) occurred. Thirty-seven members of the *Gaku Ren* in Kyoto were charged with violating the law and arrested. Soon afterwards, thirty-eight members in other cities were arrested. Some distinguished progressive professors at Kyoto and other universities were also taken into custody. After this affair, the oppressive actions by the government and the university authorities increased. Many other student organizations were prohibited. Some went underground or disguised themselves. Others pretended to be purely academic—that is, nonactivist groups for the study of social thought. Still others channeled their activities into more moderate and humanitarian areas—such as the Student Settlement House Movement and Student Cooperative Store Movement. Some students concentrated on intramural movements, instead of participating in off-campus political activities. Many students enthusiastically supported campus demonstrations against military training—the most famous of which occurred at Waseda University in 1923 and at Otaru Commercial College in 1925.

Intramural movements, called *Gakko Sodo* (school riots or school disturbances) and led by university student activists, took place in many institutions, including the high schools. Every potential source of discontent was used to organize students against the campus authorities. Authoritarian administrations, poor diet in the dormitories, incompetent professors, and increases in fees were some of the issues that led to student strikes and other agitations. Intramural movements increased rapidly after 1925, as is shown by the following table.[9]

Year	1925	1926	1927	1928	1929	1930	1931
Number of school riots	15	7	13	75	117	223	395
Number of students arrested	45	—	29	120	292	950	1,119

After the supression of political groups in 1925, student activists found a refuge in intramural movements. The Student Cooperative Store Movement appeared first in the Waseda University in 1926. It attracted many students and expanded rapidly into other schools. The Student Settlement House Movement, begun in 1923 after the great earthquake, ran labor schools and medical clinics in slum areas. Activists often tried to turn these moderate and humanistic movements into *sub rosa* leftist ones. As a result, these movements, too, were suppressed around 1930. By the beginning of World War II, almost every kind of student movement had been dismissed from the campus. Except for the officially sponsored organizations that supported the government's militaristic and imperialistic effort, student movements had gone underground.

There were always struggles in terms of ideology, power, and direction within the student movements and organizations, especially after 1925. Study or activity, revolution or parliamentarianism, Bolshevism or anarchism, humanitarianism or Marxism, pragmatism or ideology, politicalism or academism were vigorously debated. In general, the more radical and thorough ideologies seem to have attracted the activist students. Faced with the increasingly radicalized and sophisticated movements, the government and school administrators made every effort to suppress them forcefully. By encouraging sports and establishing guidance offices, they hoped to involve the student body in more "healthy and safe" organizations. They also sponsored and supported proestablishment organizations. *Kokoku Doshi Kai* (Society of Patriotic Comrades) was formed at the University of Tokyo in 1919. Its members had a markedly militaristic and reactionary orientation, and it was led by conservative professors. In the 1930's, similar student groups were formed in many schools. These rightist organizations rarely had national federation or the support of many students. Shortly before World War II, all student governments and extracurricular organizations were dissolved in favor of a purely official organization called *Hokokudan* (Patriot Student Body). All students were formally made members of this organization.

Zengakuren

In the history of student movements, the period after 1925 is described as the dark ages. Bloody struggles went on between a small number of militant activists and the police. The majority of students may have been concerned about the fate of the nation, the growing militarism, and the decline of democracy, but they were voiceless and powerless. The military defeat in 1945 emancipated the nation from the repressive political order. Just as in the *Jiyu-minken Undo* (Movement for Civil Rights and Liberty) of the 1880's and the Taisho democracy of the decade after 1910, the new postwar age of social emancipation witnessed a nationwide spread of political concerns and movements, including student organizations. While *Shinjin-Kai*, or its offspring *Gakuren*, was the core of the prewar federated student organizations, the now famous *Zengakuren* took the lead in the postwar period.

In the early postwar period, there were many demonstrations in institutions, including the high schools. The first student demonstration after the war, in fact, took place in the Ueno Girls' Middle School at Tokyo, in October, 1945, demanding that the militarist principal retire. This affair proved to be the precursor of the demonstrations insisting on the "democratization of the campus." The student protest called for purges of the militarist, "war-criminal" teachers, demanded that the liberal or progressive professors who had previously been dismissed be brought back, encouraged the participation of students in school administration, advocated selfgovernment of dormitories, recommended the abolition of official student-guidance systems, and the like. "Defend the students' life," another slogan of the time, implied a struggle for better conditions, decreased tuition, increased scholarships, more school buildings and dormitories, and a discount for student travel. In the broader polity, the Law for Maintaining the Social Order was repealed and its servant, the *tokko keisatsu* (special police for political thought), abolished. The Communist Party was openly recognized, and labor unions were encouraged. The inflation, the scarcity of food and shelter, the heavy destruction from the bombing, and the economic isolation of the nation—all contributed to the destruction of normal life. And it is not surprising that most students seem to be concerned with social and economic issues and participate enthusiastically in political movements.[10]

The most important of Japanese student movements, the *Zengakuren* (an abbreviation of *Zen Nihon Gekusei Jichikai So Rengo*, All Japan Federation of College Student Governments), was organized on September 18, 1948, with affiliated units in 168 national, 31 municipal, and 61 private universities. *Zengakuren* had 300,000 members in 1948, when the total enrollment in all the higher institutions was about 440,000. The first central committee was controlled by the Communist Party.[11] The agreement adopted at the foundation assembly of *Zengakuren* in Tokyo read as follows:

> *Zengakuren*, with the objectives of realizing all justifiable demands of all students by democratic methods and of contributing to the foundation of a democratic Japan through movements for restoring education, shall emphasize the following programs: 1) security and improvement of student life, and equal opportunities for education; 2) defense of academic freedom and national culture; 3) thorough democratization of educational administration; 4) security of right of autonomy of faculties; 5) unification and enlargement of students' fronts; 6) defense of peace and democracy; and 7) support of all other kinds of movements necessary for realizing the federation's objectives.

In October, the Ministry of Education issued to each institution a circular entitled "On Student Political Movements." This circular declared that the study of politics and freedom of criticism should be encouraged on the campus, that individual students should be free to belong to a political association, but that educational institutions should be places for study and order and not centers of political struggle. Educational institutions should be politically neutral, and branch organizations of political parties and cooperation between workers and students should be discouraged. This statement reflected the government's attitude toward the student movement. The new plan for boards of trustees proposed, under the University Act, the introduction of outside powers into the academic administration. Students opposed this change with the slogan, "movement for defense of education," and progressive professors, schoolteachers, workers, and journalists assisted them in their efforts. Widespread political disorders linked to international tensions followed demonstrations around this university issue.

The opposition between the Occupation Forces and the government, on the one hand, and the workers, students, and "progressive intellectuals," on the other, became increasingly clear. The former pressed for a so-called "Red purge" in all spheres of the nation, especially education. The proposal to establish boards of trustees and to transform the national universities into local public institutions on the American model was interpreted as an attempt to weaken academic autonomy and freedom. In an order of July 15, 1950, the American General Headquarters prohibited a students' strike and demonstration. These actions stimulated the students' anger and led to more militant activities. Defense of freedom, democracy, and peace against "American imperialism" became the slogan of the movement. The outbreak of the Korean War in 1950, followed in 1951 by the signing of the Peace Treaty at San Francisco, which contained a U.S.-Japan Mutual Security Pact, could not but involve the nation in the Korean conflict. The international tensions of the period helped, therefore, to polarize Japanese politics inside as well as outside the university.

Except for the first postwar years, there has been a continuous history of student political movements both on and off the campus. The movements have seized on every possible issue. These range from purely institutional matters—for example, increased fees and the University Act—to purely political or international matters, such as the Vietnam war and the nuclear test ban. Each of these issues has led to general and enthusiastic movements. *Zengakuren* became well known because of its violent demonstrations in 1960 at Tokyo's Haneda Airport against the Mutual Security Treaty, an event which made it impossible for President Eisenhower to visit Japan. The slogans, "Down with Premier Kishi" and "Against *Ampo*" (the Pact) were heard everywhere. Almost every day, over ten thousand students demonstrated at the Diet, in the streets, or at the airport. Violent struggles went on, and many students were arrested or injured. About half of Japan's students participated in the general strike against *Ampo*. In spite of strong student opposition, the Security Treaty was finally renewed, although Premier Kishi was forced to resign his post.

Since 1960, the student movements have declined in strength, perhaps because of the economic prosperity or the more effective university administration, the factional conflicts in *Zengakuren* or the general sense of failure that followed the *Ampo* struggle. Students have recently resembled a politically apathetic mass concerned only with their individual lives.[12] The professional leaders have tried to awaken the students' political consciousness. Although they have had some success from time to time, no mass movements on the scale of those in 1960 have taken place since. The Waseda situation discussed earlier did not stimulate comparable movements at other schools. One would be rash, however, to see in the present situation more than a period of transitional armed peace. The strains caused by the Vietnam war and the tension between the U.S. and Red China are becoming more difficult for the Japanese to deal with. The explosive U.S.-Japan Security Treaty will come up for revision in 1970. Campus-based political struggles will necessarily reappear in the near future. The rapidly increasing numbers of students face economic uncertainty as to their future, and many will prove receptive to political radicalism.

It is difficult to compute the frequency of student unrest, but the following table demonstrates the three stages of postwar student movements up to 1960.[13] It can be readily noted that intermural and extramural movements increased relatively as well as absolutely over time.

	1st Period (1945–47)	2nd Period (1948–50)	3rd Period (1951–60)
Intramural Movements	117 (90%)	217 (59%)	137 (26%)
Intermural Movements	9 (7%)	119 (32%)	379 (51%)
Extramural Movements	4 (3%)	27 (9%)	124 (23%)

A high frequency of demonstration in a given period, however, does not necessarily indicate that there is more enthusiasm or more intensity

Name of Happening	Number of Student Participants		
	Meetings	Demon-strations	Strikes
I. Intramural movements			
A. Student Festival, Waseda (May, 1947)	3000		
B. Restoring Private Education, Waseda (April, 1946)		6000	
II. Intermural movements			
A. Restoring Education (June, 1948)	10,000 (100)		
B. Against Raising Fees (June, 1948)			200,000 (150)
Against Raising Fees (Feb., 1956)		6000	
C. Defense of Education (Nov., 1948)	4000 (50)		
D. Against University Act (May, 1949)	35,000 (23)		200,000 (140)
E. Against Eells Speech (Sept., 1950)	5000		10,000 (40)
F. Against Students' Suffrage at Home (Oct., 1953)		3000	
III. Extramural movements			
A. For Overall Pace Treaty (Oct., 1951)	8000 (16)	7000	
B. Against Rearmament (Feb., 1952)		5000	
C. Against Law Prohibiting "Destructive Activities" (May, 1952)	8700	3000	8700
D. Against U.S. Asama Base (June, 1953)		3000	
Against U.S. Sunagawa Base (Oct., 1956)		3000	26,000
Against U.S. Okinawa Base (July, 1956)		2500	
E. Against Two Educational Acts (May, 1956)	10,000	10,000	250,000 (150)
F. Against Law Evaluating Teaching Efficiency (April, 1958)	4400		21,000 (60)
G. Against Institution for Moral Education, Nara (Sept., 1958)	1300		
H. Against Law of Police Activities (Oct., 1958)	3500	1000	29,280 (60)
I. Against Nuclear Testing (May, 1957)	1000 (30)	18,000	43,700 (168)
J. Against Revision of U.S.–Japan Security Pact (Oct., 1959)	20,000	5000	300,000 (90)
K. Down with Kishi (Oct., 1959)			350,000 (90)
Down with Kishi (April, 1960)		35,000	250,000 (90)*

( )* indicates number of schools that participated.

in movements. It is also important to note that the number of universities and students increased radically during this period. Demonstrations may be small and may occur separately in many places on diverse issues. The attraction of a movement for the general student population can, however, be seen by the number of students participating. Since the main types of activity are meetings, demonstrations, and strikes, it is necessary to estimate how many students participate in various types of movements. There are little reliable data available, but I have tried to make some estimates based on various reports.

It is clear from these figures, which are far from complete, that students can be interested in and mobilized for various kinds of movements.

The number of students formally under the control of *Zengakuren*, when compared with the number of students engaged in activities and the total student population, constitutes some sort of index of the intensity of the various movements. The number of students under *Zengakuren* control is, however, difficult to estimate. The percentage of schools and students holding membership in *Zengakuren* is presented in the table below:

Year	A	B	% (A/B)	C	D	% (C/D)
1948	110	592	18.6 %	220,000	453,917	48.5 %
	or 272		or 45.9	or 300,000		or 66.1
1949 Feb.	312	769	40.6	300,000	398,340	75.3
May	394	769	51.2			
1950 May	200	884	22.6		405,310	
June	210	884	23.8			
1952	57	516	11.0	132,215	501,912	26.3
1953	57	454	12.6		511,124	
1956		496		190,000	624,397	30.4
				or 200,346		or 32.1
1957		500		250,000	637,591	39.2
1958 May	111	503	22.1	285,000	649,314	43.9
Sept.	110	503	21.9	300,000		46.2
1959	110	511	21.5	266,000	673,394	39.5
				or 300,000		or 44.6
1960		525		300,000	709,878	42.2

Note: A. Number of schools affiliated with *Zengakuren*
B. Number of all institutions of higher education
C. Number of students affiliated with *Zengakuren*
D. Total number of students in universities

Roughly speaking, about a fifth of all higher institutions and about a third of all college students in Japan are at least formally or nominally affiliated with *Zengakuren*. This means that the colleges with larger enrollments are more likely to affiliate and that about half of all Japanese students may have participated in a *Zengakuren* movement, such as the struggles against the revision of U.S.–Japan Security Pact.

Factionalism is inevitable in most political movements, but it is perhaps most common in student movements, because students tend to be idealistic and puritanical and to cling to ideological principles. Strong national organizations require bureaucratization and an emphasis on formalism and professionalization of leaders. These, in turn, lead to a greater distance between the leader and the follower. The factional struggles for internal hegemony stimulate increased radicalization, dogmatization, and further factionalization. Each leftist political party seeks to exert control over the student movement, thereby increasing the sources of factionalism and internecine disputes within the movement.

Postwar Japanese student movements are not an exception. Various factions in *Zengakuren* depend, to a considerable extent, upon sponsoring political parties, which are in turn influenced by changes in the international political situations. This is especially the case with Communist-oriented students. The balance of power between the U.S.S.R. and Red China, between Stalinism and anti-Stalinism, has had considerable effect upon the factionalization within *Zengakuren*. In 1950, the theory of peaceful revolution was criticized by the Russian Party as contrary to Marxism-Leninism. The Communist Party split into two main factions, with the victory for the militant revolutionaries. After the death of Stalin in 1953, the Russian Party gradually became more moderate, while the Chinese Party began to insist upon armed revolution. At the general meeting of the Japanese Party in 1955, the principle of "beloved Communism" was adopted. These changes in world Communism had great impact on the direction of the student movement. In *Zengakuren*, the armed revolutionists defeated the peaceful ones, so that the conflict between the Japanese Communist Party and *Zengakuren* became clear cut. The leaders of *Zengakuren* were dismissed from the Party as Trotskyists.

This consideration of the Japanese student movement indicates that student movements are likely to arise during periods of rapid social and political change. In Japan, students were particularly active during the Meiji period, in the Taisho democracy, and after Japan's defeat in World War II. All these were periods of considerable social stress and change in Japan. Progressive intellectuals, workers, and students have cooperated with one another to resist the ruling elite. Students have been especially conscious of their own power either as prospective leaders or as a mass movement. They consider themselves an *avant-garde* social-reform movement. As their ideal or objective becomes broader and harder to attain, their movements are liable to become more radical. This can be seen typically in the history of the *Shinjin Kai* and the *Zengakuren*. The type of movement that attracts the greater number of students must be concerned directly with campus matters, such as fees, military training, or academic freedom.

Thus, there seems to be a cycle in Japanese and other student movements. Campus-based issues, particularly those involving threats to academic or political freedom, frequently stimulate widespread participation in student movements. The leaders of such groups are inevitably led to see wider, more radical national objectives. As they build a national movement, they lose contact with their local bases of support. Inevitably, therefore, the national movement declines and fractionates, and a period of relative weakness and passivity eventuates. This may in turn be followed by a new cycle involving new generations of students.

After a relatively long period of weakened intermural movement, the Japanese people have been struck by the revival of militant and violent activism since the middle of 1967. These outbursts are concerned mainly with the governmental policy toward the Vietnam war. Premier Sato left Haneda in October, 1967, in order to talk with President Johnson about the war. The Japanese people, especially the intellectuals and the progressives, were concerned that the Sato government was uncritically involved in the dangerous policy of the United States. In fact, Sato claimed at the White House that Japan agreed with the American policy in Vietnam in every aspect. As the bombing in North Vietnam escalated, as the struggles became more hopeless, and as the international public opinion became more unfavorable toward the United States, Sato's attitude toward world politics gave the Japanese people a feeling of uneasiness. This was expressed by journalists and politicians, but Sato seemed to pay it no attention. The militant students tried, in this context, to stop Sato's departure for America in October, 1967; to stop a U.S. atomic carrier, the *Enterprise*, from putting in at Sasebo in January, 1968; to hinder in February the development of the New Tokyo International Airport at Sanrizuka (which they said would serve as an American Air Force base); and to stop the opening of the

		Distance Between Government and People	
		Short	Long
Distance Between University and People	*Short*	I	II
	Long	III	IV

American Army hospital at Ohji in March. More than a thousand students belonging to the so-called *Sanpakei Zengakuren* (*Zengakuren of three factions*) were involved. Armed with cudgel and helmet, they engaged in warlike actions against the police, and many were wounded and arrested. The public opinion toward their guerrilla tactics was not necessarily favorable, but the students are convinced that they are the only patriots who can keep the nation from the "corrupt imperialism" and that radical militancy is the only way to correct the dangerous direction of the government. The more forceful the suppression, the stronger their conviction and their belief in violence. The public, although criticizing the violence, shared the students' resentment, dissatisfaction, uneasiness toward governmental policy. Thus, the student movements are sometimes supported and justified in terms of their inner motives. In this manner, the intermural movements have been escalating and perhaps will continue to do until 1970, when the U.S.–Japan Security Pact is to be revised.

The history of Japanese student movements suggests that a typology can be proposed to show the relation between the broader social and political context and student political activism. Let us assume that student political movement is determined by two main factors— namely, distance between government and people, on the one hand, and distance between university and people, on the other. Four types of status of university or student in the nation concerned can be deduced.

Distance between government and people is determined mainly by the degree of democratization of the polity and the degree of national consensus or integration of the people. The former refers to the development of parliamentarianism, the consideration of public opinion in decision-making of the government, the existence of legal and effective channels for expression of the wishes of the people, and so forth. The latter means that national objectives and interests are recognized by the overwhelming majority of the people, that there exist no fundamental

311

opposition and polarization in the nation, and that the government—whether democratic or not—represents the integrated people. Take, for example, a colonized nation acting in union around the provisional government with independence as the supreme aim, and a wartime nation unifying around the government with victory as the sole goal. In both cases, there exists an identification of the people and the government, and the distance between them can be said to be short, even though the government is totalitarian or despotic. Conversely, even when parliamentary procedures are fully developed, at times the interests of two sectors are too far apart to make compromise likely, and the distance between the government which represents one sector and the remaining sector is great. In such cases, antigovernmental movements are likely.

The second dimension—namely the distance between university and people—has two main aspects. One is the gap or lag between the university culture and the national culture. For example, in a colonized country, where the master nation in Europe established a university to propagate and indoctrinate the Western ideology and technology to the natives, the distance is so great between the Western culture taught at the university and the tribe culture that students are keenly conscious of the backwardness of their own country and the necessity of its modernization as well as independence. They feel inferior to but also resentful toward the Western culture. Such attitudes can lead to a political movement for independence and a revolt the *status quo*.

The other aspect of distance between the university and the people refers to the opportunity for access to university. When the door for higher education is equally open to the people of any social origin, or university enrollment expands greatly, the distance between the university and the people is necessarily shortened. In such cases, the gap in culture and value between the university and the larger society is generally small, and students are influenced by public opinion. Although apathy is often characteristic of a mass society, students sometimes initiate federated movements like trade unionism owing to an awareness of their power as a result of their increased numbers, to the growing sense of alienation in the bureaucratized university, and to economic interests of greater numbers of students from humble origins. When the distance between the university and the people is great, when the university is *for* and *of* the elite, students are generally conservative. Conservatives cannot be militant unless gravely threatened by the opponents, and they tend to be individualistic. In the aristocratic academy, the radical political movements are hardly developed, and social or traditional student organizations are likely, although a few sensitive lower-class students and a few humanitarian upper-class students may be admitted and devote themselves to political movements. In Japan, the distance between the university and the people is short, but the distance between the government and the people is long.[14]

1. Mombusho (Ministry of Education), *Waga Kuni no Koto Kyoiku* (Tokyo, 1964), p. 141.

2. According to a national survey of annual income of the families of college students made by the Ministry of Education in 1963, the distribution of students among national, municipal, and private universities in terms of their economic level can be seen.

	Less than 300,000 yen	300,000– 900,000 yen	More than 900,000 yen	Average Income	Total Number of Students
National	13.0 %	60.8 %	26.2 %	763,843 yen	192,290
Municipal	6.5	58.3	35.2	912,486	29,980
Private	5.2	44.1	55.9	1,329,485	434,210
Total	7.5	49.7	42.8	1,000,480	656,480

Adapted from T. Kawaguchi, *Shin Elite Shiritsu Daigakusei* (Private University Students, The New Elite; Tokyo, 1966), p. 125.

It is one of the problems of Japanese higher education that students in so-called *Bunka-Kei* (humanities and social sciences) are more numerous than those in *Rika-Kei* (physical sciences and medicine), who are needed more in the age of industry and technology. The opposition between these two categories of science is discussed in C. P. Snow, *The Two Cultures: A Second Look* (Cambridge, 1964). The proportion of students in the two *Keis* is different in different kinds of colleges in Japan, as shown in the following table for 1958.

	Bunka-Kei	Rika-Kei	Others	Total
National	90,405	86,808	19,316	196,529
Municipal	16,063	12,570	3,995	32,628
Private	370,026	133,379	30,187	533,592
Total	476,494	232,757	53,498	762,749

Source: Adapted from Mombusho, *Higher Education in Japan*, pp. 34–35.

3. See "Understandable Motives of Student Movements," *Asahi Journal* (July 19, 1964), pp. 12–17; also M. Nemoto, "Logic of Waseda Barricade," *Keizai Orai*, Vol. 18, pp. 172–79.

4. In my article, "*Zengakuren:* A Japanese Case Study of a Student Political Movement," *Sociology of Education*, Vol. 37, pp. 229–53, and also "Comparison Between Pre- and Post-war Student Movements in Japan." *Sociology of Education*, Vol. 37, pp. 59–70, I classified the types of student movement into three groups: in-campus, co-campus, and extra-campus, which are the same as those used here.

Type	Origin	Field of Activity
1. intramural	spontaneous and natural	within a particular campus
2. intermural	intentional and deliberate	with students in other universities
3. extramural	intentional and deliberate	with non-students off the campus

Type	Degree of Organization	Size	Relative Number of Participants in the Student Body
1.	least-organized	small	great
2.	most-organized	large	smaller
3.	less-organized	large	smallest

Type	Duration	Concern	Object of Ultimate Attack	Radicalness
1.	short	immediate and academic	university authorities	moderate
2.	longest	academic and political	government	most radical
3.	longer	political and social	political regime	radical

Type	Leader	Distance Between Leaders and Followers	Chance of Success
1.	amateur	small	great
2.	professional	greater	smaller
3.	professional	greatest	smallest

5. Some 1700 publications relevant to student movements in Japan were classified and listed in my article, "Bibliography of Student Movements in Japan," *Educational Studies of the Faculty of Education, Hiroshima University*, Vol. 11 (1963), pp. 97–143.

6. M. Nigai, *Nihon no Daigaku* (Higher Institutions in Japan; Tokyo, 1965), p. 47.

7. S. Inaoka and S. Itoya, *Nihon no Gakusei Undo* (Student Movements in Japan; Tokyo, 1961), p. 54.

8. Mombusho, *Gakusei Shiso Undo no Enkaku* (History of Student Ideological Movements, 1931), p. 35.

9. Adapted from S. Takakuwa, *Nihon Gakusei Undo Shi* (History of Student Movements in Japan; Tokyo, 1955), p. 156. A lot of surveys of the participant students by the Ministry of Education and other offices during the second stage are available. In general, the students involved in the movements in the prewar period came from the middle class and had better achievement. See for example, T. Okada, *Shiso Sakei no Genin oyobi sono Keiro* (Causes and Processes of Getting the Leftist Ideology; Tokyo, 1935).

10. According to a survey done by the Ministry of Education in 1948 among 6801 samples of college students, 63.8 per cent said they found great difficulties in continuing their schooling mainly owing to economic reasons. T. Arai, *Kiki no Gakusei Undo* (Student Movements in Crises; Tokyo, 1952), p. 39.

11. Gakusei Mondai Kenkyusho (Institute for Student Problems), *Sengo Nihon Gakusei Undo Shi* (Postwar History of Student Movements in Japan; Tokyo, 1960), p. 15.

12. Professor Tsuyoshi Ishida of the Hiroshima Institute of Technology conducted research into the college students' attitude toward student movements in 1966. Some of the findings are cited below (unpublished data).

	Strongly Agree	Slightly Agree	Don't Know	Slightly Disagree	Strongly Disagree	No Answer
In general, student movements are run only by a few activists.	20.9%	31.1	29.1	10.5	4.2	4.2
Students should not have demonstration parades for political matters.	14.8%	27.4	24.9	21.1	8.5	3.3
Students should not strike for political matters. (Total—1769)	18.5%	31.8	24.4	15.5	6.2	3.6

13. See Shimbori, *"Zengakuren."*

14. The author develops the above typology in "Why Are Student Movements Intensified?" *Chuo-Koron,* Vol. 83, No. 5 (in Japanese; May, 1968), pp. 242–255.

WILLIAM K. CUMMINGS

THE CONSERVATIVES REFORM
HIGHER EDUCATION

A striking feature of modern Japan's development has been the role of conservative rulers in proposing and carrying through radical innovations. The very revolution to establish the Meiji state was accomplished by a segment of Japan's feudal aristocracy. And in more recent years, the vast social changes underlying the Japanese economic growth "miracle" have been engineered by a conservative establishment of big businessmen, bureaucrats, and politicians.

The modern Japanese university was established by the government in the nineteenth century "to teach such science and technology as satisfies the requirements of the state and to study such science and technology in depth" (Article 1 of the Imperial University Ordinance). Since the creation of the Imperial University, conservative governments have promoted two major waves of reform—during the mid-Taishō period and during the American Occupation. In 1969, following two decades when only one national university was established, the Satō cabinet announced a government plan to establish twenty new univer-

William K. Cummings is Associate Professor of Sociology at the University of Chicago.
Reprint from *The Japan Interpreter*, 8, no. 4 (Winter 1974), pp. 421–431, with permission of the author and publisher.

sities, each radically different from the existing national university mold. The Tsukuba University law which passed the Diet in September 1973 is the härbinger of Japanese higher education's third reform wave from above.

The 71st Diet Session

In Japan's short history of parliamentary government, the 71st Diet session was surely one of the most bizarre. Because of his impetuosity in domestic politics and forces largely beyond his control in international affairs, Tanaka Kakuei dropped from an all-time high of popularity for a Japanese prime minister to a record low. Despite their mutual antipathy, the progressive parties agreed to consolidate their opposition against all conservative-sponsored bills, regardless of their content. Aiding them in this effort was the commitment of Kōno Kenzō, president of the Upper House, to guarantee the impartiality of the deliberations—a commitment he had made two years earlier when he resigned from the LDP as a condition of becoming president. And to test the opposition's will, the conservatives decided, following the failure of their election reform bill, to push through not one, but four additional important bills simultaneously. It was no wonder that the 71st session was extended twice for a total period of two hundred and eighty days, the longest Diet session of the postwar period.

The Tsukuba bill was only one of the government's four important bills, and it would be difficult to say how much of the opposition's objection was to the bill itself and how much was due to the opposition's decision to block all conservative legislation. It is significant that the National Universities Association, which had opposed earlier government attempts to reduce university autonomy, did not officially oppose Tsukuba—nor did it approve. However, this association is composed of administrators and according to a later survey, it did not reflect the negative attitudes of the majority of staff at national universities. Two large groups of professors signed petitions of protest, and intellectuals filled the mass media with their opinions on the bill, largely critical.

After lengthy, penetrating debates and the "forced passage" of the bill in the committees of the Lower and Upper houses as well as the plenary session of the Lower House, it was finally enacted in a "normal" session of the Upper House. Only the Democratic Socialists among the opposition were present for the final vote. On October 1 Tsukuba

University was officially founded and that same day Miwa Tomoo, former president of Tokyo Education University from 1963–68, was appointed the first president. By 1977 all of the present faculties of Tokyo Education University will be moved to Tsukuba to complete Japan's most notorious new university.

The Issue of University Autonomy

The staff of the first Imperial University and of all subsequently established national institutions have been government officials appointed by the minister of education and subject to both the privileges and responsibilities of that status. The president of the Imperial University was appointed by the emperor and the deans of the respective faculties were chosen by the president and the minister of education. Almost from the beginning of the Imperial University, conflicts developed between scholars who strove to advance truth and liberty and the state, which was concerned with national development and solidarity. These conflicts came to a head in 1914 when Sawayanagi Masatarō, a distinguished and strong-willed educator, was appointed president of Kyoto Imperial University and almost immediately dismissed several faculty members. The university's outrage, led by the Faculty of Law, was only stilled by the resignation of Sawayanagi and the reinstatement of the dismissed professors; the next year the government agreed to allow both Kyoto and Tokyo Imperial universities to select their own presidents and deans. While this change was not codified in law, it became a cardinal principle in the emerging Japanese conception of university autonomy. The faculty meetings (*kyōjukai*) composed of the full professors of each university faculty and responsible for most university decisions, including the selection of personnel, were the principal organs enjoying the new autonomy.

In the formative years, the autonomy was fragile and the universities went to unusual extremes to maintain it. Thus as Japan approached war and the national government expressed displeasure at the "dangerous thoughts" of professors such as Minobe Tatsukichi (1935) and Kawai Eijirō (1938), the universities asked these professors to resign in order to avoid formal government action. Some scholars approved of the government pressure, but many began to feel there was a fundamental contradiction between the goals of the university and those of the state.

These scholars nursed their doubts throughout the repressive war period, but almost as soon as the war was over the more outspoken began agitating for greater freedom from government control. Partly in response to this agitation and also in keeping with its policy of democratization the occupation authorities sought to strengthen the autonomy of universities and to reduce the role of the central government in education. The new Constitution declared that "academic freedom is guaranteed" (Article 23) and the Fundamental Law of Education stated "education shall not be subject to improper control . . ." (Article 10). New regulations were issued providing universities with the authority to select their officers and academic staff, subject only to the automatic approval of the government.

The occupation-promoted reforms were admittedly sometimes ambiguous. Furthermore, in the late 'forties the Japanese government, with the clear support of the occupation, attempted to restrict the autonomy of national universities by making them responsible to boards of trustees (1948) and later to a national universities committee (1951) composed in part of non-scholars. However, strong opposition on the part of students and scholars, and political allies in the progressive camp forced the government to abandon these "reforms," leaving the tradition of university autonomy intact.

Thinking back on the occupation, one concludes that its greatest legacy to higher education was the transfer of real authority from the relatively conservative Ministry of Education to the conservative-dominated but nevertheless pluralistic National Diet. Under this new system of authority, the government has found it much more difficult to promote change. Even its campaign to create higher technical colleges in the mid-fifties was delayed several years due to opposition. In reaction against the major role of university intellectuals and students in the anti-U.S.–Japan security treaty movement of 1958–60, Prime Minister Ikeda Hayato proposed to increase the role of the central government in the administration of the national universities. His university control bill would have given the minister of education the power to veto the men that each national university selected as its president. However, once again the universities coordinated their views and gained the support of the progressive parties to oppose the government reform, and Ikeda was persuaded to drop his legislation.

The Student Revolt of the Sixties

As the student revolt of the late sixties began to gain momentum, conservative politicians once again began to review university policy.

On the one hand were the hawks who urged strong measures to punish individual student demonstrators and their universities. On the other hand, a moderate group advised the government to give individual universities the chance to settle their own disputes and develop self-reform plans while the government worked on its own long-range plan for a fundamental reform of the entire educational system. The latter group prevailed initially, and in June 1967 the government asked the minister of education's Central Council on Education to study fundamental reforms.

Meanwhile the student revolt continued to escalate and, at least to many conservative politicians, the universities' inability to solve their disputes became all the more evident. Consequently, from mid-1968 the government began to prepare legislation to end campus disruptions. A bill was presented to the Diet in May 1969 and enacted that August, as the Law of Provisional Measures Concerning University Government by a "forced vote," against seemingly adamant opposition. Despite vigorous public opposition, it was apparent that many in the progressive camp and the universities were privately in favor of the law. Compared with versions prepared by the conservative hawks, the law was quite moderate: the First Article stated that the aim was to "determine emergency measures which shall be taken *to assist the independent efforts by universities* to restore order . . ." The law authorized the minister of education to issue written recommendations (*kankoku*) to the presidents of national universities only if they failed to solve their disputes within a period of six months. If after receiving these recommendations, a university was still unable to solve its problems, the minister of education, in consultation with a Special Council on University Problems, was empowered to take firmer action.

Some months later the government presented a second bill to the Diet which proposed government aid to subsidize the operating costs of private schools. This bill was readily approved in May 1970, breaking a century-long tradition of government neglect of private education, and since that time the government has substantially increased its aid to private institutions. By 1973, government aid to private universities amounted to one-eighth of their operating expenses; at institutions with medical and science faculties, the percentage was more than one-fifth. Taken together, these laws served to effectively defuse the student revolt. Since 1970 campus disputes have been infrequent and have usually terminated quickly.

Reform Fever and the Tsukuba Concept

During the peak of student revolt the nation's attention was riveted on the campuses. In addition to the Central Council on Education's study of fundamental reform, the various political parties, business groups and other public associations began to review the performance of Japanese education for the first time since the occupation. A major theme of these establishment discussions was the need for Japan to develop "new universities" with radically different modes of organization and government. Experiencing pressure from the government above, from these outside organizations and from the students below, individual universities began to consider self-reform. Between 1967 and 1970 over five hundred reform reports were issued by various organizations. Among universities, the University of Tokyo and Hiroshima University were the two most prolific. In July 1969, however, Tokyo Education University surpassed its two rivals by declaring that its "A Concept of a New University at Tsukuba" was the reform plan which it intended to carry out.

The details of the university described in the Tsukuba Concept were indeed radical. In the first lines, the report stated that the new university would be "opened to society." To this end, the report proposed the formation of a new kind of university corporation with outsiders included on the governing board; in addition, it recommended that some outsiders be selected by a university-wide personnel committee to assist in the evaluation of specific personnel cases. The report proposed the elimination of traditional faculties (*gakubu*) and their replacement by multi-disciplinary schools "for the purpose of teaching" (later called *gakugun*), and "complexes" for the coordination of research (later called *gakkei*). In addition, the report recommended the establishment of research projects that could be created and dissolved as they achieved their objectives. University staff would hold multiple appointments in these separate organizations, with provision for some to concentrate full-time in one area before rotation to another. For the government of the university, a complex system of committees was recommended starting with staff meetings at the operational levels and moving up to functionally differentiated committees, each chaired by a vice-president for research, teaching, building and grounds, and student affairs. The highest deliberative body would be the university senate composed of elected representatives and several ex-officio officers appointed by the president. Final authority on all matters would rest with the president whose powers were considerably strengthened relative to the situation in existing national universities.

From Campus Move to a New Concept

To appreciate how Tokyo Education University came to its momentous decision, we must go back to the occupation period when the institution was founded. At that time, the Ministry of Education was faced with the task of consolidating existing higher educational institutions to conform to the occupation's new university system. To create Tokyo Education University, it consolidated several institutions including the prestigious Tokyo Arts and Sciences University (Tokyo Bunri Daigaku) established in 1929 and the Tokyo Higher Normal School founded in 1887, and appointed former ministry official Shibanuma Naoshi as president. While Tokyo Education University existed as a legal and administrative entity, there were severe internal cleavages from the start between those representing the proud traditions of component institutions, between those trained at different universities, and between those committed to different political philosophies. Furthermore, the several component institutions from which Tokyo Education University had been established were physically located on different campuses and many of their buildings had been damaged during the Tokyo fire-bombing. The one common bond of this new institution was its aspiration for greatness. President Shibanuma did an admirable job in developing the school's physical plant, but was unable to reduce the internal cleavages of the university.

From 1956 the task of establishing internal peace fell on the shoulders of the new president, Tomonaga Shin'ichirō, a distinguished physicist and 1965 recipient of a Nobel Prize. Tomonaga instituted a governance procedure that provided maximum respect for the opinions of each faculty: according to the "Tomonaga principle," the university made no major decision until all the faculties in separate votes approved the decision and authorized their senate representatives to support it. In 1960, following this principle, the university decided to move to a new location where all the faculties could share a common campus, expand, and acquire new research facilities. While the site of the new campus was not decided, the university felt that a successful move would serve its quest for greatness.

Following the election in 1963 of Miwa Tomoo as the university's third president, the Ministry of Education asked if the university would like to move to the new Tsukuba Research City, which Kōno Ichirō, minister of construction, was planning. President Miwa indicated the university's interest and appointed a committee to study the feasibility. Each faculty was also asked its opinion. The decision on Tsukuba proved difficult. The site is sixty-seven kilometers from Tokyo with only mediocre rail links, thus making commuting to and from the metropolis difficult. If the university moved, except for the hardiest commuters, all the faculty and staff would have to give up their Tokyo homes and the other benefits of the metropolis including side jobs, easy access to large libraries, chances for association with other Tokyo intellectuals, and the pleasures of Tokyo night life. On the other hand, the new campus would be spacious and skillful bargaining might bring exciting new research equipment. Moreover, the city would consist mainly of other research organizations and their staffs, resulting in a homogeneous class composition. There would be no factories to pollute the air. These advantages and disadvantages weighted differently for the respective faculties, but clearly offered little to the Faculty of Letters (a faculty composed of both social science and humanities disciplines). For the Faculty of Education, the balance was mixed but those members who maintained close relations with the Ministry of Education were in favor of the move. The remaining faculties of Science, Physical Education and Agriculture decided they had more to gain by moving, though there were dissidents in these faculties as well.

In 1967 the Ministry of Education asked Tokyo Education University to commit itself one way or the other, and it was from this point that the university began to experience grave internal conflict. At President Miwa's request, a senate meeting was held on June 10, 1967 to discuss the move. The faculties of Letters and Education representatives expressed reservations about the move; they would be happy to allow the other faculties to go if they could stay at the present campus for some time. The *broad terms* of this proposal were acceptable to the other faculties, and thus the senate approved a resolution which combined a request for land at Tsukuba with the condition that the university be allowed to retain its Tokyo Ōtsuka campus. However, according to a majority of the members of the Faculty of Letters, this resolution did not represent their specific request for a central government guarantee of the Tokyo campus *prior* to the university's decision on moving. Another way of viewing the difference was that the pro-move group, dominated by men who were themselves politically moderate to conservative, preferred to trust in the good will and generosity of the government. On the other hand, many in the Faculty of Letters felt there was little basis for trusting a conservative government, and hence the university should proceed cautiously, obtaining written guarantees at every stage of the negotiations. The issues involved and the individual motives at the time of the June decision were far more subtle than this brief summary indicates. In any case, the manner in which the decision was made strained what good will there was between the pro and anti-move groups to the breaking point. Immediately following the decision to move, students began a vigorous protest against the move and about other issues which virtually paralyzed the campus for two years.

A majority of the professors in the Faculty of Letters, feeling their opinion had been ignored by the university senate, voted on June 22 to recall their senate representatives and to send no new representatives until after the senate retracted its June 10 decision. In their opinion, developed over the course of daily meetings, that decision had been made in violation of the established Tomonaga principle of faculty meeting approval. The Faculty of Letters' stand received support from a minority of the staff in the other faculties of the university and from student protestors.

This strong position by the Faculty of Letters was greeted with disdain by pro-move leaders who charged that it had been influenced by communist agitators and that the members were thinking of their selfish interests rather than the good of the whole university. The pro-move group proceded with its plans, and in late July President Miwa appointed a Master Plan Committee to prepare for the move. No individual authorized by the Faculty of Letters was on this committee or participated in the university senate after the June 10, 1967 decision to move.

The student protest at Tokyo Education University was one of the most persistent of all those at national universities, yet with the existing decentralized government structure the university was virtually impotent to deal with it. Within the university, especially in the Faculty of Science, there were several outspoken professors who felt the university should be reorganized to centralize its administration and to improve its capacity for teaching and research. As the reform fever picked up across the nation, these reform arguments became more compelling and thus, from mid-1968, the Master Plan Committee decided to develop a plan for reorganization to accompany the move. The committee received a grant from the Ministry of Education for this purpose. Some of the committee members actively consulted with ministry officials concerning the type of reforms that would be agreeable. The reformers hoped that the combination of a move *and* reforms might be appealing to at least some among the dissidents, but they failed to understand their anti-move colleagues' "opposition on principle." In early July 1969, the Master Plan Committee presented "A Concept of a New University at Tsukuba" for formal consideration. On July 24, the senate voted to approve the document as a basis for future planning. The short period allowed for study of the report prior to the vote and the troubled state of the campus had prohibited all of the members of the respective faculties from airing their opinions. Sizeable minorities within the faculties of Agriculture, Education, and Science issued strong protests against the senate vote; the Faculty of Letters boycotted the senate vote. Despite these ruffles, the Tsukuba Concept became official university policy.

Tsukuba as a Conservative Symbol

The Tsukuba Concept arrived at by Tokyo Education University "autonomously" included plans to move to a new location, to develop radical new structures for research and teaching, to establish a more centralized administration, and to inaugurate a new form of university incorporation which would include outsiders on the governing board. All of these were top priority reform goals of the conservative government, as the Tokyo Education University reformers well recognized. The Ministry of Education immediately put its full support behind the Tsukuba Concept, and committees were appointed to work out the details.

At the time the Tsukuba Concept was announced, it received no more attention than many of the other reforms proposed by various universities. But as other universities failed to implement their proposals—for example, the University of Tokyo which was the most prolific producer of "interim" reform reports had not even one major change by late 1973—Tokyo Education University's daring Tsukuba Concept became more conspicuous. Articulate critics, many from within the university, began to attack various elements of the plan. To the credit of the reformers, they listened to some of the criticism. Thus various elements of the master plan were modified, auch as abandonment of the university corporation concept and the substitution in its place of an "advisory committee" of outsiders with virtually no decision-making power. To appease the critics following an embarrassing incident in 1973 when three faculty meetings declared they could no longer trust the president, some curbs on the administration's power were introduced, including a system for recalling the president. Despite these revisions, the final plan the university and the government agreed on a basis for presenting the Tsukuba University bill embodied a radical departure from the existing national university model.

Conclusion

The path leading to Tsukuba was a tortuous one; it took over ten years to traverse and there were several casualties among the faculty of Tokyo Education University. A major prerequisite for Tsukuba was the student revolt which kindled the nationwide university reform fever. The Tsukuba Concept was born at Tokyo Education University because of that institution's insatiable ambition, its low level of internal integration, and the room this provided for some relatively marginal professors to push the institution toward innovation and possible greatness. Over the past three years the reform faction has engaged in a series of vindictive acts against the dissident Faculty of Letters, including the failure to acknowledge promotion requests and an attempt to dismiss three of the Faculty's distinguished members. These and other actions in the Tsukuba affair have violated the traditions of academic civility and faculty meeting autonomy to the point where no one knows how many from the Faculty of Letters will ever go to Tsukuba. Few who are affiliated with the university in any faculty are happy with the Tsukuba Concept, though most are relieved that the battle is over. Former president Tomonaga expressed his regrets that the situation had become so chaotic.

The Ministry of Education has called Tsukuba a new university, as it must, in order to boost its accomplishments before the mass media and the conservative establishment. But the university is no more than old wine in a new bottle. The bottle has a radical design, with some features deserving serious attention by educators elsewhere—for example, the concept of creating totally separate organizations and administrations for teaching and research and allowing some faculty to devote full-time to one or the other of these organizations. However, the old wine will deform the bottle. Indeed given the bitter battle fought and the intention of some to continue it, it is possible that the bottle will actually break, leaving the government's reform in chaos.

Regardless, Tsukuba University is the government's greatest post-occupation triumph at the level of higher education. It represents the first time that the government has been able to make permanent changes in the basic laws pertaining to university government and organization. The changes, whose full implications will only gradually become clear, include provisions for advisory councils, vice-presidents, personnel committees, and differentiated organs for research (*gakkei*) and teaching (*gakugun*). These changes will allow a stronger administration to develop at Tsukuba University than has been customary at existing national universities. They also will provide the government with a legitimate channel, through the Advisory Council, to attempt to influence much of the decision-making at the university. The government was especially anxious to have the Advisory Council included in the legislation because the council reflects two changes the conservatives have advocated throughout the postwar period: the members of this council will be chosen from outside the university and the Minister of Education will have a veto over their selection. The government actually hoped that Tsukuba would become a university corporation governed by a board of trustees, but this more extreme reform was impossible. The Advisory Council will have virtually no formal role in decision-making, and it is likely to only marginally increase the capacity of outside groups, including the government, to influence Tsukuba—as long as the Tsukuba faculty does not want to be influenced. Thus at the formal level, the government gained a symbolic victory opening a visible channel for communication from outside, but little substantial change in the formal division of authority between the university and the state. On the other hand, the reform leaders of Tsukuba share many of the convictions of the conservative government and are prepared to listen carefully to government advice.

Now that the Diet has enacted the Tsukuba law, other universities will be able to incorporate features of the Tsukuba Concept in their structures, such as vice-presidents or a personnel committee. A major fear of the Tsukuba University bill opponents was that the government would attempt to force the Tsukuba innovations on existing institutions. In the Diet debate Ministry of Education officials insisted that they had no such intentions, and thus far there is no basis for doubting their word. In the years to come, however, the government may well "encourage" existing universities to adopt certain of the Tsukuba reforms. Such efforts could easily revive a new round of government-university confrontations. Encouraged by their success in the Tsukuba legislation, reform-minded individuals with the government will promote several additional policies over the coming years. In 1972 the government opened the first classes of the University of the Air. Only a few short weeks after the Tsukuba law was enacted, Secretary-General Kurt Waldheim conveyed to the Japanese government the news that the main campus of the forthcoming United Nations University would be located in Japan. The government has recently committed itself to substantially increase the scale of publicly supported medical education. Over the last several months the government has announced firm plans for the establishment of two additional "new universities": a physical education school sharing many of Tsukuba's organizational features and a university to provide further training for graduates of higher technical colleges and for employed technicians who want additional formal education.

Taking the various government reform plans and prospects into account, one can expect that the next years will be active ones for Japanese higher education, especially relative to the stagnancy of the past two decades. On balance, the conservatives' reforms may lead to some improvements. Without a doubt, those affecting the autonomy of universities will be strongly resisted by Japan's progressive guardians of university tradition.

THOMAS R. H. HAVENS

CHANGING STYLES OF UNIVERSITY
LIFE IN JAPAN

The year 1973 marked a century since the Meiji education reforms
and twenty-five years since the American occupation revamped
Japanese higher education. Today nearly one Japanese out of three in
the 19–23 age group is enrolled in a university or junior college, compared with fewer than one in ten before the war. The percentage of
university students proceeding successfully to the bachelor's degree
is probably higher than in any other country. Universal mass higher
education, although not yet a reality, is clearly closer at hand than
ever before in Japan's history.

The growth of a large-scale university system produced problems
as well as benefits, the more so because higher education in postwar
Japan has been used to an unusual degree as an instrument to certify
young men and women for appropriate social roles. Although campus
radicalism had a long history, the huge student demonstrations surrounding the U.S.–Japan security treaty issue in 1960 were an unmis-

Thomas R. H. Havens is Professor of History at Connecticut College in New London,
Connecticut.

Reprinted with additions and corrections by the author from *The Japan Interpreter*,
8, no. 3 (Autumn 1973), pp. 285–291, with permission of the author and publisher.

takable sign that the "massification" of Japanese higher education had reached a new stage. The sheer volume of young persons passing through the university system had produced qualitative changes in the relationships of students with one another, their teachers, and society at large.

Much happened to the Japanese university in the years after 1960, and there was little evidence that the pace of change would abate in the future. Only the brave or the foolish dared catalog the recent innovations and shifting moods of higher education in any country, above all Japan, where the modern university appeared especially enigmatic. Still, three complementary themes seemed to characterize the campus changes: democratization, diversification, and dispersal. None was peculiar to the academy itself; each was a trend generated in the overall society.

Democratization

For a long time teachers in Japan enjoyed great discretion over university policy. The attenuation of professorial prerogatives and democratization of administrative procedures after 1960 derived variously from teachers' idealism, the public relations requirements of large educational enterprises, and the general social milieu of postwar Japan, as much as from the demands of undergraduate activists (for whom on-campus changes were often mere side issues). The universities' unswerving commitment to democratic procedures made it easier for radicals to paralyze campuses, but most academics seemed prepared to accept disruptions rather than compromise due process and the open expression of moral outrage. More doubtful voices were raised when the moral content evaporated and institutions found themselves shut down by factional jostling within the student movement.

Whatever else the student struggles of the mid- and late 1960s accomplished, however, they propelled many Japanese universities toward internal administrative reforms. This process did not reach the familiar European and American apex of student participation in faculty or trustee deliberations, but it accelerated the use of secret balloting and other innovations within many university faculties. Nevertheless, older consensual decision-making patterns occasionally resurfaced when universities were gripped by crises. Whether this meant that democratization was only skin deep, or merely that old habits died hard, could not yet be known. Master-disciple relationships remained strong in the major graduate schools, which educated far fewer students than their counterparts in the United States. But there were signs that the self-renewing character of many university departments was dissipating. When institutions could afford to make new appointments to their teaching staffs, they turned increasingly to other graduate centers for candidates. This openness was especially true for science and engineering faculties, but it reached into the humanities and social sciences as well. The freedom to teach and write at liberty, guaranteed by the national constitution, seemed circumscribed only by the budget and the routine approval of colleagues for new courses. Tyrants in any country could flay scholars with the purse as well as the shackle, but political threats to academic freedom in Japan's universities seemed minimal.

Contacts between professors and undergraduates remained relatively formal, but many students perceived that the social distance between themselves and their teachers was diminishing. Respect rather than awe characterized the undergraduate attitude toward the professor. Forms of speech used in the classroom gradually became more standard, less honorific. The self-confidence of the generation studying in the universities was apparent in a new reluctance to revere professors simply because they were professors. This was true among women undergraduates as well, who formed a measurably larger segment of the campus population (although women have continued to be surprisingly scarce at certain major national universities and technical centers). Nevertheless it was still rare to find an undergraduate approaching a teacher after class, partly because both parties were busy with many other class hours and the demands of commuting, but also perhaps because the professor's office, known as a research study or *kenkyūshitsu*, still seemed too cerebral a precinct for mere students. At least some professors were beginning to post office hours at the major universities, suggesting that perhaps teacher-student relationships were softening. In short, as with administrative procedures and the composition of teaching staffs, student-professor relations had moved far toward openness since 1960.

Diversification

Japanese higher education has never been so monolithic or "routinized" as its worst critics claimed. Indeed, the postwar occupation tried to standardize many aspects of a previously diffuse university system. Variety became a motif of campus life in the 1960s and early 1970s, ranging from student styles and reading preferences to choice of curriculum and academic methodology. By then the prefectural and metropolitan universities created after World War II had matured into full-fledged complements to the older national and private institutions, and dozens of new private universities and junior colleges founded in the post-occupation period had become well established. In 1972 the proportion of students enrolled in private institutions exceeded 70 percent of the national total. The prospective undergraduate confronted an unprecedented choice of type, level, location, and apecialization for his or her university years.

Fast disappearing was the once predominant school uniform. It used to be a symbol of egalitarianism that concealed socio-economic discrepancies among classmates, but the uniform has been pretty much discarded by undergraduates in favor of the slacks, sweaters, jeans, skirts, and every other variety of casual attire—matched by every sort of hair style—found on campuses around the world. Perhaps in deference to indigenous habits, however, Japanese students seemed to launder their garments somewhat more frequently than their counterparts abroad. Undergraduates were no longer routinely absorbing the writings of Yanagida Kunio or Kita Ikki—although some still read these authors—whose selfless idealism and quest for home-grown reform appealed almost universally to students in the 1960s. Reading habits became much more diverse. If all students still patronized comic books, some read pornographic ones, others read mini-dramas, and still others read high brow satires reminiscent of "head comics" in the United States.

More substantial diversification was apparent in the subjects offered and the curricular patterns set by university faculties. The propensity toward prescribed courses lingered in many institutions, but most welcomed the Ministry of Education's ruling in 1972 that a year of study abroad could be counted toward a Japanese baccalaureate degree, and some universities began to grant credit for supervised field study in the liberal arts. No one model of undergraduate study predominated. Some universities, such as Tokyo, separated freshmen and sophomores for general education on a branch campus before bringing them to the main campus for specialization in their last two years. Others were accepting students immediately into the divisions in which they in-

332

tended to concentrate but offered general education courses within these divisions in the first two years.

Some institutions by the mid-1970s had developed substantial regional studies programs, especially focusing on Southeast Asia and America, but the concept of multidisciplinary area studies remained unfamiliar to many Japanese professors—particularly in Japan studies itself. Interdisciplinary research, especially in the social sciences but to a surprising degree in literature, education, and philosophy as well, had advanced much further in the major university centers than a decade earlier. Waseda's Institute of Social Sciences, for example, sponsored a dozen ongoing research seminars on such themes as urban administration, modern Soviet studies, national economic policy, and Japanese society under fascism—topics of interest to contemporary scholars everywhere. Elsewhere plans were afoot to create a new unit for "human environment studies," or *ningen kankyōgaku*. This proposal represented an imaginative, perhaps unique, pooling of sociologists, economists, psychologists, anthropologists, historians, political scientists, cyberneticists, and policy-oriented pure scientists for studies of man and his eco-social surroundings.

Most striking, however, was the transformed role of Marxist ideology in the 1970s. Together with its enormously fruitful contributions to modern scholarship, Marxism in the first decade or two after the war became a badge of non-reflection for some Japanese academics. Ideology sometimes imposed a methodological uniformity and interpretive consistency that precluded debate. Although Marxist outlooks never tyrannized the academic world to the degree feared by their most vehement opponents, only in recent years did the rhetorical logjam dissolve with a resulting liberation of Marxism from its formerly rigid frameworks. Once again it became a living force, to inspire criticism, to stir moral reflection, something to be shaped and redefined as an ongoing heritage in conjunction with other major world ideologies. Many Japanese scholars seemed fully as sophisticated as their European colleagues in grappling constructively with Marxism —and far less parochial on the subject than almost all Americans.

In some institutions, Marxists were nevertheless ranged in neatly marked camps against self-styled "neo-positivists" (hardly recognizable, no doubt, to the Meiji doyen of Japanese positivism, Nishi Amane). By neo-positivism scholars generally meant objective, "value-free" social science—an idea whose possibility is now widely questioned, both at home and abroad. In other institutions a multiplicity of viewpoints prevailed: some liberal, some provincial, a few Maoist, nearly all democratic as the term was used in postwar Japan. Such diversity was no virtue in itself, but it was an essential precondition to a true education, and the Japanese university had much more of it in the mid-1970s than before.

Dispersal

Less pronounced, perhaps less desirable as well, was the trend toward dispersal and fragmentation in Japanese higher education. As was true abroad, overspecialization became a danger, spurred on by the vocational demands of a high-technology economy and increasingly complex society. Humane values and general truths were sometimes hidden by the rush to acquire knowledge available only to an elite.

Physically, too, universities grew disparate. Urban campuses, already too crowded with outdated and inadequate buildings, had no room for new divisions or professional schools. The result was academic sprawl—departments and divisions in separate locations, spread throughout large cities wherever building sites were available. As a consequence, university-wide identity was lost or badly tarnished. The universities' slender library facilities were likewise scattered. Cataloging, never entirely reliable under the best of circumstances, often broke down as understaffed libraries tried to keep track of the specialized collections in the universities' respective divisions. Students and scholars alike were driven to purchase more books on their own or rely on the National Diet Library, a non-circulating depository with cataloging intricacies of its own to be mastered.

Figures published in 1973 showed that more than 60 percent of Japan's universities, with nearly 80 percent of the nation's undergraduate enrollment, were located in the seven prefectures with the largest metropolitan populations. Tokyo alone was the locale for 26.2 percent of all universities and 43.9 percent of all university students. Since few students and almost no professors lived on, or even near, the campuses, the effects on informal educational contacts were considerable. Professors at Tokyo universities routinely commuted an hour or more in each direction to their classes and understandably prized their free days for study at home. Few found it possible to be on campus daily—the more so because of publishers' deadlines and guest appearances here and there—and many went to the university only once or twice a week, their days filled with lectures to meet their teaching loads. The urban university of the 1970s was no longer merely a streetcar school; students lived in lodgings so far away that they routinely took a train, then a subway, then a bus just to get to class. This dispersal of curricular interests, physical plant, and university personnel at least provided an education of sorts in megalopolitan living, but it meant a dissipation of energies as well. Living in scattered fashion throughout the Kanto or Kinki areas made it harder for those in academic life to see each other regularly, let alone their students. The price paid for living near museums, libraries, films, theaters, government offices, and the headquarters of the future employers of graduates was a considerable compromise of the residential intimacy of the medieval college, after which all modern Japanese universities were originally modeled.

As a solution, government officials urged campus administrators to relocate in provincial areas where land is still available. A distinguished commission, headed by President Miyamoto of Tokyo University of Education, recommended plans for a new university complex in Tsukuba, Ibaraki prefecture, and on February 9, 1973 the government submitted a draft to the Diet to create Tsukuba University. The bold scheme split research and teaching by replacing the traditional faculties (*gakubu*) with three teaching divisions (*gakugun*) and nearly two dozen research units (*gakkei*). Administrative reorganization also took place. Tokyo University of Education forthwith agreed to move to Tsukuba and promised to accommodate its current students within the new institution.

On other campuses the reaction was guarded. Few urban universities were willing to trade the convenience of metropolitan life for the putative benefits of togetherness in the countryside. Faculties were understandably suspicious of state-endorsed schemes which abolished the *gakubu* and scatter its already diminishing prerogatives. Student leaders regarded the Tsukuba plan as an administrative power play to thwart activism. Universities in general were anxious lest the new model confer greater control over higher education on the Ministry of Education, and voices on the left were raised in the Diet against the potential for intellectual standardization implicit in the Tsukuba draft.

By 1977 Tsukuba University was in its second full year of activity on a hillside site larger than the area within Tokyo's Yamanote circle. The enormous campus was full of clatter from classroom and dormitory construction reminiscent of the go-go early 60s at many American universities. Clever administrators hired away some of the leading brains from rival institutions and set an early pattern of academic excellence that stymied many erstwhile critics. A special effort was begun to internationalize the curriculum, faculty, and student body—a welcome break in the notably insular character of Japan's national universities. Jealousies and doubts persisted, especially over the huge proportion of the education ministry's budget absorbed by Tsukuba each year. But for the first time in many decades, a respectable body of opinion believed that the exciting frontiers of Japanese higher education were now outside the greatest cities: at Tsukuba and at little-noticed Hiroshima University, the next target in the government's program of regional academic strengthening.

At Tsukuba, Hiroshima, and elsewhere, the styles of student life changed as dramatically in the mid-70s as Japanese society at large. Despite an energy crisis and a shrinking economic growth rate, Japan became a main focus of international culture—both fashion and the arts. Culturally the 1970s may turn out to have been the decade of Japan, as the 1960s belonged to America or the 1920s to Weimar. No country surpassed Japan's innovations in modern dance or architecture, and no society absorbed more designer fashions or imported foods. Students too underwent a revolution in life styles, with even longer hair on the men and shorter cuts on the women, smart dress aping their elders already in the work force, and flashy cars on urban campuses that lacked adequate parking lots. Boy-girl relationships matured strikingly in the mid-1970s. University women admitted having three times many male friends in 1977 as those surveyed just three years earlier, and students' partying and dating habits suddenly seemed indistinguishable from those in America and Western Europe. Equally characteristic was the new phenomenon of the "fifth-year student," or *gonensei*—typically a male undergraduate who deliberately flunked a senior year course in order to stay on an extra year in college, avoiding the reality of a tightening job market and the responsibilities of becoming an adult. Only an affluent society could produce parents rich enough, and indulgent enough, to wink at such languidness.

The Japanese university world of the 1970s changed during the years since the treaty riots at least as fast as the overall society. Like every social institution, the university reflected the worst and the best of the environment surrounding it; its strengths, no less than its pitfalls, derived from contemporary life as a whole and were not inherent in the higher education system itself. At its worst, the Japanese university was ever more crowded, impersonal, and underfinanced; at its best, it was a center of openness, vigor, and imagination—probably reaching as close to the ideal of free inquiry and the unbiased search for truth as has any other institution, either in Japan or elsewhere.

EDWARD R. BEAUCHAMP

REPORT FROM JAPAN 1976

One of the major characteristics of Japanese education from the beginning of the Meiji period in 1868 to the end of what the Japanese refer to as "the Pacific War" in 1945 was the highly centralized nature of its system of public education. A Ministry of Education (*Mombusho*) was created in July 1871, and all educational matters were brought under its control and supervision at that time. This system proved to be highly efficient, but was injected with a virulent strain of ultra-nationalism when promilitarist elements seized control of the government in the early 1930s.

During the American occupation of Japan (1945–1952) following the end of the Second World War, one of the primary objectives of the victors was the destruction of this centralized system of education, which was viewed as a fundamental cause of the nationalist fervor underlying Japan's military aggression. The only significant Japanese political group to have opposed the regime and emerged from the war with "clean hands" were the Communists, and they warmly supported American efforts at educational reform in general and decentralization

Reprinted from *Educational Forum* 41, 3 (March, 1977) pp. 373–378 with permission of the author and publisher.

in particular. However, the American efforts to foster decentralization failed, and today Japan once more possesses one of the world's most highly centralized educational systems.

It is only by viewing contemporary Japanese education within this context that one can begin to understand the acrimonious rivalry that exists between the conservative ruling Liberal-Democratic Party (LDP) and the leftist-leaning Japan Teachers' Union (JTU). This rivalry exacerbates virtually all of the current controversies which fuel the educational debate in Japan. Both the ideologies and the practical political interests of these bitter rivals serve to define their positions on the ever present educational issue of centralization versus decentralization. Although often anti-American and pro-Communist, the JTU is among the staunchest defenders of both the Japanese Constitution and the educational reforms imposed during the reign of General Douglas MacArthur. The JTU strongly favors, for its own practical reasons, decentralization as a means of reducing the control of the Tory government over education. The government for its part is frightened of the leftist political orientation of the JTU, and accurately envisions that decentralized, local decision-making would work to the political advantage of their rivals. The reality of Japan's political life is that the urban centers are the strongholds of leftist sentiment while rural Japan is the core of LDP strength. Whether the JTU would continue to favor decentralization should their political allies come to power is, of course, another question.

In light of this long-standing conflict, it came as a great surprise to both Japanese and knowledgable foreigners alike when Michio Nagai was named minister of education by a Liberal-Democrat Prime Minister, Takeo Miki, in December 1974. Nagai is a very unusual cabinet minister within the Japanese context. He is not a party politician, but a *bona fide* intellectual of wide international reputation. Perhaps the most unusual aspect of his appointment, however, is his well-known and long-standing ties to the Japan Teachers' Union. Holder of an American Ph.D. from Ohio State. Nagai is comfortable in several languages (including excellent English), and has taught at Columbia, Stanford, the University of Hong Kong, and El Colegio de Mexico before becoming an editorial writer for the prestigious daily newspaper, *Asahi Shimbun.*

Nagai, a truly international man, is distrusted by party regulars because he is not one of them, and has come under increasingly severe attack from both his fellow intellectuals and JTU members as having "sold out" to the power structure. His efforts at changing the direction of Japanese education are not appreciated, either by the LDP or the JTU.

The single most controversial reform initiated by Nagai is the so-called *shūnin* system which creates several quasi-administrative positions in elementary and secondary schools that are roughly equivalent to that of department heads in an American context. The ministerial ordinance establishing the system was issued in December 1975, and provided that "Under the supervision of the principal, the *shūnin* engage in liaison and coordination work and also gives guidance and advice on the formulation of educational plans and other school affairs." Since issuing this ordinance, Nagai has repeatedly stressed that *shūnin* are not to be viewed as supervisors possessing the power to issue orders, but merely as advisors and coordinators who will pass on to other teachers the wishes of principals in the interest of a rather vague "school management harmony."

The reaction of the JTU to this decision can only be described as instantaneous and violent. The union views the establishment of the *shūnin* system, correctly in the opinion of many neutral observers, as yet another attempt by the government to further control of the schools and their teachers. The union retaliated with a series of mass demonstrations and a number of limited, but illegal strikes in an unsuccessful attempt to force the government to back down on this issue.

In the view of the JTU, perhaps the most insidious aspect of the *shūnin* system was the establishment of a new category of teachers with close ties to the school administration who received a separate financial allowance for their added responsibilities. One influential newspaper, the *Yomiuri Shimbun*, suggested editorially that the *shūnin* system "permits providing an additional allowance" to those teachers over forty years of age who constitute the single "largest age group," and who need a supplemented income. The union, on the other hand, sees this as "salami tactics" by the government, and envisions from seven to twelve teachers in *each* school being "bought off" by the government in this manner. This would result, the union contends, in a decline in union membership and strength. There does seem to be some evidence that gives credence to the union view. Up until the last decade, both principals and head teachers were allowed to be union members until the government declared them ineligible to belong to the JTU.

This *shūnin* system became effective with the opening of the new academic year April 9, 1976. Each elementary school principal was to appoint a *shūnin* to head the department of instruction, plus a *shūnin* for each of the school's six grade levels. The principals were also to appoint heads of business affairs and health programs. In addition to these positions, junior high schools were expected to appoint a guidance counselor. At the high school level, a department head for all subjects taught was appointed, in addition to the positions found in the junior high school.

At last count only about half of Japan's forty-seven prefectures had agreed to cooperate in the implementation of the *shūnin* system. Yokohama Mayor Ichio Asukata, chairman of the pro-leftist National Association of Reformist Mayors, spoke for his organization and, probably, most of the opponents of *shūnin* in mid-January 1976, when he stated that "Education must be neutral, and the implementation of the *shūnin* system is a political problem, for it plays a leading role in making the country into a fascist state." The issue is still not resolved, although the government appears to be ever so slowly gaining the upper hand in this issue, as it has in similar conflicts in the three decades since the end of World War II.

Another long-standing issue in Japanese education is the Ministry of Education's method of selecting textbooks for use in the schools. Traditionally, the government has exerted tight control over the textbook selection process, and this tradition survived the reforms of the American occupation.

Undoubtedly, the *cause célèbre* of the textbook controversy has been the so-called "Ienaga Case." In June 1965 Professor Saburo Ienaga, a well-known historian at the Tokyo University of Education, filed a damage suit against the Ministry of Education following the ministry's rejection of his Japanese history textbook on the grounds that it contained several hundred "defects" that needed correction before the text could be approved. Charging that the textbook selection process violated the constitutional provision guaranteeing freedom of expression, and that his academic freedom was infringed, Professor Ienaga asked for approximately ¥2,000,000 in damages.

In June 1967 Ienaga initiated a second suit when the university rejected a fifth revised edition of his *New Japanese History* textbook on the grounds that it contained objectionable passages dealing with the mythological origins of Japan, the Meiji Constitution, and the origins of World War II, among other things. In a 1972 interview, Ienaga defended his textbook against ministry criticism:

This is nothing more or less than what the old pre-war governments were doing—promulgating an official history of Japan. The Ministry doesn't like anything lengthy about the China incident ... it doesn't like mention of the colonial status of Taiwan and Korea in the old empire or much detail at all on the interwar period.

In July 1970 the Tokyo District Court ruled in Ienaga's favor on his second (1967) suit. The court held that the way in which the Ministry of Education operated the textbook selection system violated both the Constitution and Japan's Fundamental Law of Education. In July 1974, however, the same court ruled in Ienaga's original suit (1965) that it was legal for the government to examine the contents of potential school textbooks submitted by authors.

The second Ienaga suit which was decided in his favor in 1970 was appealed by the Ministry of Education, and in an unexpected decision the Tokyo Higher Court, on December 20, 1975, dismissed the ministry's appeal by reaffirming the lower court's decision. The Tokyo Higher Court decided that, in the Ienaga case, the ministry had abused and overstepped its administrative discretion. Although gratified with this decision, Ienaga and his supporters were chagrined at the court's failure to rule on the constitutional issues involved in the case. The ministry immediately appealed this decision to the Supreme Court, and many Japanese would not be surprised if the more conservative justices on that court overruled the Tokyo Higher Court. In any event, when a definitive decision is forthcoming, its effects on Japanese education will be profound.

A more immediate concern (especially to the young people most intimately affected), is the current bleak employment situation facing university graduates. As in the United States, Japan has been experiencing an economic recession which forces both the government and business firms to curtail short-term expenditures sharply and to plan long-range spending more carefully. These widespread cutbacks were vividly reflected in employment recruitment for March 1976 graduates of Japanese universities, and triggered great concern among students, parents, and politicians who were facing an election in December 1976. Until very recently, graduating seniors had been assured of satisfactory employment in an expanding economy.

Since the 1973 oil crisis, however, economic growth in Japan has come to a virtual standstill, and in 1974 registered its first negative growth rate (minus 0.5 percent) since the end of World War II. This has led many of Japan's largest and most prestigious firms to retrench by paring their employment levels to meet the new economic realities. This cutback has primarily taken the form of reducing staffs by attrition and hiring new employees only where absolutely necessary. Belt tightening has also adversely affected experienced workers, who find it increasingly difficult to find new positions.

It is not only the private employment sector outlook which is gloomy. The traditionally intense competition for government employment has also increased. In October 1975 the Tokyo Metropolitan Government held its entrance examination, but nearly one half of the 11,500 applicants failed to turn up to compete for the 470 job openings. The Japanese mass media had given a great deal of publicity to the large number of applicants for the relatively few jobs, and this apparently discouraged all but 5,870 persons (50.8 percent of those signed up) from taking the examination. Following the examination, the press reported that the "competition rates," based on the number of applicants, were 43.5 times for college, junior college, and university graduates, and 6.3 times for senior high school graduates, resulting in an all time high average of 24.6 times.

Up through March 1976 the short-term future appeared especially bleak. Several reputable employment surveys, conducted in early 1976 for national newspapers, predicted that job opportunities for March graduates would be far fewer than in the past. In fact, only a handful of the 150 major and medium-sized business enterprises in Tokyo hired more university graduates than in 1975, and two dozen of them did not hire any university graduates in 1976.

In addition, two factors complicate the gloomy employment situation described above. The first is the propensity of firms to offer positions only to graduates of a very small number of prestigious elite universities, primarily state-run institutions such as the University of Tokyo, and a few private schools, especially Keio and Waseda.

This educational fact of life lends credence to the fear of graduating students of less prestigious private and provincial universities that they are discriminated against in employment opportunities. For example, in the fall of 1975 one newspaper described how an unidentified prestigious private university (rumored to be Keio) reported that there were already 8,800 job offers for some 1,600 of its students who want jobs. This works out to be 5.6 job offers per student. On the other hand, mammoth Nihon University, a private Tokyo university with upwards of 80,000 students, has been notified that only 320 out of over 1,200 major firms listed on the Tokyo Stock Exchange are willing to consider its graduates for employment next spring.

The second complicating factor in the Japanese university employment problem results from the increasingly vocal demands of some Japanese women for more equitable treatment in the job market. Although women comprise more than half (about thirty million of a total of about fifty-three million) of the labor force—mostly in clerical and service jobs—they are often the first to lose their jobs when an economic slump occurs. Many firms complain that women look at post-university employment as temporary until finding husbands. Many Japanese employers apparently agree with a professor from Kyoto, Dr. Yuji Kaida, who contends that, "If you consider company work as a meal, men employees are the main course, and women are the dessert." In any event, Professor Kaida maintains that if women want to work, "they should find work after graduating from high school" and not clutter up the university employment market.

In face of both current economic realities and the widespread attitudes reflected in Professor Kaida's comment, Japanese women students have organized a campaign to lobby the government and business firms to provide more jobs for women graduates. Pointing out that the number of job offers for graduating women in 1976 was only one-fourth of that for the corresponding period of 1975, the newly formed liaison committee of The Society to Think About the Employment of Women College Graduates denounces the current situation as discrimination of the worst kind. The results of their initial efforts have not been promising. The students who made the rounds of various governmental and business offices to present their case were refused the opportunity of meeting with the men in charge.

Japan is an energetic and well disciplined society, but the specter of thousands of unemployed and underemployed university graduates— men as well as women—who feel disillusioned with society is enough to send a chill through thoughtful people who remember the 1930s. The government seems quietly concerned and searching for an answer, but no relief appears on the horizon. In the meantime, many of the nation's most talented young people wonder if they sweated through entrance examinations and four years of college for nothing.

Student extremists in Japan continued their violent activities over the past year. Divided into various radical factions, based on their own version of ideological purity, these radical groups often spend as much time attacking each other as the society they all purport to want to overthrow.

In the first three months of 1976 alone, there were fourteen reported incidents of intrafactional violence. One of the most unusual attacks occurred late in 1975 when six, steel pipe-wielding female radicals attacked a rival faction coed in a restroom at the Tokyo Women's Christian College in Tokyo's western suburb of Ogikubo. A few months later another especially vicious incident took place in the early morning hours of February 28, 1976. At that time a group of five male *chukakuha* (Middle Core) faction members, armed with steel pipes, broke into the apartment of a *Kakumaruha* (Revolutionary Marxist) faction member, where they inflicted serious injuries upon their ideological victim, his wife, and even his two year old son.

The most serious and sensational terrorist act occurred on March 2, 1976, when a powerful time bomb that had been constructed from a fire extinguisher and placed in Sapporo's Hokkaido Prefectural Government Building exploded as innocent government employees were arriving for work. In killing two persons and injuring eighty-four others, the East Asia Anti-Japanese Armed Front claimed that they acted to strike a blow against "Japanese imperialists" who oppress Japanese "minorities," including the Ainus, Hokkaido's indigenous people.

This act of what one newspaper called "ideological idiocy" reflects a growing minority problem in Japan. Although usually described as having a highly homogeneous population, Japan also possesses significant numbers of *Ainu* (mostly in Hokkaido), as well as the socially outcast *burakumin* (represented by an increasingly militant Buraku Liberation League) and smaller groups of Koreans and Chinese. As in many Western societies, idealistic students often take on the minority's cause as their own.

These are only a few of the issues which plague Japanese education today. Others which can only be mentioned briefly include the relatively small but growing Women's Movement and its multifaceted implica-

345

tions for education; the financial crisis faced by Japan's private universities; the perennial problem of the system of entrance examinations to Japan's universities; the recent Organization for Economic Cooperation and Development (OECD) report that severely criticized Japanese social science research for being too abstract and not responding to legitimate social demands; new trends in using television and radio in a government-sponsored "University of the Air"; the problems and prospects of the new United Nations University situated in Tokyo; and the "new" problem of educating Japanese children of businessmen and diplomats overseas. All of these issues and more are important elements in the ferment that is endemic in Japan's contemporary educational system.

Part III

Some Possible Future Directions
of Japanese Education.

Probably the most interesting, yet the most difficult, aspect of any study of Japanese education is projecting its future. Certainly no individual, especially a non-Japanese, is capable of "predicting" what Japan's future holds with any degree of accuracy. We can, however, look at how those who control or influence Japanese education would like to shape it over the next several years.

Since the end of World War II and the emergence of the *Nikkyoso* (the Japan Teachers Union) as a potent opposition force to the educational bureaucrats within the *Mombusho*, a fierce ideological battle has raged between these two rivals. In July, 1975, the *Nikkyoso* published their views on "What Japan's Educational System Should Be," which is very critical of both the existing system and the government's approach to it.

The other side of the coin, the "official" government view of the future development of Japanese education is reflected in the report of the Central Council for Education (1972), *Basic Guidelines for the Reform of Education.* The Japan Teachers Union calls for a fundamental restructuring of education; however, the Central Council for Education accepts the basic structure as sound and advocates fine tuning.

The future of Japanese education cannot be predicted, but the contributions comprising this section clearly suggests how the two major educational protagonists of Japan view it in the context of the interests of the groups they represent. Perhaps this is all that one can reasonably expect.

What Japan's Education
Should Be

Our Idea and Standpoint of Reform

I. Idea

A. IDEA OF EDUCATION

1. Education as the Right—a Right of the People

Education is a life-long right of all the people. We, the Japanese people, have been assured it to be a fundamental idea of national education since the end of World War II. Until war's end education was one of the people's three major duties along with taxation and conscription. The ruling circles took advantage of education for mobilizing manpower among the broad masses in order to enforce their policies for capitalizing and militarizing the nation.

Therefore, mentally and physically handicapped boys and girls were alienated and exempted from school enrollment under that compulsory school system. In schools it was emphasized to teach feudal morals and emperor-centered history as well as gymnastics for military training; girls were trained to be mothers of brave soldiers in future.

The postwar reform in education aimed to subvert the dominant idea of "compulsory" or bureaucratic education. The new Constitution solemnly declares that all the people have a right to education in Article 26, and guarantees academic freedom in Article 23. Education is no

Reprinted from JTU-Council on Educational Reform, *How to Reform Japan's Education* (Tokyo: JTU, 1975), pp. 33–45, with permission of the publisher.

longer to be our duty but a constitutional right for all the people. Education is also to be provided not only in a school system, but in every opportunity and every place.

A fundamental change of idea, however, is not always followed by a change of realities of education. The right to education is not yet completely secured even for school-aged children: a lot of handicapped children and youth have been left alone out of a public school system as we see in Part One, I "Realities". Furthermore, our school system today can scarecely meet the people's urgent needs in general.

If education is a right of men, it must be enjoyment for him as every right should be. Access to truth without any restriction would be a joy for all, especially for those who have long been deprived it. But now we are afraid to say that our children and youth are really enjoying learning in school as their right to access to truth. In fact our schools are rather painful system for children; they are obliged to cram enormous knowledge unsystematically and unscientifically, only wishing to get good marks in examinations under the ability-first policies of the government.

Our schools today are still nothing but only places to go to reluctantly and obligatorily as they were in prewar days. Then, what we have to do is quite clear; we have to make our schools be institutions where children and youth can be willing to go and learn joyfully.

For this purpose we must keep, first of all, education firmly stand on the base of the Fundamental Law of Education, which the reactionary forces have been trying hard to be a mere scrap of paper as well as the Constitution, for they are disadvantage for them. It is important for us to examine first what education means for men and society.

2. Education and Its Value

a. Education of of Man—Personal Growth and Social Progress

A man is a social and historical being as well as a natural one. Not only formed by nature and society, men can also reform them positively. Through these processes men can change themselves infinitely. If we may call this change human development, we cannot evaluate it with the results of its achievement but with its vitality to how to change.

The present life affected by past will orientate future, a hope of which also encourages us now. It is important for all, especially for young people, to live their present life vividly with future hope, wishing full development of their possibilities. Because education is the very work to help and encourage men to develop their possibilities, it is essential for all, especially indispensable for children.

Our task is to secure children's present life wholesome and rich for their future development through education. Every child has infinite possibilities to be developed, which often extend so marvelously beyond men's thought. Education must be realistic enough to meet the present social and cultural needs, but also ambitious enough in hoping unpredictable future development of children. Those who are in teaching profession must realize their heavy responsibility for shaping personality, and try to foster in themselves deep reliance and humbleness to the possibility of human beings. Teachers and educational administrators should caution themselves against arrogance and selfishness, with which they will debase education and cause enormous damage to children and society tomorrow.

b. Educational Value

In former days education was monopolized by the privileged minority, but gradually schools for the masses were developed in order to meet their growing needs for education. In modern days a public school system for all has been developed in many countries according to wide recognition of human rights.

The fundamental human rights to cultured life naturally demand educational opportunity for all in their every stage of development. Cultural heritage of every race and of human beings as a whole, once monopolized by the privileged class, has been gradually shared by all the masses.

In human development, however, much emphasis should not be put on acquiring various knowledge but on fostering scientific, intellectual, and sensitive mind through that knowledge. When children learn, they will find a new wonderful world of unknown before them. As watching the stars in the sky or insects on the earth, children will be astonished and interested in wonders of nature toward scientific approach. Education must encourage children in their discovery and new intellectual world. The existing culture can only be valuable when it contributes to children's wholesome development; however, today

351

a lot of parents know that children would be damaged harmfully if they are crammed with heaps of existing knowledge and estimated only by how much they acquired it.

When we think of what education and educational value should be, we cannot help but be generous in recognizing various senses of value in education, because the rigid existing sense can no longer meet children's various demands for developing their possibilities to the full. There would be no education where there is no confidence in humanity and individual possibilities with various senses of value.

It is only in a society of freedom that education can fully prove its worth to develop each individual personality. Under a standardized, controlled educational environment individuality can never be developed freely and multifariously. It is essential for school today to restore freedom in society and school in order to fulfill its primary purpose.

3. Aims of Education—Our Image of Desirable Personality

Now we will examine exactly what personality we may think desirable in educational work. When we teach, we usually have a certain expectation to those whom we teach, although having to guard ourselves not to make such expectation a barrier to children's growth. Educational work would be dull and monotonous if we lack such reasonable wishes based on our ideas and principles of education.

First of all we want ourselves and also our children to be the people who firmly stand on the basis of the Constitution and the Fundamental Law of Education; both of which we have established after the war with an ardent wish for peace and justice, expressing universal principles to be respected and special historical tasks to be carried out by the Japanese people in the Constitution and the Law. Today we must put more emphasis on this problem, because the reactionary forces are trying to deteriorate the Constitution and the Law, the ideas of which have not yet been prevailed completely among the people.

Let us examine some of the major characteristics which we think desirable.

a. One who loves justice

According to the Fundamental Law of Education, one of the main aims of education is to make a man who loves justice. We used to hesitate to refer the term of justice, as we once were indoctrinated militarism and mobilized to the aggressive wars under the name of fulfilling justice on the earth.

But now we can tell what is injustice or unrighteousness: it is to intrude into other countries; to oppress, subordinate, or discriminate others; to do everything with a selfish aim regardless of others. We find a lot of unjust problems of poverty, misery, and selfishness causing the environmental pollution, the skyrocketing prices of commodities, and frequent occurance of a family suicide.

We hope our children to be persons who will respect justice, be enraged at unjust realities, and do their best for prevailing righteousness throughout the country and the world.

b. One who respects others, rejecting discrimination and loving labour

Could we fully understand the idea of respecting man's life and dignity in the new Constitution? We had or still have a shameful history of discrimination against the Korean, the Chinese, the Okinawan, the Ainu race, and the inhabitants of "unliberated hamlets" called Buraku. In our society today those who are mentally or physically handicapped are still often contempted and rejected, and at the same time in general those who cannot get good achievements in school are supposed to be of inferior personality under the ability-first system.

One of our major tasks in education is to teach children to reject any discrimination of race, sex, or ability. An aptitude of discrimination is closely related to disregarding of labour. It is essential for us to love labour by which we can be human beings distinct from animal.

c. One who loves truth

What does it mean by "loving truth" stated in the Fundamental Law of Education? Our schools had long been distributing the knowledge which was often unsystematic and sometimes distorted especially in the subject of history by the authorities. Now we have to establish academic freedom and the people's subjecthood in learning, while creating scientific, active and practical manners.

Education must be founded, before everything else, on truth. Especially in this time of technical innovation what we need is not fragmental subdivided knowledge, but essential principles for creative thinking. Under the nation-wide environmental pollution and disruption today, we have to rebuilt our country with a new vision of respecting man's life and harmonizing society and nature, avoiding a stopgap measure with narrow skill and information.

In the post-war reform of education, most of the false knowledge in school textbooks in pre-war days was largely revised and corrected. But recently the Ministry of Education, through the course of guidance and the authorized school-books, has been emphasizing to teach only idealistic and superficial matters, while carefully rejecting disadvantageous facts for the government such as the aggressive wars, the environmental pollution, or the poor administration in social welfare.

We must disclose and accuse such dangerous plots, but teach children very truth necessary for their growth, as fostering in them scientific manners in discerning truth. One of our desirable characteristics to be aimed is, therefore, a man of loving and searching after truth.

d. On who is full of vitality and sensitivity

In order to build better society and culture we should be vital and sensitive enough, although our present circumstances are too dark and hard. Sensitivity is essential for a man, because it provides him not only a sense of beauty but also a warm delicate mind of considering others. We could have our life really human when we are full of fellow feeling with one another sharing joys and sorrows. At the same time we need an indomitable spirit vital enough to overcome difficulties in life. Parents and teachers always have to mind to train children's bodies and souls unyielding to any hardship.

We also cannot but think of what labour means to men; when working together, a man can get fellow feeling mutually as co-workers, and he feels a vital life in himself. Labour is a primary desire of a man by nature. Our ancestors described this desirable character in the traditional saying of "Graceful mind in healthy body." Following their wisdom we hope our children to be sound in mind and body as stated in the Fundamental Law of Education.

e. One who wishes for international solidarity

In the Constitution it is clearly proclaimed that "We desire to occupy an honored place in an international society striving for the preservation of peace, and the banishment of tyranny and slavery, oppression and intolerance for all time from the earth." In the world today there still are wars, oppressions, racial discrimination, and a lot of people who are deprived of their freedom and are in suffer.

We, once oppressed the other peoples and were ourselves suppressed under the arbitrary authorities, wish our children to be a generation that can sympathize with the suffering peoples of far countries and step forward eliminating the causes of suffer, with joining in international solidarity for peace and democracy. Nationalism, in its exact meaning of loving one's country, is useful for international solidarity, when it helps to make a country peaceful and democratic. Both of nationalism and international solidarity, stimulating each other, are to be essential for our desirable characters.

B. IDEA OF AN EDUCATIONAL SYSTEM

1. A Principle of Justice in Education

Now let us consider our fundamental idea of a school system in order to actualize our general idea of education. Justice, to which we referred as one of our desirable characters, should also be a fundamental principle in our school system.

The post-war reform in our school system called "6-3 grade system" —exactly 6-3-3-4 (elementary, junior secondary, senior secondary, college, respectively)—has essentially aimed to provide equal opportunity for all. It tried to have children study as long as possible under a single-track school system instead of the double one in former days, with a same curriculum in a same school according to their resident districts without any discrimination of status, class, property, or sex.

However, the political situation changed after the San Francisco Peace Treaty in 1951, and the high-economic growth policies were accelerated through the 1960's. The government and the financial circles projected together a readjustment of school system, devaluating the democratic 6-3 system, preaching their convenient theories of "equal opportunity", and advertizing their "ability-first" policy.

In the old society where the social order was stabilized by status and property, with which educational opportunity followed, the idea of "ability-first" was a revolutionary slogan as well as "equal opportunity" against any discrimination except ability. The ability-first policy played a certain role for democratization of society and education in a certain period of time, as long as it emphasized equality of men.

But according to the development of capitalixm it has gradually shifted to overemphasizing ability which industries just needed, and at last it introduced a new discrimination of ability in society. In a capitalist society "equal opportunity according to ability" means nothing but mechanics for alienating the inferiors. Under this situation schools become a system of selecting children to be classified with ability. Just as an orange sorter selects oranges into each grade of A, B, or C with its respective price and destination, our school classify children for each destination appointed by the demands of industries according to their school record of "ability". Then, children are forced to compete with one another and kick others down with the strong guidance of self-interested parents who love their children blindly and some teachers who believe competition is best in learning. The ability-first policy has inevitably brought hot competition into school system, while rejecting the principle idea of "mutual help and respect" in the Fundamental Law of Education, and excluding those who cannot take well to competition labeling deficient.

As a matter of course the ability-first policy has all prevailed into whole society of ours, because the principle rule of capitalism demands it not only in education but also in society as a whole. It is a regular method of keeping social orders for the dominant class to establish a hierarchy system in society according to man's fidelity or ability useful for them, and for this purpose they manipulate public once by sham-democratic rules or another by force. The financial circles, the most dominant in our society today, are advocating their naked excessive demands for labour and profit under "the man-power cultivating project". The financial circles worked upon the Ministry of Education to reorganize the educational system more efficiently along their ability-first policy. This policy of ability-first with its plausible propaganda, is the very root of all disasters in education today.

Under this policy the elite at the top of the social hiarachy system must sacrifice humanity instead of ability, because to be the elite is nothing but to be hartless, intolerant, and to kick their fellows down for their success. It must be a caramity for the people to have such elite in the important positions of national policy-making. In this respect also we cannot agree with the government's plan to make universities be a finish course for selected elite in the cause of "university-industry co-operation". We must have our universities widely open to the masses through self-reformation by all staffs of every university basically.

On the other hand, for handicapped children at the opposite end to the elite, a school system plays a role to exclusive them in order to keep the hiarachy system solid, although the government is publicly propagating a reform plan for the education of the handicapped children.

Against the government's educational policy based on the distinction of ability, we must declare a principle of justice in education for full and wholesome development of every child. Equal educational opportunity should provide everyone with access to education without any discrimination such as of social status or family origin. In a capitalist society the "equal" opportunity is almost closed to poor children, and they say it is proper for the rich to have rich education but for the poor to have poorer one according to their capacity. Our society can never assure everyone, especially to the poor and the handicapped, of his full development. We want everyone to be completely guaranteed to satisfy his educational needs in a school system which is not to be like a sharp tapering ladder, but a broad public way.

Furthermore, because of the principle of justice we do demand education to be more full and complete for the "less talented" by the fact itself. The rule of "according to ability" is historically recognized as a modern equal idea in economic distribution. But could we say, simply applying this rule to education, that those who have much ability can get much more educational opportunity than those of disability? Is it fair to say that poorer and shorter education will be good enough for ths handicapped or mentally retarded children according to their disability? On the contrary they must be tained more carefully and long enough to be able to overcome their difficulties.

In the present school system most of mentally and physically handicapped children are excluded from compulsory education and deprived of their right to education. There is very few school for them except benevolently settled ones; and such schools usually have no high school course in which education for the handicapped children can be fully extended. "Education according to ability" in the third article of the Fundamental Law of Education must be construed in this sense, although there are many administrative authorities that have failed to understand it, only keeping the predominant idea of the survival of the fittest.

Once and again, we must fairly recognize "education according to ability" as an idea of "education satisfying every need of development": it must not be a rule for discriminating the handicapped, but for much longer care and instruction for them; the leavier they are handicapped, the more they should be helped.

It will be meaningless to discuss about a rule of equal educational opportunity for all without referring to equality in society as its prerequisite. Wishing our children to love justice, we should create an educational system on the basis of a principle of justice, which implies "education satisfying every need of individual development", while continually keeping scientific approach to the fundamental or structural problems of society.

2. The People's Right to Education and Academic Freedom

a. The right to education and learning

The people's right to learning is a prerequisite of the right to education. The right to learning is one of the fundamental human rights such as right to live, development, the pursuit of happiness, and work. It is also inseparable from academic freedom and the pursuit of truth. For children and youth the right to learning is essential to their growth and development, and for adults it is a demand for continual life-long education.

Our right to learning directly comes from an idea of popular sovereignty. It secures the people to demand their fundamental and life-long education as well as academic and intellectual freedom. The people's right to education is a general idea which demands the government to respect the people's right to learning and its effective implementation.

b. The right of children and youth to learning

The people's right to learning is first to secure full development of children and youth as one of their essential needs. Children of course have the same human rights as adults', but they themselves have their peculiar demands different from grownups because of their immaturity. However, their immaturity cannot be recognized as of lower capacity than adults', but of unpredictable possibilities for future growth. With help and instruction in family, school, and community children are expected to grow and choose spontaneously their future course in life. If children are deprived of their right to learning, they may become too ignorant to demand their rights when grown up, and sometimes it can be harmful to society: you can imagine, for example, how a political illiterate will work with his vote. Thus, the children's right to learning is a pre-condition to all the other human rights.

To secure every right of children is closely related to whether fundamental rights of their parents to cultured life is implemented or not: parents must be guaranteed civil rights to freedom and education for themselves and for their children's wholesome growth.

c. Parents' obligation in children's education and its trust

A child is born and nursed in a family. We know that education in infancy plays a basic role in men's intellectual growth and character shaping. A child with hearty care of a mother or a nurse will grow in rich sentiment. Family environment and disciplines also play significant educational roles in children's growth. Therefore, it is a natural responsibility of parents to foster and educate their children. We must recognize that the responsibility of parents is to secure children's human rights to growth and education, although once it was accompanied with a dictatorial authority under a feudal family system. So, parents have a due right to accuse and reject anything that tries to interfere in their performance of this duty.

In society today, parents entrust part of their children's education to school which can give more systematic, organized instruction than each home. In this sense, school is to make parents' duty socialize in order to give children collective experience in learning and living under professional guidance. Parents entrust their children's education to schools and teachers, expecting them to provide quality education based on science and truth with highly professional knowledge and training. If schools and teachers cannot meet this demand but fail to secure children's wholesome development, parents should accuse them and request their improvement or reform. The obligation to guarantee children's human development is accomplished in mutual help and criticism between parents and teachers.

d. Teachers' obligations and their academic freedom

Under a public school system today, children and youth grow through a whole activity in school or class. All school staffs, not only teachers in charge, have to be organized in one aim-having body for securing desirable conditions for children's growth and quality education based on humanity and science. It is a primary task of school staffs, especially of teachers, to do their best to propel children's growth through their professional, creative activities inside and outside of class. For this purpose teachers should have scientific knowledge on children's development, and train themselves continuously for better teaching.

Teachers, as initial performers and drivers of educational science, should be completely guaranteed a right to freedom of research and educational practice. Without this guarantee, there will be no education and its progress in its real sense. In order to fulfill their obligations, it is essential for teachers to closely join with professional research workers and educators in the movement for establishing autonomy in curriculum-making and selecting textbooks as well as what and how to teach and evaluate.

e. A right and role of a collective of school staffs

It is important for a collective of school staffs to which degree they have acquired their freedom and democracy at work in order to fulfill their obligations. For the sake of establishing a democratic group of the staffs, each staff must be guaranteed academic freedom in his work, and each individual work of research can be systematically discussed and practiced in his group with mutual help and criticism among themselves and also parents.

A democratic group of school staffs will never be developed without a movement of demanding fundamental labour rights. Educational research work and its practice can be successfully propelled under a vivid labour movement of educational workers. Through such educational activities that make children of working class develop to the full, firm solidarity can be established between educational workers and the other workers. When all educational workers can recognize the important role of such activities as a driving power of their unionism, a teachers' union movement will develop further in quality and quantity.

With this viewpoint it is necessary for all school staffs to examine more carefully how to be a school management, a staff meeting, or collective research activities in school.

f. A community control in education

Education, a creative activity for securing children's right to learning and human development, is required to be autonomous, or neutral we may say, from any authoritative control, while asking parents and the inhabitants to participate in establishing democratic conditions for education.

Today an idea of a community control in education has a reasonable ground for its stand, because public schools are essentially financed at public expense, that is, tax of the people. In a community control, citizens can learn how to exercise their political right in popular sovereignty. It is nothing but the people's demand for taking back public education from the government in order to restore its primary sense of "public", which has been often misunderstood for "of the government" in our society. We should promote decentralization of educational administration, especially demanding to revive a public-elective system of education boards as well as endeavouring to reform activities in a Parent-Teacher Association and to participate in a local educational administration.

g. Public education and the State's responsibility

A community control or decentralization in education, however, can never mean of releasing the State's responsibility for educational finance under the present conditions. On the contrary, the State's responsibility will become much heavier for enriching and distributing educational budget in considering a principle of justice in a school system and of children's right to education, although any additional official control must not follow after. Our public schools are poorly equipped in general from nursery schools to colleges; they stand out in sharp contrast to a striking growth of the gross national product and a huge amount of the military budget. Under such conditions, the people have been urging the State to fulfill its responsibility in education.

h. The people's demand for self-education with teachers' co-operation

The people's right to education and learning will be developed further in a movement for demanding self-education, which is practically drived by workers, farmers, fishermen, and citizens in each community. The masses of people are now organizing their educational demands of themselves and also of their children into a mass nationwide movement. Teachers should firmly join with this movement and reflect the people's demands in their educational activities. We could not completely keep our right to education untill we have established a firm solidarity among the broad masses, workers, and teachers.

Our idea of education and its system above stated is not one-sided or partial view, but that already examined and discussed in a mass movement for peace and democratic education, and recognized to be precious heritage of the age-old struggle of man to education. Only such a movement and demands of the people can support and drive forward our democratic reform of education, and further enrich our idea of education.

II. Standpoint

Having a lot of problems to be solved in our education today, we must at first choose which principles are available to solve them. Therefore, in the previous sections we have tried to make our essential idea clear in considering the present conditions, contradictions, and demands in education.

Now, on the basis of that idea we are going to examine our blueprint in detail for solving the problems. In considering the concrete plan, we think it necessary to keep the most basic standpoints of ours in mind, lest we should be confused with a lot of pressing problems and fail to recognize a whole aspect in education.

We can summarize our standpoints in the following five:

A. THE IDEA OF THE POST-WAR EDUCATIONAL REFORM AND THE 6-3 SYSTEM

In discussing educational reform, the first premise is how we estimate the primary idea of the post-war reform and its bearings thenceforth. Although the government have been taking a negative attitude for it, we think the primary idea of the reform being debased often by the government's policy is still having or rather increasing its democratic value today.

We can never forget that all of the people standing amid the bombed ruins immediately after the war firmly made up their minds to have no more war but to establish a peaceful country. The bitter experience of the people under fascism has correctly led to a universal principle of mankind for peace. The people's resolution was represented in the ideas of popular sovereignty, renunciation of war, and respect of fundamental human rights in the new Constitution, and these were also the major principles of the post-war educational reform.

Reffering more precisely, the post-war reform aimed to create democratic education for peace and truth, and to secure the right to education for all, rejecting the former militaristic education. It has established a single-track school system with 6–3 graded compulsory education, doing away with all educational discriminations under the former double-track system, respecting spontaneous activities of children and students, and securing their democratic rights. It also aimed to propel the people's cultural and educational activities in each community. It placed a heavy responsibility on the State and the local self-governing bodies for preparing favorable educational conditions, and established publicly-elected education boards for decentralization of education.

These reform plans have been largely deformed during three decades after the war by the government's reactionary education policy, but the essentiai idea of the reform have gradually taken root deep into the people's movement for democratic education. To respect the principles of the post-war reform is not to stick to them blindly, but to develop them effectively in our present movement.

Revaluating the important role of the 6–3 school system in our educational history, we will newly recommend it to be developed correctly for democratic education. The 6–3 system was once highly estimated by the Ministry of Education itself calling it an epoch-making approach to democratic education. As recognized in UNESCO's report on "Secondary Education in the World" in 1961, the great role of a 6–3 system in education, which was originally established in part of the U.S.A., is to be a pioneering attempt in this century to reform an old stratified school system in the West since the eighteenth century. It was not a peculiar idea in the U.S.A. alone, but also seen in many of the Western countries. In Japan it was also supported before the war by some educators, such as Noguchi Entaro or Abe Shigetaka. The major demand of a 6–3 system in those days was to open wide the exclusive secondary education to the people without discrimination of sex. This demand was inherited and developed into the post-war movement for "public high school for all" and for equal educational opportunity for mentally and physically handicapped children. Thus an idea of a 6–3 system has been developing into a demand for a human right to education today from a simple request of high school career in early days.

However, shortly after its establishment, the 6–3 system in Japan has been partially rectified by the government calling it "too radical" or "just unwelcome offspring of the Occupied Forces": high schools and colleges were diversified into each streaming course to begin with setting up a system of higher technical school under the policy of "high economic growth". In 1971, furthermore, the Central Council for Education which is a consultative organ of the Minister of Education summitted a report on overhauling reform of the 6–3 system. The revisionists are insisting that the 6–3 system can no longer meet the demands of a modern technological society. That is to say, it is not efficient enough to their "economic high growth" policy.

We will frontally oppose the government's reform plan which takes economic growth prior to all. On the contrary, we believe that the essential principles of the 6–3 system must be secured for real human development of all children. It may not be necessary for us to insist on the grading of 6–3–3–4 in the school system, and we could find any other suitable grading fit for children's growth if it is necessary. But we rather think that a rough-and-ready revision of the present 6–3 system will bring much confusion and more harm than good under thypresent government's policy, because it has been accepted by the masses during almost three decades with its democratic ideas in spite of the government's various devices for deterioration.

Now we must properly develop the 6–3 single-track school system for securing a right to education of every child including, of course, the handicapped, while constantly seeking for more democratic and quality education as long and rich as possible under an equal condition. On the basis of the principle of the 6–3 system, we must also develop the pre- and post-compulsory education as well as adults' educational and cultural activities in a community, co-ordinating them one another.

B. TO INTEGRATE EDUCATION AND WELFARE

Secondly, we will emphasize to have a wide and integrated vision on the problems around education and welfare, in order to ensure a children's right to learning equally and completely. We cannot discuss educational problems without knowing the exact living conditions of the people, especially of children. During these ten-odd years our living and cultural conditions have been drastically changed and damaged under the national "high economic growth", and the bittest damage has been given to the weak and a younger generation. Therefore, there is much attention increasing among the majority of the people for securing their privileges in education and welfare.

Notably, there is a strong demand for integrating a nursery school and a kindergarten. It must not be confined to only a administrative unification, but be developed to establish creative principle and system for wholesome growth of infants in examining critically the existing government's policy of education and welfare.

Besides, there are a lot of educational problems closely related to welfare: how to secure children's summer camps and swimming classes during vacation as well as adequate playgrounds for children outside school; how to be desirable school lunch, school sanitation, and safety in school; and urgent problems of after-school caring for so-called "door key children", of education for the handicapped children, of the children living in the discriminated areas called "Buraku", and of the existing evening lower-secondary schools outlawed under the present rules. All of these problem must be urgently but deliverately solved with a coherent and comprehensive standpoint.

The first to be accused is the bureaucratic administration in the children's problems kindergartens are under the control of the Ministry of Education, but nursery schools are under the Ministry of Health and Welfare because they are supposed to be for poorer children. There exists undoubtedly a discriminative idea to children from the very beginning of their life under the national policy. In general, the Ministry of Education has a chief concern on the children being "normal" in mentality, health, and family environment, while treating lightly the problems of the handicapped and the poor children. Therefore, those who seem to be "abnormal" have been almost deprived of their right to education under the name of "exceptional" or "disqualified" children. They are rather under the jurisdiction of a benevolent standpoint of the Ministry of Health and Welfare or of a corrective view of the Ministry of Justice. On the one hand the government's educational policy has rejected a view of welfare, and on the other the welfare policy has neglected children's educational opportunity. There are a lot of deserted children in a dark valley between the government's policy of education and that of welfare; while many progressive teachers and citizens, criticizing such realities have been sincerely endeavouring to propel each movement for improvement, such as a settlement movement, a liberation movement of the discriminated areas called "Buraku", and a guidance through children's composition about their living conditions.

Education in school is seriously threatened today by the nation-wide disruption of living and cultural environment in each community and home. Our education will never be reconstructed and developed without an effort to revive educational energy in a family, school and community as well as to promote welfare in society. No one can deny this especially when he sees problems of so-called "underprivileged" children. Education should be essentially examined in view of maintaining and promoting the people's minimum standards of wholesome and cultured living. Under the environmental disruption today many of the people are fighting to secure their rights to living and to human development with a strong demand of education as its nucleus.

On the other hand, welfare is generally supposed to be a public activity for assisting persons who need help. Including this narrow sense we must now put emphasis upon an exact idea of welfare in terms of the Constitution stating "In all spheres of life, the State shall use its endeavors for the promotion and extension of social welfare and security, and of public health" in Article 25. When thinking of this, we must also acknowledge our right to education and to work inseparable from one another. (in Article 26 and 27 respectively)

It will be our important task to unify education and welfare without any traditional prejudice. Therefore, we have to examine more scientifically the real situations of our education and welfare. The problems of children's education and welfare would actually concern much more to adults than to children themselves. We must co-ordinate the problems of children's education and welfare with those of adults' permanent education in the whole movement of securing a right to living.

C. TO ESTABLISH COMMUNITY CONTROL IN EDUCATION

Thirdly, a community control in education is to be a must in our reform plan of a school system. It is important for us to examine why it has not yet established in our society although it was one or the major principles of the post-war educational reform under the Fundamental Law of Education.

The pre-war public school system since the Meiji era had been carried forward under the Imperial Rescript on Education, the essential idea of which was to sacrifice an individual life to the Emperor without any reservation. It was administrated by a strong centralized system with having each local authority as a mere branch of the central government. There was no idea of local autonomy, and of course, public education was never considered as the people's right.

After the war the people has taken over the sovereignity, repealed the Imperial Rescript on Education, and established the democratic Constitution and the Fundamental Law of Education, which defines an aim of education to "bring up the people who respect individual dignity and love truth and peace" (Preamble), "to develop fully each personality" and to foster "builders of the peaceful state and society" (Article 1). In the reform of educational administration, a public-elective system of education boards was newly started in order to concretize three essential principles of the reform:—democratization, decentralization, and independency. The main object of a new board system was "to have school administration managed by the just will of the people in accordance with the real local conditions, on the basis of the realization that education shall not be subjected to improper control, but it shall be directly responsible to the whole people" (Article 1, the Education Board Law).

However, the long-dominated idea of nationalism and centralism in education hampered this newly born principle of local autonomy in education. Furthermore, the local autonomy was often deprived by the State under the name of a welfare state owing much obligation to the people or of promoting efficiency in educational administration. In 1956, the government forcibly enacted a law for replacing a public-elective system of education boards with an appointment system.

We, aspiring to a democratic educational system with principles of justice and freedom in education, will consider "local autonomy" or especially "community control" most important in educational administration. As generally known, a "local autonomy" system is "a best school" for people to know what democracy is. Especially in a community control system democratization of education will be much accelerated with having every citizen realize himself as a master of their society. A community control system in education will never be realized unless the people's right to self-education is secured and available means are systematized in order to reflect directly the people's demands of education. For achieving this purpose our present tasks are: to have democratic management in the Parent-Teacher Association, to demand a local educational council of the citizens' attendance, and to revive a public-elective system of education boards. A community control in education does not necessarily mean that all educational problems in a community must be charged on citizens alone. Needles to say, a close co-operation between citizens and professional staffs in school is indispensable for democratic education.

It is essential for full development of children to have school staffs active enough in their professional work which stands on the basis of liberal, creative, and scientific manners in educational contents and methods. In this view, autonomy of school staffs as well as their academic freedom must be guaranteed. Autonomy of school staffs, or a self-governing body in school should be established on the solid foundation of mutual co-operation, while having each staff carrying on his own activity. Parents, citizens, and school staffs in a community must be united in a firm solidarity for establishing real community control in education.

D. EFFECTIVE IMPLEMENTATION OF FREE PUBLIC EDUCATION

Except compulsory education of nine years, the pre- and post-compulsory education owe much to private institutions, the fee of which costs much higher but their educational conditions are not always better than public schools, because the public institutions are too few in number to meet the demands of entrance. Besides, even in public higher institutions a personal expenditure is so expensive that children of the poor almost give up their higher education. We think such unequal situations must be reformed on the basis of a principle of justice and of a constitutional right to education.

Our compulsory school system established in the beginning of the Meiji era charged at first its expenditure and obligation for setting and managing schools on local authorities, and since 1900 the school fee has been free. Today not only the fee but also textbooks are free to all compulsory school children aged from 6 to 15. Under the Emperor System in the pre-war days a free compulsory education was enlarged not with a democratic idea but with a national demand for demobilizing large man-power for economic and military growth of the State. After the compulsory primary school there were a few middle and higher public institutions with a minimum parents' charge in order to train a certain leaders in society, and especially in normal schools the tuition was completely free. As the popular demand for higher education was gradually increased, a lot of private institutions were established with all costs charged on parents.

After the war a principle of the old system was reformed, and compulsory education are no longer the people's obligation but their right to be guaranteed by the State. Under this democratic principle the post-compulsory education should have enlarged to meet a large demand of the people by establishing public institutions as many as possible, and there should have left little chance for a "moneymaking" private school to survive. But the government supinely failed to adopt an available policy with the result of tremendous differences in conditions and tuition between the public institutions and the private ones. The same situation is seen the pre-compulsory stage of education: very high cost of parents' charge in private kindergartens and extremely small numbers of public ones.

We, insisting on the urgent reform such situation, never intend to have all private institutions place under public management. It would not be realistic and impossible. It would be available that some citizens or religious groups will establish and manage an educational institution with much better condition and lower parents' charge than the public one. But under the present circumstances a respectable management of a private school cannot but usually lead to a financial crisis.

Therefore, our present task is to demand a State subsidy system to private institutions to be conditioned equal to the public ones. At the same time we must also demand to build much public institutions to enroll more students in number than those of private schools. In referring to colleges and universities, it must be necessary to reverse the present ratio of students: 75 per cent of all the students are in private institutions and only 25 per cent are in public ones.

Finally in future, we expect to have all of our public education to be completely free in charge under public responsibility. With this viewpoint it is to be our present task to have all public and private institutions subsidized much more fully in every stage from infant education to college level, as well as in every vocational and in-service training institutions.

E. TO PROMOTE DEMOCRATIC PLANNING OF EDUCATION

Last but not least is to formulate a progressive project for democratization of education. As we know, no one can create Japan's education but the people themselves. We must not admit the government to reform a school system arbitrarily and authoritatively. On the contrary, we should urgently propel a grass-root movement for democratic planning of education under close co-operation among parents, teachers, educators, and the broad masses of the people.

In every part of the country the people are accelerating their educational propaganda with various demands: requiring more nursery schools, establishing a semi-public-elective system of an education board, or fighting against amalgamation and abolition of small schools. Furthermore, in a labour union movement workers are demanding for democratization of a schooling system within an enterprise and for in-service technical training. At the same time, educational workers are propelling their spontaneous curriculum-making movement; for example, how to teach the intentionally omitted themes in school books such as of atomic-bombing in Hiroshima and Nagasaki, of problems in Okinawa, of liberation of "Buraku", or of environmental disruption.

Against such movement of the people, the government is trying to have education put under a strong control so that it may be more effectively utilized for the capitalists' economic growth and for controlling national consensus freely. In concretizing this scheme, the government has made a certain long-range economic projects, namely the New National Development Plan and the Socio-economic Development Plan. Moreover, the government has been interfering an autonomous plan-making of each local self-governing body by having it follow the government's model. The educational policy is, of course, taken into these projects.

More urgently, therefore, against the government's policy the people's educational demands must be organized in the powerful mass movement for establishing a democratic, scientific, and comprehensive plan concerning a school system, curriculum, and educational finance and administration. Especially it is urgently important in the problems of building various institutions for educational, cultural, gymnastic, and welfare activities. We will have much questions to be considered such as how to concretize citizens' participation in plan-making, how to be allocation and management of such institutions, or how to reform drastically the financial charge problem between the State and local self-governing bodies.

No self-governing body alone can achieve its educational reform of a school system without the nation-wide mass movement of the people for demanding a fundamental change in the State's educational policy. From this point of view, the National Alliance for Democratic Education, now growing everywhere in the country, would have a historical task with its unique activities. Starting with a daily-life demand, we should have our movement develop into a nation-wide educational propaganda with more scientific, democratic, and step-by-step projects.

Basic Guidelines for the Reform of Elementary and Secondary Education

The need for the reform of elementary and secondary education has been recognized for some time. But full agreement has not been attained on the problems of education at these levels or on their causes. As a prerequisite for considering future reform, the Council has, therefore, aimed to clarify these problems and the situations in which they arise in today's school education. The Council's conclusions are presented in "I. Central Problems in Elementary and Secondary Education".

Owing to society's effort over the last 100 years, modern school education in Japan is equal in quality to that of other advanced countries. Furthermore, school education has contributed greatly to our nation's development. However, if we merely rest upon tradition and do not make positive efforts for the future, school education will become an obstacle to future social development. It is wrong to think that the contemporary school system which was hurriedly established under the supervision of the Occupation Administration during the unusual situation following World War II will be satisfactory for all

Reprinted from Ministry of Education, *Basic Guidelines for the Reform of Education: Report of the Central Council for Education* (Tokyo: Ministry of Education, 1972), pp. 7–23, with permission of the Ministry of Education.

time. Today, we are confronted with an entirely different set of problems, the challenge of a new era which mankind has never seen the likes of before. If education is to be of value in this new era, we must try to comprehend not only current problems but also the problems which will emerge in the coming years. And based on this understanding, we must adopt a flexible attitude and enthusiastically reform our school system. Proposals for such reforms are indicated in "[Section] II. Basic Guidelines for the Reform of Elementary and Secondary Education."

I. Central Problems in Elementary and Secondary Education

As was indicated in the discussion of the basic problems of human development, it is necessary in today's society for every individual to develop the strength of personality to live an independent self-controlled existence. This strength does not come simply from learning various knowledge and skills. Rather it comes as the individual's personality develops to the point where it has the capacity to integrate these various abilities and talents in a meaningful whole. The objective of education for the development of personality should be to help people acquire the abilities for building a satisfactory and spontaneous life, for adapting to social realities, and for the creative solution of difficulties. The Japanese people, showing tolerance for the values of others, should realize their national identity, and on the basis of the rules of democratic society and their national tradition should contribute to the peace of the world and the welfare of mankind through the development of a distinct but universal culture.

Thanks to the post-war educational reforms nine years of compulsory education have become established, equality of educational opportunity has been promoted, and the educational level of the people has been significantly improved. There is no doubt that these reforms together with the educational heritage have been the basis for the school system's considerable contribution to Japan's socio-economic development. But today the school system is faced with the problem of how to cope with the qualitative changes that have occurred as a consequence of quantitative expansion. Also there are many problems in the school system which stem from the hasty reforms introduced in the unsettled situation of the post-war occupation. On the basis of our evaluation of school education's past accomplishments and the need for it to accomplish new tasks, we conclude that the main objectives in the reform of elementary and secondary education can be summarized as follows:

1. *As elementary and secondary education provide the basis on which the individuals develop throughout their lives, importance should be attached to pupils developing their personalities to the full and acquiring an understanding of their nation. To do this school education must be improved so that teaching takes account of each individual's development, using methods which flexibly take account of both the normal stages of human growth and the special characteristics of individual students.*

(Explanation)   Ideally, education aims to cultivate fine personalities and to enable individuals to develop their potentialities to the fullest extent so they can realize desirable objectives. At the same time, as stated in the Fundamental Law of Education, it aims to cultivate citizens for a peaceful nation and society. The individual does not exist in isolation from State or Society. He is only able to develop his individuality and demonstrate his creative ability within the context of the cultural tradition of the society where he lives. If these facts are ignored, cultural discontinuity and mounting confusion will be inevitable. In order that individuals can enjoy the security to freely pursue their diverse values, a democratic social order is necessary. It is the task of public education to foster individuality while at the same time instilling the common basis necessary for cultural continuity and social order. Then, the development of an enriched individuality will become the foundation for the creation of new culture for the nation and the world.

Educational systems necessarily reflect the social demands of the period when they were founded. A system, which was suitable for one time needs to be changed as the time change if it is to play its role in developing human potentialities to the fullest extent. Improvement in school systems and educational contents should be based on the results of studies of human development.

Individuals are different, both in their inherited predispositions and in the nature of their development, and, therefore, the same educational method will not suffice for all even if the same subject matter is being taught. In particular, during the period when individualized growth is being promoted, neither the contents nor the methods of

374

education should be uniform. Because of the over-emphasis on formal equalities, at present, there exists an unfortunate tendency for students not to learn even the basic essentials and to graduate from school after completing only superficial studies. This tendency is particularly noticeable in the upper secondary schools to which a large percentage of the age group are now advancing.

2. *It is the government's responsibility to maintain and improve the standard contents and level of public education, to guarantee equality of opportunity in education, and to work towards the diffusion and development of the kind of school education the public demands. In order to fulfill this responsibility, the government must take proper actions based on a long term view of educational development, enlisting the understanding and support of the people.*

(Explanation)   Some people emphasize even today the idea which was proposed at the time of the post-war educational reformation that the national government should play only an advisory role in educational administration and should confine its activities in education to improving the external environment of education. These people think that government intervention in the contents of education was responsible for leading the people to accept narrow-minded nationalism during the pre-war years. Nevertheless it is an important task of the government to insure that all the people receive a minimal basic education in keeping with the national ideals stated in the Constitution, to see that this education meets appropriate standards with respect to content, and to make continuous efforts to introduce improvements in this education.

It is also important that the government guarantees equal opportunities for education to all the people and responds to the justifiable demands for education of different social groups.

In carrying out these tasks, the government should insure that its programs reflect what the people hope to find in the educational system. The execution of the programs should be based on long-range planning.

3. *Especially in elementary and secondary education, it is the educator who determines the substance of education, but it is increasingly difficult to attract good teachers for these levels. As much will be expected from*

school education in the future, it is necessary to take comprehensive steps to improve the conditions for training and rewarding school teachers so that highly-qualified people will join the teaching profession and will conduct their education with confidence and pride.

(Explanation) In this country, the teaching profession has traditionally been held in high regard and trust. Yet in recent years the conditions of teachers have declined relative to other occupations requiring similar training. Furthermore, higher education has been slow in developing teacher training courses. Consequently young people do not find the teaching profession very attractive.

Education deals with the highly complicated processes of human physical and mental growth, and has to integrate philosophic concepts with scientific methods. Research into education has to be conducted which will help us better understand how to succeed in these difficult tasks, and the professional level of those engaged in education should be maintained as high as possible.

It is necessary, moreover, to improve the training and working conditions of teachers so that young people who choose the teaching profession may be encouraged to participate in inservice training to improve their professional skills and so that teachers will be able to feel confidence and pride in their social status.

II. Basic Guidelines for the Reform of Elementary and Secondary Education

1. Developing a School System Adapted to the Different Stages of Human Growth

In order to study measures for resolving the problems in the current school system and to implement gradual educational reform, experimental pilot projects must be carried out with the following aims.

(1) Experiment with ways to improve the effectiveness of primary education by establishing institutions which provide continuous education for youths from the ages of four or five through what is now the lower years of elementary school.

(2) Establish an institution which provides a consistent program of secondary education as an experiment to find a solution to the problems caused by the current division of secondary education into lower and upper schools, and introduce educational guidance as well as diversified courses

376

so that students can plan their studies according to their abilities and interests.

(3) *In addition to the two experiments above, other experiments such as linking the upper grades of elementary schools with the lower grades of lower secondary schools and the upper grades of lower secondary schools with upper secondary schools should be attempted.*

(4) *Extend the idea of the educational program offered at present in the technical colleges, i.e. a consistent set of courses covering both secondary education and the first stage of higher education, to other subject areas and educational establishments.*

(Explanation)   The interim report presented by the Central Council in June pointed out that the current school system is in several respects poorly adapted to the natural process of human development. One point is that there tends to be similarities in the stage of development between the children of kindergartens and pupils of lower grades of elementary schools, and also between pupils of upper grades of elementary schools and pupils of lower secondary schools. Another point is that the division of secondary education into lower and upper secondary schools cuts it into small pieces, and may have undesirable influences for the maturing youths. The report also pointed out that the way of dividing school levels also has great influence on the relationships in a given school between boys and girls in different stages of development.

Various proposals have been put forward for sweeping reforms to solve all the problems of the educational system at once, but it is necessary to analyse those specific conditions which could ensure their ultimate success. There have been instances in Japan's past when sweeping educational reforms were undertaken, borrowing from the experiences of other countries. Today, however, all the countries are in the process of looking for proper ways of solving the problems of the educational system mentioned above.

Therefore, it is necessary to find new devices which will minimize the disturbance coming with reform and to develop an educational system particularly suited to the actual conditions of this country.

The experimental pilot projects will consist of trials to find the best combinations of educational reforms for the future. The pilot projects will institute variations on the present school system in order to clarify on a scientific basis their relative effectiveness in promoting human development. The projects shall be carried out over a period of about ten years in order to gain an accurate and penetrating understanding of the results. Whether to expand the systems studied in the pilot projects on a nationwide basis, to establish them parallel to the current system, or to drop them should be judged after the results have been studied.

In carrying out the experimental pilot projects the following practices should be observed. First of all, a system should be established to make continuous evaluation of the results of the projects by a professional organization. The cooperation of educators, researchers, and administrators, in the preparation of surveys is indispensable for the success of these scientific experimental programs. Secondly the experimental schools should not be limited to one type of area, nor should they include only one type of student. It is important, too, to make it possible for the pupils finishing the courses of the experimental schools to move to schools of the regular system without difficulty. In the case of launching an experimental public school in a school district, it should be possible for those who do not wish to go to this experimental school to go to a regular school of their own choice.

The aim of (1) is to study the various possibilities of group education during childhood. It is aimed at drawing specific conclusions about the problem of linking present kindergarten education with elementary school education, and at evaluating the proposals to lower the age at which elementary education might be started (bearing in mind the increasing precocity of small children) and to consider the possibility of developing young children's abilities more effectively by involving them in the educational process at an earlier age.

Referring to (2), it is pointed out that the current practice of dividing secondary education into lower and upper levels, both of short duration, disrupts the growth of young people during adolescence and creates problems for the students in choosing courses that will be useful for their future. Opportunities for teachers to observe and guide students are also curtailed because of this practice. A study of concrete measures which can be used to guide students in choosing the type of education most suitable to their aptitudes is necessary. The selective mechanism of entrance examinations should be replaced by those measures.

Somewhat different from the experiments proposed in one and two above would be the combination of the upper grades of elementary school with the present lower secondary school, and the combination of the upper grades of the present lower secondary school with the present upper secondary school in new educational institutions. The purpose in establishing these various combinations would be to discover the system best suited to respond to the different stages of development of pupils. There are various other proposals including one to make lower secondary school four years and upper secondary school four years. These need to be given careful consideration in connection with the results of the experiments of (1) and (2) and further study of the present school system.

In connection with (4), in view of the striking achievements of technical colleges, it is proposed that this kind of education should be extended to cover specialized fields which, at present, are excluded, since this kind of education, freed from the bad effects of the entrance examination, can put more emphasis on the development of the personalities of young people. As technical colleges increase in number and variety, we must review the functions of vocational courses in the secondary schools and consider various new possibilities for providing education of this kind.

2. Reforming the Curricula in Accordance with the Characteristics of Each School Level

The curricula offered at each school level should be consistent and should aim at giving pupils the basic educational skills needed for living in Japanese society as well as developing their individual, creative personalities. At the beginning the emphasis should be placed on the learning of certain standardized, fundamental, well chosen essentials. After this step the school system should allow individuals to choose the courses best suited to their particular abilities and interests. From this viewpoint the following need further examination:

(1) Promotion of consistency in the curricula offered from the elementary school to the upper secondary school, careful selection of curricula contents, and further examination of the classification of subjects taught, especially so as to improve basic education in the elementary school.

Especially in the lower secondary school, it is necessary to discover ways for teachers to observe students and, based on careful consideration of each student's individual characteristics, to provide students with the guidance they need to select their future courses. While students at this

379

stage will still receive some common courses, this is the point where their educational careers will begin to differentiate.

(2) Diversification of the curricula of upper secondary schools to enable students to choose courses suited to their particular abilities and interests. In this context, while the courses are diversified, it should be made easier for individual students to transfer from one major to another as their abilities develop and their interests change. The system should also be structured so that students may advance to schools of a higher grade from various courses.

(Explanation) Curricula have been improved, but in the current situation, in which nine years of education are compulsory and more than 80 per cent of lower secondary school pupils advance to the upper secondary schools, new thinking on curricula is required. The idea of teaching a complete set of courses at each school level should be abandoned and attention focused, rather, on consistency of the educational curricula as a whole, that is from kindergarten right through to the time individuals leave the educational system.

A number of defects are pointed out at present: curricula are too extensive at the level where only basic education should be emphasized, an unnecessary duplication of curricula occurs between different school levels, an emphasis on formal equality ignores individual differences at the upper secondary level, and the physical strength of pupils is under-developed in spite of the general improvement in their height and weight. Cultivation of fundamental abilities at the stage of elementary education is important. The role of Japanese language teaching to give students the basic ability to transmit their culture as well as to enable them to think, to express themselves, and to better communicate should be emphasized. The role of mathematics to give the students a basis for logical thinking also should be emphasized. Particularly for the lower grades it is necessary to think about forming curricula better suited to the different stages of pupils' development without being confined to the current division of subjects. It is especially important at this stage for the pupils to acquire the basic attitudes necessary for life and learning through integrated development of their intellectual, emotions, motivation, and physique.

Upper secondary school education faces various difficulties in providing effective education that is responsive to the wide diversity in the abilities, aptitudes and interests of students. It is necessary to investigate the possibilities of making available to general course upper secondary schools, which most of the students are enrolled in, a wide selection of courses from which they can choose in accordance with their academic progress and the crystallization of their interests. Pupils' abilities and interests should not, in this context, be taken as static, however, and pupils should have the chance to change their courses as the need arises. So that pupils from such courses, as well as from the vocational courses, should be able to proceed to higher education, those in charge of higher education must provide links between such courses and higher education and amend their method of selection of applicants accordingly.

3. Improvement of the Students' Guidance in Selection of Courses

The difficult but important task of education is to guide students to select suitable courses at each level of education. While hoping that individual students will develop new potentialities, it is necessary to recognize their demonstrated abilities as objectively as possible. To do this effectively however, schools require the understanding and cooperation of individual families and society in general.

(Explanation)   In upper secondary schools the majority of students choose to take the general course. This is partly because of the better chances that it offers of proceeding to higher education, and partly because, on graduation from lower secondary school, most students still do not know what they want to do in the future. Far too many students of the general course choose easy courses, and consequently graduate from the upper secondary schools without having completed adequate studies. This suggests a need, as stated above, to institute diverse courses even within the general course and to make provisions so that students who have ability may proceed to higher education from any of the courses. This will eliminate the present situation where some courses are terminal and prevent students from proceeding to higher education.

Even these measures will not solve all the problems. However diverse the courses offered, students will not change in their tendency to converge on specific courses if, at the same time, adequate guidance is not offered. In this country, those who are admitted to any type of course are allowed to proceed to a higher level of class or even graduate on the basis of extremely unsatisfactory results, and students are inclined to take theoretical and prestigious courses even if they acquire little of use from these studies. Such being the case, there is a danger that the significance of course diversification will be lost.

Both students and society will lose if such a situation remains unchecked. Even if students feel satisfied with such a state of affairs while at school, it is likely that they will feel severely disappointed later if their education proves of no real use. Those in charge of education should also realize that their main task is to help students understand the importance of determining their own futures for themselves with a clear mind instead of devoting themselves to competition with others.

It is important, therefore, to prepare diversified courses to meet different abilities, aptitudes and interests and to assist students in the choice of their courses so that their studies may be of real value. Since the performance of such a task requires a specialist's knowledge and training, it is important to make efforts continuously to improve the ability of teachers to offer students constructive guidance. Simultaneously, the understanding and co-operation of the students' homes and of society in general are vital to the successful execution of such a task by the school authorities.

4. Improving Educational Techniques in Order to Develop Students' Individual Abilities and Interests

The success of education depends not on what is superficially studied but on what is actually learned. In this learning process, teaching skills and techniques are as important as the content and level of education offered.

It is very important, therefore, to make the best use of teaching techniques which can be adapted to individual abilities and interests at each school level in order to ensure the attainment of educational objectives. To this end, the following measure should be given particular attention:

(1) In order to provide effective education which will both conform to educational objectives and prove suitable for individual pupils' characteristics, measures for more flexible class management such as "instruction by grouping" should be considered.

(2) So that students can pursue their studies in a rational manner and in a fashion suited to their individual characteristics, measures which in-

crease opportunities for individual study should be considered.

(3) *Measures to develop a flexible system with simultaneous guidance given to students of different grades should be considered as this may be more effective than giving guidance to students of one grade at a time.*

(4) *Measures to allow exceptional students to skip some grades in high school and enter higher educational institutions at a comparatively early age should be considered.*

(Explanation) Because different students have different bases of knowledge and experience and the understanding and the advancement of learning may differ depending on individuals, there are many cases where differentiated educational techniques need to be employed for pupils who have the same educational objectives. Such individual differences are not given, however, but change according to the educational objective at stake.

"Instruction by grouping" has in the past been branded as counter to the spirit of education and has encountered opposition; it was previously understood as a method for providing different levels of education for students by means of grouping them on the basis of tests into advanced and inferior groups. But this is an overly narrow interpretation of this procedure. Educationally speaking it is worse to treat all students the same than it is to take account of their differences. What is important is to avoid making student groups inflexible, to move students from group to group as needed according to different educational objectives and to use the teaching techniques most appropriate for each individual student, especially for those students whose scholastic level is lower than average. In addition the classes composed of various types of students must be handled so that the educational function of group life is not impaired.

It is important in education to enable all students to advance their understanding by individualized instruction. Today, therefore, efforts are being made to introduce teaching machines and other such devices. Research into the use of such devices should, of course, be encouraged, and these new teaching methods will require continual evaluation, with an assessment of the merits and demerits of each. Of particular interest are the changes they will bring to class studies and contact between students and teachers. As the introduction of the teaching machines will possibly be of great use for the improvement both of individualized learning and existing teaching methods in general, it is necessary to make efforts to find more practical ways of using these machines and of popularizing them throughout the school system.

In opposition to the traditional practice of breaking education and instruction into grades, the so-called "non-graded system" has been proposed in which individualized instruction is offered to students according to the degree of their progress. This proposal is worthy of consideration. As far as the students' progress to higher grades is concerned, exceptional measures should be permitted in the case of students who have shown special ability and whose mental and physical maturity deserves accelerated advancement from an educational viewpoint. This is the way to respect individuality.

In order to improve education by means of instruction by grouping and individualized learning as mentioned above, it is also necessary to improve the distribution of educational personnel and facilities as well as to take actions to raise the aspirations and abilities of teachers.

5. Maintaining and Improving the Standard of Public Education and Equality of Educational Opportunity

The government should reform the administrative and financial arrangements which regulate education in order to ensure equality of educational opportunity with attention, in particular, to the following:

(1) *Maintaining curriculum criteria and other educational standards at an adequate level and improving them by means of continuous re-examination in the light of changes in society's needs.*

(2) *Ensuring the public nature of private schools so that they play an important role in public education, improving their educational conditions, and relieving students in these schools of their extra financial burdens.*

(3) *In keeping with the diversification of employment opportunities, more flexible means of education should be provided for young people already at work.*

(Explanation) It is important for the Government to improve and upgrade the contents of the existing system of education while at the same time conducting a vigorous research program on directions for reform.

It is evident that the desired outcome of higher standards in education depends largely upon the creativity of the educators themselves. It, however, is necessary for the government to designate the minimum criteria for proper curricula in order to ensure that the efforts of the educators are consistent with the purpose of public education as stated in Chapter I and to guarantee that education of adequate quality will be provided throughout the nation. Furthermore it is important to establish standard in terms of the composition of classes, the number of teachers in a school, school facilities and equipment, and teaching materials in order to ensure effective educational activities. Therefore it is necessary to set required standards as well as to make plans for their upgrading. Research must be carried out continuously so that these educational criteria may be regularly revised in the light of new research findings on the effectiveness of education and in response to changing social conditions.

The proportion of private schools among kindergartens and upper secondary schools is large and there are also many private elementary and lower secondary schools with their own unique features. In general because of the managerial difficulties there is a tendency for private schools to provide inadequate educational conditions or impose an excessive financial burden on parents. The private schools share, with the public schools, an important role in public education. To leave them in such a plight will result in substantial inequalities of educational opportunity. Taking these conditions into account, financial assistance similar to that available to the public schools should be extended to the private schools except those which do not desire it and investigations should be made into the feasibility of advising private schools concerning requisite educational conditions and coordinating private school education with local educational programs.

In accordance with economic growth and with changing supply and demand in the labour force, working conditions are constantly changing so that some workers lose jobs and others have increased free time. It is, therefore, necessary to develop more flexible part-time education and upper secondary correspondence courses in terms of the schooling period, educational content, and educational structure so that greater numbers of workers can continue their education.

6. The Positive Expansion and Development of Kindergarten Education

In view of the importance of education for small children and the popular demand for kindergarten education, the government should act-

ively promote the following measures for the improvement of kindergarten education:

(1) *Declare that all 5-year-old children who so wish may be enrolled in kindergartens, and make it the obligation of municipal authorities to establish sufficient numbers of kindergartens to achieve this objective. Financial aid from the national and prefectural governments will be necessary for this.*

(2) *Together with the measures explained in* (1), *coordinate the geographical distribution of kindergartens so that both public and private kindergartens can adequately play their respective roles and at the same time take necessary financial measures in order to enrich the quality of the education and decrease the expense of enrolling kindergartens.*

(3) *Improve kindergarten curricula on the basis of research on pre-primary education.*

(4) *Change-over from individually-operated kindergartens to incorporated kindergartens in as short a period as is possible.*

(Explanation)   It is important for the future to decide how homes and schools may together carry out the education of small children, since education in the early years of life is known to affect a person's entire life significantly. Many people recognize that it is especially important for the future development of children of pre-school age to provide an experience of group life which is not available in the home.

Along with this effort for expansion, possible improvements in the critieria of kindergarten curricula require examination based on research studies. It was in order to investigate new possibilities of the future in this field that we suggested the experimental pilot project stated above in (1) of I in this Chapter.

However we must wait for some time until many youths have been trained in these new pre-primary educational institutions before conclusions are formed with respect to their merits. In the meantime measures for the promotion of kindergartens, the principal contemporary organization for pre-primary education, are required. Today the popular demand for kindergartens is strong. It is necessary to promote the expansion and improvement of kindergarten education. In order to eliminate differences of geographic distribution of kindergartens and to promote equality of opportunity as soon as possible, the first target should be to guarantee the opportunity of enrollment to all five year old children who wish to go to kindergartens.

The main problems related to the implementation of the policy are how to adjust the relationship between public kindergartens and private kindergartens and the relationship between kindergartens nursery schools. At present 70 per cent of the kindergartens are private and the geographic distribution of these kindergartens is very uneven. In order to accommodate all the children who wish to go to kindergartens it is necessary to make it the responsibility of the cities, townships and the villages to establish public kindergartens where there is a shortage. At the same time the quality of both public and private kindergartens should be improved and some measures should be taken to subsidize private kindergartens so that the financial burdens of the parents of the private kindergartens will be equal to those of the parents of public kindergartens, and the educational level of the private kindergartens can be maintained as high as in the public kindergartens. For this purpose the national and prefectural governments should provide the cities, townships and villages and the private kindergartens with strong financial assistance. In doing so the local governments must provide the administrative guidance necessary for adjusting the capacities of the public and private kindergartens with an overall view to ensuring that the education in the private kindergartens is consistent with regional educational planning. Consideration should also be given in this context to the enrolling of children of 3 or 4 years old in kindergartens.

Those children which now are sent to nurseries under the welfare program of the Ministry of Health should as a provisional policy also be allowed to go to kindergartens. But the nurseries should be encouraged to upgrade their educational programs so that they eventually can achieve recognition as kindergartens.

As kindergarten education becomes more widespread, it is necessary to conduct research on educational methods and curricula for this level and based on the results of this research to raise the quality of education. This will necessitate an improvement in the depth of training of kindergarten teachers. Furthermore amongst the private kindergartens, individually owned schools should be turned into incorporated organizations as soon as is possible so that their legal position is firmly established.

7. Positive Expansion and Improvement of Special Education

It is an important responsibility of the government to guarantee equality of educational opportunity to all the people according to their ability. There are people who are mentally and physically handicapped and not suited to study in ordinary schools or to be taught with the teaching methods of ordinary school education. To provide the opportunity of special education for these people the government should take administrative and financial steps as soon as possible to implement the measures described below.

(1) Hold the cities, towns or villages responsible for establishing a sufficient number of special classes to accommodate all the mentally retarded children so that they can receive compulsory education.

(2) Diversify the forms of education so as to meet the various needs of the mentally and physically handicapped children. This would include sending teachers to those children unable to attend school because of medical treatment or other reasons.

(3) The government should take a more active role in improving the facilities for special education by means of establishing institutes for children with dual handicaps of a serious kind, etc.

(4) Improve the treatment of the mentally and physically handicapped children through earlier discovery and training of them, improvement of the facilities for their education after compulsory education, and through promotion of closer cooperation between the diverse authorities responsible for the mentally and physically handicapped.

(Explanation) Special education, so far, has been developed by the efforts of enthusiastic educators and volunteers. Though it has gradually attracted public attention, administrative measures for it are still insufficient. The situation should be improved immediately in keeping with the national ideal that all people should be respected as individuals.

The School Education Law has been in effect for more than twenty years, but the provision of compulsory education by means of special schools for the three types of handicapped children (mentally retarded, physically handicapped and physically unfit) has not been carried out yet. It is necessary to carry this out as soon as possible. It is also necessary to secure equal educational opportunity for those children who are mentally weak but not retarded by requiring the cities, towns and villages to open special classes for them. Opening special classes for the children with weak-vision and hearing should also be promoted.

For children who have difficulty in attending school because of the need of medical treatment or other reasons, the practice of sending teachers to teach them should be positively promoted with thorough consideration given to educational contents and teaching methods. For those who, though mentally or physically handicapped, are fit to be educated in normal classes, the system of sending visiting professional teachers to the classes where they study should be made a standard practice.

Children with dual handicaps should be educated by opening special classes in the special schools. The number of these children, however, is not many and the educational method is not well-developed yet. Therefore the government should establish institutes for those unable to attend special classes with thorough consideration of the matters related to medical care and protection.

The education of the mentally and physically handicapped children in their infancy has a great influence on their later development. Therefore it is an urgent need to consider the establishment of a system where necessary diagnoses and guidance can be provided so that these children can be identified early and provided with special training. In order to strengthen their adaptability to the society and to help them become more independent in the society, post-compulsory education, for instance in the senior years of the special school for the handicapped should be further expanded in the future. These children should not be forced to attend school with the same regularity as ordinary children. Special consideration should be given to allow flexibility in accordance with the extent of their handicaps and their abilities and aptitudes.

Furthermore the mentally and physically handicapped children need not only education in the narrow sense but also medical treatment, protection in terms of their living, and training for social independence. Without these, education can not be expected to have any effect. But these latter affairs are administered under different authorities, and it is hard for the schools to keep close contact with these various authorities. Therefore the government needs to commit more efforts towards integrating the various authorities which play some role in the lives of the handicapped.

To advance the expansion and improvement of special education as described above, efforts should be made to create a better understanding of special education among the members of the broader society. In addition it is important to train exceptional teachers with the ability to give proper guidance in response to various handicaps, and to establish a system to promote scientific research on these problems to provide a basis for the improvement of educational content and methodology.

8. Improvement of the Structure of Management within Schools and the Administrative Structure of Education

In order to establish a structure within each school which can perform integrated activities in the pursuit of the objectives of public education and which can hold itself responsible to the public, appropriate measures for reforms should be considered with emphasis on the following:

(1) Establishing an administrative organization within schools in which the responsibility for various school activities is properly divided, thus ensuring a lively and well-organized school program under the guidance and responsibility of the school principal.

(2) Unifying the system of local educational administration so it coordinates public and private schools.

(3) Devising means for hearing the criticisms and wishes of the people concerning education so that these can be incorporated in educational policy and administration.

(Explanation)   As it is the individual teachers who conduct the practical activities of education in schools, the promotion of their spontaneity and creativity is an important element in making education lively. In order to realize such a state of education, a system where all the teachers can participate positively in developing the goals and plan of their school and in carrying these out should be established. It is the school principals' responsibility to maintain the cooperative unity of the school as a whole and exert leadership properly to upgrade education. Furthermore it is indispensable to improve the system of school management so that the part each teacher should take in school activities is clearly defined, and fits into an organizational structure where smooth cooperation is possible.

To meet these requirements an administrative and teaching staff organization should be established which consists of the assistant principal, the chief instructor, the head teacher in charge of each grade, the subject director, the chief counsellor etc., in accordance with the type and size of the school as well as the nature of these posts.

As stated previously, private schools, along with public schools, play an important role in public education. In order to secure equality of educational opportunity for all the people, it is necessary to introduce administrative and financial measures which result in the unified coordination of public and private schools at the local level. This will facilitate better regulation of the geographical distribution of schools and the maintenance of uniform educational standards in the respective local areas. This means that, for this purpose, it is necessary to integrate the educational administration of public and private schools which is currently performed separately by the prefectural boards of education and the governor. As an interim measure, steps should be taken to promote closer relationships and coordination between the two organizations, and at the same time steps should be taken to reform the structure of the boards of education so that they can give adequate guidance and assistances to the private schools.

It is also pointed out that problems arise from requiring every city and village to form its own board of education as many are not able to function well. This matter relates to the problem of whether the current towns and villages are the proper units for local self-government. In any case expansion of the units for educational administration should be given serious consideration.

Because the government's educational policy and its administrative measures affect all the nation's children, special consideration has to be given to their continuous improvement. It is necessary in considering improvement to understand what the people at large think about governmental policies, what criticisms they have, and what their hopes are. Better means need to be found to incorporate the will of the public in policy changes.

9. The Training and Recruitment of Teachers and the Improvement of Their Status

As the role of teachers is going to be increasingly important in the future, the following measures should be comprehensively enforced to secure the best possible teachers for the educational system and to improve the quality of their work as well as their social and economic status.

(1) In principle, the teachers of elementary education and a certain per cent of the teachers in secondary education should be trained in institutions of higher education with special curricula for that purpose hereafter called "teachers college". On the other hand distinguished teachers should be secured by means of inducing the graduates of ordinary universities with high qualification into the teaching profession. In doing so, measures should be taken to balance the demand and supply of teachers of the different areas throughout the country.

(2) In addition to improving the teachers colleges as explained above, the

government should take appropriate steps to train teachers and to expand the financial aid system for students in order to secure necessary teachers for compulsory schools.

(3) It may be necessary to consider a system in which prospective teachers are put on trial for about one year in an actual teaching situation and employed on a full-time basis only if their performance proves satisfactory. This will improve the training program and the new teachers will develop more self-confidence and a higher level of teaching ability under these conditions.

(4) A system of licensing talented individuals who, although they may not have proper teaching certificates, are sufficiently erudite and experienced must be extended in order to invite them to teach in schools.

(5) Means must be found to establish institutions of higher education designed for advanced educational research and teacher training, and a system should be started which gives teachers graduating from these institutions a special status and a salary in accordance with that status.

(6) As teachers' pay, improvement must be made to keep the teachers' salary at a level high enough to attract distinguished persons into the teaching profession, and at the same time to create a salary scale which will provide teachers with suitable increases in salaries as their abilities become more specialized and their administrative responsibilities are increased.

In addition, since the people put a high value on education and expect much from the teachers, it is desirable that teachers form their own professional organizations and makes efforts to improve their skills through mutual exchanges of experience. In this way the teachers may earn the respect and trust of society and public recognition that the teaching profession is a speciality based on highly developed skills and a firm professional ethic. If the teachers will make efforts to improve their quality continuously by means of such training, their constructive opinions will be socially accepted and meet the people's expectations of them.

(Explanation) The teaching profession essentially requires a high level of specialized competence. It requires in addition to the basic qualifications of an educator, for instance, a thorough understanding of human growth and development, professional knowledge concerning subject matter, and practical teaching techniques. An ability to co-ordinate all of these is also required. This ability and these skill need to be continuously developed in the process of teacher training, recruitment, in-service training, and re-education.

At the stage of teacher training, elementary education and secondary education should be considered separately. As is the case in most countries, it is essential to train teachers for elementary education in a special course of teachers colleges, as these teachers need to teach all the subjects and to give proper educational guidance with an integrated understanding of the growth and development of infants and children. On the other hand it is often thought that the teachers colleges are not necessarily required for training the teachers of secondary education as these teachers teach their own special subjects. In fact, there have been many distinguished teachers who are graduates of ordinary universities. But the education in lower secondary schools which is now compulsory and the education in upper secondary schools which now enroll more than 80 per cent of the age group faces new problems which differ from those in the pre-war middle schools. Therefore both the lower and upper secondary schools need some teachers who have had special training in methods of teaching and guidance and who therefore will have the knowledge necessary for responding to the diversity in the interests and abilities of youths at these levels. For these teachers, education in teachers colleges is very important. The teachers colleges need not always be national colleges.

Recently the mobility of population between different areas is increasing. In the light of this fact it is a necessary to consider measures to establish cooperation between the national government and local governments in order to adjust to the shifting demand for teachers in different areas.

The government should promote major improvements in the teachers colleges where change is long overdue through securing high quality teachers and other staff. It is also the responsibility of the government to develop a plan to insure that compulsory schools receive a certain per cent of their teachers from the teachers colleges in order to guarantee the supply of teachers of high quality, and financial assistance to students at teachers colleges should be expanded in order to make studying there more attractive. There also is a system where university students obtain the qualifications to become teachers in a designated course through taking special courses and participating in practice teaching. This system, however, has tended to be a formality and has not functioned effectively. To improve this is an other important task.

What is necessary for upgrading the quality of teachers and improving their training is changes in the process of recruitment, in-service training, and re-education. In order to strengthen the self-confidence and the attitudes of teachers towards their profession, it is most effective to give them training in an actual situation at the start of their employment under the guidance of their seniors, as is done in many professions today. For appropriate implementation of this scheme, creation of a system should be considered where persons who are receiving this training are given a special status. In doing so the method of recruitment and the treatment of these persons should be given due consideration. At the same time establishment of some institution to organize the training is necessary, and the numbers of teachers that schools are allowed to employ should be made large enough so the training scheme can operate smoothly.

There are many persons among the ordinary people in the society who though they did not intend to be a teacher at the beginning of their career actually have the ability to be excellent educators. In addition, those who have acquired necessary knowledge and experience through their professional life in various fields can make a great contribution to education. It is important to make it feasible to attract such persons into the profession. It should be made easier to give teaching licences to those who are sufficiently qualified but without a proper teaching certificate. This could result in a decline of the undesirable effects caused by the exclusiveness of the teaching profession and could make education more lively and broadminded. It will be desirable to make good use of this system especially in the fields of industrial and special education.

It is also important for the teachers to enrich their experiences, to continue their own training, and to brush up their professional skills in order to uphold the quality of their education. Therefore it is necessary to establish a system to give treatment in terms of professional status and salary to those who have special achievements as teachers, who have advanced training at graduate schools, and to others who carry out research on education of a high level. This will make it possible to improve the teachers' professional level and socio-economic status, and also to provide the teachers colleges with staff experienced in teaching.

Teacher training is in principle the responsibility of the higher educational institutions of the first category (University). But in practice a considerable per cent of teachers in elementary schools and nursing teachers are graduates of junior colleges. Therefore taking into account the balance of demand and supply in the future it would be appropriate to give approval to the graduates of the second category of higher educational institutions (Junior College) to be teachers.

These measures are to improve the teachers quality through the process of training, recruitment and in-service training. For these measures to function effectively, above all, distinguished persons should be invited into the teaching profession and.those who are in the profession should make continuous efforts. To guarantee an improved system, first of all, the salary level of teachers should be made higher so that qualified graduates go into the teaching profession. So far teachers' salaries have been based on the principle of seniority. In order to encourage the efforts of teachers it is necessary to establish a salary system in which teachers can be paid in accordance with their professional performance and administrative responsibility.

The above stated structural reforms are the basic conditions which enable excellent teachers to be trained and retrained in the profession. Nevertheless the most valuable educational achievements will depend on the spontaneous creativity of the educators themselves. They will exert these creative efforts if they feel confidence and pride in the teaching role. It is the job of the teachers' professional organizations to promote and encourage such efforts. It is hoped that the teachers' organizations will, as in other countries, try to improve the professional level and contribute to the development of education by means of upholding the professional code which is of such importance to their activities, and by making constructive proposals. In addition, all the teachers as well as the professional organizations of teachers should make efforts not to introduce political activities into education lest the neutrality of education should be infringed and the order of the school should be destroyed.

10. The Promotion of Research on Educational Reform

In view of the present, rapid pace of change and the pressing need to improve the quality of education, a center must be set up to promote and integrate research which pertains to educational reform, as well as to carry out a special program of research and development on education.

(Explanation) The most pressing educational problems confronting society today, as well as those anticipated in the future, are not particularly new, but we still are not clear on how we can solve these problems. Furthermore, extensive study is required of possible ways to conduct the reforms described above. These tasks include, for example, an integrated understanding of the various academic disciplines on child growth, a comprehensive assessment of individual ability from various viewpoints, the development of new educational techniques based on theories of the learning process, knowledge of ways to improve the educational environment in schools, and so forth. Unless such problems are solved, it will not be possible for education to play its proper role in society.

These fundamental problems of education involve the study of human beings. It is almost impossible to make a proper investigation without an overall coordination of all the relevant fields of study including education. Especially the results of research in the fields of philosophy, psychology, sociology, medical science, and engineering are indispensable for the development of educational theory and methodology. Nevertheless it is becoming more and more difficult for the different fields of learning to be coordinated owing to the increasing specialization of learning.

There are numerous researchers and research institutes on education in Japan. But research to show the proper direction for educational reforms is not being promoted in a systematic way or with clear objectives. In addition neither the organization and conditions for research nor the treatment of researchers are sufficient to attract many good people to the field of educational research. To take measures to improve organization and finance and to secure qualified researchers are the first steps required for upgrading the quality of education.

For the achievement of the goals of the reforms shown in these *Guidelines* it is necessary to make clear the theoretical and practical tasks of research and to promote integrated research and development through the cooperation of distinguished researchers in related fields. This is also an essential condition for carrying out the pilot experimental projects mentioned in (1) of this Chapter in a proper way. The results of the research and development will be of fundamental importance for the formulation of an educational program for the future.

For this purpose the establishment of a "Research and Development Center for Education" is needed. This center would promote qualitative innovation in education and the popularization of its results. It would also choose subjects of research for long-term educational reform, allocate research funds for education, coordinate research activities, and improve the network of communication for educational research and development among schools, research institutes, and universities in different areas.

SELECTED BIBLIOGRAPHY

Part I. The Roots of Contemporary Japanese Education

I. *Basic Works*

A. **Bibliographies**

Beauchamp, Edward R., "Historical and Social Dimensions of Japanese Education," *Educational Studies*, 5, 1–2, (1974), 11–16.

"Bibliography of Asian Studies," *Journal of Asian Studies*. Annually since 1957.

Eells, Walter C., *The Literature of Japanese Education, 1945–1954*, Hamden, Connecticut: The Shoe String Press, 1955.

Passin, Herbert, *Japanese Education: A Bibliography of Materials in the English Language*, New York: Teachers College Press, 1970.

———, "Japanese Education: Guide to a Bibliography of Materials in the English Language," *Comparative Education Review*, 9, 1, (1965), 81–101.

Shulman, Frank J., *Japan and Korea: An Annotated Bibliography of Doctoral Dissertations in Western Languages, 1877–1969*, Chicago: American Library Association, 1970.

Stucki, Curtis W., *American Doctoral Dissertations on Asia, 1933–1966*, Ithaca: Southeast Asia Program, Department of Asian Studies, Cornell University, 1968, (3rd revised edition).

Teichler, Ulrich and Friedrich Voss, *Bibliography on Japanese Education: Postwar Publications in Western Languages*, Pullach bei Munchen: Verlag Dokumentation, 1974.

Ward, Robert E. and Frank J. Shulman (eds.), *The Allied Occupation of Japan, 1945–1952: An Annotated Bibliography of Western-Language Materials*, Chicago: American Library Association, 1974.

B. General Works

Anderson, Ronald S., *Education in Japan: A Century of Modern Development*, Washington, D.C.: United States Government Printing Office, 1975.

Aso, Makoto, *Education and Japan's Modernization*, Tokyo: Ministry of Foreign Affairs, 1972.

Cleaver, Charles G., *Japanese and Americans: Cultural Parallels and Paradoxes*, Minneapolis: University of Minnesota Press, 1976, chapter 8.

Hall, John W., et al., *Twelve Doors to Japan*, Englewood Cliffs, New Jersey: Prentice Hall, 1965, chapter 9.

Jansen, Marius and Lawrence Stone, "Education and Modernization in Japan and England," *Comparative Studies in Society and History*, 9, 2, (1967), 208–232.

Kazamias, Andreas and Byron Massialas, *Tradition and Change in Education*, Englewood Cliffs, New Jersey: Prentice Hall, 1965, chapter 6.

Kaigo, Tokiomi, *Japanese Education: Its Past and Present*, Tokyo: Kokusai Bunka Shinkai, 1968.

Keenleyside, Hugh and A. F. Thomas, *History of Japanese Education and Present Educational System*, Tokyo: Hokuseido Press, 1937.

Kobayashi, Tetsuya, *Society, Schools and Progress in Japan*, New York: Pergamon Press, 1976.

Lebra, Joyce, et al., *Women in Changing Japan*, Boulder, Colorado: Westview Press, 1976, chapter 8.

Lombard, Frank, *Pre-Meiji Education in Japan*, Tokyo: Kyo Bun Kan, 1913.

Nakayama, Shigeru, et al., *Science and Society in Modern Japan*, Cambridge: MIT Press, 1974.

Passin, Herbert, *Society and Education in Japan*, New York: Teachers College Press, 1965.

Shipman, M. D., *Education and Modernization*, London: Faber and Faber, 1971, chapters 8–11.

Schwantes, Robert S., *Japanese and Americans: A Century of Cultural Relations*, New York: Harper and Brothers, 1955.

II. *The Historical Context of Modern Japanese Education*

A. Tokugawa Period (1603–1868)

Craig, Albert M., "Science and Confucianism in Tokugawa Japan," in Marius B. Jansen (ed.), *Changing Japanese Attitudes Toward Modernization*, Princeton: Princeton University Press, 1965, pp. 133–166.

Dore, Ronald P., "Talent and the Social Order in Tokugawa Japan," *Past and Present*, 21, (1962) 60–72.

Hall, John W., "The Confucian Scholar in Tokugawa Japan," in David S. Nivison and Arthur F. Wright (eds.), *Confucianism in Action*, Stanford: Stanford University Press, 1959, pp. 268–301.

Kobayashi, Tetsuya, "Tokugawa Education as a Foundation of Modern Education in Japan," *Comparative Education Review*, 9, 3, (1965), 288–302.

Murayama, Masao, *Studies in the Intellectual History of Tokugawa Japan:* Tokyo: University of Tokyo Press, 1975.

Rhee, Song Nai, "Educational Modernization in Tokugawa Japan: The Case of Kagahan," *Comparative Education Review*, 14, 2, (1970), 144–151.

Spae, Joseph J., *Ito Jinsai: A Philosopher, Educator and Sinologist of the Tokugawa Period*, Peking: Catholic University Press, 1948.

B. Meiji Period (1868–1912)

Beauchamp, Edward R., *An American Teacher in Early Meiji Japan*, Honolulu: The University Press of Hawaii, 1976.

Blacker, Carmen, *The Japanese Enlightenment: A Study of the Writings of Fukuzawa Yukichi*, Cambridge: Cambridge University Press, 1964.

Burnstein, Ira J., *The American Movement to Develop Protestant Colleges for Men in Japan, 1868–1912*, Ann Arbor: School of Education, University of Michigan, 1967.

Craig, Albert M., "Fukuzawa Yukichi: The Philosophical Foundations of Meiji Nationalism," in Robert E. Ward (ed.), *Political Devel-*

opment in Meiji Japan, Princeton: Princeton University Press, 1968, pp. 99–148.

Fukuzawa, Yukichi, *The Autobiography of Fukuzawa Yukichi*, (Translated by Kiyooka Eiichi), Tokyo: Hokuseido Press, 1934.

———, *An Encouragement of Learning*, (Translated by David Dilworth and Hirano Umeyo), Tokyo: Sophia University Press, 1969.

———, *An Outline of a Theory of Civilization*, (Translated by David Dilworth and C. Cameron Hurst), Tokyo: Sophia University Press, 1973.

Hall, Ivan, *Mori Arinori*, Cambridge: Harvard University Press, 1973.

Japanese National Commission for UNESCO, *The Role of Education in the Social and Economic Development of Japan*, Tokyo: Ministry of Education, 1966.

Kikuchi, Dairoku, *Japanese Education*, London: John Murray, 1909.

Koizumi, Shinzo, "The Teacher and the Nation: Fukuzawa Yukichi and Keio University," *Japan Quarterly*, 5, 4, (1958), 462–467.

Maruyama, Masao, "Fukuzawa, Uchimura and Okamura: Meiji Intellectuals and Westernization," *Developing Economies*, 5, 1, (1966), 594–611.

Nagai, Michio, "The Development of Intellectuals in the Meiji and Taisho Periods," *Journal of Social and Political Ideas in Japan*, 2, 1, (1964), 28–32.

Sansom, Sir George B., *The Western World and Japan*, London: Cresset, 1950, chapter 15, section 3 (pp. 450–467).

Scheiner, Irwin, *Christian Converts and Social Protest in Meiji Japan*, Berkeley: University of California Press, 1970.

Shiveley, Donald H., "The Japanization of the Middle Meiji," in Donald H. Shiveley (ed.), *Tradition and Modernization in Japanese Culture*, Princeton: Princeton University Press, 1971, pp. 77–119.

Umetani, Noboru, "The Role of Foreign Employees in the Meiji Era in Japan," Tokyo: Institute of Developing Economies, 1970.

C. Prewar Education

Brown, Delmar, *Nationalism in Japan: An Introductory Historical Analysis*, Berkeley: University of California Press, 1955, Especially chapters 7–10.

Caiger, John G., "The Aims and Content of School Courses in Japanese History, 1872–1945," in Edward R. Skrzyplzak (ed.), *Japan's Modern Century*, Tokyo: Sophia University Press, 1968, pp. 51–81.

Hall, Robert K. (ed.), *Kokutai no Hongi: Cardinal Principles of National Entity of Japan*, Cambridge: Harvard University Press, 1949.

———, *Shūshin: Ethics of a Defeated Nation*, New York: Teachers College Press, 1949.

Kobayashi, Victor N., "Nationalism and Educational Progressivism in Japan, 1900–1941," *Educational and Psychological Review*, (Bombay, India), VI, (1966), 82–92.

Lamott, Willis C., *Nippon: The Crime and Punishment of Japan*, New York: John Day, 1944, chapter 4.

London, Kurt, *Background and Conflict: Ideas and Forms in World Power*, New York: Macmillan, 1945, chapter 12.

Maruyama, Masao, *Thought and Behaviour in Modern Japanese Politics*, New York: Oxford University Press, 1963, chapters 7–10.

Mitchell, Richard H., *Thought Control in Prewar Japan*, Ithaca: Cornell University Press, 1976.

Morris, Ivan I., *Nationalism and the Right Wing in Japan*, London: Oxford University Press, 1960, especially "Introduction" by Maruyama Masao.

Murthy, P.A.N., *The Rise of Modern Nationalism in Japan: A Historical Study of the Role of Education in the Making of Modern Japan*, New Delhi: Ashajanak Publications, 1973.

D. Education and Reform During the American Occupation (1945–1952)

Adams, Donald and Mamoru Oshiba, "Japanese Education After the Americans Left," *Peabody Journal of Education*, 39, 1, (1961), 9–12.

Adams, Donald, "Rebirth of Moral Education in Japan," *Comparative Education Review*, 4, 1, (1960), 61–64.

Dore, Ronald P., "The Ethics of the New Japan," *Pacific Affairs*, 25, 2, (1952), 147–159.

Duke, Benjamin C., "American Educational Reform in Japan Twelve Years Later," *Harvard Educational Review*, 34, (1964), 525–536.

"Education in Japan," *Journal of Political and Social Ideas in Japan* (entire issue), 1, 3, (1963).

Hall, Robert K., *Education for a New Japan*, New Haven: Yale University Press, 1949.

Kawai, Kazuo, *Japan's American Interlude*, Chicago: University of Chicago Press, 1960.

Kobayashi, Victor N., *John Dewey in Japanese Educational Thought*, Ann Arbor: School of Education, University of Michigan, 1964.

Nishimoto, Mitoji, "Educational Changes in Japan After the War," *Journal of Educational Sociology*, 26, (1952), 17–26.

Oshiba, Mamoru, "Moral Education in Japan," *School Review*, 49, 2, (1961), 227–244.

Report of the United States Education Mission to Japan, Washington, D.C.: United States Government Printing Office, 1946.

Report of the Second United States Education Mission to Japan, Washington, D.C.: United States Government Printing Office, 1950.

Sansom, Sir George B., "Education in Japan," *Pacific Affairs*, 19, (1946), 413–415.

United States Supreme Commander Allied Powers [SCAP], General Headquarters, Civil Information and Education Section, Educational Division, *Education in the New Japan*, 2 vols., Tokyo: SCAP, 1948.

PART II. SELECTED DIMENSIONS OF CONTEMPORARY JAPANESE EDUCATION

A. Pre-University Education

"As the Twig is Bent, *Japan Quarterly*, 17, 3, (1970), 248–252.

Bethel, Dayle M., *Makiguchi; The Value Creator: Revolutionary Japanese Educator and Founder of Soka Gakkai*, New York: Weatherhill, 1973.

Brameld, Theodore, *Japan: Culture, Education and Change in Two Communities*, New York: Holt, Rinehart and Winston, 1968.

Caiger, John G., "Ienaga Saburo and the First Postwar Japanese History Textbook," *Modern Asian Studies*, 3, (1969), 1–16.

De Vos, George and Hiroshi Wagatsuma, *Japan's Invisible Race: Caste and Culture in Personality*, Berkeley: University of California Press, 1966.

De Vos, George, et al., *Socialization for Achievement: Essays on the Cultural Psychology of the Japanese*, Berkeley: University of California, 1973, chapters 14–15.

De Vera, Jose M., *Educational Television in Japan*, Tokyo: Charles Tuttle, 1967.

Dore, Ronald P., *City Life in Japan*, Berkeley: University of California Press, 1958, chapter 14.

404

————, "Textbook Censorship in Japan: The Ienaga Case," *Pacific Affairs*, 18, (1970), 548–556.

Duke, Benjamin C., "Ministry Condemned for Censorship," *Times Educational Supplement*, 2898, (1970), 1204.

"Examination Hell," *Japan Quarterly*, 20, 2, (1973), 131–135.

Gross, Carl, *Sokagakkai and Education*, East Lansing: Institute for International Studies, Michigan State University, 1970.

Iriye, Akira (ed.), *Mutual Images: Essays in American-Japanese Relations*, Cambridge: Harvard University Press, 1975, chapter 8.

Kobayashi, Victor N., "Japan's Examination Hell," *Educational Forum*, 28, (1963), 19–23.

Mitchell, Richard H., *The Korean Minority in Japan*, Berkeley: University of California Press, 1967, chapters 7–11.

Miyauchi, Dixon Y., "Textbooks in Search for a New National Ethics in Japan," *Social Education*, 28, 3, (1964), 131–137.

Ogata, Kazuko, "Mothers and the Textbook Controversy," *Japan Christian Quarterly*, 37, 2, (1971), 80–82.

Osborn, Robert, "Tamagawa-Gakuin: A Vision of the New Education in Japan," *Teachers College Record*, 71, (1970), 660–671.

Rohlen, Thomas P., "Violence at Yoka High School: The Implications for Japanese Coalition Politics of the Confrontation Between the Communist Party and the Buraku Liberation League," *Asian Survey* 16, 7, (July, 1976), 682–699.

Shikaumi, Nobuya, *Culture Policy in Japan*, Paris: UNESCO, 1970.

Singleton, John C., *Nichu: A Japanese School*, New York: Holt, Rinehart and Winston, 1967.

————, "Urban-Rural Comparisons in Japanese Education," *International Review of Education*, 13, 4, (1967), 470–482.

Thurston, Donald, *Teachers and Politics in Japan*, Princeton: Princeton University Press, 1973.

Vogel, Ezra, "Entrance Examinations and Emotional Disturbances in Japan's New Middle Class," in Robert Smith and Richard Beardsley (eds.), *Japanese Culture*, London: Methuen, 1963, pp. 140–152.

Wada, Shoji, "Japan's Academic Career Cult," *World Yearbook of Education, 1969*, London: Evans, 1969, 291–297.

B. Students and Higher Education

Austin, Lewis (ed.), *Japan: The Paradox of Progress*, New Haven: Yale University Press, 1976, chapter 3.

Azumi, Koya, *Higher Education and Business Recruitment in Japan*, New York: Teachers College Press, 1969.

Bakke, E. Wight and Mary S., *Campus Challenge: Student Activism in Perspective*, Hamden, Connecticut: Archon Books, 1971.

Battistini, Lawrence H., *The Postwar Student Struggle in Japan*, Tokyo: Charles Tuttle, 1956.

Blewett, John (ed.), *Higher Education in Postwar Japan: The Ministry of Education's 1964 White Paper*, Tokyo: Sophia University Press, 1965.

Burn, Barbara, *Higher Education in Nine Countries: A Comparative Study of Colleges and Universities Abroad*, New York: McGraw-Hill, 1971, chapter 9.

"Coping with Student Disorders in Japan," *Minerva*, 8, 1, (1970), 116–135.

Cummings, William K., "The Japanese Private University," *Minerva*, 9, 3, (1973), 303–324.

Dore, Ronald P., "The Future of Japan's Meritocracy," *Bulletin of the International House of Japan*, 26, (1970), 30–50.

Duke, Benjamin C., "Conflict and Turmoil Within the Japanese University," *Malaysian Journal of Education*, 7, (1969), 778–782.

———, *Japan's Militant Teachers: A History of the Left-Wing Teachers Movement*, Honolulu: University Press of Hawaii, 1973.

Duke, Benjamin C., "The Struggle for Control of the Japanese Universities," *Journal of Higher Education*, 35, (1964), 19–26.

Feuer, Lewis, "The De-Authorization of the Elders: The Zengakuren of Japan," in Lewis Feuer, *The Conflict of Generations: The Character and Significance of Student Movements*, New York: Basic Books, 1969, pp. 199–214.

Fuse, Toyomasa, "Japan," in M. S. Archer (ed.), *Students, University and Society*, London: Heinemann, 1972, pp. 212–245.

———, "Student Radicalism in Japan: A Cultural Revolution?" *Comparative Education Review*, 13, 3, (1969), 325–342.

Kitamura, Kazuyuki and William Cummings, "The 'Big Bang' Theory and Japanese University Reform," *Comparative Education Review*, 16, 2, (1972), 303–324.

Krauss, Ellis, *Japanese Radicals Revisited: Student Protest in Postwar Japan*, Berkeley: University of California Press, 1974.

Lifton, Robert, "Youth and History: Individual Change in Postwar Japan," *Asian Cultural Studies*, 3, (1962), 115–136.

406

Nagai, Michio, *Higher Education in Japan: Its Takeoff and Crash*, Tokyo: University of Tokyo Press, 1971.

Organization of Economic Cooperation and Development, *Review of National Policies for Education; Japan*, Paris: OECD, 1971.

Packard, George, *Protest in Tokyo: The Security Treaty Crisis of 1960*, Princeton: Princeton University Press, 1966.

Pempel, T. J., "Evaluating Japan's Mass Higher Education," *Japan Quarterly*, 18, 4, (1971), 449–454.

————, "The Politics of Enrollment Expansion in Japanese Universities," *The Journal of Asian Studies*, 33, 1, (1973), 67–86.

Shimbori, Michiya, "Zengakuren: A Japanese Case Study of a Student Political Movement," *Sociology of Education*, 37, 3, (1964), 229–253.

————, "Comparison Between Pre- and Post-War Student Movements in Japan," *Sociology of Education*, 38, 1, (1963), 49–70.

————, "Student Radicals in Japan," *Annals of the American Academy of Political and Social Sciences*, 395, (1971), 150–158.

Smith, Henry DeWitt, II, *Japan's First Student Radicals*, Cambridge: Harvard University Press, 1972.

————, "The Origins of Student Radicalism in Japan," *Journal of Contemporary History*, 5, 1, (1970), 87–103.

Teichler, Ulrich, "Some Aspects of Higher Education in Japan," *K.B.S. Bulletin of Japanese Culture*, 114, (1972), 1–16.

Tsurumi, Kazuko, "Some Comments on the Japanese Student Movement in the 1960's," *Journal of Contemporary History*, 5, 1, (1970), 104–112.

Tsurumi, Kazuko, "The Japanese Student Movement: Group Portraits," *Japan Quarterly*, 16, 1, (1969), 25–44.

————, "The Japanese Student Movement: Its Milieu," *Japan Quarterly*, 15, 4, (1968), 430–455.

"University Reform in Japan," *Minerva*, 8, 4, (1970), 581–593.

Vogel, Ezra (ed.), *Modern Japanese Organization and Decision-Making*, Berkeley: University of California Press, 1975, pp. 304–330.

PART III. SOME POSSIBLE FUTURE DIRECTIONS OF JAPANESE EDUCATION

Axelbank, Albert, *Black Star Over Japan: Rising Force of Militarism*, Tokyo: Charles Tuttle, 1972.

Brzezinski, Zbigniew, *The Fragile Blossom: Crisis and Change in Japan*, New York: Harper & Row, 1972.

Huddle, Norie, et al., *Island of Dreams: Environmental Crisis in Japan*, New York and Tokyo: Autumn Press, 1975.

Kahn, Herman, *The Emerging Japanese Superstate: Challenge and Response*, Englewood Cliffs, New Jersey: Prentice-Hall, 1971.

Organization for Economic Co-operation and Development, *Review of National Policies for Education: Japan*, Paris: OECD, 1971, Especially parts two and three.

Matsushita, Konosuke, *Japan at the Brink*, Tokyo: Kodansha International, 1976, especially part II, pp. 77–112.

Tanaka, Kakuei, *Building a New Japan: A Plan for Remodeling the Japanese Archipelago*, Tokyo: The Simul Press, 1972.